Textbooks in the Kaleidoscope

A Critical Survey of Literature and Research on Educational Texts

Egil Børre Johnsen

Textbooks in the Kaleidoscope

A Critical Survey of Literature and Research on Educational Texts

Translated by Linda Sivesind

Scandinavian
University Press

Scandinavian University Press (Universitetsforlaget AS),
0608 Oslo, Norway
Distributed world-wide excluding Norway by
Oxford University Press, Walton Street, Oxford OX2 6DP

Oxford   New York   Toronto   Dehli   Bombay   Calcutta   Madras   Karachi
Kuala Lumpur   Singapore   Hong Kong   Tokyo   Nairobi
Dar es Salaam   Cape Town   Melbourne   Auckland   Madrid and
associated companies in Berlin   Ibadan

Oxford is a trade mark of Oxford University Press

Published in the United States by
Oxford University Press Inc., New York

© Universitetsforlaget 1993

ISBN 82-00-21506-7

Published with grants from the Norwegian Research Council and the
Norwegian Non-Fiction Writers' and Translators' Association (NFF)

British Library Cataloguing in Publication Data
Data available

Library of Congress Cataloguing in Publication Data
Data available

Printed in Norway by
A/S Foto-Trykk, Trøgstad 1993

For Anna-Clara

Staring incessantly at the background, I rotated the kaleidoscope ever so cautiously, so cautiously. I was amazed by how the rosette gradually changed. Sometimes one small piece would move almost imperceptibly, yet have the most violent consequences. The patterns were both dazzling and disquieting, and soon I longed to exact the secret of the device. I opened the one end, counted the glass bits and pried the three small mirrors from the inside of the cardboard casing. Then I remounted the mirrors, but I only put three or four glass bits back in. The interplay now yielded far more modest results; the patterns no longer held any surprises. But now it was easy to follow and understand the patterns! And now it was easy to understand why the kaleidoscope gave so much joy and pleasure!

André Gide: *Si le grain ne meurt*, 1926.

Kaleidoscope, invented in England in 1817, an optical instrument in which, thanks to an arrangement of reflecting surfaces, one sees loose bits of colored glass, bits of feathers, etc., form the most strange and wonderful geometrical patterns. Used in actual practice to compose patterns. The images change infinitely by rotating the tube so the bits form new constellations in relation to the mirrors. Kaleidoscope images can be movingly beautiful and their initial effect can be astonishing and surprising - but in the long run they are tiring, monotonous despite all their variety.

Dreyer's Young People's Encyclopedia, 1949.

Preface

This book is a critical survey of textbook literature and research. Although so much textbook research has been done thus far that this survey cannot pretend to cover all of it, the material is still not so extensive as to preclude the survey from covering the most important results and trends in textbook literature and research reports published in Danish, English, French, German, Norwegian and Swedish.

The part of the work done in 1990–92 has been funded by the Norwegian Research Council for Science and the Humanities as part of the Council's program for research pertaining to the passing on of culture and heritage. The project may also be viewed as a preliminary part of the efforts being made in several countries to determine what must be done to win recognition for textbook research as a separate college or university discipline.

It took several years to collect the material covered. I could not have managed to collect and collate it without the help of many colleagues. My special thanks to Staffan Selander of the Textbook Institute at Härnösand, Sweden, to Richard Bamberger at the Institute for Textbook Research in Vienna, to Alain Choppin at the National Institute of Educational Research in Paris and to the members of the Norwegian Non-Fiction Writers' and Translators' Association Textbook Committee. The management and staff at the Research Library of the Norwegian Educational Library have provided invaluable assistance. I would also like to express my gratitude to Boel Englund (Stockholm), Tomas Englund (Uppsala), Jean Osborn (Urbana-Champaign), Ian Westbury (Urbana-Champaign), Arthur Woodward (Rochester), Stephen Heyneman (Washington, DC), Ian Michael (Bristol), Chris Stray (Swansea),

Karl Peter Fritzsche (Braunschweig), Gisela Teistler (Braun-schweig), Gerd Stein (Duisburg), Horst Strietzel (Berlin), Brigitte Reich (Berlin) and Egbert Dietrich (Köthen).

I want to thank my editor, Anne Turner, as well as Karl Øyvind Jordell, Leif Longum and Oddvar Vormeland, for their constructive criticism of the manuscript. One severe and most important critic has been my translator, Linda Sivesind. My very special thanks to her. The large number of book titles from so many different countries has created certain technical problems. English, French and German titles have been listed in their original languages. The titles of works written in Nordic languages have been translated into English and occur only in English in the text proper. This has been done partly to save space and partly to achieve a certain uniformity. In the bibliography, on the other hand, titles are listed by their original Nordic-language title, followed by the English translation in parentheses.

His, March 1993
Egil Børre Johnsen

Contents

Introduction
by Alan C. Purves
The University at Albany

Textbooks have been with us for many centuries. Among the incunabula exist a number of religious and secular textbooks. *Orbis Pictus* of Comenius is frequently mentioned as among the first illustrated school texts, but it was preceded by many with and without illustration. In most of the world they have come to be an integral part of education and literacy, so much so that we almost forget they are there. The Qu'ran is a textbook in the religious and literacy instruction of Islamic youth. The cookbook in nearly every literate household is a textbook. The manual accompanying software and hardware as well as every new appliance is a textbook. Although he focuses on the textbooks used in formal and secular schooling, in this volume, Egil Børre Johnsen undertakes a painstaking summary of the analysis of their presence, their design, and their effect in schools in Europe and North America. This excellent analysis combines four inter-related issues on which I shall offer some comments from a trans-Atlantic and mother tongue perspective: the very existence of textbooks; their content, their design, and their relation to instruction. My perspective is also that of a person who has spent some time composing and compiling textbooks for schools and universities as well as doing some research on their effects.

I should also mention a fifth issue, the influence of state purchasing or publishing, which leads to issues of censorship and politics around the textbook industry. In the United States we have witnessed the inclusion of creationism as a topic in biology; Germany saw the deliberate anti-semitism of textbooks in the 1930's, and the de-Nazification of the textbooks in the late 1940's.

Textbooks exist within a political context no less than do schools; we cannot discuss either as if they were representations of an isolated entity called "pure knowledge" or "pure pedagogical practice". Johnsen's analyses frame textbooks within this ideological context.

For educators, particularly educators in the mother tongue and the social sciences, textbooks have had a mixed reputation, although fewer critics have challenged their importance in technical subjects and many of the sciences. I have lived through two rounds of attacks on textbooks in the mother-tongue curriculum in the United States. The first was the "paperback revolution" of the 1950's and early 1960's; the second is the "whole language" movement of the late 1980's. Both declared the end of the textbook. The claim was that paperbacks or trade books would supplant the anthology-based text series by providing greater variety and flexibility of literary works to teachers and students. A parallel movement in the social sciences argued for the use of original source materials. While the claims of variety and flexibility cannot be denied theoretically, there was a practical side to those textbooks that helped them to survive their challengers. Normally the anthology costs less, whether it be the school or the pupil that purchases it. The challengers flourished in times of prosperity; when a recession comes, the textbook tends to return. Even though the cost of permissions has soared, it is still lower than the cost of individual volumes. The cost of maintaining a school library has also risen sharply; and the library does not allow for multiple copies. In the United States, copyright laws have virtually prohibited teachers from providing class sets of duplicated materials. The next challenge to the textbook will, I think, come from the electronic media, and it remains to be seen whether the low cost and easy portability of the textbook can be matched or surpassed. On-line access to multiple texts may be simple, but copyright and other costs may again allow the textbook to survive as an inexpensive alternative.

Related to the existence of textbooks in schools is the question of content; from which question, to my mind, two issues arise: timeliness and selection. In the sciences in particular, information and experimentation offer the practitioner a constantly changing universe. Such is also the case in the more contemporary parts of history and literature. The textbook takes about two years to produce – although desk-top publishing can shorten the process somewhat. In many schools, the life of a textbook is about five years. Taking publishing time and shelf-life together means that the content of a text book can be up to seven years old, and perhaps seven years out-of-date. Schools could be sued for malpractice if up-to-date information is a criterion of schooling. In the United States and, I suspect, other countries as well, literature texts suffer from an additional conservatism on the part of teahers who much prefer to teach the poems and stories that they know. A publisher dare not devote more than 20 percent of the total pages to new selections. It is for this reason that there has been relatively little change in the selections in United States anthologies, as Applebee (1991) has observed.

A second aspect of content is selection. A textbook necessarily represents a perspective, a point-of-view with regards to the material. That perspective will dictate such matters as selection, sequence, and emphasis. It also affects the very language of the textbook (as Johnsen explores in detail). The problem of selection has become particularly crucial in literature, where the issue of canon and its relation to culture has become a political as well as a pedagogical issue. The creator of a literature textbook, like the teacher in the classroom, must make a selection from the vast array of texts. So too must the writer of a history or a science text. Any selection results from preference, whether it be taste, interest, a sense of what is pedagogically sound, a sense of what is appropriate for the age or training of the students, and, in many cases, availability of the material in copyright or the public domain. All of these play their part in some mix. Generally, the authors of textbooks do not make their criteria known and they do not suggest its arbitrary character. That they should is the argument of many, particularly Suzanne de Castell, whom Johnsen cites frequently. That they do not cite their criteria comes from a sense that the textbook is authoritative or definitive, a position that can no longer hold. It may be more or less rational, more or less fashionable, and it may give the illusion of authority and definition, but readers and teachers are finding themselves increasingly free to be skeptical.

Some textbooks are beginning to announce their limitations and the authors are beginning to be fittingly humble. It is a trend that I hope will continue.

Related to the selection and ordering of content is design. The textbook is a complex visual display of information, one in which the graphics may play as great a part as the verbal content. Often textbook analysts and critics are unaware of this design. The information is embedded in a page and that very embedding may indeed shape how the information is perceived. In the United States, for example, a literature textbook usually surrounds the poem or story with an introductory page or more, a set of "literal" and "inferential" comprehension questions (usually indistinguishable upon close analysis), a section on vocabulary and a set of directed activities for writing or discussion. In Europe, by contrast, the literature is often separated from this paraphernalia. One can infer that the two presentations reflect and inculcate different approaches to the notion of literary text and to what is expected of the stuaent reader. History and science texts are similarly cluttered with material that may be more confusing than enlightening to the student. Some material may be boxed; some may be contained as captions to illustrations; some may be color-coded. The cues as to which information is more important are often subtle for the unwary and unprepared reader.

The design of textbooks is partly the matter of chance and history and partly the result of deliberate instructional planning. The margins in some science and mathematics textbooks are deliberately widened so that students may enter calculations. Type size reflects an untested notion as to what is most readable by groups of students of different ages. Presumably older students have greater visual acuity and so can read texts in smaller fonts with less leading. Illustrations are often inserted not with instructional aims but with aims that are related to some notion of page design.

The final aspect of textbooks, and the one that Johnsen devotes much penetrating analysis is the role of the textbook in instruction, and particularly the relation of the textbook to the teacher. There was a period in the United States and elsewhere, when publishers and instructional designers wanted to create "teacher-proof" textbooks. These were to be books that would fit into an "instructional system". The teacher was to be programmed to use the books in precisely the way that the authors and editors had designed. It is this "systems" approach to textbooks, particularly basal reading series and introductory mathematics series, that has caused the most anger on the part of critics. Those who examined the effects of these approaches soon learned that the system was far from perfect. Teachers were able to transmute the most teacher-proof texts. Questions that were to stimulate discussion were transmuted into factual recitations. Plans were sabotaged by the very fact of the classroom and its inhabitants.

Johnsen reviews the various studies of textbook use, which show nicely the relation of the textbook to other facets of instruction. We can appreciate the myriad uses that textbooks enjoy; some as proof from the teacher and some as clay in the hands of the teacher. Some are in the center of the classroom, being the focal point of instruction. Some are in the center in a different way, being a reference tool for the teacher and students. In my studies concerning the curriculum and instruction in written composition, the pattern of use of the textbook is far from consistent even within a country. There are also differences among textbooks: some are grammars, some are rhetorics, some are instructional texts. Generalizations are difficult indeed. Textbooks in mother tongue are indeed ubiquitous. Whether their ubiquity is accompanied by uniformity in use is another matter.

Textbooks are indeed a kaleidoscope, and we should not see them as being a single image or even a single refraction of the light of instruction. How we view them depends on who we are, what our view of curriculum and instruction may be, and what our view of knowledge and learning may be. Egil Børre Johnsen's magnificent volume causes us to rethink and review our perception of one facet of the world that surrounds us.

Chapter I

Introduction

Background and Objectives

It is difficult to pinpoint the place of the textbook in literature, not least because the textbook may well be our most composite literary product. Although this is especially true of the writing, development and distribution of textbooks, it also applies to genres and target groups, as well as to the ways we read and use textbooks.

It is equally difficult to pinpoint the essence of textbook analysis. The subject originated after the end of WW I, and thus far analyses have employed a wide range of objectives, means and methods. As far as subject matter is concerned, textbooks and, by inference, textbook analyses cover the entire spectrum of topics. Nonetheless, the approaches taken by textbook analysts must of necessity be interdisciplinary. Linguistics, pedagogics, philosophy, history, sociology and psychology are just a few of the traditional disciplines applied in combination in textbook analyses.

Despite its now considerable scope, the phenomenon of textbook analysis has never been established as a separate college or university discipline. There are internationally recognized basic texts that outline the entire technical process involved in the development and production of textbooks (Richaudeau 1986), but no comparable theoretical systems have been established for textbook analysis as a field of research with status as a separate discipline.

There may be several explanations for why the field has consistently remained supplementary or complementary. Hartmut Hacker (Hacker 1980) points out that following WW II the focus on the textbook as a medium was redirected toward audio-visual media. He also contends that the combination of private sector production and public sector approval has detracted from textbooks' appeal as research objects.

The lack of any more organized initiatives may also be seen as a consequence of the attitude the educational community has officially adopted toward textbooks. Today a number of countries have curricula for primary and lower-secondary schools which literally never mention the word textbook. For example, the word rarely appears in the 306-page Norwegian primary school curriculum and then only as one of several items on lists of classroom paraphernalia. Otherwise, there are sporadic public debates about content or the lack of books in certain subjects, etc. Yet the debates rarely suggest the elimination of textbooks, although there are exceptions (Duneton-Pagliano 1978, Quéréel 1982, Bonilauri 1983).

Still one question regarding the future of textbook research looms large in the West: Are we sure that schools benefit from using textbooks? As long as most of the support for the answer "yes" is no more than a positive assumption based on long traditions, booming sales and growing consumption, the dilemma remains the same; we hesitate to apply terms like science and research to a field whose existence has not yet been sanctioned.

In countries such as the former Soviet Union and GDR, textbooks have constituted the cornerstone of school system didactics during the past few decades. One of the great system builders in the Soviet Union, Dmitri Sujew, admonishes that every socialistic teacher and educator must spurn any Western notions that involve the elimination of textbooks (Sujew 1986). In 1990 the revolution in the GDR led to the replacement of social science and contemporary history textbooks. Owing to the unresolved problems and consequences entailed by the change, the situation calls for more research (Fritzsche 1990, Zückert 1990).

Textbooks are a type of composite literature collocated and compiled by several interested parties (specialists, authors, publishers, authorities) and they are intended to serve several user groups (teachers, students/pupils, parents). The motives are not the same for every group. The correlations between the different groups' criteria are frequently overlooked in evaluative analyses (Wain 1990). We still lack viable research on the question of whose criteria are measured (to the extent the analysis is descriptive) or should be measured (to the extent the analysis is normative, like most analyses). By applying different parts of the same analytical system, one and the same textbook could theoretically be judged brilliant and worthless at the same time. If so, this indicates that analysts could tailor their methods to suit their purpose. But where do such methodological templates originate, and how universal are they? How universal can they be for textbooks in dozens of subjects at different levels at different times?

The uncertainty prevailing with regard to such questions is the starting point for the following critical survey. The work may be regarded as a preliminary contribution to the efforts now being made in several countries to define the terms and conditions for textbook science as a separate discipline in higher education. My objective is to catalog as many as possible of the different perspectives taken in such research, and to present approaches and results with an eye to future research projects.

In Chapter VI, I present an analogy concerning the kaleidoscopic nature of textbooks - and of textbook research. This phenomenon also emerges through form and content in my book. Parts of the discussion are condensed and encyclopedic; the use of "mentioning" and fragmentation is no less absent than in textbooks. But then, I have taken this liberty when writing a *survey*. Today, I would never have taken the same liberty when writing a textbook.

The Textbook Concept

The term *textbook* is neither precise nor stable:

> What is a textbook? Several answers are possible. Rather than cling to one of them, I suggest that it is more useful to consider the various degrees of restriction they impose. For example, if we confine the word *textbook* to books produced for use in instructional sequences, then we exclude books whose authors did not intend such use. When a copy of Shakespeare's plays, even a plain text, is brought into a classroom and used for teaching, it becomes, in a sense, a textbook. Rather than excluding such cases from view, we should distinguish them. Here the available English vocabulary can help by enabling us to distinguish *textbooks* from *schoolbooks*. The former term may be reserved for books written, designed and produced specifically for instructional use, the latter for books used in instruction but less closely tied to pedagogic sequences.
>
> The distinction between textbooks and schoolbooks is not just the epiphenomenon of a scholastic exercise in definition. It is the sedimented product of an historical process which can be traced in the histories of the words. *Schoolbook* is first attested in the 1750s, and more commonly from the 1770s. *Textbook* does not appear until the 1830s. Its predecessor *text book* is much older, and denotes the text, usually Latin or Greek, used for instruction. (Stray 1991, p. 1.)

The definition of a *textbook* may be as general as to include other books made and published for educational purpose, or even any book used in the classroom. The textbook may also be a subset of

an even broader and increasingly more commonly-used term –
teaching media. Catalogs touting today's products can give the
impression that schools have turned into huge teaching media
centers. Books should or may compete with and/or complement/
supplement other media. But even if one's aspirations are limited
to books, it is becoming difficult to maintain an overview. One
reason for this is the increase in the number of titles that qualify
for formal approval as reference books or textbooks, based on
approval schemes or other forms of control or purchasing schemes.
Another reason is that the term textbook is in the process of
becoming unofficially extended, thanks to developments on the
office equipment front. Photocopying has become a matter of
routine, and it will soon be commonplace to retrieve information
from databases for direct use in the classroom. It is also
conceivable that schools will eventually experience a media
situation similar to today's situation at colleges and universities,
i.e., the term "textbook" will be applied to a growing variety of
functions in differentiated, individually-tailored teaching situations.
In theory, a novel can be required reading, a study reference or
supplementary reading in disciplines such as literature, social
science, history and psychology. At the same time, a sort of
"underground literature" is emerging, although it is difficult to
register. Photocopied manuscripts and offprints, combinations of
self-made materials and materials produced by others, a little of
this and a little of that, are being collocated to serve new aims;
pirate editions and promotional editions meld together to form a
new type of book stock. Many teachers have become compilers or,
if you will, textbook authors. In many ways the situation is
reminiscent of the compilation of anthologies, which are often on
the borderline between textbooks and non-textbooks.

Without taking any particular stand on the role of textbooks in
the classroom, and without reference to studies limited to analyzing
the use of specific textbooks, there is thus reason to contend that
the closer we get to our own time, the less reliable are the results
of analyses of the use of specific *textbooks* as universal
descriptions of all aspects of the teaching situation.

Two of the most comprehensive studies discussed below
(Sigurgeirsson 1990, DsU 1980:4) employ very broad definitions

of the term "teaching media", which they subdivide into basic texts, manuals, workbooks, reference books and exercise books:

> After starting out with a very narrow definition of teaching media, our discussions brought us to the realization that we really ought to employ a wide definition of the term: "All material used in teaching". (DsU 1980:4, p. 191.)

A more exhaustive discussion of the term teaching media is available in Norwegian (Gravem, n.y.). The author reviews the ideas prevalent in different countries during the 1960s and 1970s. He points out that a general, more pragmatic definition evolved during the 1970s, when teaching media became bearers not least of certain aspects of locally planned educational programs. But "this involved normative views - practice veered off in another direction" (p. 50). Gravem stresses the problem of fuzzy, inconsistent definitions of the term teaching media. He attributes the problem to one specific condition, i.e., that education's " 'sphere of reality' is largely man-made. (...) In this context teaching is but one element of a complex structure, and it can hardly be expected that the phenomenon can be studied on the basis of "internal" consistency alone." (P. 51.)

The lack of any general consensus on evaluation criteria for textbooks and teaching media can probably be interpreted as symptomatic of the situation Gravem describes. His description of the "sphere" is applicable to textbooks, teaching and knowledge, all three. Regarding the areas of *teaching* and *knowledge* in this connection, I would refer to my discussion in the chapter *The Use of Textbooks* (pp. 157–160).

In my survey consisting of all accessible research material, the word "textbook" is used in a narrow as well as in a broad sense, depending on the nature of the research. Problems in the use of the term will, furthermore, be discussed in my chapter on registration (*Appendix*, p. 351). Certain chapters also indicate how the definition of the term may determine both the development and the use of textbooks. This is especially clear in the chapter entitled *Approval and the Textbook Concept* (p. 281), as well as in the discussion of the French *parascolaires* (p. 307).

Material and Structure

Most of the material used here has originated in Germany, France, the Nordic countries, the UK or the USA, although important contributions have come from a number of other countries as well. Quotations from the Nordic languages, as well as the lengthier French and German passages, have been translated.

It is imperative to point out that the term research has occasionally been extended to its broadest possible definition. The survey also includes articles and brief presentations of a fairly unpretentious nature, mainly because the number of large-scale works is limited and because part of the goal has been to present the broadest possible survey of the viewpoints taken.

The most comprehensive collected bibliographical survey compiled thus far was written by Woodward, Elliott and Nagel, and entitled *Textbooks in School and Society* (1988). Some of the 467 articles and books on the subject are based on analyses, while others are not. All are in English and most come from the USA. The titles have been arranged in two main chapters containing two and three sections respectively:

Textbook Producers and Consumers

I   Textbooks and School Programs.
II   The Production and Marketing of Textbooks.

Evaluation and Criticism of Textbooks

III   General Discussion and Special Topics
IV   Subject Matter Content Coverage
V   Ideology and Controversy

This outline says something about one tradition which has been more pronounced in the USA than in any other country, i.e., production and marketing. The topic listed last (ideological studies), which takes up no more than 15 of the 140 pages in the book, is the one that has dominated textbook research in the former West Germany. In contrast, didactics and methodology have dominated the field in countries such as the former East Germany and Norway.

One possible way to achieve a more universal perspective on the subject – irrespective of national traditions and historical development – is to separate the large number of titles and studies made in the various countries into the following three main categories:

1. Ideology in textbooks.
2. The use of textbooks.
3. The development of textbooks.

1: Textbooks, or sets of textbooks, are produced as a single unit, a product intended to provide information about a particular subject. The question of what is written between the covers, particularly the underlying philosophy extolled in the books, has been the main focus of textbook research to date. Readers and textbooks in history and social studies have been the targets of content analyses that survey the selection of material and the attitudes taken in the presentation.

2: In the school the textbook is the main instrument used for teaching. Several researchers have therefore investigated how books are used by teachers and pupils. This research has frequently been based on questions regarding textbooks' authority, accessibility and effectiveness. On the whole, this approach is certainly not as common as the content analyses in the first group, although in relative terms it has seen more rapid growth over the past decade.

3: Textbooks have a long "life cycle". They undergo a process consisting of conceptualization, writing, editing, approval (by the publisher and/or public bodies), marketing, selection and distribution before landing on a pupil's desk. Both singly and collectively, these areas have been studied in different countries and contexts, but the scale of this type of research has been relatively modest.

Many studies are limited exclusively to one of the three main areas. In addition, a significant number of studies fit into one of the main categories even though they may touch on the two others. As certain works encompass two or three of main areas, they are mentioned in several chapters. Some repetition of author names and titles has been inevitable.

Thus the material has been divided into three main parts (chapters II–III, IV and V). I begin with international research traditions, giving pride of place to the ones with the longest tradition (historical and ideological analyses of content (chapters II–III)). It would have been logical also to start with the development of textbooks (chapter V). For several reasons, however, this chapter comes as the last one. The question of how books are being used (chapter IV) is linked to the question of their ideology (chapter III). Furthermore, the development of textbooks is a field where research activity has been relatively modest. It also involves issues and approaches with which I am not very familiar as a researcher.

Each main chapter of the survey presents approaches and results, then concludes with a brief commentary on procedures in the studies and, sometimes, suggestions for further solutions. These headings are called *Perspectives*. They do not claim to be exhaustive analyses of the material previously presented. The material is too wide and the ideas too varied and too numerous for such a task. My work is written with the intention of providing a survey which in its turn may initiate action. Therefore, I am less concerned with identifying weaknesses than with emphasizing possibilities. Research which in my opinion may add to further development, receives the widest mention; particularly, I have endeavoured to stress those ideas which point forward. For this reason, the content of *Perspectives* has not been restricted to my own conclusions. Where I see fit, I have included particularly enlightening contributions from other scholars.

The sections under the heading *Perspectives* have set out the premises for the conclusions in the chapter *Conclusion*.

Chapter II

Historical Investigations

It can be difficult to differentiate between historical and ideological investigations, but such a distinction is made in this survey. Historical investigations include studies which have no express ideological aims and which explicitly apply historical viewpoints of a fundamentally different nature. In addition, the source material must consist of books that are historical in the sense that they are no longer in use, or of such books compared with titles in use when the investigations were carried out. Consequently, historical investigations may include monographs, biographies, general genre histories, or histories of particular subjects or disciplines insofar as these may be gleaned from the books.

Individual Works/Authors

There are few comprehensive studies of individual works. Any individual books that have received much attention have nearly always been titles that have dominated their times. They might be readers such as P.A. Jensen's or Nordahl Rolfsen's (Sanderud 1951, Sletvold 1971) in Norway, classics such as Noah Webster's dictionaries and language books (Johnson 1904, Carpenter 1963) in the USA, standard works such as von Rochow's *Der Kinderfreund* (Tischer 1970) in Germany, or readers like Bruno's (Maingueneau 1979) or historical works such as Lavisse's (Nora 1962) in France.

Common to all of these titles is that they are included in comprehensive, general studies. This is not a question of monographs. Books about individual authors and their works exist only as exceptions. One example is McGuffey and his readers, which dominated the US school system for more than a century (Vail 1911, Minnich 1936).

Other prominent series of readers have also been analyzed over a period of time - based on the readers' degree of readability. The authors investigate how this changes with new editions and new editors. When an individual work is discussed in the literature on textbooks, the point of departure is usually more educational or philosophical than historical or biographical. Characteristically, the only large-scale monograph about a single textbook title that I have come across concerns Selma Lagerlöf's geographical reader, the tale of Nils Holgersson (Ahlström 1942). This story is mostly fiction, and it acquired a significant reading public outside of the school as well. One thorough monograph, although on a more modest scale, is Lars Furuland's analysis of *The Primary School Reader* (Furuland 1987, see page 241). In France there is a rare example of *constructive* textbook criticism - with an historical perspective - based on a particular work. G. Bruno's reader, originally published in 1877, was called *Le tour de France par*

deux enfants and dominated the market throughout three generations. Both the protagonists were boys. In 1978-79 Anne Pons
published *Le tour de France par Camille et Paul, deux enfants
d'aujourd'hui*. Pons follows in Bruno's footsteps geographically,
but challenges what she regards as prejudices. Just as a curiosity,
I might mention that Munksgaard, the Danish publisher, has chosen
to include some facsimiles of old school books in their history
book series for primary and lower secondary schools. The facsimiles are to be used as a basis for exercises in which pupils are
asked to evaluate language and presentation (Holm 1986).

The two most comprehensive studies of Swedish and Danish
history instruction (Andolf 1972, Møller 1986) do not concede the
authors/works that have dominated the classroom (Pallin, Schotte
and Munch) a correspondingly dominant position.

There is a remarkable lack of comprehensive, independent
historical analyses of individual titles or authorships. There may be
several explanations for this. Perhaps investigators have been
restricted by a tradition that limits such comprehensive individual
commentary to fiction. Or perhaps the primary, but less than
flattering, explanation is that individual textbooks do not constitute
a sufficiently rich or distinctive material for it to be natural to
undertake more extensive analyses. In any case, the fact that no
individual textbook has been found worthy of analysis on a higher
level may be seen as a symptom of low literary status. The view
that there is no analytical apparatus capable of dealing with
individual works must be seen against this background. Strictly
speaking, however, such a model was proposed in Lee J. Cronbach's work already in 1955 (Cronbach 1955).

One of the few exceptions is Turid Henriksen's study of the
development of foreign language education in Norway (Henriksen
1989), which is specifically based on an analysis of Sigurd and
Gunnar Høst's French books through three generations. The
analysis addresses the special literary and subject didactic
characteristics of the books and looks at their contents in relation
to social development and production conditions. In principle, this
is an approach that saw a breakthrough in a number of literary
communities in the late 1960s.

Genre Histories

The history of textbooks themselves, i.e., the story of what they have contained and of how they have been put together and looked at various times - of their distinct literary character - is a rare phenomenon, limited in most countries to the history of readers.

As mentioned, however, there is a limited tradition in the USA (Johnson 1904, Nietz 1961, Carpenter 1963). Ian Westbury has outlined how Comenius' textbook from 1658, *Orbis Sensualium Pictus*, has been normative for the formulation of Latin textbooks in the USA right up to our own time (Westbury 1982). In Denmark, Gyldendal published a book to commemorate its 200th anniversary of textbook publication, which contained four historical essays that presented more than 130 titles in chronological order (Skovgaard-Petersen 1970). Harald L. Tveterås made a major contribution in Norway when he wrote almost 100 pages about the textbooks published by Cappelen throughout a period of nearly 150 years (Tveterås 1979). The titles are systematically arranged by subject and presented chronologically. The book includes information about the authors and provides some background information, placing the various titles within the context of both cultural and publishing house policy. The work is one of a kind in Norway. Even though the book deals with the country's oldest and for quite some time largest textbook publisher, its significance is limited because of this relationship.

If we include literature on the history of textbook production and textbook policies in this group, the USA stands out for having independent and relatively old traditions. In 1931, The National Society for the Study of Education published a book devoted to the textbook in instruction (NSSE 1931). In the main, it deals with the textbook as a moral and economic link in the societal system.

J. W. Ong has written a dissertation on the historical role of textbook culture in the development of the school's transmission of knowledge (Ong 1958, mentioned here on the basis of Westbury 1982). Ong's point of departure is the art of book printing, and he points out how it changed the conditions for teaching. In the 17th and 18th centuries, the medieval processual method of learning, characterized by dialogue and direct intellectual contact, was replaced by

> (...) the *mastery* and *memorization* of the fixed bodies of knowledge represented in books. Ong argues that this development, which he associates with the work of the French scholar, Peter Ramus (1515-72), and the associated movement of Ramism, had the effect of shifting teaching (and intellectual work itself) away from a "person world" (associated with voice and auditory perception) to an "object world" (associated with visual perception). He links the development of both "subjects", within education and the related movement of "encyclopaedism", and modern science, with its concern for the understanding of an ordered "objective" universe, to this development of the "textbook" tradition. (Westbury 1982, p. 7.)

This viewpoint is referred to here because it is unusual to allot such an important role to textbooks in the history of schooling, where tradition emphasizes educational philosophy, laws, plans and/or political systems to explain fundamental changes (Engelsen 1990). Ong's work is also unusual because of the emphasis it attaches to textbooks' physical role.

Anthologies

If we delve deep into the educational system and far back in time, we encounter a genre problem that also affects registration:

> It is difficult, however, and will perhaps prove impossible, usefully to make any general distinction between works written

with a specifically pedagogical purpose and those written for entertainment. (...) This is especially true of stories and verse written for children; it is also true of anthologies, from which it can be more concisely illustrated. A group of 27 eighteenth-century anthologies, inspected at random, ranges from collections made without stated pedagogical intent to those which are offered as school texts. (Michael 1979, p. 202.)

Books devoted to the history of genres are extremely rare. Such books might very likely represent a valuable approach in some subjects. In his book about mother tongue instruction in England, David Shayer looks at the selection of literature, mainly in light of the traditional conflict between classical and contemporary literature (Shayer 1972). He also calls for an evaluation of the relationship between fiction and non-fiction in the selections (pp. 171-179). He does not go into the anthology as a genre in that context. Nevertheless, he asks whether the selection of literature can be influenced by tradition; whether the anthology as a genre helps determine the selection, and possibly even part of the reader experience.

The grounds for claiming that genre determines content - in the field of anthologies for example - was established by Dora V. Smith (1933), Patrick Quéréel (1982) and Boel Englund (1991), among others. One central issue, if this is true, involves the relationship between an established and vital genre tradition on one hand and new curricula (with new objectives and revised methods) on the other.

Nick Jones has written an essay on the development of poetry anthologies in Great Britain since the 1950s (Jones 1983). His intention was to investigate how the selection of contemporary poetry has changed in recent decades. His focus is the "pattern of values with which each anthology is necessarily inscribed" (p. 40). Jones systematizes the material with the help of an anthology typology which is particularly interesting because it includes published selections of literature from both within and outside of the school system. The model is composed of three groups: "First Order anthology" is "polemical", "innovative" and "partisan"; it is consciously exploratory and rejuvenative and can often manifest itself in magazine form. "Second Order anthology" is "judicial"; this is where the greats are firmly enshrined and a few new candidates assessed. "Third Order anthology" is school anthologies. They are

> (...) almost entirely distinct from those through which the main poetic tradition is established. A *Third Order anthology* is produced by an educational publisher (Harrap, Arnold, Murray), and is aimed directly and exclusively at the school market. It is therefore essentially a *distributive* anthology, which aims to select, from the available tradition, a body of work conforming to the highly specific perceived requirements of a targeted (and captive) readership, which may be further identified by age-band and "ability level". (P. 44.)

Rather than dividing the material into time periods, Jones writes about the form and function of anthologies in general. He develops this further in a later essay in which he works out a general genre description of the school anthology (Jones 1984, pp. 69-72). Two core characteristics are the poems' length (they are short) and the consistent recurrence of the same poems and authors.

There is a German work which, like Jones' essays, is partly historical and partly descriptive. It is the most thorough and copious work on the anthology as a genre that exists in German: *Die deutschsprachige Anthologie 1-2* (Bark - Pforte 1970). This analysis, like Björck's work (see page 372), includes all types of literary anthologies and does not single out school anthologies. A major portion of it, however, is Dietger Pforte's 120-page discussion of the principles for editing anthologies. This is a profound analysis with viewpoints that are directly applicable to school anthologies. The study itself is also outstanding. Bark and Pforte have registered 1998 titles, which have been systematized by structure. Then the text selections in all the anthologies have been systematized by theme, literary form and readership. The latter comprises the categories profession, interest group and age.

Together with Pforte's analysis, this survey makes up the first volume. Volume 2 is a collection of articles. Most of the articles have some kind of historical approach. They deal with everything from religious anthologies to collections of political election propaganda. One special feature is that they include several more socio-literary contributions from bookdealers and publishers.

Another noteworthy characteristic of the work is that one long article deals with how anthologies were "received" by various periodicals in the last century. Gerhard Trott writes about the comments anthologies received during three different periods; around 1813-1815 (during the wars of independence against Napoleon), just before and after 1848 (the February Revolution) and around 1870-1871 (the Franco-Prussian war) (Trott 1970). The point of departure is that "socio-political changes in the social substance affect production and the design of the anthology and its reception in journalistic publications." (P. 246.) The article discusses the reviews under the heading "Socio-political Anthologies". But before he arrives at this point, Trott writes an introduction: "The Anthology as an Expression of Apolitical Awareness". Here he claims that anthologies with proclaimed non-political goals also must be considered to be "socio-literary objectivizations" (p. 249) of and within the society in which they are published.

Historical anthology studies have also been conducted in the Nordic countries. One example is Annica Danielsson's doctoral dissertation "Three Anthologies - Three Realities" (Danielsson 1988), which discusses the three readers that dominated the Swedish upper secondary school from 1945 to 1975. Danielsson, too, emphasizes the question of what national or societal image emerges from the text selections. Like Göran Andolf and Karin Tarschys, she wishes to illuminate several aspects of the subject's development and therefore draws upon material from school history, school policy, socio-literary and genre theory in her presentation.

In the first, traditional reader, which held sway until into the 1950s, Danielsson draws attention to the same pattern of God-fearing patriotism that Herbert Tingsten found in history books and readers (see page 102). Then that "reality" gave way to a more international and social-democratic direction throughout the 1960s. In the 1970s, the leading anthology was influenced by the consumer society and the book itself assumed in many ways the characteristics of a supermarket, including a hitherto unthinkable range of literary qualities, genres, cultures and topics.

Taken to the extreme, the term anthology includes the so-called *school editions* of classical and/or modern literature. They comprise booklets or books containing texts specifically adapted for school use. As a rule, they deal with one author; more rarely with epochs or movements. France has especially rich traditions in this area. Julia Lilienthal investigated a selection of anthologies, attaching emphasis to the educational approach to classical literature (Lilienthal 1974). Her objective was to "reveal the general characteristics of the genre and their literary-didactic principles" (p. 3). Lilienthal studied extra-textual enhancements, lay-out, commentary, evaluations and information in the form of quotations of secondary literature, for example. She placed the greatest emphasis on series of questions and problems. She drew conclusions about "die pädagogische Fiction" which supports the contention that the inclusion of fiction in a text adapted for school use in some way or another attaches some sort of additional authorship to the literature.

History of Particular Subjects

Textbooks play a supporting role in some studies of this type and a main role in others. Some of the most important are classified here according to that scale; that is, the most textbook-oriented studies appear last.

In Karin Tarschys' comprehensive work on Swedish as a school subject (Tarschys 1955), textbooks are little more than a backdrop for a general briefing on official statutes, curricula, educational policy and educational debate. In a Norwegian thesis on the evolution of physics as a subject in secondary schools, textbooks are dealt with in chronological order in a separate survey chapter (Engeseth 1984). Textbooks are less peripheral in a standard work on the teaching of English as a foreign language, *A History of English Language Teaching* (Howatt 1984). This survey covers the period from the renaissance up to modern times. It is distinguished from most other such studies in that it includes fairly detailed biographies of the authors. There is one clear tendency in the presentation which is quite common in historical surveys, especially those involving mother tongue or foreign language teaching: The earlier we find ourselves in history, the more important textbooks are as primary sources. The best example of this is Ian Michael's standard work in this field (see page 373). The further we progress into our own century, the smaller the relative percentage of pages devoted to textbooks. One primary reason for this is, of course, that textbooks in the 17th and 18th centuries faced few of today's competitors in the form of curricula, periodicals, polemical literature, research reports, methodological guides and other printed teaching aids. A possible contributory cause may be that school history researchers anno 1980 do not attribute the same importance to their own or their children's textbooks as they do to 300-year-old books that are almost impossible to obtain. If so, this may have a simple psychological explanation, but it may also be an expression of the prevailing attitude - of the age and of the academic environment - to such books.

In his treatise on history instruction in the upper secondary school (Andolf 1972) Göran Andolf uses the same broad variety of materials as Karin Tarschys and A.P.R. Howatt. But whereas Tarschys consistently and Howatt increasingly use sources other than books, Andolf's work goes a long way in the direction of a pure textbook analysis. Approximately four-fifths of the book deals with textbook texts and circumstances directly affecting them.

Andolf's analysis embraces a period of 145 years (1820-1965), Tarschys' one of over 100 years (1800-1912). Andolf has therefore had access to an even more comprehensive corpus than Tarschys. That books are Andolf's most important source for the history of the discipline is also apparent from a methodological factor. Quantitative measurements from a number of text categories taken from textbooks are the basis for the most important of his conclusions.

Tarschys and Andolf undertook historical studies from approximately the same time period and with access to the same kinds of source material. The goals for their investigations were also the same: to describe the subject's contents seen in relation to the prevailing mentality at any given time, in terms of ideology and methodology, behind and within the subject.

In this context we are concerned with two fundamentally different attitudes toward the relationship between textbooks and subject (history). To the extent one can speak of traditions in textbook research, Tarschys represents the line that sees textbooks as important secondary sources where one finds verification of ideas, systems and regulations. Her paramount goal is to expose this superstructure, and her work is largely based on sources other than textbooks. Textbooks nevertheless acquire a central position thanks to their exemplification or documentation function. The presentation of the development of mother tongue instruction in Great Britain in this century, which is most predominantly based on textbooks, is entirely in keeping with this view. David Shayer

(Shayer 1972) writes about English teaching, particularly at the junior and secondary level, from 1900 to 1970. His point of departure is clear:

> It would be almost impossible to determine in exact detail (by visiting several hundred schools over whole terms) the kind of English teaching which is going on in this country now, in 1971; still less is it possible to say exactly what kind of English work was going on in the nation's classrooms in 1910, or in 1925, or throughout the decade 1900-1910. In the absence of such direct observation we must fall back on other forms of evidence, almost wholly of a written kind, which can provide information at second-hand. (...) I refer to such items connected with English teaching as method books, textbooks, examination papers and syllabuses, Board and Ministry Reports, the memoranda of other official and professional bodies, and the comments and statements of informed contemporary opinion. (P. 1.)

Shayer's study is arranged by decades. The chapters are based partly on official statements and reports, partly on general educational trends during the period, and partly on statements from people who played major roles in the subject. The book may be regarded as a long essay. It gradually becomes apparent that the personalized model which Shayer depicts in this way is woven through with textbook titles. But based on the author's point of departure, the books are neither regarded as a separate literary tradition nor as anything but transformations of viewpoints found in method books (which are often mentioned along with examples from textbooks). The textbook titles are generally presented in large groups and used as symptoms and "fair game" in the hunt for longed-for verifications; their justification consists largely in the fact that they are mentioned.

Göran Andolf, who completed his study 17 years after Tarschys, but at the same time as Shayer, represents a newer trend whereby textbooks are regarded as the most reliable sources for learning about what thought processes and motives have actually predominated, and about what implications this has had for content. That, in turn, means that content analysis is the most important means of shedding light on the subject's ideological and methodological development. The question of the choice and use of method thus becomes a far more central issue for Andolf than for Tarschys or Shayer.

In Jørgen Møller's study (Møller 1983), the role of textbooks as a source of information on the history of the subject of history is as dominating as in Andolf's. Møller has:

> (...) created a survey of the history books available for upper secondary school during the past hundred years, has noted the dissemination of the books, and has tried through the books (in connection with approval schemes, etc.) to form a picture of the content and character of history teaching and history scholarship - and to note their relationship to research. (From an introduction to the book by Søren Kjørup, then member of the National Humanities Research Council. (Kjørup 1983, p. 15.)

Møller's departure point is thus identical with Andolf's. Møller divides his material into three main groups: Formalia (laws, schemes, etc.), teaching materials (primarily textbooks) and polemical and general literature on educational theory (pp. 23-24). Like Andolf, Møller performed extensive registration work. As far as methodology is concerned, however, he differs from his predecessors in many ways (see page 378). It might be appropriate to mention by way of conclusion that neither of these two textbook analyses uses the word "textbook" in their main titles. However, Andolf mentions the word in the subtitle ("Teaching and Textbooks 1820-1965").

Andolf's subtitle could also have been applied to a large-scale older study from the USA. Tyler Kepner's survey of textbooks in geography and history in American schools from 1784 to 1922 is one of the rare examples of investigations that used the books primarily to uncover trends in the development of teaching methods (Kepner 1935):

> In this survey the writer proposes (1) to trace the interrelations between methodology and textbooks in geography and history, (2) to describe briefly the chief characteristics of significant

textbooks, for technique cannot safely be dissociated from organization, and (3) to call attention by implication to those pioneers in textbook writing whose names should be better known. (P. 143.)

Kepner believed he could decipher the shifting view of teaching and methodology during the period. On this point there was no complete congruence between the subjects. Notwithstanding, there were so many common characteristics that the classifications could be done in much the same way in geography (the first attempts 1784-1821/ "educational" geography 1821-1850/ "philosophical" geography 1850-1890/ thematic and region-oriented geography 1890-1921) and history (the first attempts 1787-1822/ "educational" history 1822-1850/ the advent of the large series"1850-1890/ theme-oriented history books 1890-1921).

As is apparent, the classification has not been carried out according to uniform criteria, something the author himself points out in his discussion of the registration and selection problem. Underway, however, Kepner gives examples of the degree to which one can or cannot use textbooks for a subject as a basis for drawing conclusions about the development of education and educational philosophy. Two certain conclusions drawn from his own investigation are: First, that there is a mutual influence between books and methodology and that the balance of power between them varies and, second, that throughout the period geography books have been far more strongly influenced than history books by educational trends (p. 172).

Staffan Selander takes a big step further in the same direction as Andolf, Møller and Kepner. (Selander 1988; see page 80). In addition to sharing their view on the importance of textbooks as sources for subject viewpoint and method, he chooses a few books and a few passages from each of them in order to show what changes have occurred in the course of 50 years (1925/1975). The work of Peter Damerow, who has investigated the image of geometry as a subject, as reflected in various textbooks from the period 1960-1980, is based on a similar principle (Damerow 1980).

Such solutions are rare insofar as studies of the histories of particular subjects are concerned. There are titles that discuss five to ten books, but not two. A broader perspective is achieved if one chooses two titles from each year, such that each pair represents two different countries: What do they have in common and what is different in the development of the subject in two different countries during the period in question? Such a study is currently underway; it concerns Swedish and French literature anthologies for the upper secondary school level from the 1920s and 1980s (Englund 1991).

One relatively common type of investigation involves comparing the development of a subject, syllabuses and curricula with the development of textbooks, with an eye to the degree of correspondence. The 1970s saw an increase in the criticism of textbooks in the USA, both on ideological and educational grounds (Library of Congress 1981). Curricula were changed in state after state. Against this background a number of studies were undertaken in the 1980s that compared books from the 1960s with those from the 1980s. There is an outline of a dozen such studies in David Elliott's article "Textbooks and the Curriculum in the Postwar Era: 1950-1980" (Elliott 1990). The investigation focuses on books in history, social studies and mathematics. According to Elliott, books have seldom been changed to conform to the new intentions about fostering pupils' independence and critical sense. To the extent that changes have occurred, they have chiefly taken place on the technical level.

It is evident from Elliott's outline that several such studies have not covered more than 10 to 15 years. Some might feel this is too short a time span. Nevertheless, it is clear that there has been no contemporary or immediate change in the (school) authority/subject expertise/publisher relationship.

Two recent Swedish analyses are less critical of textbooks as literature and more directly trained in the direction of subject history. In 1989 the Institute for Educational Text Research at Härnösand published a special issue of the periodical SPOV. It contains several contributions on textbooks, two of which are devoted to the subjects needlework for girls and nursing. In the first area three different authors' teachers' guides, published at different times (1892, 1919, 1932), were analyzed from a subject history perspective (Trotzig 1989). Then, in an article on five textbooks in nursing, the books' presentation of nutrition and food preparation was analyzed from a corresponding perspective (Heyman 1989).

Gerhard Meyendorf's account of the history of chemistry books in the secondary school in Germany during the past 150 years is unique (Meyendorf 1989). The work is limited by the fact that post-1945 textbooks from West Germany were not examined. In other respects it is a very comprehensive survey in which the author emphasizes the interaction between the subject - both in and out of school - and the books:

> Through the presentation of the history of textbooks in chemistry, other features of the history of the subject itself emerge. This corroborates yet again the view that textbook analyses can provide a great deal of information about the objectives, content and form of the teaching for which these books are intended. (P. 130.)

In Meyendorf's analysis the books are regarded as both influenced and influencing. The venue is a process of historical development which, in grossly simplified terms, has gone from the lexical to the pupil-friendly ("a book for the pupils"). Like Tarschys and Andolf, he stresses the importance of subject didactic and methodological literature. But Meyendorf believes that development trends can only be explained by comparing them to social conditions and general political development, educational philosophy, school policy and book culture. Thus the elucidation of the history of the subject of chemistry and of chemistry books involves a very complex process.

One salient question, which is not discussed separately or as a matter of principle either by Meyendorf or in other historical investigations, is the question of textbooks' potential for supplementing other sources and developing general historical perspectives.

History of Particular Disciplines

Textbooks have been used as source material for studies of how particular disciplines have developed within a subject, but extensive investigations are rare. There are many studies that deal with strictly limited topics, but their objective is to see how the topic is represented at a given point in time in various books for the same grade level and/or to measure what pupils retain of the material. As an example, comprehensive measurements have been taken of what pupils comprehend and learn on the topic of evaporation and the water cycle as it is presented in natural science books in the former West Germany and East Germany and Hungary (Nestler 1990). But such comparative studies seldom have an historical focus. The same is true of studies of history textbooks: History studies are only based on large units, such as whole subjects, long periods of time or large stocks of books. Strongly delimited topics, shorter individual texts or one title are rare in this context. However, the fact that such approaches could actually be fruitful was demonstrated by the science philosopher Nils Roll-Hansen in an introduction to a reprint of G. C. Raff's *Natural History for Children* from 1831 (Roll-Hansen 1988). The distance from the perception of nature in our own day is shown to be both so great and so small that it in itself is worth examining. More important than the cultural history dimension however, is the fact that the text from 1831 is normative in a way that illuminates the problem of descriptive versus normative in modern presentations of biological issues. Raff's natural history was not an authorized textbook, even if it was probably to some degree used as one - something which in turn invites reflection over the relationship between non-fiction books for children and textbooks for children.

The question of historical studies of disciplines is connected to educational level. There are few such studies from primary school. One must go some way up in the system before subjects are split into disciplines, insofar as they are ever regarded as anything other than one integral discipline. Even the term discipline has become more controversial in recent decades. Yet it is clear that at least some of the most comprehensive school subjects have traditionally had what has been perceived as disciplinary divisions. It is also clear that more specialized "disciplines" are accompanied by a greater awareness of the relationship between school subject and academic subject. In the sizeable bibliography of Woodward, Elliott and Nagel (1988), "arithmetic" is listed under the main grouping "mathematics". There, reference is made to a study which reviewed 153 elementary books published between 1900 and 1957 (Dooley 1960). The goal was to investigate which aspects of the arithmetic presented in the textbooks were affected by new research results and which were not. The author found that writers and publishers were quick to incorporate the new - often within five years after incontrovertible new material was available. But this was always on the condition that the new material was "clear, concise and exact" (bibliography p. 99) - that it in one way or another had to reach the authors in a *popularized* (*my* expression) form. A number of important innovations in the subject did not get into the books because they had not been adequately adapted.

Disciplines within Mother Tongue Instruction

Mother tongue instruction is the most typical example of a multi-discipline subject. Further, what this subject calls a "discipline" usually corresponds to a "subject" at a higher level. Grammar and literary history are separate academic subjects at colleges and universities, not only at departments for linguistics and literary science, but also at the separate institutes for mother tongue and foreign language instruction. Instead of "individual disciplines", perhaps one ought to speak of studies of more delimited subject or topic areas. With a view to a subject like mother tongue instruction, grammar, writing skills and literary history would thus be prominent in the sense that they have received a certain amount of attention in the field of textbooks.

Elementary reading training, with a vast number of historical primer studies, dominates the field. However, many would insist that reading must be considered more as a separate subject than as a discipline.

The problem of subject/discipline has been thoroughly dealt with in a study made by William Riley Parker: "Where do English Departments Come From?" (Parker 1967; see Applebee 1974, p. 16.)

Grammar Books

Although one cannot speak of any general tradition, studies on the evolution of the grammar book have been made in certain countries. As early as 1929, Elizabeth Baker's study of the development of "elementary English language textbooks" (Baker

1929) was available in the USA. It analyzed changes that occurred from 1840 to 1929, but has not since been followed up. This is remarkable in that mother tongue instruction, especially the discipline of "grammar", has played a major role in the various states' curriculum guidelines for English. There is no rich tradition in this area in Germany either, although they do have standard works that have exerted influence on grammar book studies in other countries, e.g. Hans Glinz' work on sentence elements (Glinz 1969).

There is a stronger tradition in France. Some of the French studies make little distinction between levels, especially for the 18th and 19th centuries. Others try to limit themselves to school grammars, for example, although it can be hard to distinguish school grammars from other grammars, especially those published in the centuries prior to our own. In this field André Chervel's work, *Histoire de la grammaire scolaire* (Chervel 1977) is the standard. The exposition is chiefly a description of the relationship between academic subjects and school subjects. Chervel's thesis is that much of the descriptive grammar and the information about fundamental grammar problems has been lost from school books. On the other hand Chervel finds a positive correlation in the opposite direction. He shows that the repeated efforts to make school grammars understandable and functional, in both the 19th and 20th centuries, has been an important impetus to research. But trends in research and views on language have only superficially been embodied in grammar books. According to Chervel, this is mainly attributable to educational considerations, first and foremost the requirement that grammar books should help teach writing skills, especially orthography. The book has the subtitle: ... *et il fallut apprendre à écrire à tous les petits Français* (... and all French children had to learn to write).

In this way Chervel's survey becomes a study of what can happen when science is popularized. Since this also deals with a science in which more than one movement or school of thought has always exerted influence, the study also raises questions about educational policy. Chervel personally comes to a conclusion that is typical for grammar book studies, whether they are undertaken with an historical or contemporary perspective: Grammar as a separate discipline should, and can, enrich both linguistic ability and reading pleasure. Yet it does not appear to have done so, and it still does not appear to be doing so.

France's other sizeable work on school grammars builds on Chervel's study to some extent. This is Stéphane Karabétian's *Théories et Pratiques des Grammaires* from 1988. The work primarily consists of a systematic historical survey and a classification of grammar books based on their educational approaches. Like Chervel, Karabétian considers the relationship between "old" and "new" with a certain skepticism as to the frequency of updating.

In the Nordic countries, Frøydis Hertzberg presented her doctoral dissertation " '– and this Science has been named Grammar' " in 1991 (Hertzberg 1990). One-third of the study is an historical account of syntax in the tradition of school grammars throughout 300 years. Hertzberg's point of view is primarily linguistic, but she also uses the history of school conditions in her description of the changes that have occurred. The books are analyzed in light of domestic debate and European trends against the background of developments in the school system in general. In line with this interdisciplinary approach, she finds an inner trend that is primarily connected with "a transition from pure word analysis to pure sentence element analysis", and an outer line attached to "the mother tongue grammar's position as an educational and research discipline" (p. 118).

In another large segment of her dissertation Hertzberg comments on the relationship between new and old as she sees it, based on the debate surrounding the discipline's role in mother tongue instruction:

> (...) one cannot help but be struck by how features from earlier times suddenly pop up again as new. Still, this does not mean that history repeats itself. In the interplay between ideas and material conditions, any period of history can display characteristics that are quite genuine for that particular period, and an argument which is presented at one point in time might have a completely different meaning than if it were presented fifty years later. (P. 319.)

Bernt Fossestøl has investigated the descriptions of word classes and syntax in Norwegian grammars from the 1800s (Fossestøl 1987). Norwegian authors published more than sixty titles during this period, and "Nearly all 19th century Norwegian grammars were intended for use in school" (p. 51). Fossestøl tries to uncover the grammatical train of thought, its preconceptions and development, as it emerges in the books. His objective is not primarily to evaluate the books as teaching aids. However, on that point Fossestøl concludes with an observation that corresponds to Chervel's: "On the whole, grammars that do not pretend to be scholarly will nearly always serve to confirm views that are already well established in research. In actual practice, they will therefore come to function as a defense of the preceding generation's stylistic and linguistic ideals" (p. 262).

It is apparent from the introduction that Fossestøl regards his study as a history of the subject. (P. 7.) He points out that interest in subject history has two sides. First, one wants to discover the background for the currently prevailing views. Second, one wants to determine what views and scientific parameters one's predecessors worked under: "That is, both the real history of the subject and the way of writing about the subject come into focus" (p. 7). The latter viewpoint complements Hertzberg's emphasis on the importance of an interdisciplinary approach.

Indirectly speaking, school grammars may be regarded as a way of writing about the subject, and the science-popularization dichotomy is an important theme for both Chervel and Fossestøl. However, at one point Fossestøl touches on another descriptive function that such books have, or that they *could* have:

Despite the debate (i.e., about language and philosophy), in which several authors eagerly participated, it is a remarkably unbiased world we meet in grammars. In pedagogical terms, they are rather stereotyped, and the examples cited are not very closely connected to contemporary reality, but they often have a clear moralistic purpose. (P. 52.)

Fossestøl's investigation was never intended to deal with precisely this point. Looking at grammar studies as a whole, however, it is remarkable that no one has elected to investigate the world or "reality" delineated by all these examples. If patterns exist, they should command interest in terms of education, ideology and cultural history. And should no such patterns exist, that is also an important characteristic - *inter alia* for the assessment of the influence exerted by the examples used in the various systems and paradigms.

Writing Skills Books

One problem for anyone who wants to carry historical studies of school grammars forward into our own time is the trend toward books that combine an introduction to grammar with extensive practical exercises. During the past few decades, the discipline "language writing skills" has become a regular feature or a major component of such grammars. However, several European countries have traditions of separate writing skills or composition books that go back more than one hundred and fifty years. They include everything from exercise books, which need be nothing more than reprints of old examination papers, to workbooks or theoretical and/or practical introductions to the art of writing. When one considers the prestige and weight attached to the discipline with regard to examinations and grades, it is surprising that such books have scarcely been examined in an historical perspective. In their bibliography of textbook research in the USA, Woodward, Elliott and Nagel (Woodward, et al., 1988) make the following comment:

> The fact that there are only two articles in this section appears to illustrate very well the problem, mentioned above, of the textbook not being recognized as an important factor influencing the quality of classroom instruction. (P. 16.)

This point loses some of its weight, though, when we realize that this same bibliography devotes several pages of references to textbook analyses in each of many other disciplines. The question of why exactly basic writing skills books are underrepresented may possibly be attributable to some extent to the fact that these books have been presented and perceived as teaching aids and workbooks.

Yet this situation also applies to comparable publications in a number of other subjects, not least science and mathematics, where quite a bit of such literature *has* been analyzed, even historically.

The two authors referred to in the American bibliography are B. von B. Donsky (Donsky 1984) and D. H. Graves (Graves 1977). The former has investigated three popular basic English composition books from three different periods between 1900 and 1969. He finds the treatment of form and sentence structure unchanged. On the other hand, he identifies a clear trend toward placing greater emphasis on oral rather than written usage. Graves compared eight basic books from various levels and periods. He concluded that as far as the question of presentation method was concerned, it had not changed or developed since the turn of the century. (Just ten years later a new study would show a different result. Debate and concern about written culture and functional illiteracy in the USA in the 1980s (Hirsch 1987) gave rise to an avalanche of new writing skills books based largely on so-called creative and/or process-oriented writing theory.)

In the introduction to his standard work on the history of the school essay in Germany, Otto Ludwig discusses the source material (Ludwig 1988). He decries the lack of primary source material, that is the essays written by pupils themselves. He also points out many gaps in the information about how and how much writing has taken place. Accounts from teachers and pupils, reports and regulations are too few and too unreliable. The most important sources are

> The works dealing with the didactics and methodology of essays, the manuals, guidelines and recommendations for teaching stylistics and essay writing, rhetoric and stylistics for school use, the countless example books which came on the market, especially in the 19th century, contain so many references to teaching that they form a basis upon which the history of the school essay may be built. (Pp. 5-6.)

Of these sources, Ludwig, like Tarschys, emphasizes didactic and methodological expositions. Textbooks appear sporadically in literature lists and are to some extent part of the presentation, occasionally under separate headings. Ludwig also analyzes the train of methodological thought independent of the topics, content or attitudes in the essay texts.

Books on Literary History

Books on literary history have had a wider distribution than pure grammar books in upper secondary schools in our century. Despite the fact that most Western European countries have produced a fair amount of research literature on literary criticism and the writing of literary history in recent decades, no research has been done in the area of literary histories for the school - at least not in Scandinavia. In the introduction to his study "On Books on the History of Norwegian Literature" (Kittang-Meldahl-Skei 1983), Per Meldahl writes that he especially wants to investigate

> (...) that portion of Norwegian literary historiography that has contributed to *creating* a tradition. This chiefly means that we limit ourselves to the more "professional" literary history writing. Little will therefore be said about literary histories for school use, which are, of course, also a part of Norwegian literary historiography. Let us nevertheless mention that school books (anthologies and literary history commentary) play a significant role when the writing of Norwegian literary history begins to find its form. (Meldahl 1983, p. 113.)

The relationship between the presentation in long, "adult" literary histories and in textbooks, which need not necessarily be a popularization of the former, has not been investigated. Anyone attempting to study it will encounter the problem of the boundary between academic subjects and school subjects just as Chervel, Fossestøl and Hertzberg did in connection with the history of grammars. It has sometimes been difficult recently to determine whether a grammar was written primarily to transmit knowledge to a particular age group or to present a particular view of grammar. As the above quotation suggests, it may appear as if literary histories for the school do not demonstrate as much independence as many school grammars have done. Nevertheless, Meldahl does not quite let go of the idea that the school textbooks have also played "a significant part".

In this connection, an observation made by Øystein Eek in his master's thesis on the writing of literary history in upper secondary textbooks (Eek 1982) is of interest. He points out that the concept of neo-realism was introduced and used systematically in Simon Wright Hofgaard's literary history for the school (5th printing 1920 with Hans Eitrem) before it was adopted into other literary histories (Eek, pp. 88–89). A study would probably reveal that Hofgaard's literary history exhibited a certain uniqueness, representing innovation from the very first printing.

Lars Brink's study of the literary history book's position in Swedish upper secondary schools analyzes the view of literature and the topic and author selection in the most popular books used from 1910 to 1945 (Brink 1992). His work is a doctoral dissertation which tries to ascertain why and how selections and values have changed in schoolbooks (the study also includes anthologies and school editions). Brink also tries to determine the motives for publishing new books, thus giving a composite profile both of literary canons and of editors' role in the school system.

Both Brink's study and those of others seem to indicate certain historical patterns as regards literary histories' attitude to literature and to textbook readers. This pattern is outlined by Bengt-Göran Martinsson in his doctoral dissertation entitled *Tradition and Meaning* (Martinsson 1989): The idealistic/empirical, historical and psychological/symbolic approach. It is remarkable that Martinsson's three historical literary viewpoint strata are not primarily revealed through textbooks, but through pupils' written responses throughout the corresponding period.

Perspectives

Two individual works can stand as a general summary of procedures. One is Choppin's "L'histoire des manuels scolaires: Une approche globale" (Choppin 1980). It is the only somewhat larger theoretical study that exists on the subject. (For Choppin's most recent publication, see page 151.)

The other work is Andolf 1972, which covers most of the perspectives from other historical studies. Andolf's methods and results will also be examined more closely as an appropriate transition to the next chapter where my discussion of the quantitative methods he uses in his summary are further elucidated.

A selection of Choppin's most important points are presented in this context because they illuminate several aspects of the works in the above survey and because they are generally quite applicable to historical textbook research in other countries as well:

– Authors who have written about the history of textbooks have rarely taken time to define the term "textbook". It may seem as though the general familiarity attached to the phenomenon has given it "une réalité indiscutable et des contours précis" (p. 2).
– The many designations for textbooks (livres élémentaires, livres classiques, livres de classe, livres scolaires, ouvrages classiques, manuels, manuels scolaires...) may seem arbitrary, but they are related to the development of both production conditions and legislation/approval.
– Choppin reiterates two authoritative definitions, one from UNESCO and one from *Bibliographie de la France*, and shows that they are not only at odds with each other, but that they also - to the extent that they otherwise might each be adequate on

their own - can only be applied to the situation or purpose in question, which is to quantify production: "School books are all books created for the purpose of helping to teach" (*Bibliographie de la France*, 1969); "School textbooks: books prescribed for pupils receiving education at the first and second levels" (UNESCO 1968).

- If the purpose of carrying out textbook research is to give a complete picture of the knowledge the school has transmitted through printed books, one must include both those which are expressly designed for the school and all the books which, without being produced for such a purpose, have nevertheless become school books through use and convention.
- During periods with official authorization schemes, directives and booklists will be important sources of book titles and viewpoints on textbooks. In the first place, they will tell something about the central authorities' general view on educational policy. Second, they might also say something about influence and pressure from various groups - political parties, religious bodies, educational movements and economic forces.
- Since the 1960s textbooks' share of publishers' sales have sunk. At the same time, the interest in textbooks as research objects has increased. A survey of theses for school history ("mémoires de maîtrise en histoire de l'éducation") from 1968 to 1979 shows that 24 of 283 theses were written on school books (Caspard - Huguet 1979).

Tentatively, Choppin concludes by presenting a survey of different kinds of research, both completed and neglected. In keyword form, the list is as follows:

- Content analyses have dominated French textbook research (to a certain degree studies of individual works or authors, but mainly studies of books from a particular period or on a particular theme as presented in several different books).
- The angle of approach has usually been sociological; one questioned ideologies, value systems, ways of describing society.
- Textbooks for primary school have been far more frequently investigated than textbooks for secondary school.

- The individual subjects whose development has been described using textbook analyses have comprised French mother tongue instruction, philosophy and geography, but above all history (historians and sociologists would probably encounter major problems if faced with the task of analyzing books in mathematics and physics).
- One neglected area has been the distribution of textbooks, their lifetime and place of use, their origins and their authors' backgrounds.
- Another neglected area is the study of textbooks' development as an educational tool. At one time textbooks were usually written by a single author, today almost all titles are co-authored. How and why has this come about? Are there clear trends in the relationship between school subjects and academic subjects? Between textbooks and curricula? How were the books used in their time? What do the prefaces say about this, for example? How were/are they read and used?
- Other neglected areas include the books' historical development as objects and printed matter, publishing history and approval schemes and - in a more recent perspective - the relationship between the presentation of crucial international questions in various countries' textbooks.

Göran Andolf's study (Andolf 1972) stands out among the investigations of the history of particular subjects. It is a study of history teaching illuminated primarily with the aid of the textbooks' contents. Andolf's quantitative method is generally characterized by its meticulous registration of primary and secondary sources, including the charting of circulars, regulations, ordinances, debates, etc., as well as a summary of all the material in the units of the individual chapters. His analysis is descriptive, emphasizing the following categories: The arrangement of material in the books, the selection of material and the extent to which it is representative, the use of names and dates, the use of evaluations, causal explanations, genre ("epic" versus "descriptive"; p. 317) and sources. These categories are measured by number, frequency and degree. Tables and appendices provide running documentation for the analysis. The objective is to discover what historical material pupils have read - and read most of - through the years. For example, the tables list the number of times the names of military leaders and battles are mentioned, citing the line count, in each book's treatment of the conflict surrounding the succession to the throne of Spain (p. 206). Andolf's work, published 17 years after Tarschys' history of mother tongue instruction, relies on methodological theories published for the most part after 1955 (Berelson 1952, Thavenius 1966, Holsti 1969). Andolf discusses the method in a separate chapter in which it is apparent that he places great emphasis on the scientific aspect of his work:

> Characteristic for what are usually called scientific results is that they should be independent of their authors and that they should be verifiable by others. This has not always been true of the methods of investigating text that have been common thus far. The researcher has read the text and has described it on the basis of his impressions. (...) In this way the researcher uses his own personality as a gauge, and what he reads from the gauge are his own experiences. (P. 136.)

Instead, Andolf wants the reader to be presented with information that is as accurate as possible, so he has the opportunity to examine critically the grounds for the data and the conclusions drawn: "In this way quantitative content analysis yields systematic and accurate results." (Pp. 136-37.) Andolf is certainly not without reservations regarding the method; he refers to the same difficulties that Togeby discusses (see page 125), among other things. These problems include the choice of objects for measurement and the establishment of the connection between that which is measured and that which one believes or feels it ought to describe. Nevertheless Andolf believes the method offers many advantages over "the essayistic impressionistic methods that have prevailed thus far" (p. 137); this is especially true as regards "showing how different kinds of material are distributed, i.e., the choices the textbook author has made, and the principles that lie behind them." (P. 137.)

It is not difficult to find objections to the method - or at any rate to the application of it - based on the impersonal scientific platform that is Andolf's point of departure (see above). In the introduction he writes that in their books on history teaching, authors such as Herbert Tingsten and Göran Palm proceed on "the impressions they have gotten from reading, and they occasionally support what they say with quotations. What they choose to include in each book is subjective; particularly the last two studies mentioned may be said to describe their authors better than their objectives." (P. 2.) But even Andolf builds on subjective impressions. Although he chooses among subjects and periods and justifies his choices, they are all based on the assumption that the periods and events that take up a large number of pages in books also dominate instruction. In addition, his categories change for reasons which are not always equally apparent. For example, based on line counts, the cultural aspect is more dominant in the discussion of Egypt, while the political aspect comes to the fore in presentations of the French revolution. In order to systematize material from several different textbooks when making his comparative analysis, Andolf has occasionally found it necessary to divide the textbooks' material and their arrangement of that material to accommodate the categories in his own survey. What we can be sure of is that the content and categories in the books, carefully and judiciously selected by Andolf on the basis of his reading of secondary literature, *have* had the dimensions that Andolf bases his conclusions upon their having. This is verified by measurements and tables. But that form of statistical science does not preclude the "author's" decisive influence, even in this presentation.

Andolf uses his corpus to demonstrate *inter alia* his view of the theory that the content of and objectives for history teaching can be read from the books. Ergo, he analyzes them as expressions of views of teaching - possibly. For, as he himself writes, we lack an analysis of the relationship between history as a subject and educational trends (p. 135).

We are no more certain today than we were in 1972 about the degree to which Andolf is right in his fundamental assumption that "most pupils learn more about what textbooks devote a lot of attention to than about what they neglect" (p. 1). For instance, we do not know much more about which types of language and style have had the greatest impact. Andolf touches upon this area as well, but that discussion constitutes no more than six percent of the exposition.

Göran Andolf has shown how one can use quantitative methods to describe some of the contents of textbooks and, on that basis, to say something significant about the shifting view of history in the school. However, the degree to which his empirically based analysis is an expression of actual teaching might still be an open question.

The many ways in which a subject is presented, in different books and by different teachers, make it difficult to feel that a subject's - or discipline's - "inner" history is identical with the development of the school book version. On the other hand, it would be interesting to investigate whether these books *have* their own history, some strong genre tradition which might compete with and/or determine the school version. As mentioned earlier, Chervel discusses this interplay briefly, but gives it no systematic treatment. The relationship should be clarified, not least because in the larger context of educational politics and social philosophy, one might raise the question of which view of language and reality holds the field at any given time: the school's own language and history or those of the academic subjects.

Chapter III

Ideological Research Traditions

Since textbook research trends have been quite closely linked to the progression of ideological investigations, I have chosen to present a number of national traditions under this heading. I must point out, however, that the survey is not exhaustive, neither in terms of the individual countries nor in a larger perspective. Neither does it try to register systematically the connecting links and inspirations transmitted between research communities in various countries.

To a certain extent, this section also considers directions and fields other than those that deal with ideology.

The presentation of national traditions occasionally consists of quotations from the different parties' own presentation of the tradition in question.

Historical Background

Duisburg

In the early half of the 1970s, staff members at the University of Duisburg began to take a serious interest in making systematic investigations of textbooks as political media.

The two trendsetters were E. Horst Schallenberger and Gerd Stein, both professors of political science. From 1973 to 1978, they edited and published a series of books called *Zur Sache Schulbuch*. The intense activity continued into the early 1980s, while the Institute published less comprehensive individual publications - *IfS-Impulse* - based on conferences devoted to how the question of peace, the Jewish issue and Europe were portrayed in textbooks.

The Duisburg tradition is embodied in the titles of the first and last volumes in the *Zur Sache Schulbuch* series: *Das Schulbuch - Produkt und Faktor gesellschaftlicher Prozesse* (volume 1 1973; see Schallenberger) and *Schulbuchwissen, Politik und Pädagogik* (volume 10 1977/78; see Stein). Both Schallenberger and Stein return repeatedly to the starting point for their scholarly interest in textbooks, i.e., the sharp criticism and extensive attention focused on such books by the West German media in the early 1970s.

The criticism was directed

actually far less at the textbook as a didactic medium than at the textbook
- as an object of political conflict
- as an expenditure within the framework of public education expenses
- as an investment project for publishers, i.e., as one of many goods sold in bookshops

- as an instrument of government control of teaching and education; in short: it concerns the textbooks as a POLI-TICUM. (Stein 1976, p. 25.)

The stimuli for the public interest taken in textbooks as political literature stemmed from several sources. In the 1960s educators and jurists at colleges and universities began to take an interest in the approval schemes practiced in the various Bundesländer. This interest coincided with the new school reforms which compelled parents to read textbooks carefully; some even went so far as to form action groups and protest against the use of certain titles. The anti-authoritarian educational sentiments of the times led to the publication of more class-conscious textbooks with more distinct political profiles. The biggest attention-getter was a work called *Drucksachen*, published the same year as *Onward and Never Forget* (see page 151), which shows a similar tendency. The mass media used it in a smear campaign against the political party CDU during the election in Niedersachsen in 1974 (Langenbucher - Mast 1979).

What Schallenberger and Stein wanted was, on the one hand, to conduct investigations which might shed light on textbooks as social and school media and, on the other hand, to exploit general interest in order to build bridges between disciplines such as political science and pedagogy and promote multi-perspective and interdisciplinary textbook research (Stein 1977; p. V).

This point of departure offers a far broader perspective than work on history book revision. Duisburg also spawned analyses within that tradition, e.g., a large-scale comparison of the pictures of Germany portrayed in history books in Switzerland, Austria and East and West Germany from 1945 to 1955; an investigation which concluded that the textbooks - irrespective of country - presented very one-sided views and limited pupils' chances to form their own opinions (Overesch 1978). Such a conclusion offers an entirely different perspective from that of Sprenger (see page 89), who, for example, states in another contribution in the same series that he sees the open competition in the West as a guarantee for less textbook bias there than in the East (Sprenger 1977). These examples give an indication of the range of the work being conducted at the Institut für Schulbuchforschung in Duisburg.

In many ways the work done at Duisburg has been fundamental, although it was never really completed (the Institute was closed in 1990). The IfS succeeded no better in reaching textbooks' authors, editors and users than the publications from the Institute, which were generally influenced by the editors' areas of expertise, succeeded in recruiting an influx of new scholars into the academic community. In a recapitulation commemorating the tenth anniversary of the Institute one of its board members, Michael Alloys Schillo, called for the dissemination of new knowledge (Schillo 1987). He asked how many users had been informed about textbooks' political and scientific aspects. He also asked whether the researchers had actually come up with an answer to the ever-recurring question of why there are approval schemes and why textbooks still seem to be too difficult for many pupils. In addition, he asked how many publishers' editors had been informed of the research results.

Most of the salient factors related to the objectives and experiences gained at Duisburg were discussed in Franz Pöggeler's book on politics in textbooks (Pöggeler 1985). Schallenberger and Stein are also contributors, but the book's list of contributors offers a reminder that textbook research was carried out at many West German universities in the 1980s; five different research centers are represented in Pöggeler's book, which covers a wide range of subjects and has a composition that illustrates the Duisburg ideals. In the first article, "Politik im Schulbuch", Franz Pöggeler justifies his reasons for addressing the topic. He does this by setting up five working hypotheses:

1. Political influence in teaching and textbooks is not limited to the social sciences; it occurs in all subjects, even those traditionally thought of as apolitical.

2. Hence it is crucial to distinguish between *intentional* and *functional* political influence. Basic political beliefs are even embodied in the ABCs, whose only express goal has been to teach the alphabet. This is even more obvious in song books, for example.

3. Neither textbook authors nor teachers are sufficiently aware of this. This means that biased and incorrect information can be

passed on freely; i.e., we are dealing with a functional form of political indoctrination which is also "subcutaneous", meaning it "lies under the skin".

4. Most textbook analyses which deal with influence treat textbooks used at higher levels ("vom Beginn des Jugendalters") based on the assumption that political influence ("Bildung") does not begin before that. Yet such influence starts already in pupils' very first textbooks.

5. Ideally, one would not form an overall opinion of textbooks' political form and content until one had the whole picture. But such a vantage point is not feasible. (Pöggeler discusses *methods* immediately after this viewpoint; see page 387.)

The combination of textbook analyses and the numerous textbook excerpts in the book confirms the contention set out in point 1. At the same time, the various analyses - of books in a total of seven subjects - provide ammunition for those who claim that teachers, not least at the lowest levels, should be given special courses in textbook science. Uncovering a text's explicit and implicit messages calls for procedures that require awareness and training beyond that needed for more traditional literary analysis.

The most lengthy contribution to the book is Barbara Klauss and Günther Brilla's analysis of biology books for the primary, lower secondary and upper secondary levels (Klauss - Brilla 1985). The authors point out that it is easier for readers to see the ideology in textbooks based on national socialism and marxism than that contained in West German books published after the war. Recent curricula have not offered any guidance on the relationship between biology and social issues. Yet controversial issues and opinions are inevitable within the subject's individual disciplines, e.g., sexual instruction, nature and the environment and genetics. The analysis' goal will not only be to determine whether the viewpoints on controversial issues are represented, but also to identify the form in which they are presented. This latter point refers not only to the choice of words and formulations, but also to the overall context of the statements. The book's composition, its basic attitude as expressed not least through its style, must also be examined. To exemplify this, the authors mention one condition in particular. In the former GDR, textbooks had one express, principal goal: They were to promote the development of the socialistic, classless state. Textbooks in the West are intended to build up positive attitudes toward life and society, too. Yet attitude-molding factors there are not an explicit part of the textbook ideology per se in the same way as they are/were in the East. The authors show how emotional, positive statements engender general optimism in the East German books, while West German textbooks often exhibit undertones which are directly pessimistic (p. 185).

Braunschweig and the GDR

The institute in Duisbrug has cooperated with the Georg Eckert Institute in Braunschweig; one important impetus for their cooperation was the international conference entitled "Europa im Schulbuch", arranged in Duisburg in 1977 (Schillo 1987). The conference was subsequently followed up by an institute project called "Europa im Schulbuch - Schulbücher in Europa" (Gödde-Baumann 1987).

In this area, however, it is the Georg Eckert Institute in Braunschweig that has dominated European research. The Institute has been an important venue for work in connection with the international revision of history and geography books. Today it is Europe's largest textbook institute, and it boasts a long, uninterrupted history. The Institute publishes annual bibliographies of textbook research. The list from 1988 includes 171 titles, most of them from West Germany. The majority of the titles were written by people at or associated with the Institute.

One typical feature of the Braunschweig tradition is the loyalty consistently shown to the ideals of the founder of the Institute. Georg Eckert's belief in the ability of textbooks to promote tolerance and the desire for peace has steered the Institute's work for more than 40 years, focusing on making comparative studies of how countries and the peace issue are portrayed in textbooks. Another typical trait of a more methodical nature has also helped determine the direction of these efforts. The selection of material and its presentation *in the books* have been the dominant focus of interest at the expense of questions concerning development and use of textbooks.

However, this situation began to change in the mid-1980s. The selection of topics is now more varied, and several researchers at the institute are concentrating on methodological problems. Naturally, methodology has been discussed in articles that have appeared fairly regularly throughout the history of the Institute (Weinbrenner 1986), but not with the same intensity as at the Duisburg institute from 1977 to 1987.

A few examples of recent investigations undertaken at Braunschweig may be indicative of the activity which now appears to be branching out in many directions.

In an article published in 1986, the director of the Institute, Ernst Hinrichs, discussed the relationship between research and textbooks in the subject of history (Hinrichs 1986). He examined eight currently used history books at the lower secondary level and compared their description of absolutism (Absolutismus) with contemporary, generally accepted research results produced by English, French and German historians. Such results were not reflected in the books. While contemporary research defines absolutism mainly as a *structure*, rather loosely connected to time and place, the textbooks maintain that the concept is a time-related or *epochal* phenomenon. The conclusion of the article interjects a viewpoint which must be said to pertain to educational ideology. Hinrichs seems to believe that the curricula may impede contact and cooperation between researchers and textbook authors: "Perhaps this will change in the new generation of textbooks despite the limitations imposed by the curricula?" (P. 320.)

In the article "Can't we get rid of the prejudices?" (Fritzsche 1989), the author asks "whether the fact that we can manage without prejudices is not in itself a prejudice?" (p. 376). Fritzsche explains the German preoccupation with national characteristics, prejudices and biases in history books as symptomatic of the fact that Germany's entire political culture is burdened "with a history of problems with its national consciousness" (p. 385).

The issue of *Internationale Schulbuchforschung* in which Fritzsche's article was published also contains other contributions which tell of a broadening and rejuvenation of scope, e.g., toward textbooks in subjects other than history and geography, foreign languages (see Kubanek, page 107) and of non-European conditions (the Third World; see von Laer 1989; Sperling 1989). It is also typical of this broader perspective that the Institute soon after published a book on how textbooks fulfill the requirements concerning introductions to local history and civics - *The 'little space' as a problem of international textbook research* (Hinrichs 1990). "Regionality" has become a buzzword in educational planning in Germany as well. One of the reasons for publishing the book was that little attention had previously been paid to the concept of regionality and the important political aspects it encompasses.

As a contribution to UNESCO's efforts to establish criteria for the improvement of educational materials with an international dimension, the Institute also published a report on studies undertaken and in the planning stage in this field (Georg-Eckert-Institut 1991). A report edited by the Council of Europe presents lectures on textbook analysis held at an international workshop in Braunschweig in 1990 (Bourdillon 1992).

A new question has become urgent since the reunification of East and West Germany in 1990. Should school systems and textbooks originating under a totalitarian and a democratic form of government, respectively, be adjusted to accommodate each other, or should all traditions from the totalitarian regime be abandoned? Karl Peter Fritzsche describes the problem as follows:

> Firstly, will it be possible for former citizens and experts of the GDR to be allowed to develop their own textbooks, offering the opportunity for an open discussion about the past and the present? Secondly, to what extent will the process of German reunification act as a suction pipe, producing homogeneity which will have repercussions on the West German political culture and language? This could unleash a form of semantic crusade against any terms belonging to the semantic word field including "Socialism". (Fritzsche 1990, p. 7).

A retrospective look at textbook research and textbook development in the GDR during the past few decades will provide a far stronger argument for mutual accommodation than for West German predominance.

A whole school of textbook research was developed in the GDR. *Schulbuchgestaltung in der DDR* (Autorenkollektiv 1984) may be seen as the most important manifestation of this tradition. The tradition initially became strong and well-developed because of the emphasis the regime placed on learning and education. In that connection considerable importance was attached to textbooks. The book's preface states *inter alia*:

> The textbooks in the GDR are indispensable for giving children a Communist upbringing, for preparing them for life and productive work in the future formation of the mature Socialist society. (P. 9.)

In the same preface, the authors cite the "Programm der Sozialistischen Einheitspartei Deutschlands" from 1976. The pupils are to develop so that "the thoughts and actions of the workers are characterized by the Socialistic ideology, the working class' Marxist-Leninist philosophy of life."

Such a clearly expressed ideology, practiced by a loyal body of teachers within a totalitarian state, automatically provided the following objective for those whose job it was to make the textbooks: To convey the official ideology as well as possible in books on all subjects and to maximize the efficiency of the same books as educational instruments.

It was actually possible to draw historical parallels to justify homogeneity. As recently as in 1989, a paper was presented at the 14th scientific textbook conference in Halle-Köthen in which the author indirectly placed the Marxist-liberal conflict into an historical perspective. He said that one has to distinguish between two different categories of books. Books in the first category are based on scientifically proven facts (Grundkonzeption), while those in the other are based on more liberally and eclectically selected thoughts (eklektisches Gedankengut):

> The first category comprises textbooks based on the educational concept of the Reformation, the textbooks of RATKE and KOMENSKY in the 17th century, and the textbooks of the Philanthropists in the 18th century. The second, the eclectic,

comprises the countless mass of different textbooks that are used in German classrooms. (Egerland 1990, p. 36.)

For textbook work, the GDR ideology meant that the books' attributes as educational instruments became the main focus of interest. However, this occurred as an obvious extension of the ultimate message, which primarily resulted in the emphasizing of attitude-molding material. Irrespective of whether the books were for mathematics, history or biology, there is a conspicuous tendency toward using evaluative, emotional material which is positive and constructive. A work produced by the director of the Ratke Institute in Köthen, H.-J. Schwier, is called "Methodische Überlegungen zur emotionalen Werksamkeit von Lehrbuchabschnitten im Biologieunterrict" (Schwier 1980). The ideology is also apparent in the books' evaluations of social and political conditions in the West, especially in the history books (see page 91).

A research community evolved, based on the teachers college in Halle-Köthen and the sole textbook publisher, Volk und Wissen, where head of research Horst Strietzel was a key person. The work done there has been significant in two areas:

1. The East Germans developed a systematic method of text research which placed heavy emphasis on the composition and structure of the textbook material. Financial difficulties precluded the use of many illustrations and extra-textual enhancements, but this doesn't explain why the textbook *texts* received so much attention. The explanation lies partly in the fact that the texts were accorded far more prestige than has been the case in the West, and partly in the fact that East German researchers were able to base their work on well-developed theories originating in Romania, Hungary, Bulgaria, Estonia and Poland, and especially on theories developed in the Soviet Union.

2. How much can pupils learn from such texts, and how do they learn fastest? The GDR has made attempts to answer this question using practical measurements of classroom results. Several analytical systems have been developed to obtain such

measurements, which have been far more comprehensive than comparable measurements undertaken in countries in the West.

There was cooperation with the former Soviet Union, thanks not least to Dmitri Sujew, one of the leading textbook theorists in the former Soviet Union and for years director of Moscow's foremost textbook publisher, Prosweschtschenie. His 1983 book, *Shkaalnij Utsjebnik* (*The Schoolbook*), was translated to German by Volk und Wissen in 1986 (Sujew 1986). It presents analytical models based on a holistic, Marxist-Leninist framework. As basic systematic research, Sujew's book is unparalleled in the West. Owing to traditions and the political system, Sujew is able to take the book's leading role in the classroom for granted. There would be no point in arguing against viewpoints such as the following one, excerpted from the introduction to the chapter on *Function-Structure Analysis*:

> The textbook is part of the teaching media system; it is at the very core of the system.
> Relatively speaking, the textbook is an independent system, it realizes certain functions and has a specific structure.
> The textbook is a complete system in which all parts have a special task and demonstrate independent design and form. (Sujew 1986, p. 177.)

In the USSR textbook researchers have been publishing annual editions of a series called "Textbook Development and Textbook Research" since 1974. As early as 1970, East Germany began publishing the same sort of series: *Informationen zu Schulbuchfragen*. Volume 53 from 1985 contains a table of contents from 1979 to 1984. It includes more than 500 titles, the majority of which concern text analysis, user surveys and discussions of methodology.

Both sides are obviously willing to unite the GDR and FRG traditions. Leading textbook researchers from the West have expressed their fear that research publications from the GDR and the research institutions themselves will disappear (Bamberger 1990). One sign pointing in the opposite direction is the establishment of the Wissenschaftliches Zentrum für Schulbuchforschung am Wolfgang-Ratke-Institut, which was founded in Köthen in December 1990.

The USA

One general characteristic of textbook investigations in the USA is that most of their results are presented in the form of articles and reports. Compared with the large number of such investigations, it is striking that the results of so few have been published in book form. The number of books that include several reports in the same volume is also modest.

The growing interest shown during the past two decades in textbooks as political literature follows a tradition predicted earlier by several researchers. Basic work done in this field includes Shaver's (Shaver 1965) and Fox and Hess' analyses of material on social conflicts in social studies books (Fox - Hess 1972). Shaver found the whole portrayal of US society in 93 high school textbooks to be naive and unrealistic, while the other two researchers demonstrated that social conflicts and conflicts of interest are either totally precluded from or not explained in such books. Their observation of this absence is a crucial point seen in connection with Michael Apple's studies (see page 148). In his book *Ideology and Curricula* (2. ed. 1990), the latter discusses how conflicting views in science generate knowledge, and how the exclusion of such dynamics in textbooks serves to transmit special ideologies. Works such as these of Fox, Hess and Apple have been among the most important inspiration forces for later work in Scandinavia developing in their wake.

A large number of ideological investigations were published in the USA in the 1970s and 1980s. As far as method is concerned, these studies are reminiscent of the European history textbook revision. However, Jean Anyon's investigation, entitled "Ideology and United States History Textbooks" (Anyon 1979) was published in 1979. Many regarded Anyon's study to be a "landmark in the analysis of school textbooks" (Gilbert 1989, p. 63). For this author, ideology is "an explanation or interpretation of social reality which, although presented as objective, is demonstrably partial in that it expresses the social priorities of certain political, economic, or other groups" (Anyon 1979, p. 363). Anyon reviews the presentation of economics and business and industry in history books and also focuses on the production and sale of textbooks. This last field also received special national attention in 1983 when the National Commission on Excellence in Education published a very influential report on the need for educational reform not least in the area of textbooks: *A Nation at Risk: the Imperative for Educational Reform* (Government Printing Office 1983). Ideology gradually became a question of market forces, production facilities and more or less obvious approval schemes, as much as a question of the books' content. The 30th yearbook of the NSSE was the first unequivocal expression of this (NSSE 1931).

In the USA, research is conducted at numerous institutions and spread across a wide geographical area. As far as publications are concerned, there are about ten reference centers and journals that stand out (Woodward - Elliott - Nagel 1988, p. 6). One state also stands out in this context: Cronbach's unparalleled work from 1955, the NSSE yearbooks (NSSE 1931, 1990) and Woodward's bibliography have all originated in one way or another at the University of Illinois Urbana, also the home of the *Journal of Curriculum Studies* (ed. Ian Westbury). The journal has presented a great deal of material on textbook theory.

Recent Trends in Other Countries

Sweden has dominated textbook traditions in the Nordic countries, both textbook research in general and ideological investigations in particular.

The books written by Palm and Tingsten (see pages 137 and 102) provided the impetus for textbook research at several Swedish colleges and universities. In the 1970s and early 1980s, there was a tradition of internationalism, concerned with how other countries were presented in Swedish textbooks (Gullberg - Lind 1969, O!sson 1986), and a more domestic tradition, concerned with issues such as how the term *democracy* was presented in the textbooks (Anderberg 1981).

An atmosphere of cooperation developed in Sweden between the research institutions and SiL, the State Institute for Teaching

Materials. The Institute eventually initiated a number of topic-related investigations, performed as commissioned research (e.g., Women and men in literary history, A study of political parties, How working life is described in Swedish teaching materials). The reports were based on scientific investigations aimed not at approval or disapproval, but at making even better books in the future.

As far as Sweden is concerned, it is possible to follow developments from the introduction of the approval system in 1938, to 1988. The latter year marked the presentation of the Report from the Teaching Materials Board (Ds 1988:22), which maps the textbook situation and sets out a program of action. The program contains no separate item pertaining to research, but it recommends a better approval system that sets very high standards for those in charge of examining the books. A combination of a program with correspondingly high standards and a tradition of cooperation between the senior school authorities and competent investigators constitutes a rare model, to which there are no direct parallels in the Nordic countries or other places in Europe. However, The State Institute for Teaching Materials was discontinued in the summer of 1991, and it seems clear that the newly-organized administrative system, the new School Administration, will not be involved with textbook approval.

The primary textbook research community in Sweden today is the Institute for Educational Text Research in Härnösand, headed by Staffan Selander, who was deeply involved in curriculum theory and textbook-related studies throughout the 1980s. In 1984, he published his *Textum Institutionis - the Pedagogical Web*. In it, he analyzes how texts are used in different contexts, why they are moved from certain contexts to other contexts, and what happens to them in the process (Selander 1984). Four years later he published *Textbook Knowledge* (Selander 1988), a complex analysis of a large number of history textbooks. The author discusses the textbook as a genre and the significance of social and institutional parameters for the content and form of textbooks and, based on the perspective of curriculum theory, he points out how one may develop methods for textbook analysis. This model is then applied to an analysis that reveals cognitive content patterns in history books over a period of 100 years, based mainly on the type of paradigmatic knowledge and basic images used in the books, both at the topic and the meta-level. In an article in the *Scandinavian Journal of Educational Research*, Selander has outlined part of his program as follows:

> To make textbook analysis a scientific endeavour, we make the following assumptions:
>
> [1] There is an objective world outside our minds.
> [2] Textbooks are socially determined reconstructions of this objective world.
> [3] The textbook is basically framed by the institution (e.g. the educational system).
> [4] The textbook is structured to fit institutionally defined needs, and thus it had an inner structure of its own.
> [5] It is possible to reframe the textbook analytically so that the relationship between (a) the text in the textbook and the outside world and (b) the textbook and other (e.g. scientific) texts can be traced. Thus it is possible to analyze the kind of paradigmatic thought (perspectives, models of explanations, etc.) that a single textbook or a set of textbooks represents. (Selander 1990, pp. 143-44.)

The program has been implemented at the Institute in Härnösand. The research element encompasses a number of textbook studies, some of which are connected to newspaper studies. The research deals with how the textbook presents topics such as Africa, racism, (Spov 9/1990) business and industry (Selander 1992), the ratio of text to pictures, and the books' view of knowledge and science. Moreover, the Institute is now developing courses to train textbook researchers. This will be followed up by further education courses and network programs, including reports and the Institute's own periodical (Spov 1989, Spov 1990, Spov 1991, Spov 1992.).

Austria opened its own *Institut für Schulbuchforschung*, headed by Richard Bamberger, in Vienna in 1988. In a general briefing, Bamberger describes the Institute's tasks as follows:

The Institute has been set up with the help of the Federal Ministry of Education, Culture and Sport. Since the very beginning one of its main activities has been the development of methods of textbook analysis. A number of worksheets have been drafted so far; some of them have been tested in practice and have yielded certain results.

The following relevant areas of activity may be mentioned:

1. A worksheet to *analyse whether a textbook corresponds to the age and level of pupils* and is difficult or easy to digest - with 28 items to mark and explanatory notes.

2. *Tests* to find out whether the textbook has contributed to *efficient learning* and whether terms have been understood correctly (for various school subjects).

For example 100 items spread over five tests were developed for civics education. Preliminary results show how important it is to offer political education not only through history but also across various other subjects.

3.Worksheets to *analyse textbook contents* and compare different textbooks used in Austria and abroad:

3.1 *Space analysis*: how much space is given to different countries or topics, e.g. the situation of women or of children of different social groups;

3.2 *Frequency analysis*: how often certain names and terms or topics appear in textbooks;

3.3 *Analysis of what textbooks say*: comparative interpretation of textbooks or of certain topics dealt with in textbooks.

4. Circular letters to *publishers, authors and teachers* are in preparation. The idea is to put questions about aspects of design, use and efficiency of textbooks.

5. *Prejudices and underlying assumptions* are examined in the context of content analysis mentioned above.

6. *Criteria with regard to subject matter didactics*: whether a textbook is suited for a particular group of pupils and not too difficult is a key question of research undertaken so far. Even before the Institute was set up, two projects were devoted to this problem area:

6.1   Dr. Richard Bamberger and Prof. Dr. Erich Vanecek, Research into reading, understanding, learning and writing;

6.2   Dr. Richard Bamberger, a research report (about 600 pages) about the question of whether textbooks are easy to read and useful learning tools.

7. *Analysis of the approach used in textbooks*: development of

7.1) a general textbook analysis grid;
7.2) special grids for history, geography, biology, physics and reading books in the mother tongue.

8. *Bibliography*
The Institute is busy compiling a bibliography, in particular of the literature on textbook analysis: more than 100 items.

9. Discussions with publishers, authors and Ministry experts testing textbooks aim at drawing *conclusions for the preparation, production and publication of textbooks.*

10. *Neglected areas of research*: research as to whether text-books are adequate for a particular group of pupils and easy to read. (Bamberger 1990.)

In 1971 the Georg Eckert Institute published volume 16 in its series of publications, which was entitled *Europe. The History and Topicality of Concepts.* The author, Rolf-Joachim Sattler, presents an exposition on Europe as an historical and political entity. It is based on conferences and work conducted under the auspices of the Council of Europe and consists of an exceptionally detailed conceptual analysis. Sattler's intention was to help clarify the concept in textbooks (Sattler 1971).

Twenty years later, the Institut für Schulbuchforschung in Vienna presented an investigation entitled: "Das Europabild im Schulbuch. Zum Europabegriff in den österreichischen Geschichts- und Geographiebüchern der 8. Schulstufe." (Gattermann - Gintenstorfer 1991.) The authors examined six books in each subject. They used analytical grids containing a series of different categories, ranging from text length, documentation, exercises and illustrations to the registration of occurrences of European topics and European designations. The method is quantitative, measuring "Space" and "Frequency", while the surveys are concluded with an interpretive "Summary". The summary contends that the picture of Europe presented in Austrian textbooks is arbitrary. There is no uniform concept or systematic attempt to establish cultural or political unity:

> Well, Europe is more than the EC, but most textbook authors give the EC priority. In simple terms: Eastern Europe means the East-West conflict and Western Europe is the EC!
> (...)
> An economic and political Europe, a Europe of culture and a Europe committed to human rights: In the history books we find nothing but an economic Europe! (Gattermann - Gintenstorfer 1991, p. 28.)

In the *United Kingdom*, the Colloquium on Textbooks, Schools and Society was established in 1988:

> to promote the interdisciplinary study of textbooks. Meetings are held three times a year, when possible in surroundings which are evocative of textbooks and their use. Venues so far have included the libraries of Eton College and Westminster School. Programmes are planned to include both general methodological discussion and papers on specific topics. Among those considered so far have been; the Latin grammars of Melanchthon

[16th century] and Kennedy [19th century], the writings of the early 19th-century educationist Mrs Trimmer, the mathematics textbooks of Robert Recorde [16th century], the influence of printing from plates, the Frobelian books of Mrs Walker, William Godwin's venture into publishing, 19th-century biology textbooks, the 17th-century catalogue of King's Norton Grammar School, and history textbooks at Oxford and Cambridge in the mid-nineteenth century. The Colloquium issues a newsletter, *Paradigm*, which carries both articles and summaries of papers given at meetings. It is intended to expand the newsletter to include listings of information sources, notes and queries and a research register. (Fauvel - Michael - Stray - Wilkes 1990.)

In *France*, the Institut National de Recherche Pédagogique has been and is an important center for textbook research (see Chervel, Choppin, EMMANUELLE, Tournier). So is La Socitété pour l'Information sur les Manuels Scolaires (see Huot).

Australia and *Canada* have several universities with staff members who have done and continue to do textbook research (see de Castell, Gilbert, Luke, Olson). These reseachers have established an informal network among themselves and have produced a fundamental work as a manifestation of this cooperation: *Language, Authority and Criticism. Readings on the School Textbook.* (De Castell - Luke - Luke (eds.) 1989.):

Unlike previous anthologies - which have tended to gather research and commentary from particular disciplines (for example, reading psychology, curriculum theory and development, literary criticism) - *Language, Authority and Criticism* features original articles from a range of disciplinary perspectives. Controversial matters of textbook ideological content, discourse form, and classroom use are examined by sociologists, literary critics, linguists, psychologists and educationists. Additionally, the economic and political influences on textbook publishing, adoption and censorship are considered. (Cover.)

One special manifestation of interest in Canada is the publication entitled *Embattled Books: The State of the Text* (Willinsky - Bogdan 1990). The book contains contributions from authors such as Michael W. Apple, James Moffett and Suzanne de Castell. They discuss the textbook from a financial and social perspective.

In *Japan*, the Japan Textbook Research Center in Tokyo has been in operation for some ten years now. It was founded as a research center which mainly intended to "offer the results of its research to membership publishers of textbooks, and to help any organizations or people who are now making or want to make surveys about textbooks" (*Outline of Japan Textbook Research Center* 1990). The Center's practical objective is more strongly pronounced than those at comparable insitutes in Europe. In addition to its commitment to helping to improve the quality of Japanese textbooks, the Center has a distinct international orientation. Among its publications from the 1980s are comparative studies of social science textbooks from the USA and Japan (see page 98) and one of books and syllabuses in five different countries (the USA, the UK, France, and the former FRG and USSR). In March 1990, the library boasted almost 75,000 volumes, virtually all of which have been published in Japan since 1945, in addition to a considerable collection of foreign textbooks. The Center is currently working on setting up a textbook library database to systematize all post-war Japanese titles. Furthermore, the Center has established contact with approximately 20 other nations for the purpose of exchanging textbooks (*School Textbooks in Japan* 1991, p. IV).

The University of Tartu in Estonia has a special textbook research department, which has published a composite work entitled *Problems of Textbook Effectivity* (Tartu Ulikooli Toimetised 1991). The contributions are in the predominant tradition of former Eastern Bloc countries, based on advanced systems for measuring accessibility in and the learning effect of texts.

The Nation in the Textbooks

International Textbook Revision

Traditionally, studies have been based on the desire to describe a nation's own self-image as depicted in textbooks. This brings up the need for comparison - to see how one's own country is described in foreign books and how other nations are described in the books of one's own country or of other countries.

Many such comparative and contrastive studies have been made, and most of them are firmly rooted in German research. There is one particular tradition that stands out in this school of research. It involves analyzing the content of history books across national borders. International peace efforts have provided the framework for this work. It does not focus primarily on investigations of how the presentation of certain topics has changed over the years; the main point has been to investigate the presentation of certain topics in books used at the same time in different countries.

During the inter-war years, many countries took the initiative to ensure that textbooks in history and to some extent also in geography were endowed with a content and a spirit that would encourage tolerance and stimulate the desire for peace. Most agreements were bilateral at that time; the first was signed between Argentina and Brazil in 1933. English, French and German historians were moving in the same direction, but their work progressed slowly.

The work accelerated in the 1950s, and UNESCO, the Georg Eckert Institute in Braunschweig and, later, the Council of Europe, played pivotal roles. The background and development of the efforts have been described by the English textbook author E.H. Dance in a book entitled *History the Betrayer* (Dance 1960). The work has not comprised organized, systematic research; it has been made up of separate projects through which interested historians have voluntarily cooperated across national borders to eliminate errors, prejudices and biases in the presentation of national histories and international incidents and conflicts. Following a resolution passed by the Council of Europe, in 1965 the Georg Eckert Institute was named the center for the administration of and information on the work, which is still in progress. According to the Institute's annual report for 1989, there are still cooperation agreements involving the exchange and examination of history and/or geography textbooks between 14 European countries and Africa and Latin America (no countries are specified for the last two areas).

In 1967 Otto-Ernst Schüddekopf edited *History Teaching and History Textbook Revision* (Schüddekopf 1967). It is a summary of the revision work done up to that time. Two of the articles in it were written by Haakon Vigander, a school principal who was a prime-mover in this field for a generation. Vigander points out three matters of interest. He rejects such revision work if it has not been achieved through the cooperative efforts of researchers from several countries at the same time. He also rejects it if contact has not been established with authors who are - or will be - open to changes. Finally, the changes effected through books must also be effected through teacher education: "... young teachers and would-be teachers may be got out of the old rut" (Vigander 1967, p. 64).

A more recent contribution in the tradition of history textbook revision is a collection of essays called *Perceptions of History* (Berghahn - Schissler 1987). A dozen articles on Britain, the former West Germany and the USA seek to create an awareness of the significance of critical schoolbook scrutiny. Hanna Schissler's conclusions (pp. 36-37) underline the need for continued research.

East and West Germany
(the GDR and the FRG)

As previously mentioned, Germany was and still is a major center for textbook revision research. Naturally, developments following

WWII made the work done in Germany particularly interesting. After the constitution of East Germany in 1949, pupils in the new state were given a new set of textbooks. All the books had been written recently, and one and the same book was used for all pupils at a particular level in a particular subject. How were German history and the picture of the German national identity presented in those books, compared with the textbooks used in West Germany?

This question has been thoroughly discussed by several West German researchers in volume 43 of a series of books published by the Georg Eckert Institute (Jacobmeyer 1986). The volume, which is some 600 pages long, contains six very comprehensive analyses of how Germany is portrayed in textbooks on geography, history and the social sciences in the two German states from 1949 until the 1980s (see page 142).

An early analysis of the portrayal of Germany in East German textbooks, written by Reinhard Sprenger, was published in the Institute at Duisburg's series *Zur Sache Schulbuch* in 1977 (Sprenger 1977). Sprenger's description of East German conditions is quite representative of West German attitudes toward East German textbooks, and probably of Western European attitudes toward East Bloc textbooks in general. The author starts by pointing out that since each subject is covered by no more than one title or series, the portrayal of Germany must of necessity be one-sided:

> Since this book stands and works alone, with no competition, this book and history instruction based on it give pupils a structured, one-sided picture of history, especially German history. (Sprenger 1977, p. 82.)

No one can deny that Sprenger's view has some merit in principle, but it should be added that the existence of several publishers or competing titles does not necessarily guarantee any more variety. It has been contended that the variation seen in Western textbooks is usually only of a technical nature (Johnsen 1989). While some investigations indicate that all history and social science textbooks contain similar views and ideologies, no investigations have indicated that competition results in any fundamental contrasts.

Sprenger also points out the problems encountered by a newly established state like the GDR in its presentation of pre-1949 history. For example, the books contained more international material from those times and placed greater emphasis on the historical role of the working class. As regards the brief period after 1949, the objective was also:

> formulated clearly and unambiguously: The establishment of a Socialistic consciousness on the basis of selected (with emphasis on selected) historical knowledge, which had to be based on the maxims of Marxist history and its foundation in historical materialism. (..) This applies to ideological education and upbringing. (P. 84.)

Sprenger also criticizes the malicious, one-sided portrayal of Western imperialism and the capitalist system of exploitation which appears in East German textbooks.

These viewpoints raise several interesting fundamental and practical questions for those wishing to investigate the ideologies inherent in history and social science textbooks. First: How much more "accurate" is the picture of the GDR presented in textbooks produced in the FRG from 1949 to 1989, than the corresponding picture of the FRG that appears in textbooks printed in the GDR during the same period? Second: If this question were thoroughly investigated as a basis for research and development, what ramifications would the result have for the portrayal of Germany in the new post-reunification history textbooks?

In 1990–1991, history and social science textbooks published by the Volk und Wissen company of East Berlin were removed from schools, and the books were more or less replaced by publications from West German publishing houses. Neither East German authors nor new publishing houses were prepared to write new textbooks on such short notice. Consequently, the books already in use in the West were introduced directly in the East.

This situation has not been welcomed with overwhelming enthusiasm by the other major center for textbook research in the former GDR. That academic community, which collaborated with researchers at Volk und Wissen, was located at the College of Education at Halle-Köthen. An international conference on textbook research was arranged in Köthen in November 1990. Klaus Oestreich, a member of the college staff, delivered a lecture called "Deutsche Geschichte seit 1945 in Schulbüchern der beiden deutschen Staaten" (Oestreich 1990). In association with the planned introduction of West German textbooks, a group of researchers led by Oestreich investigated 23 history books from a West German publisher. In schematic terms, their comprehensive investigation of textbook contents provides a detailed and systematic impression of what, in the West German tradition of history textbook revision, are called biases and prejudices. However, Oestreich also points out that West German textbooks contain values absolutely worth passing on and developing further. As a supplement to Sprenger's comment on the portrayal of Germany in East German textbooks (see above), it may be appropriate to cite Oestreich's description of how West German books depict the people of East Germany:

> The textbooks' descriptions of events in the GDR are often reduced to the power and hierarchical system, sufficing with conclusions, statements and initiatives delivered "from on high" by party and state officials. The people in the GDR are faceless, passive and, quite simply, misguided and oppressed. (...) It is therefore impossible to develop a balanced portrayal of "Socialism" in the GDR. There is a lack of empirically collected conclusive accounts and contemporary documents which reflect the lives of millions of women, children and men in the "Communism of shortages"; their everyday pragmatism, their express ability to improvise and their optimistic outlook on life. The people were not permanently unhappy and oppressed for 40 years. One might say that many people in the GDR have served *their* country diligently, tenaciously and unobtrusively, even though everyone did not have the same forbearance and there were many degrees of differences. (Oestreich 1990, pp. 8-9.)

The Old Germany

It is important to note that German textbook research has also been carried out at many other, less specialized, institutions since the 1960s. Horst E. Schallenberger, founder of the Duisburg Institute, published a major work as early as 1964: *Untersuchungen zum Geschichtsbild des Wilhelminischen Ära und der Weimarer Republik* (Schallenberger 1964). The work provides a survey of history books published between 1888 and 1933, illustrating how the books' views of history change chronologically in step with political developments in society at large. The author also discusses ethical interpretations of values and ideals. Even in this context, Schallenberger contends that neither ideological candor, general consensus about neutrality, nor public approval schemes can prevent textbooks from becoming functions of political values. Other major works within the same school of thought are E. Weymar's investigation of "den Geist des Geschichtsunterrichts" in upper secondary textbooks from the last century (Weymar 1961), and R. Kühnl's (ed.) work, which contains an analysis of the "Geschichte und Ideologie" in more recent textbooks in the FRG (Kühnl 1973).

Jürgen Fröchling has conducted a comprehensive analysis of the references to medieval cities found in German history books written between 1871 and 1971 (Fröchling 1978). He discovered that their presentations varied significantly, depending on which of the five different regimes they were written under (the Empire/the Weimar Republic/the Third Reich/FRG/GDR):

> The medieval city (...) is interpreted differently in each of the five social systems investigated here, in that the predominant ideology of the respective societies is clearly part of their evaluation and assignment of emphasis. (P. 100.)

Readers have also been the object of considerable historical ideological research. J. Heinssen investigated the reader "als politisches Führungsmittel im Dritten Reich" (Heinssen 1964) and P. Hasubek discussed readers in "der Zeit des Nationalsozialismus" (Hasubek 1972). The latter emphasizes the correlation between literary educational ideals and prevailing (school) policy.

As regards anthologies designed for upper secondary schools, one suspects that the selection of material and form of presentation may also say a great deal about social and literary preferences. However, these more "adult" readers number among the least investigated of all textbook types. Apart from a few theoretical studies (see page 37), major investigations of such books have only been carried out in Germany. One of the best known examples is Peter-Martin Roeder's study *Zur Geschichte und Kritik des Lesebuchs der höheren Schule* (Roeder 1961). The author presents an historical survey from the 18th century to the 1950s, primarily discussing developments in textbook content. His material is categorized by cultural periods (Enlightenment, Classicism, Romanticism, Biedermeier, the "Kunsterziehung" movement, WWI, National Socialism, Contemporary), and the presentation is largely a survey of themes, works and authors.

Hermann Helmers' work on the main trends in the development of German readers appeared nine years after Roeder's book was published (Helmers 1970). Helmers' book was organized in a manner which is just as unusual today as it was in 1970. The author renounced comprehensiveness or a thorough chronological treatment, and chose instead to concentrate on two prominent titles from each of the six periods into which the material was divided. Helmers wished to illustrate new methods of systematic investigation. He compared books from different levels by emphasizing a neglected aspect of textbook research (the didactic adaptation of reading materials), and concentrated on the reader less as a direct exponent of the flow of historical ideology than as "ein instrument der Herrschaftsausübung" (by accounting for the background of "gesellschaftlich-historischen Faktoren").

The political and social aspects of anthologies are also discussed separately in each chapter of Roeder's work. This is a common feature of German investigations and is most conspicuous in an article in Bark and Pforte (see page 39). Such a tendency supports Hanna Schissler (Schissler 1987, pp. 36-37) and Karl Peter Fritzsche's contentions that German textbooks are susceptible to ideological bias (see page 72).

Siegfried Lenz' novel *Das Vorbild* (1973) may be regarded as a striking example of Germany's preoccupation with educational ideals. The motive and plot of his story are closely tied to an assignment that directs the development of the main characters. The story involves three teachers who propose to edit an anthology for the lower secondary level. They are unable to agree upon the selection of texts to be included in the chapter entitled "The Model". Lenz employs the conflict per se and the discussions of textbooks to portray contemporary life.

The United Kingdom

John Ahier's book *Industry, Children and the Nation. An Analysis of National Identity in School Textbooks* (Ahier 1988) is in many ways unique. First, the work is distinguished by its approach. Ahier's starting point was a book by American author Martin Wiener, who presented a socio-cultural analysis of the reasons underlying economic stagnation in post-WWI England. Wiener contended that a culturally determined negative attitude toward industry and urbanization was the primary cause of the problem. Ahier wished to investigate whether or not the textbooks of the times reflected "anti-industrial values".

Ahier is also particularly thorough as regards methodology. The problem of textbook analysis is covered in a separate chapter, and discussions of the problem of methodology are frequently integrated into the other parts of his presentation:

Although this study was not aimed directly at the content and presuppositions of the Wiener thesis but did emerge from a concern for the possible educational derivations from it, it has shown the problems with such an approach to national or class cultures and schooling. Many of the textbooks that have been examined could be read as expressing the identifiable cultural essence of ruralism, but contrary images were also found when crossing the subject boundary between history and geography. The way the texts were read in this study suggested that they did not exist as expressions of some previous national culture, but as attempts to project or construct that upon which the whole enterprise of universal state schooling and its textbooks depended, i.e. an assumption that there was a naturally integrated distinct people existing within given boundaries. Combining with that the predominant practices and discourses of child development during the period, centred as they were on learning by progressive contact with the reality of nature, it is not surprising that images within the textbooks could be counted up and used as evidence for the thesis which explains, culturally, Britain's economic decline. But, in another approach, the contents of the textbooks could also be seen as indicating, in indirect and tangential ways, many of the *other* explanations of Britain's industrial decline. (Ahier 1988, p. 175.)

Ahier's conclusions are complex and detailed. He finds himself unable to respond with a definite yes or no to questions concerning clear, predominant attitudes toward cultural values in textbooks. On the other hand, he is fairly certain that the particular national portrayal drawn in the books has not prompted the need for economic innovation. When referring to descriptions of working life and industry in Japanese textbooks (Ferro 1981), for example, Ahier writes the following about books in the UK:

For almost 100 years these books have struggled to represent Britain as the safe, benevolent homeland of a united race which, because it was the first country to industrialize, has been made to appear as the only one to achieve that condition. The benefits of Britain's natural and imperial fortunes have been constantly emphasized at the expense of both labour and enterprise. With such an education in the "social" subjects few alternative economic or political realities could have seemed as attractive for children as a nation at peace with nature and its people. (P. 8.)

The USA

There is one obvious argument that favors viewing textbooks as reflections of cultural history. It has something to do with the contents of textbooks becoming public property. Looking back in time 50 years or so, one discovers that textbooks were the main source from which the general public could seek information about the world at large:

> To discover what ideas were held by the ordinary man in any period of history is one of the persistent problems of intellectual history. The ideas and ideological development of literary men can be analyzed; recent work in intellectual history has presented us with analyses in abundance. But the ordinary man, unliterary by nature, left no direct impression of the concepts he accepted. (Elson 1964, p. VIII.)

The above passage is taken from the introduction to Ruth Miller Elson's book about 19th century American textbooks (Elson 1964). Elson emphasizes that the attitudes expressed in textbooks probably have little influence on the everyday life of pupils, in that the actions of parents and teachers play a role which is at least as important. In contrast, references to subjects beyond the realm of a pupil's everyday experience may exert a stronger influence on his attitudes toward the subject:

> Conversely, schoolbook attitudes toward ideas and people remote to his experiences probably influence his thinking more strongly on these subjects and it is likely that the cluster of concepts associated with other nations in his schoolbooks would have an effect on the formation of his adult attitudes toward these nations. (P. VIII.)

The material presented in Elson's *Guardians of Tradition* is not arranged by subject, but according to four main themes that occupy one chapter each: God and nature, The nature of man, Schoolbooks and "culture", Social Experience (the last discusses social conditions and politics). Readers/primers and history books predominate, but geography and arithmetic books are also represented. All descriptions include references to the books, each of which has a code number. Code numbers appear throughout the text, with references to page number.

Elson finds that 19th century textbook texts in all subjects all had the same main objective, i.e., to strengthen the national moral consciousness in the United States. This goal was the driving force behind textbook writers throughout the entire period, making presentations distinctly normative: "Perhaps the most fundamental assumption in nineteenth century schoolbooks is the moral character of the universe - an assumption at the base of American culture in this period." (P. 338.) God rules the nation and the world, where the hard-working will be rewarded, although often only after undergoing extreme hardship. Defeat, illness and death are presented frankly and sometimes brutally in these textbooks, which make no pretense of neutrality:

> Unlike many modern schoolbooks, those of the nineteenth century make no pretense of neutrality. While they evade issues seriously controverted in their day, they take a firm and unanimous stand on matters of basic belief. The value judgment is their stock in trade: love of country, love of God, duty to parents, the necessity to develop habits of thrift, honesty and hard work in order to accumulate property, the certainty of progress, the perfection of the United States. These are not to be questioned. Nor in this whole century of great external change is there any deviation from these basic values. (P. 338.)

Another common trait in this immutable pattern is the constant comparison with nations outside the United States, or with non-white races within the United States. The comparisons never fail to end in favor of the Americans. However, Elson contends that there are clear parallels between this feature of American textbooks and the national image presented in European textbooks during the same period. This observation was confirmed by Ernst-Otto Schüddekopf, who reviewed the book in the Georg Eckert Institute's Yearbook: "If one reads the book carefully, one experiences a sense of being transplanted to the avaricious climate of the Prussian state in the 19th century" (Schüddekopf 1965-1966, p. 267). Another common characteristic that remained unchanged throughout the century is the fact that books stayed loyal to a static set of conservative social values. Neither Charles Darwin, William James, the Civil War, nor the reform movements in the 1880s and 1890s had any influence on the values or attitudes expressed in

19th century textbooks.

In the United States, the search for and discussion of the concept of nationalism has resulted in a long series of books about literary canon. In 1972, the National Council of Teachers of English published a critical survey entitled *Searching for America* (Kelly 1972). One main part of the book discusses 12 anthologies from the viewpoint of the discrimination of ethnic minorities. The other main part consists of essays on the same subject. Much of the debate is summarized in Russel Reising's book *The Unusable Past* (Reising 1986). In one chapter, Reising evaluates the selection and publication of material in anthologies relative to prevailing literary tastes at the time of the books' publication. At the same time he emphasizes the importance of market conditions and economics as factors influencing the selection of material. Reising's last point leads directly to part of the core of American textbook research, in historical terms as well.

One major document is *The Textbook in American Society* (Cole - Sticht 1981), a publication which resulted from a national conference on textbooks arranged by the Library of Congress in 1979. The papers included contributions by librarians, textbook researchers, educationalists, educational planners, teachers, culture and media researchers and publishers.

In his opening speech, chief librarian and cultural historian Daniel J. Boorstin introduced the main theme of the conference as follows:

> (...) in a free economy, a free society, the textbook is a special test of freedom. Can we provide basic books, foundation books, which present the consensus of a subject, chosen by a government agency or by agencies chosen by other agencies, and yet preserve the freedom to grow and the freedom to dissent, the freedom to be free? That, I think, is the problem we're talking about here today. (Boorstin 1981, p. X.)

On the one hand, the American tradition appears to be concerned with investigating and developing national contexts in textbooks. On the other hand, it is very concerned about those conditions of production, marketing and approval which ensure the books' distribution throughout the school system. There is a direct link between the conference held in 1979 and the publication by the influential NSSE (National Society for the Study of Education) of an entire yearbook devoted to textbook investigations in 1990. The title of the yearbook is *Textbooks and Schooling in the United States*, and it contains research reports on the connection between marketing and school policy, and between production and distribution/choice of books.

The national and market approach is summed up in the sub-title of Frances FitzGerald's book on history books, *America Revised: What history textbooks have taught our children about their country, and how and why those textbooks have changed in different decades* (FitzGerald 1979). FitzGerald is highly critical of the history books used in American schools in the 20th century. She states that for ideological or commercial reasons, history books distort or idolize the past, they bend to meaningless educational fads and they are poorly written. She attributes their continued sale to and use in the American school system to the fact that teaching is a low status profession, lacking self-confidence and less influential than many other conservative lobby groups in society. Her book, which is based on a large corpus of textbook and reference material, is essayistic and controversial. FitzGerald's contribution to critical textbook literature has probably received more attention than any other book of its kind in the United States in modern times.

Nor is the German tradition of international history textbook revision unknown in the USA. The results of the *Japan/United States Textbook Project: Perceptions in the textbooks in each country about the history of the other* were published in 1983 (Goodman - Homma - Najita - Becker 1983). This project was also based on the lower secondary level. Fourteen Japanese and 28 American books were exchanged and analyzed. Both sides discovered that the number of discrepancies was declining but that the mistakes were so significant that the study, like many other bilateral investigations, resulted in a list of recommendations for revisions.

However, compared with Germany, for example, the USA has been the site of relatively fewer large-scale bilateral historical-ideological investigations than investigations of specific issues in national books. Four such US investigations are presented here because they illustrate investigative approaches which differ from those mentioned earlier. They involve such vastly different topics as war and foreign policy, the study of evolution and racism.

W. Griffen and J. Marciano investigated how the Vietnam War was presented in 28 lower secondary school textbooks published between 1961 and 1978 (Griffen - Marciano 1980). The authors compared the books' texts with *The Pentagon Papers* and other public domain information about the war, but they found no inclination toward more frequent or more sophisticated evaluations of the war as time passed. They concluded that the textbooks "seem to conspire to construct an environment in which the truth is mangled and a whole generation deceived" (quoted here from Woodward - Elliott - Nagel 1988, p. 129). The books not only neglected several major negative aspects of the American involvement in the war, but also ignored facts and background material that supported a critical point of view.

G. Skoog has written a comprehensive report on how the study of evolution is presented in secondary school biology textbooks (Skoog 1984). The author's study is based on an earlier investigation of 83 textbooks published between 1900 and 1969. The results of that study were compared with a more recent analysis of 10 new textbooks published between 1970 and 1977. According to Skoog, the topic of evolution was either left out completely, or only mentioned briefly or casually in books published before 1960. The topic was accorded more space in textbooks in the 1960s following the introduction of new curricula. Yet for no apparent reason, evolution was once again conspicuously under-represented in the textbooks of the 1970s.

J. Janis investigated descriptions of slavery in American junior high school history books (Janis 1972). He compared two different groups of books; one group from the 1950s and early 1960s, and another group from the late 1960s. Janis believes he has found evidence that the books in the latter category were revised in an effort to include the results of modern research on American history (Woodward - Elliott - Nagel, p. 131).

As early as in 1952, C.J. Reynolds examined accounts of

immigrants in an historical perspective (Reynolds 1952). The author investigated history books published between 1861 and 1947, and was of the opinion that the prevalent attitudes could be dated, i.e., be divided into periods. Until about 1890 textbooks' attitude toward immigrants was basically "friendly". Then until about 1930, the general attitude was "critical", after which it became generally "sympathetic".

The Nordic Countries

Ruth Miller Elson's chapter on culture in textbooks is divided into two sections. First, she discusses views on and descriptions of "scholarship" and the attitude toward the full range of intellectual life in textbooks. Second, she discusses the textbooks treatment of art and literature.

In Lena Olsson's doctoral thesis,*Culture in Flux* (Olsson 1986), we find another cultural concept. The author does not expressly discuss the terms "cultural studies" or "culture". The sub-title of the book is *Cultural Attitudes in Swedish Geography Books 1870-1985*, and the culture which Olsson discusses is that of geography, i.e., mainly the differences between the customs of people from different nations. The term is indirectly defined in Chapter 5, a comprehensive discussion entitled "Cultural Attitudes", which describes the textbook accounts in the following order: By Levels (Racism, Civilization, Religion, Social Structure, Population dynamics, Technology)/Development/Selection conditions/ Presentation (Stereotypes, Illustrations and Vocabulary). In reality, the thesis covers a very wide range of concepts. The wealth of examples refers to every topic from climate, nature and economics to Elson's brand of high brow culture.

One aim of Olsson's thesis is to "shed light on the growth of our knowledge of culture" (p. 19). She has selected such a broad time perspective due to what might be referred to as hermeneutic reasoning:

I deliberately compare the contents of the older textbooks with the contents of newer, more contemporary textbooks. (...) Such a course of action is a step in the process of understanding. It casts no aspersions on the past, but rather contributes to greater insight into the present. (Pp. 19-20.)

While Elson's work may be regarded as essayistic, Olsson's thesis is systematically organized according to principles described under the sub-heading called "The Work Process" (pp. 27 - 29). After a thorough examination of "textbooks' explicitly expressed attitudes toward culture", she organized her material into pairs of contrasting themes: positive-negative, Western-non Western, European-African, Christian-Moslem, male-female, contemporary-historical. Another method of evaluating the material was to investigate "the manner in which textbook authors provided information about different peoples, their lifestyles, their religions, their political systems, etc."
One important observation is that Olsson, as opposed to Elson, did not find the same continuity in textbooks' ways of evaluating other cultures. Elson points out that the portrayal of Europe presented in 19th century American geography books was invariably two-sided. On the one hand, the Continent was referred to as an important center for the arts and sciences, while on the other, Europe was described as being afflicted by immorality and decay. Artistically beautiful Italy is described as a filthy and disease-ridden country; Italians are branded as immoral, superstitious degenerates (Elson, p. 234). As regards the earlier portion of her material, Olsson draws similar conclusions: "The investigation of textbooks' descriptions of culture shows they are based on a judgmental outlook, expressed through a rating and ranking of various peoples and phenomena." (P. 194.) However, in Sweden she finds less national self-assertion than "Western" ethnocentrism. As far as Elson is concerned, Olsson makes the following comment:

(...) on the other hand, I have not found that the source material in any way emphasizes Swedishness. In geography textbooks, Sweden is primarily presented as part of the West. Of course, in terms of quantity, one's own country is discussed most comprehensively. *As regards evaluations, however, the authors presuppose norms which are common to all Western cultures.* That I, in this case, have arrived at a somewhat different result from Tingsten, Elson and Diestel does not necessarily mean that they have arrived at incorrect conclusions. In all probability the differences are ascribable to differences in the selection of textbook material. The ethnocentric evaluations will presumably be more obvious in subjects such as history and mother-tongue instruction than in geography. (Olsson 1986, p. 148; *my* emphasis.)

Reich's summary (Reich 1989) contains points which by and large corroborate the conclusion drawn by Olsson. Reich postulated that the selection of topics dealing with general world politics would be strongly affected by "nationalstaatlichen Perspektiven und politisch-ideologishen Deutungen" (p. 265). Instead, she found she had to concentrate on a Western European consensus or "Sichtweise", which might also be said to be at least equally attributable to general educational philosophies and/or the authors' political opinions.

Olsson's broad historical reference base and numerous categories (science, school subjects, the school system, textbook content, textbook form) are reminiscent of the work done by Göran Andolf (see page 60). The main difference is that while Andolf uses books as primary sources of information about the development of school subjects, Olsson concentrates on the view of culture as one particular element of knowledge presented in the textbooks. As the use of this term is both comprehensive and rather vague in Olsson's presentation, Olsson's distance from Andolf's subject investigation is not nearly as great as it might appear at first glance. Actually, there is more difference between Olsson's work and that of Elson, whose research was based on several, more limited concepts.

National identities and national cultural expressions have also been investigated in a few other Nordic studies.

The best known study was conducted by Herbert Tingsten and entitled *God and the Fatherland* (Tingsten 1969). Like Elson and FitzGerald, he maintains a free essayistic perspective towards his material. He states in the introduction that it was not possible to discover how frequently the books were used, and that he found it difficult to obtain the desired number of textbooks from the five countries included in the study (France, Italy, Germany, Austria and the United States) in addition to Sweden. The book, which originally appeared as a series of articles in two newspapers, is written in the spirit of international textbook revision. In the preface, Tingsten acknowledges Ernst-Otto Schüddekopf and the textbook institute at Braunschweig. Tingsten's book differs considerably from much organized textbook research in that one author alone discusses material from six different countries, and in that the study adopts an historical perspective and consistently pursues one theme: Nationalism. Therefore, in spite of being incomplete, Tingsten's work may offer the most universal treatment we have of the concept of nationalism in the European school book tradition.

It is important to note that Tingsten had a special point of departure for his work. He was "especially interested in how textbook propaganda varied under different regimes" (p. 7 of the preface; all quotes from the Norwegian edition: Odden 1970). Like Frances FitzGerald, as a political journalist he more or less automatically assumes that there is a connection between political authority and the (political) content of textbooks.

According to Tingsten, textbooks from the 1800s and early half of the 1900s are thus pure propaganda for the virtues of their own countries. However, during the decade in which Tingsten wrote his book, he noted that school propaganda in all Western countries had to give way to more complex, internationally-oriented presentations. This does not mean that indoctrination and propaganda had disappeared from textbooks, simply that "nationalism has lost ground, while the idea of peace is more strongly emphasized, and democratic views are emphasized or at least used as a basis for explanations and analyses." (P. 104.) To substantiate this point of view, Tingsten quotes historian Sven Ulric Palme, who refers to the conflicts which may arise between society's express goal of teaching children to act independently and exercise good judgement, and our general consensus (and thus the potential for indoctrination) on the importance of values which emphasize particular "general patriotic virtues" (p. 104).

Svein Lorentzen investigated nationalism in Norwegian textbooks (Lorentzen 1988). In a lengthy article, he reviews material from more than 50 primary and lower secondary school textbooks written between 1834 and 1982. In the introduction, Lorentzen states that "Norwegian textbook analyses have primarily been concerned with a horizontal perspective." (P. 12.) The author wanted to break tradition by investigating Norway's "national self-image" as it has developed in textbooks over time. As defined by Lorentzen, nationalism involves "those characteristics in the history of the country of Norway which textbook authors themselves wished to present, and the way in which they were presented." (P.13.) The main objective was to "compare history books through time, and thereby shed light on changes in aspects of our national history which textbook authors wished to pass on to coming generations." (P. 12.)

Instead of focusing on individual and national achievement, Lorentzen distinguishes between the original situation of national "prudence" and "expectant optimism", periods of strong national self-esteem (before and around 1905), and later developments in the direction of more cooperation and internationalism:

> In the history books of today, it is difficult to associate the national self-image presented with a lack of either self confidence or modesty. However, the national image has clearly been weakened at the expense of the international as well as the local dimension. (P. 30.)

Lorentzen's concluding remarks may be interpreted as comments on Herbert Tingsten's investigations. The two agree that national patriotism has seen far better days in textbooks - but what of it? Tingsten refers to an historian who points out the innate conflict between ideal principles and the desire to educate and control (see above). The last quotation from Lorentzen calls attention to a new, increasingly significant dimension besides the international and national ones: The local dimension. Although Norway has had curriculum guidelines that have emphasized local culture, we have no investigations on how those guidelines have been incorporated into textbooks. However, the question has manifested itself in many countries, and a recent publication from the Georg Eckert Institute, volume 64 in their publication series, bears the title *Regionalität.*

Der "kleine Raum" als Problem der internationalen Schulbuch-forschung (Hinrichs 1990). Magne Angvik has published an article entitled "Lokal- und Regionalgeschichte in norwegischen Geschichtslehrbüchern" in the same series (Angvik 1985).

The Third World

One common problem in Third World countries is a lack of schools and teachers, a situation which magnifies the importance of textbooks. Textbooks represent the majority of works published in many developing countries. In theory, the influence of textbooks is potentially greater in developing countries than in industrialized ones, and both the World Bank and UNESCO have emphasized this in their practical development efforts. However, widespread paper shortages, generally poor economies and conditions related to copyright rules and distribution have contributed to maintaining former colonial powers' hegemony over the written word.

Today, the Third World is a motley conglomeration that also includes major nations with written traditions much older than those of Europe. Countries such as Egypt, India and Mexico have national publishing industries large enough to produce their own school books. Like the former Soviet Union, countries such as India have their own textbook theorists and systems (McCullough 1974). In small countries with languages of limited dispersion, the chances of books being produced in their own native languages remain slight. However, political conditions may also prevent national publications in large areas. Malaysia is often referred to as a prime example (Altbach - Kelly 1988, p.6).

The question of using textbooks to build a national self-image in Third World countries must be evaluated on the basis of this overall situation. In some places it may be a question of access to any books whatsoever, even books directly imported from e.g. France, the United States or the Commonwealth of Independent States, all of which had special export programs for this purpose in the 1960s and 1970s. In other places, development has progressed to the point where educational policy and textbook development have begun to become an integral part of the work toward independence. Another type of development, seen in countries such as Kenya and Tanzania, initially involves the translation of English and French textbooks into Swahili, for example. The next, more advanced step will be for native authors to write textbooks in their own languages, a development which has proven to be extremely complex. One major study indicates that textbooks produced in Kenya in the 1970s established norms and ideals which digressed significantly from the authorities' ideas: The books glorify urban culture at the expense of agriculture and a more widespread demographic structure. In Tanzania, on the other hand, textbooks are written in a conscious effort to comply with Nyerere's socialistic reform (Mbuyi 1988). In countries in which reforms are of a more long-term and directly revolutionary nature, it would appear that textbooks are quickly recruited to the service of new regimes. This has definitely been the case in the People's Republic of China and in Iran during recent decades (Kwong 1988, Shorish 1988).

On the whole, the problem of nation-building is far more complex for textbook authors in developing countries in the 1990s than it was for the 19th century American textbook writers described by Ruth Miller Elson. Nigeria and Malaysia are two countries that arrived at vastly different solutions to the problems at hand in the 1980s. Textbook texts were written in each states' respective native language in three Nigerian states. Despite official policies, the books were strongly influenced by ethnocentric rather than national thinking. Books in the Igbo language discuss Igbo culture, while books written in the Hausa language mainly refer to Hausa culture, etc. (Okonkwo 1988). In Malaysia, the central government has enforced a strict policy of ethnic amalgamation. Malaysian textbooks attempt to present a picture of a single, predominant Malaysian identity (Mukherjee - Ahmed 1988).

It is not within the scope of this survey to provide a complete picture of textbook research in areas outside Europe and the United States. Such a task would be virtually impossible. The discussion above is generally based on a collection of articles edited by a group at the Comparative Education Center at the State University of New York, Buffalo (Altbach - Kelly 1988). Most of the contributors work in the United States, although some work in other parts of the world (Nigeria, Dehli, Singapore, Malaya). It is likely that background materials are or soon will be available from more authentic sources in the near future. The question of ethnicity and national identity will probably become the central ideological issue in the debate on and the development of textbooks. In light of the mobility of populations and political structures in the world today, this problem is in no way limited to the Third World. Angela Kubanek's studies of West German textbooks for English as a foreign language represent an expansion in the point of view and material used for analysis (Kubanek 1989). The investigation covered everything written about the Third World in 180 lower secondary school textbooks published from 1947 to 1987. The study analyzed the amount of material, language and educational adaptations. Negative accounts and stereotypical, colonial descriptions were common in books written up to the 1960s and 1970s. Later presentations were more ambivalent. Recent books have attempted to correct this distorted picture, but often fail because the writers themselves lack "philosophical reflection". Their own views on the subject are unclear, and that affects their selection of material and form of presentation.

Another investigation was carried out recently by Karen Biraimah at the University of Florida: "Knowledge Control in Developing Countries: A Comparative Study of Togolese and Thai English Language Textbooks" (Biraimah 1991). Textbooks used in Togo are written by French authors and published in Paris. Thai books are written by native authors and published in Bangkok. Biraimah's point of departure was that "examples of neo-colonialism and "Western" messages would be more prevalent in the textbooks published by Western authors, while the books published in Bangkok by Thais would represent more of a "Thai" perspective (pp. 3 - 4). The results of the investigation refuted the theory:

The data in Table 2 suggest that the textbook published in Paris devoted a far greater portion of its "global and national themes" to African topics than the Thai book devoted to Asian themes. For example, over 75 percent of all global and national themes in the African text focused on African topics, while only about 22 percent were concerned with "Western" topics. In contrast, the Thai textbook devoted 57 percent of all global and national themes to Asian topics, while about 30 percent focused on "Western" themes. (P. 5.)

Didacus Jules was Grenada's secretary of education when left-wingers under the command of Maurice Bishop set up a socialistic revolutionary regime in 1979. Bishop remained in power for some four years following the bloodless coup. One of the main planks in his political platform was his educational policy, which entailed the rewriting of textbooks. Jules has studied this process, which involved the rewriting of about twenty basic textbooks (Jules 1991). His analysis demonstrates how the revolutionary situation forces an entirely different awareness of books than one sees in countries ruled by established governments; the tension is closer to the surface:

> In summary, what the Grenada experience demonstrates is that ideology is an inescapable dimension of text content and has a decisive hand in the molding of the forms not only of the text itself but also, and equally important, of the social and pedagogical interaction mediated by the text. In the case of Grenada, for historical reasons this process could not remain obscured as a dimension of the so-called hidden curriculum. The intense ideological contestation that happens in the political context of revolution ensured that the hidden was to be made explicit, if the hegemony of the former ruling classes was to be successfully contested. (Jules 1991, p. 185.)

Nonetheless, Jules also concludes by stating that:

> The struggles around the texts highlight the importance of the form and not just the content of the knowledge of the textbook. A progressive message can be contradicted or subverted by undemocratic *forms*, as form structures learning experiences (content provides substance). In transitional contexts, the politics of the text is conditioned by this dialectic. (P. 185.)

Political, Social and Cultural Conditions

Discrimination of Groups

Investigations may be largely concerned with the degree of representation individual groups have received in textbooks - that approach has the longest traditions. Yet over the past decade, the focus has turned more toward the way in which such groups have been treated (linguistically and contextually).

Already in the 1950s, Helga Stene demonstrated bias in the portrayal of women in textbooks. In a popular arithmetic textbook she found a total of 190 exercises in which a person of a given sex was featured in an active, major role. The protagonists were female in only four of those exercises (Stene 1981).

In 1977, Hjørdis Heide published the results of a study which showed how traditional sex roles were reinforced in two widely disseminated series of social science textbooks. The books' authors were all men (Heide 1977). An analysis of four textbooks in home economics for the primary grades was published that same year. The author concluded that "none of the textbooks examined fulfilled the requirements of the Curriculum for Primary and Lower Secondary Education (...)". (Solheim 1972, p. 92.)

Tone Skinningsrud and Magnus Haavelsrud investigated the theme of equality of the sexes in all social science textbooks that were authorized for use in the lower secondary school in 1976-1977 (Skinningsrud - Haavelsrud 1979). With a view to equal status, they isolated all the textual elements that explicitly dealt with the situation of women, measuring the scope of the elements. Then the authors discussed what was said in the passages thus selected from each book. The conclusion of this combined quantitative and qualitative study was that "none of the series satisfies all our criteria: Extent, completeness, various causal explanations and suggestions for strategies to improve the situation. Still, some series were better than others, depending on how one weighted the various criteria." (P. 218.)

The conclusions of these last three studies are interesting seen against the background of the Norwegian approval system for textbooks. One of the four main parts of the approval process deals with the requirement for the implementation of equality in the texts. If we move further forward in time, we find a study which concludes with a direct reference to this system: "This investigation has shown that a representative sample of Norwegian textbooks is not free of indirect discrimination of girls and women (...). Enforcement of the approval rules concerning equal status ought to be improved." (Vogt 1984, p. 67.)

In the attempt to also quantify the indirect influences in the texts, Vogt adapted a numerical method developed by American researchers (Guttentag - Bray 1976). The comprehensive research on the subject in the USA also seems to reveal a trend from a low level of awareness (Trecker 1971) toward a higher one, although the problem cannot be described as actually having been resolved (Hahn - Blankenship 1981).

Compared to the total production of textbook analyses, the subject of women in textbooks is clearly under-represented in France and Germany. One French study will be mentioned in this context because of its original form of presentation. The book *Papa lit, maman coud* (Decroux-Masson 1979) (*Pappa reads, Mamma sews*) contains five chapters in which observations and quotations from 42 primary and lower secondary school books in French and mathematics are woven into a coherent, chatty essay: The Housekeeper, Work, The Boss, The Beauty, Pearls and Marbles. The presentation is systematic, but written in a form that makes it entertaining.

At one point in *Papa lit, maman coud*, the author questions whether textbooks in France represent democracy or the opposite (p. 123). This comment is an indirect reminder of a selection problem related to textbook analysis. It is always hard to know the degree to which one can or should distinguish between topics - or levels - such as, for example, immigrants, equality of status, or democracy in social science books. One may ask why so few authors choose to take a wider perspective and deal with the representation of all groups which are supposedly discriminated. Jean Anyon addresses this in her study of how the working class is represented in American textbooks:

> Although it would have been equally appropriate to have analyzed the treatment of black history, women's history, or any other topic involving conflict between groups in society, economic and labor history was chosen partly because it has been largely ignored by those who have recently examined curriculum content, and partly because the relationships and social conflicts between employers and employees reveal basic configurations of resource and power in our society. (Anyon 1979, p. 364.)

The last remark in the quotation - that the employer-employee relationship reveals something more general about conditions in society - gives in a manner of speaking an answer to the question of wide versus narrow approach. Anyon comes to the conclusion that textbooks consistently support views that promote the interests of certain groups (those who have property and capital) and damage those of others (workers and the poor). She writes about large segments of society. But a smaller, more limited unit, perhaps even a detail, can say a great deal about the whole. Both approaches need to be evaluated in each and every case. There are examples of studies where close reading of strictly delimited subjects is not very profitable, and there are comparable examples of survey analyses.

The broadest possible approach was taken in one study of six series of social studies textbooks for lower secondary school. Elliott, Nagel and Woodward (Elliott - Nagel - Woodward 1985) seem to have worked on the assumption that such books are and will remain inadequate. They support this by demonstrating failure on six different levels. One of their levels includes two topics which might appear separately in other contexts: "Representations of women and minority group members were unrealistic" (quoted from Woodward - Elliott - Nagel 1988, p. 126). Insofar as one can speak of the primary theme of the investigation, it can almost be spoken of here as the inadequacy of textbooks.

On the subject of minorities and immigrants, it is not hard to find examples of great differences in angle of approach. One investigation of the portrayal of "black Americans" in a dozen history books published in 1983 and 1984 measured extent and came to an average of one sentence per page "devoted to the black experience" (Garcia - Tanner 1985.) A subsequent study (Ellington 1986) investigated the role "blacks and Hispanics" played in the presentation of the topic of poverty and unemployment in twelve lower secondary school economics textbooks published from 1980 to 1985. Insofar as the groups were mentioned, it was in general, descriptive words and phrases. Only half the books contained factual information about living conditions/poverty, while only a third contained factual information about unemployment in the two groups.

One of the investigations that has gone furthest in the direction of a synthesis is Christine E. Sleeter and Carl A. Grant's study of the representation of race, social class, sex and disabilities in 47 American textbooks with copyrights from 1980 to 1986. The books covered the main subjects taught in grades 1 - 8. The analyses took six fundamentally different approaches: Picture, anthology, people, language, story line, miscellaneous:

Picture analysis involves tallying who is in each picture, categorized by sex, race (Asian, American, Black American, Hispanic American, American Indian, White American, race ambiguous, and mixed race group), and disability. Pictures can be designated as individual or group pictures. In addition, racial and sex stereotypes, and the social-class background or setting, are to be noted. The anthology analysis is for analyzing each story in readers. The race, sex, and disability of the main character and supporting characters are to be tallied, and stereotypes, the social-class setting, and which groups solve the problems are to be noted. The "people to study" analysis involves tallying the race and sex of each person mentioned in the text; this is used in science, mathematics, or social studies texts. The language analysis involves examining language in the text for sexist usage, "loaded" words that contain racial or sex stereotypes, and words or phrases that obscure viewpoints or possible conflict situations.

The story-line analysis is used primarily with social studies texts. It involves analyzing which group receives the most sustained attention (whose story is being told), which group(s) resolves problems, how other groups appear, the extent to which these other groups cause or resolve problems, and who the author intends the reader to sympathize with or learn most about. Finally, other miscellaneous analyses may lend themselves to a particular book, such as analyzing race, sex, and roles of people in mathematics story problems. For each subject area, we will describe how books treat different racial groups, both sexes, the social classes, and people with disabilities. (Sleeter - Grant 1991, pp. 82-83.)

Their conclusion was negative:

Treatment of diversity in textbooks has not improved much over the past fifteen years or so, generally, although a few textbooks have improved in specific, limited ways. There was a flurry of activity to "multiculturalize"textbooks during the late 1960s and early 1970s, although that activity never did address social class in textbooks. That activity may have stopped, and we may be entering an era of backsliding, a return to more White- and male-dominated curricula. (Sleeter - Grant 1991, p. 101.)

In Europe, one particular ethnic group has been the object of more textbook investigations than any other. Representations of the Jewish people have been studied at the institutes in Duisburg and Braunschweig. The Braunschweig bibliography lists a number of issues of their periodical that deal with the subject; however, the references to the representation of Islam in West German textbooks are even more numerous.

One comprehensive study was carried out in Sweden. In 1989 the group for pedagogical text research in Härnösand (see page 80) was commissioned by the State Institute for Teaching Aids to:

chart if - and if so in what forms - one can find racism or hostility toward foreigners, or such tendencies, in teaching aids for the various stages of elementary school, secondary school and public adult education. (SPOV 9/1990, p. 7.)

The group dealt with textbooks, not teaching manuals, exercise booklets or material other than books. They also disregarded teaching and teachers. Their objective was to investigate the books as officially authorized expressions of the current norms about what is "right, fitting and important" in Swedish society. Their corpus consisted of about 200 textbooks for all grades, in the subjects of history, social science and religion, all published in the 1980s. The group consisted of a picture researcher (Ewa Romare) and three textbook researchers (Staffan Selander, Annika Ullman and Eva Trotzig).

The methodological background for the work was pedagogical text analysis as described by Staffan Selander (Selander 1988); that is, texts are viewed in light of their institutional background. They are not products and expressions of individual authors, but are governed by many forces, and thus reflect the dominant values of the school and the age. The analysis of material selection and arrangement therefore plays an important role in this study as well. But the study focuses primarily on the literary aspect. It examines language and style so that even "the significance of the insignificant" (p. 9) - words and phrases, sentence structure, parentheses - becomes important, not least because the group is particularly concerned with how phenomena and events are explained: What thought patterns and expectations lie behind the classifications and distinctions used in the texts? By analyzing such elements, the group believes it can not only reconstruct a view of knowledge and a world picture, but also uncover value judgements that are dominant but not clearly expressed or even conscious in Swedish society. The key word is mentality:

Value judgements and ideologies are usually "just"and the normal attitude is benevolent, but the lack of flexibility in the light of foreignness means that certain fundamental, but usually unconscious, patterns of thought break through - what we call mentality. In this context mentality refers to the thought patterns we collectively share, but do not normally bring to the surface. These thought patterns can, however, be reconstructed by a critical reader - by studying how things are elucidated and explained, how they are illustrated, a picture emerges of some common, prevalent perspectives in textbooks." (P. 52.)

The study concluded that Swedish textbooks anno 1989 "in a strict sense" can neither be called racist nor hostile to foreigners. In spite of that, they have serious weaknesses. The group finds that the books' presentations are full of ambiguities and confused ideas. There are no clear distinctions made between expressions such as immigrants, refugees and guest workers. Readers get information that is neither precise nor concrete enough for them to form an acceptable conceptual apparatus when the pupils try to get their bearings in the world around them. Explanations of causes and connections are often fragmentary and haphazard. The illustrations are marked by stereotypes and ambiguity.

According to this and other recent studies (Mok 1991), it is thus not the will but the ability that is lacking. This is consistent with the textbook tradition itself. The study concludes with a challenge to textbook authors and publishers to come to grips with vague and so-called neutral approximations and instead, "use narration and paradigms as tools so that children and young people are able to understand and interpret the world in a more subtle and knowledgeable way." (P. 50.)

Indirectly, the report in SPOV 9 raises the same question as Dominique Maingueneau (see page 147); whether there is a special *school language* ("discours") which preserves educational and ideological thought patterns that promote stability in the school and the textbooks, but which is poorly suited to capture or describe conflicts and changes outside of the system. One analysis that verifies such an hypothesis on the basis of more detailed linguistic analyses is Arvid Jørstad's scrutiny of selected chapters of three social science textbooks for lower secondary school (Jørstad 1979). Jørstad's study is an edited version of a thesis on language usage analysis. By way of introduction, he identifies his basic premise by using a quotation: "When analyzing a text, it is necessary to examine linguistic expression in light of the contents. But one can also do the opposite: The formulation of the linguistic expression is also the gateway and key to a description of the contents." (Roksvold 1975, p. 3.) Jørstad distinguishes between explicit and implicit statements and analyzes the presentation of various countries' forms of government by replacing authentic formulations with imaginary ones ("attitude analysis by substitution"; p. 92). His analysis of what he calls "editing" (choice of material, subject, scope and arrangement) comes *in addition to* the analysis of language usage. Jørstad also arrives at the conclusion that the text is loaded and not apolitical. Like the Swedish group that investigated racism (SPOV 9, 1990), the author ascribes such attitudes more to a tradition than to a conscious desire to influence (p. 155). This view is supported by a study which was recently carried out by Karen Biraimah at the University of Florida: "Knowledge Control in Developing Countries: A Comparative Study of Togolese and Thai English Language Textbooks" (Biraimah 1991, see page 107). Jørstad's, and more particularly Biraimah's, studies bring relevance to questions such as: What about the world picture in textbooks where language itself is the subject of study? Can ideologies and reality actually be implied through examples in grammar books, for example?

Few investigations have examined this directly, although Åke Pettersson's study of the example words in three grammars used in primary and lower secondary schools point in a certain direction (Pettersson 1987, see page 203).

Democracy and Peace

The word democracy is a revered one, often repeated in school regulations and curricula in the countries that will be mentioned here. Since the word also appears in the media and in public debate with many interpretations and shades of meaning, it is doubly important that textbooks provide explanations that will make the concept a worthwhile tool for the pupils' studies of current events.

In 1980, the Swedish Textbook Committee commissioned Thomas Anderberg to investigate references to "democracy" in three social science textbooks for the lower secondary level.

Anderberg summed up his results in a report (Anderberg 1981). He discovered that the textbooks followed the curricula faithfully but that they failed to expand on the curricula's most important universal statements. Vagueness on difficult points was simply transferred from the curriculum to the book. Cautiousness often bordered upon the meaningless; controversial points were either rephrased or omitted.

According to Anderberg, one main reason for this, in all the books examined, is that they worked too hard to satisfy three inherently contradictory requirements: The books should be written so they became part of the school's general democratic system ("the school democracy requirement"); they should give an objective presentation of the topic ("the report requirement"); and they should encourage and inspire pupils to accept and practice democracy ("the education requirement"). Consequently, the books had to avoid and evade so many factors that they lacked their own subjective, explicitly explanatory portrayals of democracy as a phenomenon. In fact, they are all variations on the same theme within one and the same more or less abstract and obscure tradition of formulation.

A few years later, Tomas Englund published a report entitled "On Solidarity and Conflict - An Investigation of Political Attitudes in Educational Materials for Social Science as well as some Didactic Observations about how Schools Encourage Civic and Political Awareness." (Englund 1984.) This title covers a large part of Englund's agenda. Englund, currently an associate professor at the University of Uppsala's Institute of Pedagogy, contributed greatly to introducing wider perspectives into textbook analysis in the 1980s. In an earlier study of social science textbooks and teaching (Englund 1981), the author emphasized that textbook investigations require frames of reference based on both curriculum theory and sociological theory. Englund's basic premise is that a school's social and political instruction fulfills a special function in a civil democracy. Four "determinants" inherent to this function decide which information will be covered in textbooks and instruction. They are "the promotion of solidarity, an integral base of knowledge, the principle of objectivity, and the establishment of the economic organization" (Englund 1984, p. 2).

In the same vein, Englund formulated four main groups of questions that are defined and developed as the analysis progresses. The three most popular lower secondary school social science textbooks used in 1984 comprise the material for the project:

Question 1: Which democratic principles and values are emphasized/dominant in the respective teaching materials and in which context(s) are they presented? What is the teaching materials' basis for evaluation (selection and structure)?

Question 2: What kind of conflicts are dealt with in the textbooks and how are they resolved?

Question 3: Which "channels" for civic influence are discussed and how are they related to positions in business and industry and society?

Question 4: How do the textbooks deal with the question of economic democracy? (Englund 1984, p. 2.)

In this way, the investigation consistently presents fundamental questions of theory. Textbook analysis becomes part of a didactic investigation leading to the question of what determines the selection of content in curricula and textbooks. Thus he goes beyond the framework of the school system and asks whether "the time element in itself, and thereby the cultural climate and issues of the day, have a certain influence on the formation of teaching materials." (Englund 1984, p. 3.)

In a comprehensive study from 1986, "Society and Civics in Swedish Schools in the 19th Century" (Englund 1986), history and social science textbooks are placed within the above-mentioned holistic framework. This and Englund's previous work all represent a methodological synthesis of quantitative and not least, qualitative procedures.

Very few studies have concentrated exclusively on how textbooks present the concept of democracy. There is no entry for the word "democracy" in the index of the Woodward, Elliott and Nagel bibliography (see page 27). In a recent survey of all publications from the Georg Eckert Institute (*Verzeichnis der Publikationen*, June 1990), scarcely more than a dozen of close to one thousand articles bear a direct reference to this concept in their titles. The survey of educational material from the Institute contains 16 "packages", including the Third World, peace, Europe and minorities. But democracy is not singled out as a separate issue. However, it is evident that the theme of democracy is either a leitmotif or one of the main elements in many investigations into how societies and governments are presented in history and social science textbooks, whether the research has been done in Germany, the United States or the Nordic countries. Nevertheless, it is remarkable that this key concept is so rarely used as a principal point of departure.

To a large extent, that same observation applies to terms such as peace and the Third World. The following discussion will concentrate chiefly on two major studies that are representative of each of these fields.

Brigitte Reich's work *Erziehung zur Völkerständigung und Frieden* (Reich 1989) is distinguished by its thoroughness. Describing the way she builds up her study thus involves presenting a survey of the central approaches taken by ideological investigations.

The first chapter justifies the investigation and selection of material, and sets forth hypotheses. Reich is a peace researcher and educator. She examines how UN and UNESCO goals regarding education as a means of promoting peace and international understanding are achieved in five English, six French and eight West German upper secondary level textbooks in history and social science published between 1979 and 1984. Reich aspires to further the tradition of history book revision, but also emphasizes Schallenberger and Stein's view of the textbook as a *politicum*.

Moreover, she aspires to show how school system structures and the textbook market influence the books' contents: "Textbooks are not viewed as reflections of a picture of a (distorted) reality, but rather as expressions of prevalent, political conceptions of "reality'." (Pp. 7-8.) Reich uses this interpretation of "text as the world" (see Gordon, page 147) in textbooks to examine two levels that include selection of content as well as language. The first level deals with "manifest content", the other with "ideological tendencies" (p. 9). Basically, this is a traditional dichotomy, but Reich is the first to include books written in three languages, English, French and German, and to treat them equally.

The second chapter examines earlier research in this field. Reich offers some criticism of the Braunschweig tradition (see page 71) and emphasizes that more recent textbooks can make use of "a broad range of questioning and investigative methods", which should study content analysis in relation to (limited) possibilities for influence as well as the entire system for school book production. Further, Reich reasons that a study of the subject "learning for peace" must necessarily be normative.

The third chapter investigates what Reich called the "frameworks": The school systems in the three countries, the position history and social science occupy in each country's upper secondary schools, curricula and curriculum planning, and the ratio between market/sales and production/content in the books. One of Reich's most important premises is that the latter ratio has a decisive influence on the books' form and content (p. 96).

The fourth chapter is a discussion of method, which examines different sociologists' views on how content analyses should be carried out. It concludes in resignation: Sociologists' theory requirements have become so complex, so specific and, not least, so tied to the research community from which they derive, that "for the individual researcher, the objective of a critical ideological analysis appears to be almost beyond the realm of possibility" (p. 114). In her analysis, however, she uses procedures taken from several methodologists, which are, in each case, adapted to the topic and questions she is examining. Reich organizes her material into four main categories: 1) The treatment of mankind's major problems, 2) The presentation of foreign nations, 3) The presentation of the United Nations, and 4) The analysis and evaluation of the causes of wars and conflicts. In the two first categories, the most important aids are the *Reference analysis* (does the topic exist?) and the *Spatial analysis* (how much space does it take up in the presentation?) In category 3, *Contextual analysis* and *Valency analysis* also come into play, and in the last category emphasis is put on more stylistic and structural characteristics

(*Prototypes, Standard structures*).

Chapter 5 comprises nearly half the publication and includes 13 highly detailed tables in addition to text. In this chapter, Reich explains observations (Ergebnisse), evaluations (Auswertungen) and interpretations (Interpretationen). The summary, which deals with each category separately, is fairly intricate and would be difficult to outline here.

In Chapter 6, which discusses textbooks of the future based on the possibilities and shortcomings revealed in the study, Reich gives a general description of her results, which correspond with Swedish research results on the presentation of the concept of democracy (see page 117):

> In addition, the results indicate that on the one hand textbooks share a common "Western European" approach. On the other, the selection of content demonstrates dependence upon the prevailing didactical views and the author's "political" opinions. (P. 265.)

Another of Reich's observations is that some textbooks limit explanations about the causes of war to static models, such as mans' innate aggression or certain nations' warring traditions (p. 249), and that the political and military aspects of the question are given pride of place in the presentation. This observation coincides with the results of an American study. Fleming and Nurse (Fleming - Nurse 1982) examined the presentation of the Vietnam War in ten upper secondary level textbooks published from 1977 to 1981, and discovered that "most textbooks offer too sketchy an account of the war, but the deficiencies are due to the neglect of certain key topics rather than distortion, dishonesty, inaccuracy or bias" (Woodward - Elliott - Nagel 1988, p. 128). This viewpoint is supported in a comparable study of the presentation of the Vietnam War in primary school history books (Logan - Needham 1985). Even more comprehensive in terms of time, span and corpus is Griffen and Marciano's examination of the presentation of the Vietnam War in 28 high school textbooks published between 1961 and 1978 (Griffen - Marciano 1980). The authors criticize textbook authors and publishers for basing their presentation solely on the government's official version, *The Pentagon Papers*, and overlooking the large number of divergent accounts.

There are many more examples from the United States that reveal similar biases. However, Englund, Reich, Fleming, Nurse and others emphasize one apparently important point: Biases and distortions are not necessarily expressions of a desire to exercise political influence, but may more likely be caused by inattentiveness and/or pedagogical-didactic textbook traditions. At an international conference arranged in The Hague in 1989 called "NATO in History and Civics Textbooks" (Atlantisch Onderwijs Paper VII 1990), Fay Metcalf, head of the National Commission on Social Studies in Schools, delivered an introductory speech during which she raised one issue that appears to be a universal textbook problem, an issue which may also create problems for "one's own":

> (...) a problem that is frequently called "mentioning". In an effort to include all the requests and requirements of the numerous districts and states, books longer and longer have been able to devote seemingly less and less space to any one topic. The leading American history textbook today - *Triumph of the American Nation* - is at 1088 pages, the longest text now available. This book devotes a total of 46 text lines, scattered over some 86 pages, to NATO, including the organization's formation. (P. 6.)

Metcalf's observation supports Michael W. Apple's theory on cultural incorporation (see page 148).

Yngve Nordkvelle has investigated the presentation of developing countries in Norwegian upper and lower secondary school textbooks (Nordkvelle 1986, 1987). His starting point was to check the correspondence between the curricula and textbook texts. Nordkvelle found quite a bit of material about developing countries, but the information was

> biased and inadequate; engendering sympathy, but containing negative descriptions of the people, cultures, economies and lifestyles in poor nations. To a great extent, the texts also avoid taking positions on moral and political issues endemic to the

problem of development. (Nordkvelle 1991, p. 2.)

As the need for clarification about the basis for ideological criticism in the investigation increased, Nordkvelle found it necessary to expand both his perspective and his methods. At first, the study was extended by analyzing the educational qualifications teachers have for teaching about developing countries. He discovered that fewer teachers colleges offered instruction in that topic in 1987 than in 1983.

After that, Nordkvelle expanded his investigation to include classroom teaching. The author observed history and social science classes on all levels in an upper secondary school over the course of a year (Nordkvelle 1988): "The authority of the text is accentuated by passive teaching methods." (Nordkvelle 1991, p. 2.)

A final expansion was made when an analysis of pupils' answers on social science and history examinations also became part of the investigation. Partial studies have been conducted on individual countries and specific problems in the Third World (see page 105), factors which will be integrated into forthcoming research at the Georg Eckert Institute in Braunschweig. However, there are few examples of investigations that cover a perspective as comprehensive as that of Yngve Nordkvelle.

Form of Government and World View

A more common type of ideological investigation than those limited to an analysis of one topic, are surveys that include topics such as democracy, peace or the Third World in more comprehensive analyses of the presentations of forms of government and the world in general.

Two comprehensive attempts have been made in the Nordic countries to examine the total content of an entire set of textbooks in the light of ideology. Both studies were inspired by the debate on indoctrination that took place during the transition from the 1960s to the 1970s (see page 137). However, they represent vastly different solutions and may serve as examples of the possible range for approaches and results. The two attempts are the series entitled PAX KORREKTIV (PAX KORREKTIV 1970-1971; Norway) and

Lise Togeby's *The Indestructible Textbook* (Togeby 1978; Denmark).

The PAX KORREKTIV consists of four booklets, each of which deals with one particular textbook; two in history and social science at the lower secondary level and two in the same subjects at the upper secondary level. Two of the booklets have one author, two have two authors. The cover and colophon pages show that the authors oppose capitalist systems and aspire "to uncover bourgeois indoctrination in the school system" (dust cover). In the preface to the first volume, Hans Fredrik Dahl writes that their intention is to help pupils and teachers recognize "what kind of book this is, what prejudices it contains, and why." None of the four booklets in the PAX KORREKTIV discuss methods or procedures. They are voluminous and to some extent highly polemical "reviews" which partly reveal errors, partly point out prejudices and partly suggest other angles of approach, formulations and textbooks for instruction. As a whole, the criticism primarily comprises the textbook authors' express convictions and assurances that they have written the books out of respect for fundamental democratic values - but they say this without defining what they mean by such values:

> (...) the textbook authors have a very superficial relationship to what they discuss, as long as they don't explain in more detail *what* they mean by "neutrality" and "not free to evaluation", and *why* the book "cannot be ascribed to a particular political view" when it is nonetheless marked by certain fundamental values. (...)
> Even if the authors to a greater extent than in the last edition point out defects in our society, they never ask whether their basic values even *have a chance of being* realized within our present social order. Based on this, we believe that the textbook may still be ascribed to a *particular* political view. (Baldersheim - Tvedt 1970, preface.)

Lise Togeby's investigation (Togeby 1978) of eight lower secondary school social science textbooks ("the junior-secondary school" in 1972) was performed at the Institute for Political

Science at the University of Aarhus. The report has one scientific author who never says anything about her own view of society or political opinions. Following an historical survey of the subject's traditions and earlier textbook criticism, Togeby presents her method, which is quantitative content analysis. She has chosen this method not only to measure the content in the books, but also to "check the possibilities inherent in the quantitative methods. Other methods could undoubtedly have supplemented the results of the quantitative investigation. However, this has only been done to a limited extent. The project has to end sometime" (p. 49). This quotation gives some indication of the dilemma that gradually crops up in Togeby's presentation, where the boundaries between the registration of the totals of coded numerical results and their interpretation become difficult. The author herself points out that one of her chapters (Chapter 10) "is almost exclusively based on a judicious close reading of the textbooks under investigation" (p. 49).

Togeby's investigation is based on a detailed system of measurement. The model also contains elements of content and form which are systematically arranged into a total of 45 tables. Measurements of topics account for no more than a small part of this material; five tables show how frequently mention is made of the welfare state, democracy, equality between the sexes, the labor market and developing countries. However, a considerable amount of qualitative assessment lies behind the arrangement of the individual tables, which go far beyond registering the number of occurrences and pages. For example, the table on equality between the sexes contains categories as ways of explaining the situation and a separate column for "General impression positive/negative" (p. 143). The tables also measure form as an approach to the material ("aspects"), views, composition, statements (positive/ negative) and style (descriptive/explanatory/ argumentative).

Togeby's conclusions are also representative for the conclusions of other investigations discussed in this chapter (Anderberg, Anyon, Hadenius, Jørstad, Nordkvelle, PAX KORREKTIV, Reich, SPOV9):

The would-be neutrality shows up in the form, since there are no deprecating statements in the books, no discussions and no positions taken or arguments made for viewpoints. Furthermore, the form is characterized by its lack of meaning-bearing elements. There are few explanations, and there is rarely any interest shown in the significance of phenomena to the distribution of values in society. Things are rarely put into a context.

This means that the social science books consist of a number of independent, concrete items of information about Danish social conditions, but these items of information are meaningless, because they are not viewed in relation to one another. The meaning or relevance of the information they carry is unclear. *Thus the books are also very difficult to study as sources of factual educational material.* (P. 206. *My* emphasis; see Kåre Lunden, page 134.)

A third investigation should also be mentioned. Already in 1969, the Swedish Textbook Committee commissioned Stig Hadenius and Claes-Olof Olsson to undertake a comparative investigation of the way in which upper secondary school history textbooks presented the post-WWI era (Hadenius - Olsson 1971). The assignment was an extension of a public debate about the world picture presented in Swedish history textbooks. The authors were to delimit the topic themselves. They did that by dividing the study into two main parts: A content analysis of the historical material from the viewpoint of "Textbooks' picture of the world" and an analysis of the level of objectivity in the books - the latter based on the following point of view: "As one of the basic rules for all teaching, the curriculum requires *objectivity*." (P. 2.) The authors employed quantitative methods. A revised edition of the report published in the *Swedish Journal of History* in 1971 triggered a debate on method (see page 142). It is appropriate here to cite the conclusion which, in addition to pointing out the lack of balance between political material (which dominates) and social and economic material (which is under-represented), confirms that "old textbook traditions seem to have had a very strong hold on the authors; the books are conventional in so many ways." (P. 36.)

In 1990, Rajoo Kamala and Margaret Rogers investigated "Content Coverage by Continent" in the four leading social studies textbooks at the middle school level in the USA (Kamala - Rogers 1991). Their investigation was chiefly quantitative, based on measuring to some extent the space the books accorded to the different continents and countries, and to some extent the representation of common political, social and cultural topics. First of all, they found great variations in the space according to the different continents and, second, no explicitly justified or implicit patterns in the choices or placement of the mention of countries or topics. As an example of the large degree of randomness, they mention that the term/topic of nuclear power is never mentioned in any of the books.

Perspectives

Ideology, Objectivity and Indoctrination

It has traditionally been presumed that reliable, practical knowledge would enhance moral standards and that high moral standards would accelerate the acquisition of knowledge, benefiting both the individual and society. These two elements have been fundamental to all aspects of education. The marriage of knowledge and high morals was to yield what the Philanthropists called the *happy* human being; what Christian Levin Sander, the Nordic countries' first professor of pedagogy, termed the *true* human being; what the Norwegian Basic School Act currently calls the *useful* and *independent* human being; and what Norway's Act related to Upper Secondary Education describes as what might be called the *useful and knowledgeable fellow human being*.

As time has passed, most countries have probably redefined the knowledge aspect but left the moral aspect unchanged. Still, no part of the dichotomy has ever been left out, despite the fact that many modern educators would contend that the balance has shifted toward the morals or attitudes aspect. Those who hold this view generally call for schools to focus more on the basics. Their viewpoint is interesting in relation to textbooks since the books, measured as the number per pupil/consumer, have become more numerous, more specialized and more comprehensive. Is it at all possible, for example, to identify certain textbook characteristics that give some indication of the ratio between the conveyance of knowledge and the conveyance of acceptable attitudes?

This question illustrates one of a wide variety of problems which can hardly be studied without considering the larger ideological implications of textbooks. An ideology is a prominent, more or less explicitly stated system of values which is constantly being defended and/or attacked. Within the context of education, it is important to examine the relationship between the various parties involved in the process of preserving and/or re-shaping ideologies. This also entails investigating the ways in which this process is or is not transmitted through the textbook corpus in its entirety. For instance: The efforts invested in creating supplementary teaching materials, workbooks and educational packages are a consequence of the curriculum requirements concerning classroom activities and practical knowledge. In turn, these requirements are a consequence of an educational policy whose ultimate goal in the 1970s and 1980s was to produce socially productive individuals. The emphasis on this requirement coincided - or seemed to coincide - with the development of productive resources. Thus the increase in the number of books and their volume (measured per pupil) *may* be justified as being part of the educational ideology.

But what roles do the various involved parties play in the process; which party is most influenced by/exerts the most influence on and in the textbook text? Finding an answer would require a thorough study of textbook selection, production and use, and any answer would have to be based on the premise that these processes are autonomous, yet mutually dependent carriers and conveyors of ideology.

In its broadest sense, ideology includes everything from individuals' personal philosophies of life to political or other far-reaching philosophies. Textbooks have been analyzed in contexts ranging from the Marxist conception of school knowledge itself as an ideology serving the interests of powerful groups, to the conception of ideology more as a system of symbols and a world view (Berger - Luckmann 1966; see Jean Anyon 1979, pp. 361-63). It is important to bear in mind the one factor which has consistently been the most common motivation for studying textbook ideology:

> The values and attitudes that are taught in schools are of obvious and central interest to the parents of school children, and to those who are concerned with the social futures that the patterns of schooling seem to foreshadow or with the world-view that the

schools seem to reflect at a given time. When the values that the schools reflect become inconsistent with the values that groups or individuals hold as important or critical to their futures, bias is often claimed. This charge reflects, however, the perspective of the person or persons making the charge: It can be made when schooling seems to threaten the rejection or denigration of traditional values of religion and morality, nationality, race or ethnicity, sex roles and sexuality and the like, or it can be made *because* schooling reflects these values. (Westbury 1982, p. 31.)

Westbury points out the duality of the motives for analyzing textbook ideologies: Studies may be motivated by the desire to promote or defend traditional values that appear threatened or by the desire to offset or eliminate the dominance of these very same values. Such motives are most readily apparent in the steady stream of contributions made to relevant public debates in a number of countries in the 1970s and 1980s. One example of the former is the work of the Gablers, a married couple from Longview, Texas. They have worked as textbook critics for more than a generation, writing regular reviews of new books. They discussed their reasons for becoming critics in an issue of the educational journal *Phi Delta Kappan* (Gabler 1982), where they claimed that new state and regional forces threaten education and society:

> What was done suddenly through government force by Hitler has been done gradually in the United States. Government force, through schools, has gradually eliminated (banned, censored) practically all books that uphold, promote, or teach the basic values upon which our nation was founded. (P. 96.)

Norma and Mel Gabler cite the following examples of values now disappearing from textbooks, values they want to mobilize parents in the USA to protect: "monogamous families, anti-homosexuality, anti-abortion, American patriotism, morality, conservative views, teaching of honesty, obeying laws, changing bad laws through a legal process, etc." (P. 96.)

A Danish pamphlet, published by literature students at Odense University with support from the Danish trade unions movement

(Christiansen, et al., 1978), epitomizes the attacks directed against many of these values. A second printing was needed almost immediately and the pamphlet was reviewed in the left-wing newspaper "Information", where the critic wrote that "we in the labor movement can only declare that we agree with these demands (for equality through education). But how can we implement them in a non-socialistic, capitalistic society, where the power is often centered not in the national assembly but somewhere else altogether?" (Mølgaard 1978.)

While systematization is certainly a must for traditional surveys and for the registration and revision of history textbooks, it will become increasingly important to distinguish between a researcher's philosophical and political position and the final results of his work. In his discussion of the methodological problems involved in textbook research, Wolfgang Marienfeld writes that many studies of ideological criticism:

(...) make clear the number of ways in which history book representations are encumbered by prejudices, contain factual errors, apply norms inconsistently, oversimplify matters, omit mention of any other possibilities, treat outsiders unjustly, etc. Yet because one cannot arrive at unequivocal assessment criteria through scientific procedures, such analyses themselves are at risk of being ideologized, and one can reduce some of the existing investigations down to the fact that they do no more than try to replace any (real or assumed) ideologies they have identified with another ideology. (Marienfeld 1976, p. 49.)

According to Westbury and Marienfeld it is important to distinguish between the ideologies of those conducting the research and the ideological features of textbook content and/or form. Commenting upon Althusser's structuralism, Rob Gilbert describes the distinction in this way:

To map the structure of an image is to construct a representation from the researcher's perspective; a critique of ideology must always be conducted from a particular perspective. This can be seen as the overlay of one discourse on another, so that the

network of problems, concepts, relationships which comprise the
critical theory throw into relief the emphases and omissions of
the discourse being criticized. (Gilbert 1989, p. 67.)

The vast majority of ideological textbook investigations have been
carried out by researchers with rather left-wing political views, and
they usually conclude with criticism of the one-sidedness and
conservatism of textbooks. In this context, "leftist" means that such
research also criticizes the books from countries dominated by
social democratic ideals and government (Tingsten 1969, PAX
KORREKTIV 1970-1971, Togeby 1978, Ferro 1981).

In a few exceptional cases, such criticism has come from the
right; a well known example from France is Bernard Bonilauris'
151-page essay *La désinformation scolaire* (Bonilauri 1983).
Bonilauri, who was the right hand man of conservative philosopher
Raymond Aron, examined history and social science books which
"circulent en majorité dans l'enseignement secondaire" (p. 7) and
found that they paint an erroneous picture of France as an
exploitative colonial power, that they underestimate the role of the
individual in society, and that they glorify social democratic
systems at the expense of liberal values. Bonilauri uses Swedish
social democracy as an example and claims that this model has
been uncritically copied by several European societies and, to the
detriment of those countries, embedded itself as an ideal in the
textbooks.

Yet regardless of departure point, there is one trait which
dominates non-polemical literature on textbook ideologies: The
more or less explicit intention of most authors and researchers is to
analyze content to determine the extent to which it promotes
freedom and equality. Another common trait is that analyses find
the books deficient on that point. Naturally, this may be because
the researchers have similar politically-motivated reasons for
criticizing the status quo. In any case, the results point in that
direction regardless of whether the method has been inspired by
history book revision, structuralism, or "practical discourse"
(Gilbert 1989, see page 145).

Still another common denominator is the underlying assumption
that textbooks influence readers. (Otherwise there would be no

reason to analyze them, unless of course the object were to examine them solely as mirrors of dominant social attitudes (see Elson, page 95)). In the 1980s the problems inherent in that assumption surfaced as user- and reader-oriented studies took the place of traditional analyses of omissions and errors in the contents. Questioning texts' readability has a long tradition, but somehow, strengthened by researchers' more recent preoccupation with investigating explicit and implicit elements of influence, this approach now tends to probe deeper and may to some degree supplant the tradition of ideological studies.

A few examples illustrate the variety inherent in different aspects of and approaches to ideology.

A classic within the tradition of history book revision is E.H. Dance's *History the Betrayer. A Study in Bias.* (Dance 1960.) This book provides a comprehensive survey of the difficulties involved in writing history textbooks which avoid spreading incorrect information, prejudice and propaganda. The primary point is to ascertain what the books do or do not contain.

Ruth Miller Elson (Elson 1964) considers schoolbooks to be a reflection of the prevailing political and cultural aims of a society. Elson's analysis of viewpoints and attitudes is based on the assumption that textbooks are the ultimate mirror of power. She refers to the knowledge contained in textbooks to prove that their overall effect amounts to an all-out campaign to promote North American nationalism. She cites many examples of self-serving distortions, mainly at the expense of the British. However, the revelation of that fact is not the point at issue. It might be said that Elson indirectly suggests that the drawing of edifying national self-portraits is of necessity an intrinsic part of the ideology of textbooks.

The research traditions of the 1960s and 1970s linked research to history and social science textbooks. In the 1990s questions related to textbooks in the natural sciences are expected to be far more controversial than the issue of how history schoolbooks should deal with Adolf Hitler. The ideologies represented in mathematics, foreign language and natural science textbooks will most likely be considered just as weighty as those contained in history and social studies textbooks.

Some contemporary researchers challenge the justification for analyzing textbook ideologies, citing the receptiveness/ willingness of pupils as the reason for their objection. Such work must surely be based on the conviction that textbooks *do have* moral and intellectual influence. In an article entitled "Worth-less Textbooks" (Lunden 1990), historian Kåre Lunden states that ill-conceived attempts at objectivity have made history books so boring that they don't interest or influence their readers. He asks *"why* contemporary writers and those in charge of public approval schemes are so demoralized that the quality of their products suffers" (p. 227), pointing out the connection between this trend and the ideologies underlying natural science and humanities research (see page 342).

According to Vitz and Starr (see Holtz 1989) textbooks have been robbed of meaning both by the left wing (which assures the removal of positive reference to majoritarian religion) and the right wing (which assures the removal of positive references to socialism and trade unions). This point of view once again raises the question asked repeatedly above: If pedagogical texts are reduced to more or less "general" presentation of facts and narrative, failing to confront alternative views in ways which do present interpretations as well as the foundation for those interpretations, they can be accused of not being truly educative at all.

The concept of objectivity in textbooks can and has been associated with several different value systems. The systems are normally of a political and/or meta-theoretical and/or educational/ psychological nature.

If a society genuinely wishes to root education in definite values and to inculcate specific attitudes, this wish will be incorporated into its high priority goals. In a pluralistic, democratic society, this means the ideal of objectivity will be incorporated into the political objectives of the educational system.

It has not proved possible to construct an objectivity model which is universally valid. Such models must be grounded in scientific theory, and the underlying premises of such theory may be or seem to be rather unclear at any given time. Besides, the natures of individual subjects may clash with ostensibly undisputable aspects of more general scientific theories. (Harbo

1978, p. 357.)

The demand for objectivity in schools must be adapted to age levels and individual qualifications. One question which comes to mind, for instance, involves the extent to which teaching independence depends on (or is at all furthered by) objectivity in the classroom. This in turn raises the question of whose and what kind of objectivity we're talking about.

The conflict between the individual and society parallels the conflict inherent in the dichotomous goal of the national curriculum, i.e., on the one hand, to foster universal attitudes such as tolerance, open-mindedness, and impartial judgement and, on the other hand, to instill definite political, national and religious values. This dual set of values was intentionally incorporated into Norwegian curricula on the grounds that neutral values are not possible if teaching and education are to maintain the desired perspective. Schools must explicitly profess certain fundamental values and they must provide impartial information about *other* value systems. The aim is not individuals without norms, but well-rounded individuals. The ideal of objectivity must be manifested by shedding light on topics, issues and problems from different angles. Education will thus become an expression of what has been called "theoretical pluralism". Theo Koritzinsky describes the problem as follows:

> The national curriculum demands objectivity, impartiality and neutrality of values. But it also demands involvement, activity, and the need to take a stand. These two sets of values: "Objectivity"and "Involvement"may be diametrically opposed to each other. Yet the national curriculum demands the presence of both values. Striking a balance between the two and determining their proportions is difficult, but necessary" (Koritzinsky 1977, p. 15).

In connection with international textbook revision in particular, it eventually became evident that language usage and the basic perspectives taken in textbooks inevitably entail interpretations right from the start. Hence it became more common during the 1970s to emphasize the formal aspect of the representation. Some

writers went so far as to maintain that the possibility of imple-
menting the principle of "theoretical pluralism" in textbooks was
of a rather hypothetical nature:

> *Textbooks* express at least formally a descriptive pluralism,
> which means an unbiased representation of several different sets
> of values. It is, however, a very easy matter to find empirical
> proof of the fact that the ideal of "theoretical pluralism" actually
> conceals a rather obvious, (but implicit) theoretical bias in
> contemporary textbooks of social science. This means to say that
> textbooks actually have their theoretical basis in a particular
> approach towards the interpretation and understanding of society.
> This basis of understanding has not been made explicit, but
> nevertheless it is expressed in unambiguous and relatively
> consistent forms, when it comes to the *contents aspect*. This is
> shown through *the choice of topics and approaches, as well as
> in the choice of linguistic expressions and concepts*. Especially
> the latter field provides good examples of the difficulties
> involved in realizing the ideal of "theoretical pluralism".
> (Leonardsen 1979, p. 40.)

The ideological debate about the nature of text in general, as well
as that of the formally approved textbook, have long ago
challenged the assumption (in positivist vein) that bias can easily
be removed and that "objectivity" can readily be agreed upon as
the goal of the pluralist society. Is it, for instance, not possible that
the very meaning of a pluralist society is that it must permit
different objective interpretations of truth?

Tomas Englund writes that the concept of objectivity can be
described by establishing a rough distinction between four groups
or "contexts" (Englund 1984). The first applies to the description
of limited phenomena, where the call for impartiality is the most
important. The second applies to the treatment of controversial
issues, where the demand for comprehensiveness is the most
important. The third applies to the democratic aims of education,
where the analysis of the relationship between the high priority
aims/values and the call for objectivity is the most important. The
fourth applies to what Englund calls "the school's latent fostering

function", where it is the relationship between the substructures that Rob Gilbert writes about (Gilbert 1989; see page 145) and the call for objectivity that are the most important.

When discussing these groups, Englund stresses the fact that they overlap. His comment to the classification may also be seen as a comment to the various points of view and statements quoted above:

> It is obvious that these contexts (1-4) cannot be completely separated from one another. Every description of a social phenomenon contains a selection of perspectives and knowledge that may often be viewed in a different way or from other perspectives. Thus the question of controversiality often depends on the "presence" of different perspectives, which in turn depends on the degree to which the social phenomenon is actually seen in a larger perspective. In a more limited sense certain "facts" must be imparted, of course, but as soon as more complex relations are to be taught there is an increasing demand for comprehensive information. (Englund 1984, p. 9.)

In the Nordic countries the debate on educational ideology started in 1968 with the publication of Göran Palm's book *Indoctrination in Sweden* (Palm 1968). The author deals with indoctrination in relation to a number of different media. One of his main chapters is entitled "Democratic schoolbooks". He characterizes the books as being a biased defense of the established order:

> If we look beyond the latest textbooks' appealing layouts and educational refinement, we rather quickly encounter a defense of the established order that rarely leaves any margin for doubt, afterthought or discussion (....). This boring of the coming generation has been given a strange name: "the education of involvement'. (Pp. 50-51.)

In the introductory chapter Palm discusses the concept of indoctrination. He points out that the term may refer to teaching or to indoctrination through teaching, but he cautions the reader against believing that all types of influence automatically imply indoctrination. His explanation proves how difficult the concept is to apply, or rather how dependent the concept of indoctrination can be on the author's (polemical) ego:

> (....) I have reserved this term for those influences which directly or indirectly involve politics or political views. (...) The teaching of the church doctrine on Trinity for instance I do not consider to be indoctrination, since this doctrine does not have any political relevance, while the priest's admonition on how to relate to authority or to work should be called indoctrination. In my opinion, indoctrination is also something done from the top and directed downwards in society, from those in power or those few who mold public opinion and down to the more or less powerless majority (...) (p. 8).

We find the same philosophy expressed slightly differently by writer and philosopher Jon Hellesnes:

> *Indoctrination* is a *bad* thing. Indoctrination implies that one lets the coming generation learn how to understand their own situation, using the ideas of the *authorities*, instead of learning how to trust their own common sense. (...) *Politicization*, on the other hand, is a *good* thing, since it does not occur as a result of some unthematical, subjective philosophical *standpoint*, as is the case of indoctrination. Politicization is committed to what is true and reasonable. Since that which is true and reasonable is not something definitive and unambiguous, politicization is of necessity connected with *dialogue*. (Hellesnes 1975, p. 18.)

One book quite unique in a Nordic context is *Indoctrination or politicization? Form and contents in the teaching of social studies at the lower secondary level.* (Age group 13 to 16.) (Haavelsrud 1979). The book examines social studies textbooks approved in 1976 for use by pupils at the lower secondary level. Six researchers evaluated the books from the following angles: The objectivity in chapters on technical development and rationalization, the time perspective of the chapters, and how the books deal with juvenile delinquency, conflicts and topics such as equal rights. In addition, the book contains a report concerning practical classroom activities and two theoretical introductory chapters which discuss evaluation criteria and the ways in which pupils may be influenced by textbooks. Altogether, the wide range of contributions in the book provides a good foundation for a comprehensive survey of problems and options within the framework of ideological textbook analysis, as assessed by political scientists.

Hermeneutic, Quantitative and Qualitative Approaches

It is important to emphasize that the term *ideological investigations* used in this presentation covers an extensive body of content analyses. It embraces all four of the main categories of investigations that Peter Meyers employed in his survey of West German research up to the 1970s (Meyers 1973). He grouped the analyses according to the following objectives:

– To eliminate the potential for conflict and pave the way for peace and international understanding.

– To find out how the books can promote democracy and tolerance.

– To examine the books to see how they glorify their own political system and condemn other systems.

– To analyze the books in order to reconstruct a political picture of the times.

A few years later Wolfgang Marienfeld made a classification system containing six categories (Marienfeld 1976). It, too, is based on the objectives of the investigations, but it also suggests new directions:

– To determine how a nation or a culture sees itself at a given point in time.

- To analyze the books from the perspective of the individual subject in an effort to evaluate them as teaching instruments.

- To determine whether the books discuss fundamental issues (historical forces, causal explanations).

- To evaluate the choice of and rationale for the material with emphasis on the perception of values.

- To conduct international history book revisions.

- To investigate how books are used in the school.

Marienfeld's survey incorporates two categories (subject/use) which I discuss in chapter IV. The same chapter also contains a partial discussion of one of Marienfeld's categories - to determine whether the books discuss fundamental issues. The boundaries between the various categories set up by the authors of the two German surveys will of necessity be quite fluid.

But how, within or across such boundaries, have textbooks been analyzed?

As late as in 1965, Georg Eckert's close associate Otto Schüdde-kopf wrote: "There are no methods or didactics for working with textbooks; such work is a pragmatic art which has developed while being done since 1918 and especially since 1945." (Schüddekopf 1965.) Some ten years later, Wolfgang Marienfeld criticized many textbook analyses for being too one-sided (Marienfeld 1976, see page 131). He did this in a lecture delivered in Braunschweig, where he described and evaluated three main types of methodo-logical approaches: the hermeneutic, the quantitative and the qualitative.

Marienfeld's descriptions are cited in this study because they deal with the procedures that dominated the field in the 1970s and 1980s. These procedures were applied singly or in combination, and they embodied the same basic concepts. The studies examined the textbook as a process, an instrument and a product. Involving both single books and book series, they also looked at the situation in various countries.

Marienfeld's survey was subsequently presented in an article in the *Norwegian Journal of Pedagogy* (Angvik 1982). The following methodological characteristics are partly based on Magne Angvik's article.

The *hermeneutic* or *descriptive-analytical* method has also been called the traditional historical method. The work focuses on the textbooks, i.e., it is source-centered. But textbooks are compressed versions of other and in turn other versions. How can it be proven that analytical conclusions about something like the de facto objectivity of a book are irrefutable? Is it at all possible to find a means of discerning the social perspective of a textbook that is so reliable that another researcher would inevitably reach the same conclusions by following the same procedure? And *if* such a means were discovered, wouldn't it simply reveal the limitations of the method? There are countless pitfalls inherent in citing textual evidence and quotations, especially when it comes to examining ideological content. The risk is least in connection with investigations of individual works, but it increases with comparative and contrastive studies. The practice of analyzing groups of books has been virtually universal, covering a long line of approaches varying from the impressionism of Tingsten 1969 to the meticulous source references of Elson 1964. Please note, however, that even Elson's selection procedures cannot be evaluated.

A *quantitative analysis of content* helps ensure scientific veracity in the sense that it produces verifiable results. The method is based on empirical research developed in the social sciences, i.e., sociology. *Spatial analyses* measure size, e.g., the number of lines/pages devoted to a particular issue. This provides an absolute as well as a relative measure of the importance an individual publication attaches to the matter in question. *Frequency analyses* measure the number of times certain phenomena are mentioned, so they provide a good supplement to spatial analyses. The advantage of the quantitative method is that the results can easily be checked. This applies more to educational investigations (types of assignments, e.g., active ones compared with passive ones) than to ideological investigations. Both the possibilities and the problems are discussed in Andolf 1972 (see page 60). He himself has taken the method to the extreme, and he specifically pointed out its primary weakness in an article published the year before (Andolf 1971). There he discusses another investigation of the picture of society presented in Swedish history books (see page 126). He exposes how unreliable that picture is because the authors have failed to justify and explain their use of *categories* and *units of measurement*. For example, the authors write that evaluations account for a total of ten per cent of the text. Andolf points out that this item of information cannot be accepted as quantification because no norm has been furnished for the scope of each individual evaluation: "for the amount of surrounding text the evaluation supposedly covers". Other weaknesses are pointed out by Lise Togeby, who has used the method herself (Togeby 1978, see page 125):

> If one accepts that one must only describe the content manifest in the text, one is soon confronted by the question of whether it is worth the effort. The problem is that the more objective and quantitative the description of the content, the less interesting it becomes. Quantitative content analyses frequently produce reliable, but trivial results. (P. 48.)

In the lecture delivered in 1976, Marienfeld advocated a synthesis which would combine the hermeneutic and quantitative methods, preserving the best aspects of both and reducing their innate weaknesses. This *qualitative method* relies on a detailed system of categorization which may include content, sources, presentation, extra-textual enhancements and assignments. The idea is to quantify qualitative elements. For example, questions which come under the category "wealth of information" may be posed. They will subsequently be graded according to scales arranged in complex tables containing systems of symbols. Such work has a strong tendency to "swell" and is most useful in connection with limited-scope analyses that cover narrowly defined topics. The most thorough example is an investigation conducted by Marienfeld and Overesch of the image of Germany and the German question (Marienfeld - Overesch 1986; see Jacobmeyer 1986). Based on a descriptive-analytical reading of the books, they established 135 content categories, which were related to a quantitative registration of "Germany" (spatial and frequency analyses). This provided the basis for what Marienfeld calls a qualitative analysis of content. It includes both ideological and didactic (extra-textual enhancements and assignments) traits. In their discussion of methods, the authors draw attention to two unfortunate limitations: First, that language and presentation fall outside the scope of their investigation and, second, that the material and procedures they used did not allow them to provide any empirical rendition of the philosophy and the world view behind the registered presentation of Germany ("Weltbild", "Wissenschaftsverständnis", "Problemverständnis"; p. 16).

A comparison between Andolf's explicitly quantitative and Marienfeld/Overesch's explicitly qualitative analyses would probably not reveal any major methodological differences (see the discussion of Andolf on page 62). Marienfeld's attempt to achieve a synthesis and his acknowledgement of the fact that the solution was not as comprehensive as he would have liked raise the question whether there may be other valid definitions and procedures.

New Directions

The option of combining quantitative and qualitative methods is far from controversial in social science circles anymore (Holter 1990), although as recently as in 1991 Kathleen Oberle claimed that:

> Over the past decade, the qualitative/quantitative paradigm war has continued in educational research. A careful analysis of the epistemological, ontological and methodological bases for the argument reveals no substantive reasons for clinging to the belief that the qualitative and quantitative paradigms are incompatible. Indeed, most of the participants in the debate elect for a combination of approaches to research. Nonetheless, despite the fact that there is evidence that qualitative research has an important role in the advancement of knowledge in education and psychology, positivist (quantitative) research is still dominant in the literature. (Oberle 1991, p. 87.)

Most textbook researchers, many of whom have social science backgrounds, begin their presentations by comparing quantitative and qualitative methods. Such comparisons have never been brought to a logical conclusion, however; thus far researchers have been satisfied with pointing out the advantages and disadvantages of both approaches and then choosing a solution which points in a more quantitative (1970s) or a more qualitative (1980s) direction. This largely ritual "apology" may be seen as symptomatic of the problem textbook research has had with scientific validity, which some would claim has become too one-sidedly tied to the social sciences. The problem of measuring content ought really to be seen in the light of general educational history and humanistic research traditions as well. Historically speaking, schools in Western countries have changed from being institutions that loyally passed on knowledge and cultural heritage to being institutions that pass on more emancipatory ideals. Thus the farther back we go in time, the less interesting it is to know if textbook analyses are geared toward assigning numbers to elements of content in order to expose fairly obvious ideological dominance. Of course, the more recent pragmatic tradition which emphasizes *practical* instruction invites measurement. But then we are talking about user studies that gauge effectiveness and acquired amounts of learning, a field of research in which the former East Germany has gone far.

The 1980s saw the emergence of criticism of traditional content analyses. One example may be found in Arvid Jørstad (see page 115), a style researcher who began his investigation on the basis of the following premise:

> There are no recipes for analyzing the attitudes that lie behind a linguistic expression, nor is there any objective method for either verifying or disproving the results of such an analysis. (Jørstad 1979, p. 154.)

Another example may be found in Caspard 1984, an historian who castigated an American study of petit bourgeoisism in French primary school books used from 1830 to 1880 (Strumingher 1983). He asked what point there is in mobilizing an overburdened analytical apparatus and drowning the reader in a "flood" of trivialities that are so conspicuous there is no need to measure them. (Caspard 1984, p. 69.)

A third example is Brigitte Reich's investigation of textbooks in West Germany, France and Great Britain. In her introduction she dissociates herself somewhat from the most common tradition in history book revision:

> (...) the common conviction that 1) the textbook comprises an important medium in the learning process and that 2) changes in textbook texts also entail changes in pupils' ideas and attitudes, had to be relinquished. (...) However, in recognizing that, one is not questioning the value and usefulness of textbook analyses and revisions; one is assessing their value within the framework of empirical, sociological research, which must also investigate a number of factors and processes, although "specialization" still remains useful. (Pp. 33-34.)

Rob Gilbert of the James Cook University in Australia has analyzed ideological textbook criticism from an historical perspective. In the article "Text Analysis and Ideology Critique of Curricular Content" (Gilbert 1989), he surveys the English language portion of such textbook research. According to Gilbert, the first step in the development of such studies was the traditional revision of history books, where

> ... the critic's task was to identify those elements of curriculum materials which departed from the ideal of objective description, analysis and explanation of "the way the world is'. However, objectivity has come to be seen as a highly problematic concept, and this traditional perspective is now regarded as a narrow view of how ideology can operate in school texts. (P. 61.)

Methodologically speaking, this tradition ("traditional approaches") has been dominated by quantitative content analyses, which Gilbert argues are "theoretically reductionist and methodologically superficial" (P. 63).

The next step in the development was "Structuralist Analysis", when researchers began to show an interest in "organizing structures of a more comprehensive but less conspicuous nature" (p. 64). There is an underlying structure that represents definite interests and which in itself produces opinions and attitudes. To uncover such structures one must ask what factors, for example, have been identified as or considered to be social problems, whether socially controversial material and possible ways of handling it are discussed, and, if so, what philosophy lies behind these choices. The analysis becomes a "semiological analysis of ideology, posits and underlying logic from which the sets of relations in meaning systems are derived." (P. 64.)

Gilbert describes a third step in the development under the heading "Text and Context: Texts and Classroom Use". Structuralism is criticized for getting bogged down in mechanical interpretations of how underlying patterns affect readers and for focusing on pre-conceived biases at the expense of the more comprehensive process during which these structures are developed, when dealing with textbook readers for example. In other words, as a product, a textbook must *also* be analyzed in light of the entire reading and teaching process of which it is a part. We are dealing with a whole "complex of discursive practices and meanings" (p. 71).

Gilbert does not reject any of the traditions he discusses. His point is to apply them expediently in light of more recent experience:

> (...) the stage is set for the entry of what has come to be known (not, perhaps, very informatively) as post-structuralism, a collection of methods which try to expand conventional concepts of language, thought and knowledge by exploring their limits and questioning their validity. (P. 70.)

A less vague formulation of the same train of thought may be found in Tomas Englund:

> It is probably possible to distinguish between descriptive, controversial and normative factors by means of analysis when examining the treatment of one specific subject by a teaching medium, but in that particular subject as a whole and, naturally,

even more so in the teaching process as a whole, these various factors make up a single entity for the pupils, that affects them in a specific way. (Englund 1984, p. 11).

This view supports the holistic interpretations of Maingueneau 1979 and Gordon 1988.

As is indirectly evident from the above, France has relatively modest traditions as far as ideological studies are concerned. One of them stands out because it has an objective and a method that go beyond those of the vast majority of ideological investigations (Maingueneau 1979). Dominique Maingueneau's study of French textbooks from the Third Republic (1870-1914) has the subtitle "discours et idéologie". The author is a linguist whose basic premise is that even grammar books are ideologically loaded. It is no coincidence that fundamental attitudes ("idéologie") are regularly reflected in the textbooks' examples and their organization ("discours"). Through a detailed analysis of one grammar and one reader in particular, Maingueneau shows how they build up a number of definite conceptions of e.g., "French", "Algerian", "African", "Fatherland" and "the People". The analysis concludes with a surprising observation, the grounds for which are presented in a chapter that is 100 pages long. School and textbooks are not only instruments for transmitting values from a society to its individual members:

> The language and expressions that textbooks and the school use about "the world" (in all circumstances) comprise, at the most profound level, a text ("discours") about the school itself. It is exactly as if everything the school proclaims first takes on meaning in the light of its own self image. That is the final paradigm; it is here that the endless stream of metaphorical processes reaches its saturation point. (Maingueneau 1979, p. XV.)

The viewpoint that the school has - and in a way becomes - its own language, has concerned researchers with philosophical, linguistic and pedagogical backgrounds. In a long article in *Curriculum Inquiry* (Gordon 1988), David Gordon uses concepts from Paul Ricoeur's and Clifford Geertz's theories about action as text (Geertz 1980, Ricoeur 1981). Gordon transfers the concept to the area education as text and analyzes what he calls "the hidden curriculum":

> The hidden curriculum is a reading of an educational text, normally performed by students. However, as Ricoeur argues, texts can be read by anyone. The question then arises: which sort of hidden curriculum is read not only by the students, but by all members of society? What sort of reading of society's experience is provided when education is a text read by all? I propose the hypothesis that education then becomes a text about society's myths and sacred beliefs. (P. 425.)

Gordon regards school and education as a "cultural text" whose deeper lying meaning is formed by society's way of reading or interpreting its own "experience". He refers to the sociologist J. W. Meyer (Meyer 1977), who claims that the schools' paramount ideology is not this or that subject or propensity in curricula or books, but the school itself, with its categorization of knowledge and people. As regards the study of textbooks, Gordon draws no direct conclusions. However, one obvious conclusion is that interdisciplinary textbook studies are necessary to reveal the hidden pattern; the paramount ideology of the school and/or society. This point may in turn be tied to Maingueneau's study, which not least by its method (see page 364) underlines the need for evaluating textbooks as a genre and seeing them and the school as a literary institution.

According to Maingueneau, Gordon, Gilbert and Englund, it is important to question the school's and society's own "cultural text" within or in addition to the individual subjects and topics in the textbooks. Political, social and cultural conditions make up a *totality* that one must take into account regardless of which subject forms one's angle of approach.

Researchers such as Michael W. Apple are especially concerned about the "cultural incorporation" entailed by an expanded definition of context. He refers to the many works which argue that the organization of knowledge for schools is an ideological process which serves the interest of particular classes. Apple, who also argues that the textbook in western society represents the indoctrination of capitalist ideology, wishes to point out that conflicts arise continually, making it difficult to determine the superordination or subordination of particular groups.

> Curricula are not imposed in countries like the United States. Rather, they are the products of often intense conflicts, negotiations, and attempts at rebuilding hegemonic control by actually incorporating the knowledge and perspectives of the less powerful under the umbrella of the discourse of dominant groups.
> (...)
> This is clear in the case of the textbook. (...) Textbook publishers are under considerable and constant pressure to include more in their books. Progressive items are perhaps mentioned, then, but not developed in depth. Dominance is partly maintained here through compromise and the process of "mentioning". (Apple 1991, pp. 25-26.)

Allan Luke refers to the same phenomenon as "incorporative power":

> The incorporative power of the modern textbook is frequently overlooked precisely because of the public volatility of past and current disputes over textbook adoption and censorship. Overt textual content has been and continues to be a focal point for dissent, as Arons and other who have examined censorship and textbooks and First Amendment rights rightly point out. (Arons 1989, *my* comment.) But despite ongoing disputes over, for example, the selection of "controversial" literature in secondary literature curriculum, or Creationism in the science curriculum, it would be erroneous to see the contemporary textbook as constantly contested. For we hear little each year about the thousands of textbooks, produced by multinational publishers in English-speaking countries, that are adopted and taught without dispute. (Luke 1991, p. 185.)

If we look at more recent curricula, we see that their objectives point in several main directions which are given equal emphasis. The school is to educate effective *and* tradition-conscious citizens in a society characterized by solidarity, but these citizens are also to develop into independent individuals capable of taking a critical look at the society in question. Since such goals apply to every subject, textbooks will not find it easy to assume the holistic view required to reconcile concerns regarding traditional edification, effectiveness and independence. In turn, this will also apply to textbook analyses: They, too, must adapt to the trinity of tradition, pragmatism and emancipation. At that point it won't be enough simply to distinguish between quantitative and qualitative methods. The need for humanistic methods of text interpretation will grow stronger as texts increasingly become forums for discussions of conflicting views. To the extent that it is possible to refer to textbook investigations' own ideology, we might say that it has to be revitalized both with regard to the understanding of content analyses, readability measurements and educational-didactical analyses. A comprehensive work by Alain Choppin, *Les Manuels Scolaires: Histoire et Actualite*, published in the autumn of 1992, supports this way of attacking the problem. Choppin gives a thorough pedagogical, economical, ideological and historical definition of the role of the textbook in France.

Consequences

Insofar as textbook criticism has had consequences, it is clear that the effects have primarily been manifested as changes implemented in connection with revisions and new impressions of established titles. By comparison, new authors in radical opposition to the established order - in schools and in society at large - rarely write new books with ideological frameworks like the one Göran Palm is looking for (see page 137).

A common argument against writing radically different textbooks in countries like Norway and Sweden is the existence of approval schemes. The issue of what preservative or preventative role such schemes can play in this national context - or in a more international one - will not be discussed here. However, some

Norwegian authors once made a rather renowned attempt at writing a history and social studies textbook "from a viewpoint in keeping with the interests of the lower classes" (p. 3). The book, entitled *Onward and Never Forget* (Bakkemoen, et al., 1974), focuses on oppression, liberation and the struggle between the classes, as defined in Marxist terms. It breaks with practically every genre tradition except the one pertaining to chronological order. *Onward and Never Forget* was never submitted for approval, nor did it ever gain much popularity in Norway or Denmark, where it was published on commission. Two of the book's creators were subsequently hired to work in the school book division of one of Norway's largest and most traditional publishing houses. The book was analyzed by Bjørklid and Pryser in an article that asks which form of indoctrination is predominant (i.e., in the mid-1970s): "We venture to allege that the form can be summed up as *accommodation*." (Bjørklid - Pryser 1975, p. 52.) This accommodation ideology, which forms a contrast to demands for politicizing/ialogue, can lead to a more administrative role for teachers and a more instructive role for the books. The authors believe such an ideology is prerequisite to the progress of educational technology. In any case the point of view is significant for illuminating the relationship between society, school authorities, publishing houses and teaching.

Of interest also are the criteria Bjørklid and Pryser use to evaluate the degree of indoctrination in *Onward and Never Forget*. On the one hand, they commend the book for "showing itself clearly for what it is" (p. 54), but then they add that one can hardly expect bourgeois history books to state in the introduction that they present history viewed from the perspective of the upper class. The latter would clash with our bourgeois ideology of equality. However, Bjørklid and Pryser also point out that the authors of the most conventional books neglect to comment on how they have assigned priorities and made selections. The two critics postulate that indoctrination exists in everything which is dealt with for no apparent reason and in everything which is omitted for no apparent reason. Bjørklid and Pryser recommend *Onward and Never Forget* only as a supplement, not an alternative to existing books:

What we see as most negative is that the exploitative point of view has led to a far too emphatic and unnecessarily black and white picture, which in some cases prevents a deeper understanding. (...) Under any circumstances the effect that this (that is, using the book as a supplement; my comment) would have on the learning process would, in our view, doubtless be to stimulate dialogue. (P. 58.)

Although dialogue is mentioned in this quotation, an overall view of the subject shows that most ideological studies have quite convincingly demonstrated the absence of any such dialogue-stimulating effect.

While there aren't many obvious examples of instances in which the results of investigations employing more ideological or literary approaches have been incorporated into official programs, they do exist. In 1988 the California State Department of Education published a report on evaluation criteria for textbooks in history and social studies (California Board of Education 1988). The report was written for publishers in particular, and its contents "should serve as standards for the statewide adoption of instructional materials in kindergarten and grades one through eight; they can also be used as guidelines in preparing and reviewing instructional materials for grades nine through twelve." (P. 102.) The most striking feature of the guidelines in this report is their emphasis on the books' literary qualities. The factors traditionally considered most important, e.g., how the books further the goals and ideas contained in the curricula, are covered in one short paragraph, which is subsequently followed by 14 paragraphs giving detailed instructions about the stylistic and compositional formulation of the texts. The outline concludes by stating that:

The ultimate test of any textbook or instructional material is to engage the imagination of the reader. No matter how graphically the textbooks are illustrated, no matter how many experts are hired to certify their validity, and no matter how many claims are made on their behalf as conveyers of skills and concepts, the textbooks will fail unless they excite the enthusiasm of the students who read them. (P. 105.)

Another form of innovative thinking was expressed by certain English historians who wanted to give textbooks a new image (Booth 1980, Lund 1990). They suggested that two new elements be introduced in an effort to supplement the traditional outline presentation. First, they advocated the inclusion of source material as a major component of the books. Second, they prescribed that presentations be written:

> (...) bearing in mind that the pupils should work with and acquire insight into concepts which are fundamental in history, but which traditional textbooks seldom make anything of: Concepts such as causality, empathy, change/continuity and similarity/difference. These are concepts on a far higher level of abstraction than revolution, democracy and dictatorship. But they ought to open to new horizons and produce a different sort of meeting between pupil and history than "traditional" history does. (Lund 1990, p. 22.)

To achieve objectives like the one conceived by Lund ("produce a different sort of meeting between pupil and history") we would need radically new and improved approaches to the "art" of writing textbooks, approaches indicated in analyses such as Armbruster - Anderson 1984, Crismore 1984, Julkunen 1990 and Åhlberg 1991 (see page 213).

Chapter IV

The Use of Textbooks

Introduction

An analyst may approach "books in use" in any number of ways. Approaches will be determined by a number of factors which may or may not be independent of one another, but which will all be based on certain notions about objectives, means and educational practice. Schematically speaking, most of these notions will fit into one of three main categories, depending on whether they deal with concepts based on teaching, textbooks or knowledge.

Teaching takes place at school, although it is to some extent followed up at home. Today it is officially accepted - in curricula and among educators - that the school's primary objective is to provide a venue for cooperation, student-centered and teacher-centered teaching and personal development, although this view puts the role of the textbook in a controversial light. It is therefore common to question the extent to which teaching is textbook-centered. Some say that not using textbooks is a prerequisite for independence as a teacher, while others base their teaching on new textbooks that endeavor to promote independence. As to the former group, however, textbooks are often "avoided" by copying parts of them into these "independent" teachers' own programs, and it is not at all uncommon for the latter group of teachers to exercise a great deal of discretion in relation to the officially adopted text. Views expressed in connection with debates and polls are one thing; in such contexts, publishers often respond to the accusation that their textbooks dominate the classroom situation by postulating that teachers only choose books that fit their needs. What actually takes place in the classroom is something else entirely. The situation has been described as follows:

Textbooks are hopeless no matter how you approach them. They're supposed to provide stability and continuity in studies, but can't be used during planning. They control the classroom situation to the extent that not using them is seen as a sign of independence. They also exert so much control that they have to be regulated by conditions laid down in a national control system. But they do not exert enough control for the author to be able to assume that teachers will follow them. (Johansson 1988, p. 35.)

There will probably always be a plethora of opinions, ranging from vehement disagreement to concurrence, about the relationship between an explicit teaching ideal - as formulated in curricula or in teachers' minds - and actual practice. The magnitude of the variations will depend on the correspondence between theory, as expressed in curricular objectives, and reality, as experienced in teachers' training, school working environments and teaching staffs. The time factor plays an important part in this context. First, all but the smallest schools are staffed with teachers of different ages and educational backgrounds. Second, there is some disagreement as to how long it takes for the comprehensive new ideas introduced in new curricula to filter through (Strømnes 1987). For example, the curriculum for primary and lower secondary education in Norway mentions the word "textbook" very few times in its 306 pages. In every case, the word occurs simply as an item on a list of equally-ranked or high-priority teaching aids. How can this be interpreted, except as a clear signal? In light of that, it is surprising that textbook sales have increased since the plan was introduced. Although not based on empirical evidence, it therefore seems logical to assume that textbooks still occupy a central position in teaching. The most recent curriculum was introduced in 1987 however, so it has not yet had adequate time to filter through into practice. Nonetheless, it should also be safe to assume that the frequency and manner of using textbooks varies according to teacher, subject, level, school, student and home. As there are many different ways of using textbooks and as teaching is a complex situation, it is particularly difficult to draw any general conclusions on the basis of studies that focus on the books in use.

(As for the implications of the textbook concept, I refer to the discussion on page 24.)

The term *knowledge* has been substantially expanded in a large number of Western countries during the past few decades. Although pupils are supposed to learn facts in all school subjects, they are also supposed to develop a special understanding of each individual subject as well as certain skills and general attitudes.

At the same time, the sheer volume of knowledge and the number of channels of information are proliferating so explosively that scientists have seriously begun to examine the need for what has been called *unlearning* (Lærum 1991).

This picture is further complicated by the fact that knowledge is used as a polarizing term in the political debate about the school system. Apparently impassable schisms have evolved between those who claim that pupils no longer receive any core knowledge and those who take a broader view of knowledge. Such a conflict does not necessarily follow political dividing lines. It also exhibits some of the traits seen in the debate for and against grades, where there are divided views within several political parties. Insofar as it is valid to say that it is possible to learn anything about fact/non-fact oriented knowledge from curricula, there are national divisions. At the upper secondary level, for example, the subject of literary history comprises a considerably larger body of knowledge in France than in Norway, while Austria's history curriculum and history books are much larger than those used at the primary and lower secondary level in Great Britain.

If we add that subject distinctions continue to exist despite attempts at integration among certain disciplines, it becomes clear that if studies of "books in use" refer to measurements of what is taught, one might ask whether the phenomenon is quantifiable at all. What is there to measure? Compare this with the situation when textbooks are written and developed. What is to be taught? A look at new textbooks in the Nordic countries, for example, will show that they tend to pass on facts, train skills and instill certain attitudes. This is also reflected in the books' linguistic and physical presentation. The books contain an increasing proportion of personifying and emotional texts, while technology has made it possible to package this growing body of facts in an attractive, often compact form. Almost all modern textbook publishers constantly strive to strike a balance between facts, skills and attitudes.

The same uncertainty may be exemplified by a relationship that deals with researchers', teachers' and pupils' evaluations of textbooks. Countless evaluative systems have been devised at individual schools as well as at the national level. But none of the models have yet achieved authoritative status or been declared normative or routine by any of the bodies that select school books, for example.

Anyone who answers yes to the question of whether the passing on of knowledge can be measured will have to deal with one last discussion before starting to take measurements. This second discussion involves the relationship between textbooks and teaching as a whole: Is it at all possible to isolate books as a separate, measurable part of the classroom process? Although systematic classroom observation has some rather spurious aspects (Clark 1991), it is possible to measure a variable such as *time* quite accurately. Some people cite such measurements as their only grounds for contending that teaching is textbook-centered. But if we move one step further and measure knowledge *acquisition*, we encounter methodological problems deriving from our point of departure: What is knowledge - in and/or outside textbooks? Our means of measuring will provide the answer to the question and to some extent determine the nature of the knowledge to be measured.

As regards the terms "teaching", "textbook" and "knowledge", we see a trend which places distinct, fairly narrow constraints on our perspective if the studies are to represent reliable measurements on the one hand and, on the other, there is the question of whether we shouldn't take a broader approach if such investigations are to perform any valid function.

The following survey divides the studies into three groups, depending on whether they deal with *control, accessibility* or *effects and effectiveness*. The question of textbook control is dealt with first because the answers are so significant to the results achieved in the other two groups. Extensive use and strict control will amplify any damage done by poor accessibility and improve otherwise bad teaching if accessibility is good. Under certain circumstances, a comparable correlation will apply to the relationship between control and learning.

There is also another important distinction between the first group and the other two. Studies of textbook control have often focused on teachers and publishers, i.e., on teacher training and practice and on publishing house traditions and ideologies. Many critical analyses of biases in material selection and presentation are based solely on the assumption that the books are read, trusted and used by many teachers. The other groups tend to focus more on the books' suitability for use as teaching materials, i.e., their focus is on the pupil. To some extent the studies examine the language and/or the methods used in the books (accessibility), and to some extent they try to pinpoint what pupils can or may have learned from them (effectiveness).

Control

Control per se is a complex concept. It can have both positive and negative connotations. In principle, reading and using literature may entail freedom and dialogue as well as control. Ideally, control would be deliberate and positive if well-qualified, experienced teachers opted to remain loyal to the content, structure, methods and philosophies of a textbook because it was consistent with their own and other talented colleagues' mature views on educational goals in all these areas, and because their pupils like to read it. If a less well-qualified, less discerning teacher in another class chooses the same book and the same course of action, control will still be a positive factor, albeit for different reasons. However, if the teachers at a school, out of necessity or ineptitude, base their teaching on books (approved or not) which pupils reject, we see a negative form of control ascribable more to the school's budget than to the books' status or quality. We see an even more blatantly negative form of control when teachers fail to prepare their pupils for the pitfalls found in many of the textbooks the pupils use as independent sources of information for reading on their own, working in groups, using workbooks or doing homework. In isolation, textbooks may also contain a potential for negative control due to unreliability, incomplete contexts, structures inconsistent with the subject's basic premises, methods that conflict with important objectives for work routines and/or imprecise/vague use of language.

In a separate report for the DsU 1980:4 project (see page 385), Christina Gustafsson makes a clear distinction between positive and negative control. She found that in theory and to varying degrees also in practice, textbooks:

(...) exercise negative control:
- as regards material selection and sequencing
  when the teaching medium is not based on the logical structure of the subject
- as regards language
  when the pupils don't need to understand the language of the teaching medium
- as regards learning
  when pupils do well merely by memorizing the words in the textbook when basic skill like speaking and writing are not called for
- as regards ideology
  when there is no discussion about the values expressed in the teaching medium
- as regards methods
  when the teaching medium "forces" users into certain routines.
  (Gustafsson 1982, p. 96.)

Considerable Control?

What is possible in the field of use studies, is to examine finite situations and uncover tendencies toward control. This has been done, though only on a modest scale. The following investigations are mainly arranged according to the different aspects of teaching they have measured. The dominant factor in this context is the consumption of time.

Birger Bromsjö examined social science teaching and textbooks in Swedish primary and lower secondary schools in the 1950s (Bromsjö 1965). First, he had teachers make lists, ranking the subjects included in the curricula and noting how much classroom time they wanted to devote to each of them. He subsequently compared these data with measurements of time consumption and schedules in relation to the books. For example, when the distribution of teaching time actually followed the book even when the teacher had different priorities (time/scope) than those expressed in the book, the teaching was defined as textbook-centered. Bromsjö found no strong, general tendency in that direction, but he did find that some factors which had received little priority on the teachers' lists dominated the classes to an extent that corresponded to the priority they had been given in the textbooks.

Certain other similar time measurements point in the same direction without posing a problem of method. One obvious question concerns the extent to which the amount of time devoted to a topic can serve as a measure of influence. Bromsjö and others have used quantitative methods to show that the sequencing of material in the books can affect teachers' own sequencing. But the question of how much the material selected, presented and read controls teaching in terms of influencing pupils' attitudes and knowledge acquisition will remain unanswered because time cannot be used as the only valid or absolute measure in such contexts.

Ten years later Ulf P. Lundgren studied textbook control in mathematics, history and social science in upper secondary school (see Johansson 1988, p. 10). He compared three factors: the number of pages in the textbooks, the lesson units as planned by the teachers and the classes as they were actually taught. He found the correlation to be greatest between the books and the lesson plans. Still another observation led Lundgren to assume that teaching was significantly textbook-centered. He compared the sequencing of topics and points in curricula, books and classroom teaching. In mathematics, only three of 22 classes deviated from the pattern suggested by the books. In social science, eight of 17 classes deviated from the books and in history 25 of 39 classes departed from the books' sequencing. These figures led Lundgren to conclude that the books exert control, but that the control varies according to the topic structure of the subjects themselves.

Time use and the organization of teaching time were employed as units of measurement by Danish scientists in the 1970s, when they studied the teaching of knowledge subjects at the middle and lower secondary level in a total of 125 classes in Copenhagen (Jensen 1975, Jensen 1977). The classes were observed for two-week periods over a considerable period of time. The measurements distinguished between class instruction, group work and individual work. Moreover, they distinguished between categories of textbook functions which were in turn related to the three main types of teaching. This allowed Jensen to operate with four types of control: teacher-centered, pupil-centered, teacher and pupil-centered and textbook-centered. The last category proved to occupy more than one-third of the time used in middle school and about 15 per cent at the lower secondary level. Control was defined on the basis of what the pupil was actually doing, which once again entails a quantification based on the pattern used by Bromsjö. The question was, and therefore still is, whether it is possible to measure any control other than the directly observable control physically manifested in the classroom.

The tendency to perceive textbooks as exerting a great deal of control is confirmed in one of the two largest Nordic studies in this field: Ingvar Sigurgeirsson's "Inquiring into the nature, role and use of curriculum materials in Icelandic schools" (Sigurgeirsson 1990). The measurement of time use plays an important part in this study as well, although Sigurgeirsson also incorporates other important factors.

The study was motivated by the authorities' desire to renew an outdated book stock. The aim was as follows: "The teaching materials were to serve as a foundation for teaching methods, where the main emphasis was to be placed on the pupils' independent study, a stimulating school environment, inter-disciplinary teaching, various inductive teaching methods and creativity." In other words, the material included teaching media in all subjects, new teaching media developed according to new curricula and national teaching media that dominated in virtually all the country's schools.

The method involved observing 20 classes at 12 schools (for a total of about 1000 hours), interviewing teachers and pupils and sending out questionnaires.

Some of the main categories were time use, types of teaching aids, the questions posed by teachers and the texts, types of pupil activities, the interdisciplinary nature of the work and teaching methods; then the categories were further subdivided.

Here are a few of the most important conclusions as Sigur-geirsson himself has summed them up:

Published material plays a decisive role in most classrooms. Approximately 60 % of teaching time is spent working directly with the material. In English: 96 % of teaching time. In mathematics and social studies: 75%. Teaching materials aren't used at all in 20% of the classes.

The material is generally reviewed page by page.

Teachers' manuals are not used much. No more than 5-10% of the teachers use teachers' manuals to any great extent.

Only limited use is made of materials such as overheads, video, slides, games and other teaching aids.

The teaching methods are one-sided.

The material controls what happens in the classroom *to a large extent - only* not in the ways envisioned by the authors when they wrote the material! (Sigurgeirsson 1990, pp. 2-3.)

The DsU 1980:4 investigation, one of the most comprehensive studies made in the Nordic countries besides Sigurgeirsson's, is part of a project entitled "The Market for Educational Materials" (see page 385). The mandate was "to investigate the control exerted by teaching media during the teaching process and to discuss how such control can be avoided or decreased." (P. 15.)

The investigation was set up in two stages. The first consisted of preliminary studies and was mainly intended to test methods. It consisted of observing and analyzing the classroom situation during 39 hours of instruction in different subjects and classes and at different levels in the two municipalities that were later to take part in the main studies. Christina Gustafsson, head of the project and author of the report, described the preliminary studies in a separate report (Gustafsson 1978). Two important observations were noted: it proved to be very difficult to separate the role of teaching media from other factors involved in teaching and, in contrast to the plan inherent in the mandate for the study, there was little point in summarily defining textbook control as a negative phenomenon. Teaching media are aids and, as such, they have a function that is positive rather than negative, both in principle and in practice.

Like Sigurgeirsson, Gustafsson relied on observations and interviews. The main studies comprised observations of 217 classes in Swedish, English, natural science, social science and electrical teletechnology at different schools in the two different municipalities. Although few classes were investigated in each subject, several lessons were monitored in each class. For practical reasons, it was decided not to use tape recordings and transcripts, but to employ a printed form on which the observers made notes during the classes, arranging the material into five categories: Time (spent on different types of teaching media and other activities), pupil grouping (organization of the class and teaching), materials (classifying all the teaching media used), content (of the teaching media), and comments (mainly evaluations of the textbook control effect).

On some points the results show a certain correlation with Sigurgeirsson's findings. Gustafsson can also rank the subjects on a scale based on the role played by the teaching media in a certain subject (English) in terms of time, method, content and learning. In other subjects (social science), on the other hand, she describes this role as being very modest in the same areas.

Like Sigurgeirsson's, Gustafsson's investigation concludes that the teaching media probably have little effect on the methods employed in the classroom. However, an example will show how difficult this factor is to measure. Like all other studies in this field, Gustafsson's investigations concluded that reliance on textbooks is most dominant in foreign languages; according to her observations of English classes in the sixth grade, 71 per cent of all classroom time was spent on the textbooks. One of the English teachers, who was observed for a total of 12 hours, used books almost all the time. She relied not least on workbooks, in which a typical drill consisted of dialogues intended for the pupils to work together in pairs. But the teacher chose her own method; she played the one role, while the whole class played the other. This was obviously the teacher's method of preference; she disregarded the most important other drill models in the workbook entirely. How *controlled* is such a teacher, and how much control does the book exert on the pupils when such procedures are followed? (This example is taken from Johansson 1988, p. 12.)

Insofar as it is possible to talk about a general control effect across the boundaries between disciplines, levels and teachers' personalities, Gustafsson also concludes that this effect is primarily a factor of content as expressed by the selection and sequencing of material. Yet she is far more cautious than Sigurgeirsson in naming teaching media control as the force that generally predominates in the classrom: "The question is not *whether* but *how* teaching media exercise control and that is an effect of the interplay between the teaching media, the environment and the individuals involved." (P. 196.)

Norwegian researcher Svein Lorentzen studied the development of social studies at the lower secondary level (Lorentzen 1984). Lorentzen, who based his findings solely on teachers' own responses to questionnaires, found that the majority of them made extensive use of textbooks; most of them also responded that they viewed textbooks as "very important" in social science, history and geography. In contrast, supplementary literature and AV equipment were not used much. One of Lorentzen's conclusions was especially interesting in light of what was said earlier about the importance of taking the point in time and lapse of time into account when evaluating the results of use studies (see page 158):

> Of the teachers who had teaching experience prior to the introduction of the National Curriculum, nearly two-thirds stated that they had made "some changes" in their selection/use of teaching materials in social science after the implementation of the National Curriculum.
>
> Only some 6 % responded that they had made "significant changes", while nearly 20 % answered that they had made "a few changes" in this aspect of their social science teaching.
>
> As far as teaching materials are concerned, a significantly larger percentage of women than men reported that they had made "signficant changes" in their social science teaching following the introduction of the National Curriculum (Lorentzen 1984, p. 326.)

Lorentzen's report may also be viewed in conjunction with a more recent Swedish report: *Knowledge of the World around Us: Knowledge Subjects. Background, Description of Teaching, the Fostering of Democracy* (Svingby - Lendahls - Ekbom 1990). The report is part of a major national school evaluation project based mainly on knowledge and skills.

As in Lorentzen's study, the Swedish questionnaires asked

teachers about their actual use of and attitudes toward textbooks. The responses showed a strong degree of agreement in both areas. Nearly half of the 157 teachers surveyed stated that they used textbooks every day, while about the same number answered that they used textbooks weekly. Almost 80 per cent felt that textbooks were either "very important" or "important" in history and geography. By contrast, only about 20 per cent felt the same way about social science textbooks. This agrees with the comparable results of all the studies referred to in this chapter. A similar degree of correlation is also apparent in teachers' manuals and workbooks, which were not used much. The results of the Gothenburg studies confirm the results derived from other studies on still another important point. The extended teaching media concept has not caught on in practice in the area of AV equipment (radio/TV). New technology has not had the planned effect on pupils' "discovery" of their local environment.

Little Control?

The tendency to want to look at textbooks as relatively dominant control instruments is not universal. A number of studies have also been made that point in the opposite direction. Relatively extensive measurements were undertaken in the Netherlands recently in a study covering more than 700 primary and lower secondary schools (Reints - Lagerweij 1989). The results indicate to some extent significant teacher independence in relation to teaching media. The time teachers spent on books when planning and in the classroom varied from an average of 62.9 per cent in geography to 31.3 per cent in social science. Ten per cent of the schools did not use textbooks in mathematics; the percentage was higher in several other subjects, particularly foreign languages. (This last observation deviates substantially from the results published in DsU 1980:4; see page 167.)

The Dutch investigation also examined how teachers used the books in four core subjects in primary and lower secondary school. They divided methods of use into three categories: Eleven per cent of the teachers followed the books page by page. Nearly half allowed the books to dictate the structure of much of their teaching, but they supplemented the books with their own materials. For some ten per cent of the teachers textbooks were just one of several equally important sources. However, many different combinations of the last two methods of use were practiced by roughly 20 per cent of the teachers. Ten per cent of the teachers did not use textbooks at all.

The most comprehensive investigations of textbook control were conducted in the USA. In 1988 Donald Freeman and Andrew Porter presented a study entitled "Does the Content of Classroom Instruction Match the Content of Textbooks?" (Freeman - Porter 1988). They worked with seven mathematics teachers in primary and lower secondary schools in three school districts. The teachers kept teaching logs and were interviewed. On the average, they spent about one-third of the lessons on textbooks. More than 80 per cent of all classroom time was spent on the topics/problems found in the books, but there was a great deal of individual variation on this point. Although the sample comprised just seven teachers, researchers found it was possible to divide them into three main groups according to their use of and attitudes toward textbooks. One group followed the book faithfully, lesson by lesson, using little or no time on supplementary material. Another group followed the plan and progression in the book, but was selective about the texts. And the third teacher group broke up both the structure and content by adding supplementary material. The division into three groups corresponds to the grouping used by Lee J. Cronbach (see page 181). Freeman and Porter, who have conducted a series of studies on the teaching of mathematics in lower secondary school, distinguish between the main kinds of *choices* every teacher has to make. They are referring to the choice of topic, the time set aside for a topic, which pupils are to study the material, the sequence of the topics, and the goal of the teaching (how much should be understood/learned?). Rather than discussing "control", Freeman and Porter write about "teachers' adherence to textbook copies", which they view as a function of the strength of their perception of or belief in the authority of textbooks. (This discussion is based on the review presented in Stodolsky 1989.)

Based on this point of departure, the question of textbook function becomes a question of teacher function. In light of the emphasis Freeman and Porter place on content and topic, the way in which topics are defined will also be decisive. The broader the definition, the easier it will be to show a correlation between textbook and teaching. The narrower the definition, the greater the distance.

Freeman and Porter's approach to the problem of control shares one feature with the other use studies mentioned above. None of them say much about the relationship between the authorities of the teacher and the text, as perceived by pupils/parents. They also overlook or avoid the "balance of power" between teacher and text: What about the effect of the "intermediate" language that emerges when the teachers speak at the level between the book and the pupil, and which might, for instance, be analyzed from a socio-linguistic point of view? The question has been posed by Australian and Canadian researchers who have presented almost diametrically opposed views on the balance of power between teacher and textbook as far as influence is concerned (Luke 1989 and Olson 1989; see page 173).

As mentioned above, several researchers point out that groups or types of teachers use textbooks to different degrees and in different ways. This situation has motivated several people to question the reasons for such differences. Some have discussed teachers' education (Ball - Feiman-Nemser 1988) in this perspective, while others have emphasized the grade level (Lorentzen 1984; Tournier - Navarro 1985). In both cases, many studies indicate that independence increases and the time spent on textbooks decreases in direct proportion to the grade level being taught. The grounds for this conclusion are rather vague and uncertain, however. As early as in 1930, William C. Bagley studied the practices followed in 539 classroom hours in 30 different states (Bagley 1931). He drew the conclusion that the strongest determinant in the teacher-textbook relationship was not necessarily education or level, but seniority. Svein Lorentzen's questionnaires examined the same criterion, but he arrived at the opposite result (Lorentzen 1984, p. 372). Adding criteria such as the teacher's specialties and his/her motivation for becoming a teacher, level and practice, would probably complicate matters further.

Susan Stodolsky (Stodolsky 1989) is probably the one who has made the most direct claim that textbooks generally play a fairly modest part in relation to instructional content and progression. She examined the teaching of six mathematics teachers and six social science teachers in the 5th grade (Stodolsky 1988). Her results tallied with Freeman and Porter's:

> In sum, our cases suggest that teachers are very autonomous in their textbook use and that it is likely that only a minority of teachers really follow the text in the page-by-page manner suggested in the literature. Use is much more varied than usually suggested, particularly when one considers more than just the topics contained in the books. Even with regard to topics, we found, as Freeman and Porter did, that what teachers teach is in the book, but they do not teach everything that is in the books. Thus, math textbook content tends to place something like a cap on content coverage in classrooms, although putting something in a book does not guarantee instruction will be devoted to it. (Stodolsky 1989, p. 176.)

One of the points of the study is that some aspects of the teacher-textbook balance differ significantly in mathematics and social science. This has often been taken for granted in earlier literature, in that studies have assumed that social science teachers were more independent of the textbooks than mathematics teachers, who were believed to be bound to a certain pattern of progression (problem by problem and assignment by assignment). Stodolsky arrived at a more differentiated result. While it is true that the use of supplementary material is far more common in social science than in mathematics, she found that when a text is used during a class in social science, it is followed very closely; its "topical sequence is usually preserved (...). More skipping and departure from text sequence is found in math." (Stodolsky 1989, p. 181.) This page by page faithfulness in social science is confirmed by Yngve Nordkvelle's observations (Nordkvelle 1991).

In her article "Is Teaching Really by the Book?" (Stodolsky 1989), Stodolsky's conclusion also indicates an explanation as to why investigations and teachers have so overwhelmingly perceived textbooks as controlling. She points out that most of the studies have focused on basic books in reading skills, and that we may be overly hasty when we draw general conclusions from those results. Moreover, she contends that "The faulty assertions have also been bolstered by a lack of direct observation or other systematic data with which to verify or refute them." (P. 182.)

The Authority of the Text

The question of the text's degree of dominance is a question of the authority of the text. In educational cultures such as those in Western countries in the 1800s and well into our own century, teaching frequently revolved around reading aloud, memorization and verbatim repetition from books. The authority of the text was indisputable and undisputed; consequently, concepts such as "accessibility" and "effectiveness" were never on the agenda. Today textbooks still possess attributes which lend them authority, despite the fact that they are just one of a multitude of media inside as well as outside the classroom. Although an author's name is given, somehow textbooks don't seem to bear what Roland Barthes has called a personal "signature" (Barthes 1977). Coupled with their official "neutrality", this lends textbooks an impersonal authority. Regardless of cultural period, the fact that textbooks don't consist of discourse elevates them above criticism and lends them "great authority", as David R. Olson claims in a number of analyses (Olson 1989). Olson, too, recognizes that more devotion to dialogue and greater opportunity for more personal, conversational language have broken down what he quotes de Saussure in calling "the tyranny of written language". At the same time, he feels that the ability to "speak a written language" (Olson 1977, p. 270) is still our ultimate goal as we advance through the educational and examination system.

Olson's view has been challenged by Suzanne de Castell, Carmen Luke and Allan Luke (de Castell - Luke - Luke 1989), who claim that written language/textbook texts alone carry little authority today. First of all, there is a teacher in the picture as long as the anonymous texts need to be interpreted and second, behind a teacher, there is the system:

> We have argued for a more interactive and pragmatic explan-
> ation of text apprehension whereby meaning is contingent on the
> interaction between the reader's prior knowledge, the institut-
> ional setting within which the reading task is situated, the
> teacher who teaches the text and the distinctive features of the
> textbooks per se. This relationship, we have noted, is delimited
> and constrained by the rules of schooling which position teacher,
> text and student in hierarchical levels of power and authority.
> (De Castell - Luke - Luke 1989, p. 258.)

In a comment to the criticism from de Castell, Luke and Luke,
Olson points out that the most important point is not to measure
the degree of authority carried by the respective elements, but to
reveal the existence of two more or less parallel structures. "To me
the structure of language and texts is neither subordinate nor
superordinate to the social structure. A change in one is likely to
change the other and vice versa" (Olson 1989, p. 262). This last
statement implies that the evolution of media and communications
technology and its consequences on (textbook) language will in
turn influence social conditions. This warrants new types of text
studies because the language in and style of the texts are indicative
of what schools and society associate with truth and authority at
any given time.

The point made by de Castell, Luke and Luke has been carried
to the extreme by Maingueneau and Gordon, who consider school
language as being somehow superior to textbook language - the
school is its own language (see page 147 and page 148). Jean
Anyon's studies indicate that one and the same text can have vastly
different meanings and interpretations, depending on social context
(Anyon 1981). In Sweden, Ulf Lundgren deals with this question
in a book called *Organizing the World* (Lundgren 1989). It is a
study of curricular theory which discusses the language used in
curricula, schools and textbooks. Lundgren's work is based on
theories put forth by Bernstein (Bernstein 1971) and Halliday
(Halliday 1973). He asks how evaluations and knowledge are
selected and organized; parts of the analysis examine how a

specific curriculum and a specific teaching medium compare with organizational parameters with regard to control of teaching. At the end of his book, Lundgren writes that studies of linguistic interaction in the classroom (teacher-book-pupil) provide a foundation for the development of theories about which premises control which teaching. But such a theory "cannot be placed in a simple, rigid structure. The complexity inherent in the various relationships is far too great." (Lundgren 1989, p. 227.)

Like other researchers referred to in my book (Michael Apple, Pierre Bourdieu, David R. Olson, Ian Westbury), Lundgren strongly underlines the necessity of tying the analysis of ecucational processes to general theories of education and its function in society. However, if such overall and holistic theories in the sociology of knowledge, culture and education are mingled into pieces giving each party only its kaleidoscopian fragment *in the textbooks themselves*, with constant incorporation as an issue stronger than that of change, one might question the starting point for textbook research. Should such research be organized primarily in relation to categories established by theorists in the sciences of sociology and education? Or would it be functional to start looking more systematically also for categories more directly connected with the textbook as a *general* as well as a special form of literary expression? It is my opinion that the latter possibility has not been exploited to the same degree as the former. I try to follow up this point of view in the two next chapters (*Accessibility, Effects and Effectiveness*), as well as in my final chapter (*Conclusion*).

John A. Zahorik demonstrates the teacher-book complexity in his investigation of the relationship between textbooks and teaching styles (Zahorik 1990 and 1991). He based his work on that of K. Hinchman (Hinchman 1987) and D. Alverman (Alverman 1989), both of whom distinguish between three types of usage that also display a strong correlation to three teaching styles. The textbook may be perceived and used as a) a source of facts to be learned ("coverage"), b) a source of different types of activities ("textbook based activities") and/or c) a basis for interpretation and discussion ("higher level interpretation/reference"). Hinchman and Alverman based their work directly on observation of teachers, while Zahorik used questionnaires. All the investigations confirm that textbooks are used extensively and conclude that the ways of using them range from a) to b) to c). Zahorik goes one step further by investigating the connection between teaching style and the books on the one hand, and teachers' own "ideological belief" on the other. He cautions against attaching too much importance to conclusions drawn on the basis of questionnaires, but, referring to the teachers in group c), claims: "The text-thinking teachers had different beliefs about students, knowledge, and teaching than the other types of teachers" (Zahorik 1991, p. 186). Hence Zahorik gives the following answer to the question of textbook dominance: "If and how the teacher uses the textbook follows teaching style rather than dictates teaching style." (Zahorik 1991, p. 195.) For Zahorik, the issue is not whether people are for or against using textbooks, but how teachers can adapt the books to their own teaching style. Indirectly, this view supports Suzanne de Castell's claims about the necessity of working on the attitudes of teachers and pupils to textbooks (see page 201).

Work done in the field of readability has tended to pay increasing attention to pupils' qualifications as readers, while focusing on the division of responsibility between textbook and teacher. Analyses conducted by linguists and educators such as Maingueneau, Lundgren, Olson, de Castell, Luke and Luke have placed textbook, teacher and pupil in a socio-linguistic triangle where the question of authority, and consequently that of control, becomes one of several rather mercurial forces that work together or in opposition at any given time.

Perspectives

Most of the investigations mentioned here, as well as the majority of a number of smaller-scale investigations not mentioned in this survey, conclude in one way or another that textbooks have had and continue to have a strong controlling position in the classroom. It is essential, however, to be aware that such conclusions are based on observations, polls and other kinds of surveys, each of which somehow has its own built-in limitations, especially practical ones. In addition, both positive and negative connotations are conferred on the key word "control" when it is used to describe approaches to problems.

The answer to the question of textbook dominance may be summed up in five points:

First, in terms of volume, textbooks do dominate classroom instruction if one measures the total share of classroom time during which textbooks of one kind or another are in use.

Second, one might speak of a general dominance if one accepts teachers' information on the use of textbooks and their general attitude toward them, as expressed in polls.

Third, textbooks can only be assumed to have a certain degree of systematic influence on teaching methods.

Fourth, the question of textbook control is especially difficult to answer with respect to its implications for the subject matter. (The problem of ideological influence and the question of learning effect is discussed elsewhere (see page 158 and page 226).)

Fifth, and this also involves methods, the investigations often overlook the question of textbook type. This may be due to practical problems, but no one can claim that researchers haven't been aware of the problem. It was addressed in the very first known example we have of an English-language, educational periodical which devoted an entire issue to the topic of textbooks. In a special issue of *Phi Delta Kappan*, Francis St. Lawrence first dealt with the question in 1952 (St. Lawrence 1952). The subject was high school biology and 170 teachers were interviewed. The results were particularly interesting in a time perspective. A great deal of supplementary material was used and applauded, while attitudes to textbooks were generally negative. In other words, the investigation pointed in a different direction from the use studies conducted in the 1980s.

It can be difficult to distinguish between the use of *whether* and *that* in Freeman and Porter 1988 and Stodolsky 1989. Right from the start the stated objective - to determine whether specific, analyzed material controls the teaching - may seem to imply a general complaint of textbook dominance. Other analyses in the same area take a less clearly expressed position on the use of textbooks. This applies to some of the studies mentioned earlier, including Bromsjö 1965 and Lundgren 1969 (see Johansson 1988), as well as to the large-scale Dutch investigation (Reints - Lagerweij

1989). Lorentzen 1984 and Svingby - Lendahls - Ekbom 1990 also maintain neutral positions. Note that in the last two studies the use of books was only addressed as one of many elements within the framework of more comprehensive investigations. The objective was to examine many elements of control in context, something which may mean right from the start that each individual element receives less attention than it would get if it figured more prominently in the investigation.

Regardless of their opinions about the phenomenon of dominance and regardless of their point of departure, investigations have been affected by the notion that textbooks can be improved as subordinate teaching aids. They are there to serve the controlling teacher who enjoys freedom of choice, and they are not intended to stake out too much of the teacher's course. In a few exceptional cases, textbooks have been examined with the clearly stated intention of making them better suited to control teachers' methods of working (Sigurgeirsson 1990). The studies are otherwise colored by the prevalent educational view that the teacher, independent of controlling forces outside the school (with the exception of laws, plans and rules), is or should be the principal determinant of the teaching. In such analyses, normative and descriptive passages therefore intertwine, but the problem is always more or less clear: How can presumptively neutral descriptions, i.e., the analyses, be used to ensure high quality teacher-controlled teaching?

In this context, it is vital to bear in mind that control has mainly been measured as a quantitative factor, with time use during classroom teaching as the primary unit of measurement. Time use also plays a part in studies that focus on teaching plans (the teachers' plans as opposed to the plans set out in the textbooks/ teachers' manuals), the selection and sequencing of material (teachers' as opposed to textbooks'), method of reading (controlled by teacher/group/individual), type of textbook and subject (the three last groups have rarely been investigated).

Accordingly, the material associated with the textbook texts has largely consisted of classroom observations based on taking notes and/or completing forms, personal interviews and questionnaires. In total and in relative terms, teachers are more strongly represented than pupils in the interview and questionnaire material.

All the investigations seem to be based on the generally implicit assumption that the teacher is the principal determinant of what the books do for the pupils or what the pupils do with the books. If so, this must be related to the fact that almost all the studies use time as their unit of measurement. The teacher decides how classroom time is to be organized. Further along in the system, on the other hand, the teacher has no say about the curricula or examination - an examination where the books may threaten to eclipse the control of the teacher in terms of work and content.

Larger scale investigations, such as DsU 1980:4, Reints-Lagerweij 1989 and Sigurgeirsson 1990, use all the above-mentioned types of material. Each of them also uses a combination of "hermeneutic", "quantitative" and "qualitative" methods (see page 139).

This may be exemplified by the Swedish investigation. One of the main tables (DsU 1980:4, pp. 154-55) distinguishes between five types of control effects (see page 163). Each of the groups is ranked according to a four-step scale: Strong influence/tendency toward influence/weak, irregular influence/very weak influence. These degrees, which were given for seven different subjects, are based on very precise calculations which make it possible to determine percentages. Moreover, they include the researchers' evaluations of interviews and talks. To some extent, however, assessments made initially preclude attaching any importance to later observations. The table covering the distribution of working methods (class instruction, group work and individual work) indicates that teacher-centered teaching dominates. But there is no discussion of the degree to which this is related to the textbook dominance otherwise pointed out by the investigation because it is assumed that no such relationship exists.

There is a conflict inherent in this, as in the other investigations that combine measurements and interviews, involving the relationship between what teachers say they think/do, on the one hand, and what they do, on the other. Apart from Bromsjö 1965 and Lundgren 1969, who both point out that classroom time may turn out differently than expected, the investigations appear to assume a high degree of concordance between statements about teaching plans and the teaching itself. If such concordance actually exists, it would indicate that researchers should use less time on resource-intensive classroom observation and more time on talks and interview analyses.

The DsU investigation was based on notes taken in the classroom. The idea was originally to complete the notes with tape recordings, as was done in Sigurgeirsson 1990. The goal was to supplement the early experience gained from such recordings. After a test run using only notes, the research group came to the conclusion that this method in itself was sufficient. The observers felt convinced that their presence in the classroom did not influence the teaching. In addition, the group gave up the idea of focusing on statistical analyses and focused instead on the style and content of the reports from individual lessons (217 lessons adding up to 8,680 minutes). Instead of attempting to produce quasi-scientific documentation, they decided to describe their own individual reports, which were subsequently computerized, in a way that might be called semi-documentary:

The form of qualitative report we decided upon is mainly of a descriptive nature. Based on the notes jotted down during observations, we've produced a brief, verbal description of the progression of each and every lesson we observed. The focus of these qualitative descriptions has not been so much on teaching materials as on describing the context in which the various teaching materials are used. Without overstating our case by using too many evaluations, we have intentionally tried to maintain a personal style in these reports. (DsU 1980:4, pp. 21-22.)

Sigurgeirsson 1990 observed more than four times as many classes as DsU 1980:4 and conducted a far greater number of interviews (official and unofficial), in addition to making tape recordings and using a special analytical scheme. Despite having far more documentation than DsU 1980:4 and Reints - Lagerweij 1989, Sigurgeirsson found less variation between teachers and classes, and from subject to subject. Sigurgeirsson had, and used, completely different ways of processing his data than the researchers in the Swedish investigation, but his analytical scheme was more than 15 years old (The Sussex Scheme for Curriculum Analysis; Eraut 1975). At the same time, a study conducted by Ball and Feiman-Nemser (see page 311) shows that more impressionistic procedures are used even when technical equipment is available: Just six women, teachers selected by age, sex, skin color and academic background, took part in the study based on notes and surveys. On the other hand, they were monitored for a period of two years.

As mentioned by way of introduction, investigations on textbook dominance are mainly related to how teachers use the books in planning and teaching. All investigations stress that practices differ considerably from teacher to teacher. An attempt has been made to systematize such differences using a very old form. It dates from 1950 (Herrick 1950), but it was the object of more far-reaching theoretical discussion by Lee J. Cronbach (Cronbach 1955) and later used for more recent research (Woodward and Elliott 1990). Cronbach distinguishes between three main levels of lesson planning. Teachers at level III readily and immediately accept the textbook's presentation of a subject; they use material from the textbook and the workbook, and they let their year's teaching schedule follow the book. Teachers at level I discuss the educational views inherent in the curriculum with colleagues, they draw on the local community and pupils for material, and they plan their year in cooperation with their colleagues and pupils. Teachers at level II are somewhat less book-oriented than those at level III, but less progressive than those at level I. The assumption that these variations exist, if not as clearly as outlined here then at least clearly enough for each level to encompass a significant number of teachers, may or should influence every investigation and evaluation of textbook control. Logically speaking, traditional teachers' roles should thus suggest that textbooks control when the teacher wants them to control.

However, such a pattern also raises the question of what group(s) textbooks are actually written for, insofar as publishers and authors have such an (approximated) pattern in mind. With the exception of Zahoric 1991, there are no pure textbook analyses that discuss the control power of different types of textbooks in the hands of different types of teachers. Nor do we know very much about the position of textbooks in pupils' work or in their consciousness. Beverton 1986 identified considerable differences from subject to subject for seventh graders (see page 199). An investigation conducted by Sosniak and Perlman confirms Beverton's findings. Sosniak and Perlman recorded interviews with 24 and 25 high school students in history and English/mathematics, respectively. They held informal interviews toward the end of the school year. The students were guaranteed anonymity, and they knew that the teachers would never have access to the material. The authors found that most of the teaching was based on textbooks, but that the extent of use as well as the attitudes of the student varied from subject to subject and to some extent from class to class: "The data we have collected tell a variety of stories about high school students' experiences with the core academic disciplines" (p. 428). They point out that students represent a virtually untapped source:

> Observing classroom activity without attending to the *interpretations* of the participants for whom those activities have been structured may well result in missing, or misinterpreting, important elements of practice. Students have been sorely neglected as a source of information about the practice of schooling in the US. It behoves us to become more respectful of and responsive to their perceptions of their experiences, perceptions which we as adults may be unable to identify or understand without students' help. (Sosniak - Perlman 1990, p. 440.)

The absence of pupil reactions in the investigation of the books' control effect implies more than just a narrowing of perspective. It may also be seen as symptomatic of the total absence of a methodical theory in the field of control. One reason for this is that non-physical book dominance is extremely difficult to gauge. It is also probable that there is a two-way cause and effect relationship between little theory and few investigations. Yet this does not explain the lack of interest in what the readers think of textbooks; in how willing they are to let themselves be taught and educated by the texts incorporated there.

One rare exception is Lars Sigfred Evensen's doctoral dissertation on the way in which teachers and pupils experience problems in language and literature courses at the lower and upper secondary level (Evensen 1986). Using a very comprehensive polling apparatus and highly complex statistical processing systems, the author measures views on and attitudes toward the teaching situation as a whole. Pupils' opinions of their textbooks in English and Norwegian is part of the investigation. The pupils' answers to a number of questions concerning their opinions on the books allowed the author to identify certain tendencies:

> The teachers and pupils in both subjects gave teaching materials a slightly positive rating. Nonetheless, Chapter 8 reveals several problems. A majority of the pupils felt there was a great deal of dry, boring material in the books and that the exercises were monotonous; they wanted to see a more pronounced pupil profile that would encourage more interest, e.g., by means of more creative exercises.
>
> The lack of creative exercises is also clear in the teachers' materials. In this context the problem of differentiation is also central, especially in the materials used to teach the subject of Norwegian. Viewed as a whole, however, the results on teaching materials indicate that the "interest" dimension is the most significant problem. (Evensen 1986, p. 435.)

Insofar as homework is assigned and followed up, textbooks will also occupy an important position outside the classroom. Depending on current trends and the subject itself, publishers tend to shift back and forth a bit in the way they adapt their textbooks for home use. It is remarkable that textbook use in individual user situations - at home or, for that matter, at school - has failed to capture the interest of researchers who have studied the books' functions. Granted, language and accessibility have been studied, but very few investigations have focused on the school-home dichotomy. One exception is T. Sticht, who wrote an article called "Understanding Readers and Their Use of Texts" (Sticht 1985) in which he claims that texts function in entirely different ways in the two use situations, meaning that they call for entirely different skills in order to be understood and utilized.

Accessibility

The numerous articles and essays criticizing textbooks have been and continue to be dominated by two main schools of thought. One involves exposing erroneous information and ideological biases. The other involves language and style; presentations are described as heavy, difficult, bad and boring. But the two areas should not be regarded as mutually exclusive. Erroneous information and ideological biases *may* be a part of and a result of poor language as well as of wrong facts. Conversely, it isn't very productive to uncover biases in texts if in turn the same texts lose influence due to linguistic inaccessibility. (By these examples I do not imply that poor language or wrong facts are necessarily the main or only sources for ideological bias.)

The majority of the investigations in this section are book analyses which have no parallel in use investigations. They are primarily based on other research results, not least from readability research and learning theory. Most of the investigations deal with language and to some extent also with the selection and scope of the material included in the texts. Some also discuss or deal exclusively with arrangement and lay-out, methods, illustrations and extra-textual enhancements.

Vocabulary and Syntax

Non-empirical articles and essays have not been included in the following survey, which is arranged so that the earlier the investigation is mentioned, the narrower the scope of the problem. Investigations that take a broad approach are mentioned last. This system also ensures a certain chronology of presentation.

One of the first vocabulary studies was conducted in 1941 by

Arnulv Sudmann (Sudmann 1978). He tested the word comprehension of 886 children in grades 5 to 7 in Oslo. The material included 20 words such as metal/colony/trust/statesman, all taken from a chapter about antiquity in the children's history book. The tests were performed after the material had been read and reviewed in class. The children were given every opportunity: They were not required to define the words, just to use them in sentences. They were drilled in the method ahead of time. Less than half the children proved that they had understood as many as 50 per cent of the words.

Kathrine Simonsen broke new ground when she conducted a comparable investigation in upper secondary schools in Norway (Simonsen 1947). She claimed that graduates (age 19-20) mastered little more than half the more uncommon words used in the textbooks at the 1st year level (ages 16-17).

This investigation also dealt with the words in isolation. One frequently criticized problem with such investigations is that the words are taken out of context, another is that there is a difference between passive and active word comprehension. One of the pioneers in this area, Norwegian educator Helga Eng, addressed these problems:

> We see that children (grades 3 to 7) have very little ability to form a correct picture of an abstract word taken out of context. (...) This result comes as no surprise. We tend to think it doesn't matter if children don't understand every single word, they will get the general idea from the context. The investigation showed that context helped children understand only a small fraction of the unknown or tenuously perceived concepts. (Eng 1912; quoted from Sudmann 1978, p. 28.)

Recent research appears to bear out Eng's views on the limitations of context as an instrument for more or less instant understanding of the wholly or partially new words that arise in a context.

In recent years the Center for Science and Mathematics Education at the University of Oslo has worked with the language used in science textbooks. Their efforts have been based on questions and answers such as these: "Does the word *acid* mean anything to upper secondary school students? Most of them know the definition of acid, "a substance that gives off protons", but the term carries few connotations for them. They don't associate many *properties* with acids. In my opinion, they haven't really gained an understanding of the term acid." (Ringnes 1986, p. 15.) One of the most thorough analyses of concept learning, Dittmar Graf's study of the subject of biology and biology books at the lower secondary level, confirms Ringnes' opinion of existing textbooks' limited potential to serve as conveyors of conceptual comprehension (Graf 1989).

A number of English-language investigations from the 1970s and 1980s also concluded that what has been assumed to be a simple vocabulary, well-adapted to the relevant age group, may have just as profound an effect on complexity as sentence structure does. Harold Rosen posed the same critical question as Vivi Ringnes (see above) about words such as *revolution, therefore* and *correlation* in the history books (Rosen 1972). Larger-scale British investigations which point in the same direction are "The Readability of School Biology Texts" (Gould 1977), *Readability in the Classroom* (Harrison 1980) and *Learning from the Written Word* (Lunzer 1984).

Studies of textbook language have developed both in depth and breadth in recent decades. The most portentous change evolved in the late 1980s in the guise of a systematic discussion of methods and criteria for language-based textbook evaluation (Davies 1986; see page 219). Further, it became increasingly unusual to treat vocabulary and syntax as separate entities. Many people have also finally recognized the necessity for applying different models to different subjects, a situation proven by a comparative analysis of the language used in textbooks in geography, biology and geology conducted by linguists at the École Normale in Lille (Darras - Delcambre 1986).

A new attitude is evident already in the title of a collection of articles edited by Michael Marland, *Language Across the Curriculum*. In his contribution, Marland attributes much of the "problem at school" to the problem of text:

The first problem at school is the sheer quantity of new words and new ways of putting things. As the pupil gets older this accelerates - indeed some attempts to lighten the load for the immediate post-primary years have the effect of making the mid-secondary language incline so steep as to be unsurmountable by many. Either way the vocabulary expectations of the new specialized curriculum are very heavy.

(...)

The reading material in different subjects is startlingly different, each subject from the other and all from fiction. It is not only the vocabularies that are different. The predominant paragraph patterns are quite different. (Marland 1982, p. 74.)

This expansion of perspective can be illustrated by investigations conducted in one particular subject. For a number of reasons, mathematics is an obvious choice. The subject has a well-developed sign and symbol language that does not preclude the use of prose texts. Still, the amount of text has been modest enough to make mathematics easier to study than most other subjects. The textbooks underwent fundamental changes in the 1970s and 1980s. The use of consecutive text increased steadily. Consequently, several researchers wondered whether declining mathematics results could be due as much to poor reading skills/poor texts as to a real decline in mathematical skills. That question has also been posed in a way that is relevant to all school subjects: What proportion of math instruction is really language instruction?

A report called *Language and Vocabulary in Mathematics in Sweden* (Björnsson - Dahlkvist - Edstam - Jarne 1967) was published in 1967. Consisting of three sections, it describes the vocabulary used in math books, gives an account of pupils' comprehension of that vocabulary, and discusses the issue of how the language used in math problems affects pupils' ability to solve them. The material consisted of three popular textbooks used by third graders. The vocabulary descriptions show wide variation in the amount of text, which accounts for a significantly lower percentage of one of the books than of the other two. The study also deals with other variables such as the ratio of separate words to the total number of words, the percentage of mathematical terms used in all the books and in each book separately, the ratio of words that occur only once (a figure as high as one to four for mathematical terms), high frequency words (where the percentage of repetitions is so high that researchers describe the language in one of the books as "very monotonous" (p. 133)), a comparison of the vocabulary used in the math books with the vocabulary used in other children's literature (where the distinction was especially prominent for pronouns, conjunctions and negations, which occurred far more frequently in other literature than in textbooks).

Finally, the vocabulary was described within the context of the sentence, using a method that in many ways experienced its breakthrough with this investigation: The readability index (LIX), which is based on the percentage of words more than six letters long (long words) and average sentence length. Generally speaking, the difficulty of a text is directly proportional to its LIX value. The books in question scored 27, 27 and 30. The last figure applied to the book with the least text per problem, the briefest explanations, many single occurrences of words and the fewest high frequency words. Researchers found these investigations telling enough to characterize the textbook in question as not as good as the two others.

One important feature of the Swedish investigation is that the description of the vocabulary was approached from several different angles, all of which were explained and tested prior to the main investigation. Another important feature was the follow up, which encompassed two other equally comprehensive investigations; one attempted to test pupils' comprehension of the texts in the same math books, while the other studied the possible correlations between the language used in the math problems and pupils' ability to solve them. In very general terms, the comprehension test instructed pupils to underline any words they did not immediately understand. The test was adjusted against comparable word list tests. Approximately 400 different words in the books were classified as difficult based on the criterion that four or more pupils in each class did not understand them. The vast majority of the words were long, many (more than one-third) were mathematical terms, and most of them were abstract. In addition to those 400 words, 900 others were not understood by two or more pupils per class. One observation that contradicts the view of Helga Eng (see page 186), was that the pupils in the control group with (the same) words out of context underlined some 50 per cent more words. This could indicate that the presence of a meaningful context eases word comprehension considerably. However, in light of the more than 1300 "difficult"'" words in the textbooks, the researchers felt justified in deeming the language used in the textbooks unsatisfactory.

The last investigation (concerning the relationship between language and problem-solving) was a "multifaceted problem" (p. 137). A severely limited procedure was selected: The test involved two sets of problems in which the problems and answers were the same, but the text in one set had been re-written/improved by the researchers themselves to conform to the experience gained from the first two investigations. The results may be summed up as follows; 1) The re-worked version resulted in a larger number of correct answers, 2) The improvement was notable at every skills level, but especially among the slowest learners, 3) Changing text relating to mathematical terms resulted in relatively greater improvement than other types of linguistic intervention. In this investigation, too, pupils were asked to underline the words they didn't understand. The test consisted of more than 30 problems, all of which were the most frequently underlined in the original version. The pupils marked 669 words in the original texts, but only 275 in the re-written texts.

One remarkable aspect of this investigation is its exceptional thoroughness, which provides immediately applicable results in a limited field. Another and at least equally remarkable trait is that the investigation was not concluded with the writing of the report. It was designed for teachers and was arranged so that the investigations could be supplemented and elaborated by individual teachers and by schools.

Nearly 20 years later Andrew Rothery wrote an article called "Readability in Maths" (Rothery 1986). He looks at the status of readability in light of research and textbook development in the 1970s and 1980s. He refers to series of investigations that confirm the results of the Swedish investigation, e.g., the correlation between vocabulary and math comprehension. A.R. Nicholson found that pupils at the lower secondary level all understood the word "multiply", while only one in five understood the word "product", used in the mathematical sense (Nicholson 1977). Rothery has included a summary of readability testing methods in *Children Reading Mathematics* (Rothery 1984). The most familiar method in the USA is the so-called *cloze procedure*, which was introduced by W.L. Taylor in 1953 and subsequently developed by others. The main principle is to leave out individual words and mathematical symbols in a text. The reader is instructed to fill in the blanks; generally, a score of 40 - 60 per cent indicates satisfactory accessibility. Americans developed the system further, until it became strongly reminiscent of the Björnsson study. Kane, Byrne and Hater (Kane 1974) emphasized the distinction between three classes of words: Ordinary words, mathematical words and mathematical symbols. Based on this, they designed a readability formula, which, by the way, Rothery finds unsuited for the subject of mathematics as taught in Great Britain. Rothery is generally very skeptical about such formulas:

> Perhaps the greatest inadequacy of all such formulas is that in their attempt to be widely applicable, they lose the ability to help with detailed professional problems. For instance, if a teacher is to help pupils in the use of a particular text, it is important to judge its vocabulary in terms of words which are familiar to those particular pupils. (...) In fact a sensitivity to the issues involved would be more helpful than the knowledge of a readability score for a passage. (...) Clearly some significant factors affecting readability are such that they cannot be readily qualified. (Rothery 1986, p. 126.)

Such skepticism does not imply that Rothery rejects formulas. He summarizes his article by pointing out the importance of certain research results derived from readability studies. In the field of vocabulary skills, for instance, this applies to the difference between ordinary words and mathematical words, but it also applies to the difference between words used in the ordinary sense and the same words used in a different way, a way which may be inaccessible within the context of the subject. In the field of syntax, there is growing acceptance of the theory that sentence length per se is no criterion for accessibility; long sentences can be easier to read than short ones (Perera 1980, Harvey 1982). As regards mathematical symbols, it comes down to things as common, but little researched, as the ratio between the concentration of the expression and readability, or "spatial structure" (e.g., the difference between a2 and 2a). As regards extra-textual enhancements, it concerns the use of lay-out, examples, tables and illustrations. Rothery compares the presentation of the same topic in two competing textbooks published the same year. The language is obviously more clear and readily accessible in Book A. On the other hand, Book B does a better job of illustrating the phenomenon in question.

Like the researchers in the Swedish mathematics investigation, Rothery does not see the systems for measuring accessibility as exhaustive, but as a foundation for gaining insight that must be put into practice. Teachers who strive for "perfection" must act as researchers in relation to textbooks as well as to pupils.

The Institut für Schulbuchforschung was founded in Vienna in 1988. This was largely thanks to Richard Bamberger, who until that time had been doing readability research on children's and young people's literature. In collaboration with Erich Vanecek, Bamberger has written an analysis of the problem of readability that provides a thorough introduction to the measurement systems developed in the USA and Europe (Bamberger - Vanecek 1988). In the early 1980s, Bamberger and Vanecek investigated readability in primary and lower secondary level textbooks in several different subjects. They developed and used more than a dozen formulas which took a large number of different linguistic factors into account - including those beyond the word and sentence level - factors that were tested in roughly 500 texts for several different subjects and at several different levels from the fourth through the twelfth grades. The measurements were summed up as follows: The degree of linguistic difficulty in the books was often one or two levels higher than the grade for which the books were intended. The discrepancy was especially pronounced at the fifth through the eighth grade levels. Based on their readability quotients, many books intended for use in the fifth grade belonged in the eighth grade.

These results stirred up a public debate, and the formula model was therefore expanded further. A new round of tests included factors such as print face, typography, information density, reading speed, reading situation and motivation. The result showed such a strong degree of correlation with the first investigation that the researchers felt they had shown that linguistic analysis in itself was a reliable measure of accessibility (Bamberger - Vanecek 1984). Almost concurrently, East German researchers presented measurements of reading difficulty that entailed comparable criticism of books in the GDR (Starke 1983).

Sylvia Danielson studied the language used in a total of 15 textbooks in the subjects of physics, social studies and Swedish (Danielson 1975). The books were used at the lower and upper secondary levels. Altogether a relatively random sample was selected, including 19 lengthy texts from the 15 books. An analysis was made of 400 sentences and 4000 words in each text.

Danielson had certain reservations about traditional readability tests. The most important of them may be summed up as follows: Repetitiousness makes much of the material that cannot be understood out of context understandable afterall. Analyses of "incomprehensible" sentences in a paragraph may overlook earlier explanations that would have provided sufficient information for accessibility. The testing situation (testing the pupils) entails such great practical limitations that the linguistic factors "measured" do not occur frequently enough in the sample. It is not feasible to judge the effect of one linguistic factor in relation to other linguistic factors on the basis of non-fabricated texts. Strictly speaking, this can only be measured reliably using specially designed texts in which one factor can be altered, while the others remain constant.

Since Danielson's material consisted of printed texts, she chose another approach, i.e., describing the similarities and differences between the texts with a view to topic and educational level. Within this framework, she mainly limited herself to nouns for studying vocabulary and to passages with just one sentence (the dominant type of sentence in the books) to study syntax. At the word level, the investigation focused chiefly on abstracts and certain types of compounds. In the area of syntax, the study looked at sentence type and structure in addition to sentence length. As far as sentences alone are concerned, Danielson refers to one of the main views propounded by Schlesinger 1968 and Platzack 1974: Long sentences, or the intertwining of several (long) sentences in a passage, are not in themselves sufficient grounds for proclaiming poor accessibility. On the contrary:

> (...) sentences that are too short can have an adverse effect on readability. (...) Among the other texts that I examined in the initial phase of the investigation, I found one textbook in materials science for the first year of upper secondary school which averaged 11 words per sentence. In certain paragraphs the average sentence is 9 words long, i.e., the average sentence length which, according to Platzack's results, is relatively more difficult to read than texts with longer average sentence lengths. (...)
> If sentence length in itself is not as important as many would like to think, then it is unfortunate if accepted beliefs about the importance of sentence length entice authors to believe that their problems can be solved by using shorter sentences, rather than by looking at content. (Danielson 1975, pp. 130-31.)

There is reason to emphasize that Danielson's study neither shakes nor is intended to shake the position of the large body of documentation produced by readability researchers in the 1960s and 1970s that established once and for all that formulas such as lix, fog and cloze are well suited to calculate the degree of readability. It is also clear that the methods applied in empirical, data-based linguistics, for instance, can provide detailed descriptions covering not only vocabulary and syntax, but also morphology (Schuyler 1982, Mikk 1990). The more linguistic aspects that can be revealed in that way, the more questions will arise. Nonetheless, one question will probably remain unanswered no matter how systematic such descriptions become. Danielson's concluding discussion contends that such descriptions of existing, printed text in use are limited by not saying enough about the reasons why a particular word or sentence earns a particular readability quotient. To sum up the investigations of Danielson and others, it might thus be said that measurements of vocabulary as well as syntax are measurements whose results indirectly reveal the need to examine these two factors in connection with other text elements. Such a change in perspective occurred in the 1980s.

One of the first to address the problem was linguist and educator Harold Rosen of the University of London. He stressed that while a number of models had been developed to deal with linguistic analyses of textbook language, there was no analytical instrument for "the psychology of understanding and using it. We need a dimension which embraces both the linguistic and the psychological components. Until we know more about it let us call it the personal-impersonal dimension." (Rosen 1967, p. 104.) While investigations made prior to the 1980s were rather linguistically-oriented, and frequently limited to elements such as vocabulary or syntax, linguists and reading experts gradually grew more interested in Rosen's personal-impersonal dimension. Two publications represent milestones in this area: Gillham 1986 and de Castell - Luke - Luke 1989; see page 199 and page 84.

Style and Structure

In the preceding section, the term syntax was mainly linked to investigations that focused on sentence length and/or the number of sentences, in a passage for example. Formulas such as LIX flourished in the 1970s, only to lose ground later. Some researchers have gone as far as to contend that the only practical result achieved was to "lix" textbook texts into showing a relatively uniform level of inaccessibility (Johansson 1988, pp. 22-26).

A more comprehensive text study would also include analyses of textual cohesion, within each sentence, from sentence to sentence, from passage to passage, from paragraph to paragraph and among the larger units which combine to form the final text.

Such a method would expand the parameters for evaluating the language used in textbook texts, but it would also increase the degree of uncertainty regarding approach and measurement. Some of the most pronounced problems in this context are the text concept, the scientific ideal, and the relationship between form and content in that special educational context in which the textbook belongs. The following survey of investigations will demonstrate how, in different ways, these studies have addressed such problems by selecting approaches which are sometimes narrow, and sometimes very wide indeed.

New Trends

The 1970s saw the publication of a number of new books in "knowledge subjects" (history, geography, social science and natural science) in Norway. Several of the books proved too difficult for many pupils. This led some publishing houses to compile simplified versions, meaning there were two versions of the same book sets on the market, an A set and a B set. Anne Hvenekilde compared two such sets that were marketed by a major publishing house (Hvenekilde 1983). She used traditional methods to measure vocabulary and syntax, but she also analyzed the conjunctional and adverbial characteristics of the texts. Although the revision of the A texts consisted in length reduction, it also involved language revision. Hvenekilde showed the result was often a more difficult text because the well-planned cause and effect logic of the original text was destroyed and not adequately replaced in the B-sets.

While working on a project involving textbooks in Norwegian for foreigners, Hvenekilde discovered that the authors had gone so far in their quest for simplicity that they arrived more or less right back where they started - with an inaccessible text. She therefore went on to study 4th and 5th grade knowledge subject textbooks written for children who have Norwegian as their native language (Hvenekilde 1986). She studied only one set of books, but it was a set that had dominated the market for several decades. First, Hvenekilde proved that the paragraphs were organized and connected to one another in a way that often impeded understanding through context - *inter alia* by repeatedly mixing sentences and lines as textual units. Second, she found numerous places in the books where it was unclear whether the reader was being confronted with texts containing facts (reference texts) or narrative texts; in this context, she discovered "simplifications" that entailed breaks in logical text structures. Third, she found a number of contraventions of conventions related to information structure (for example, unmotivated switches between old and new information).

In conclusion, Hvenekilde makes a comment which is very apt for the investigations surveyed in this section:

> However, analyses such as this one can only form a point of departure for hypotheses concerning what pupils find easy and what they find difficult. To find out for sure, we need empirical investigations to study how the various features of the texts affect pupils' understanding and acquisition of knowledge. (Hvenekilde 1986, p. 25.)

This quotation is reminiscent of a factor which was indirectly addressed earlier in this chapter, namely that researchers have concentrated mainly on the books' texts - and not on the readers' use of them. The following may be interpreted as a rebuttal to that tradition:

> The fact is, we have little understanding of the effects of a uniform, ubiquitous application of readability criteria, for what students find difficult to read is influenced by what they have read and what they have been taught. It is meaningless to say a text is difficult; it is difficult *for someone*. Whether a text is difficult depends on the reader as well as upon the text. (MacGinitie 1981, p. 285.)

The above quotation is taken from a book based on a conference held in New York in 1981: *Learning to read in American schools: Basal readers and content texts* (Anderson - Osborn - Tierney 1981). As mentioned earlier, research into the linguistic accessibility of textbooks has traditionally been dominated by reading teachers and readability researchers who have mainly studied the materials used to teach reading in grades one through nine. The New York conference, which was attended by the foremost readability experts in the USA, may be viewed as part of that tradition. At the same time, however, it represented a departure from the tradition in that it heralded new directions. This applied to three areas in particular: The first was the disparity between reading ability, the content of readers and books in other subjects (knowledge subjects and workbooks in general), and curricula. The second involved the constraints in and misuse of readability investigations ("Davison, Green, and MacGinitie presented rather convincing evidence for avoiding the use of readability based and contextually sensitive means for testing texts." (Tierney 1981, p. 560.)) The third stemmed from the criticism in the second area and concerned the deficiencies inherent in the narrative technique and the authorial role in the growing number of cases in which publishers and authors had tried to break old patterns.

One of the main points made at the conference was that the problem of reading and text comprehension must be removed from the domain of the reading teacher and put into the domain of all teachers in all subjects, and that this must be done on the teachers', pupils' and relevant subjects' own terms. Exciting stories, glossaries containing many detailed explanations and workbooks with differentiated batteries of exercises are not enough in any subject:

> The programs' reliance on story context and independent use of the glossary as methods of vocabulary development are at best appropriate only for the most motivated and competent readers. Children most in need of vocabulary development, the less skilled readers who are unlikely to add to their vocabulary from outside sources, will receive little benefit from such indirect opportunities. (Beck 1981, p. 19.)

Two of the investigations included in the conference report stand out in this context. Jean Osborn presented the first, truly comprehensive analysis of the workbook genre since St. Lawrence 1952 (page 177) based on documentation which revealed such widespread use of workbooks in some subjects that their importance vied with that of the basic textbooks. Osborn reviewed several hundred assignments in 20 workbooks at different levels in different subjects. As a readability researcher, she concluded that "workbooks are the forgotten children of basal programs" (Osborn 1981, p. 130). Osborn subsequently followed up this work, *inter alia* through a recent investigation on what pupils learn from the workbooks (Osborn - Decker 1990, see page 229).

At the same conference, Thomas Anderson and Bonnie Armbruster presented the results of an investigation which encompassed textbook texts and pupils' work with them. The researchers sought to reveal aspects of the text which demonstrated "comprehension and learning differences" (Anderson - Armbruster 1981, p. 377), with special emphasis on textual structures which are common in the subject in question. This project was also followed up in the course of the 1980s; see page 209.

The report from the New York conference is an important manifestation of textbook (language) researchers' propensity for studying more holistic textual structures. Another manifestation is a composite work entitled *The Language of School Subjects* (Gillham 1986), which is an extension of the viewpoints in the New York report, corroborated by more recent British research. The entire book is based on the attitude expressed in the contribution by Andrew Rothery (see page 191): Educational text research is also the responsibility of the teacher and part of the instruction. The contributions are all written with that in mind. They consist of research reports adapted for further processing.

One of the key results and viewpoints in the book is that teachers and pupils have completely different ideas of what it means to read a text. There is also a qualitative distinction made between two groups of pupils (the "purposeless approach" and the "metacognitive approach"). This was demonstrated by Marian Tonjes, who works in the USA and is the only contributor from outside Great Britain. She stresses the difference between *learning to read* and *reading to learn*. The approach to the two activities varies, both when authors write and when pupils read the textbook texts (Tonjes 1986, p. 69). Teachers are generally not aware enough of this in individual subjects, and that represents quite a problem inasmuch as it was long since proven that each subject has its own special textual pattern and that such patterns, in turn, call for special reading strategies (Smith 1964).

Sue Beverton reports on a "reader-centered", i.e., not "text-centered", investigation of the status of textbook reading and pupils' motivation (Beverton 1986). One hundred and sixteen seventh graders, all of whom attended the same school, kept logs of what and how they read for a period of five weeks. Most of the subjects were textbook-centered: English, geography, history, mathematics and natural science. Altogether, the pupils' reading material comprised 108 different titles, 72 of which in the subject of English, and six of which in mathematics. The grade level is at the crux of this study. Beverton discerned a general attitude among the pupils which coincided with an attitude noted in other investigations (Lunzer - Gardner 1979, Richmond 1979, Heather 1981, Ingham 1982): "The fun goes out of reading (...) between primary and secondary schools" (p. 35). Beverton believes this is related to the textbooks' change in character at this level and to differences in school reading policies which are manifested at the same level. Most of the reading in primary school was fiction, and it was often a group activity. The situation was rapidly reversed in lower secondary school, where emphasis was placed on non-fiction - then too as the most common form of "whole-class-work" (p. 36). At the same time, the reading of fiction at this level gradually became less a class activity and more an individual activity, often tied to the school library. The total number of titles read, fiction and non-fiction alike, was clearly reduced.

If it is correct that the status of (textbook) reading declines as the educational level rises, and that the critical point lies in the transition between primary and lower secondary school, then this, on the basis of Beverton's observations, should offer a starting point for interdisciplinary investigations and discussions of genres and textbook language in all subjects. Mother-tongue instruction is especially interesting in this context. Eighteen of 72 titles in English were textbooks, the rest were fiction books and supplementary reading from the school library. The pupils described English as a subject without coherence; the many textbooks make English "a widely-spread, free-floating subject; even if highly book-oriented, it is not book-specific" (p. 28).

In *The Language of School Subjects*, Katharine Perera (Perera 1986) presents an analysis of the language in 25 paragraphs of approximately 100 words each from the genres of textbooks and narratives, excerpted from books intended to be used by pupils aged 9 - 13. She analyzes two levels: "Discourse-level differences between fiction and non-fiction" and "Sentence-level differences between fiction and non-fiction", in the order listed here (i.e., the whole before the part). Perera's book investigations confirm Beverton's pupil survey. She demonstrates significant deviations, but she does not reject the transition to more fact-oriented reading - or cogitative writing - at higher levels. On the other hand, like Beverton, she advocates the need for radical changes in the transition from the lower to the higher level. Such a transition can only be effected by developing textbook prose, reading routines and written work.

Suzanne de Castell (de Castell 1990) points out one significant condition which is both the reason for and the potential answer to the problem of reading material transition from primary to lower secondary school:

(...) it is with expository rather than with literary texts that students have the greatest difficulty.

School textbooks, however, are not primarily literary texts, and this is increasingly so as students move from the elementary to the secondary grades. So although there is much that is promising in current work on interpretation, the authority of the teacher, the author function, and the role of the reader, this work applies primarily to literary texts, whereas school textbooks are less often literary texts and more often what I shall henceforth call "fact-stating" texts. These require, it is argued here, a separate and different treatment. (P. 76.)

Beverton's and Perera's investigations both point out the textbook situation for mother-tongue instruction as a fundamental problem. In a paper delivered at the 15th International Schoolbook Conference in Köthen in 1990, linguist Hans-Wolfgang Lesch from the University of Lüneberg said the same thing. He had analyzed 17 language books in German for grades three to nine, published by seven different publishing houses. Lesch confirmed that the selection is now so large that a single publisher may publish up to three different grammars for the same level.

His analyses showed that grammar books differ appreciably in terms of linguistics, educational philosophy and pedagogics: "Using such different grammar books has fatal consequences for pupils, especially if they change schools because they move or advance to secondary school" (Lesch 1990, p. 1). Like Beverton and Perera, Lesch pointed out the consequences this could have for reading and writing in general. He drew the conclusion that either all members of the teaching profession in Germany had to be molded into a corps of linguists or that the new Ministry of Culture should, at the earliest possible date, accord all teachers and pupils in both East and West "the benefits of using just *one* school grammar". (This last point falls outside the parameters of this chapter, although the question of its practical consequences is obvious when many results point in the same direction.)

To illustrate new and broader approaches to linguistic usage in textbooks, I have chosen to take a closer look at studies related to the following three topics: The *"reality"* of the text, its *metadiscourse* and the structure of *causal explanations*.

The "Reality" of the Text

The question of which "reality" textbooks represent or are intended to represent is especially germane in the context of grammars. Their content is not given or limited in the same way as in textbooks in chemistry or geography, or in books for foreign language instruction (the country and culture) or in mother-tongue books in language history, literary history or anthologies. Grammars deal with themselves insofar as the examples they use are primarily intended to illustrate linguistic structures. Consequently, a relative clause is acceptable in the book to the degree that it illustrates the typical or atypical characteristics of the sentences to be explained in the paragraph in question. Theoretically, this is the only absolute criterion, but grammar book authors' field of vision is not quite so limited in practice. Nonetheless, the selection and use of examples in school grammars have followed certain conventions. If we ignore the older tradition which was largely based on fictional role models, the examples are to be simple and ordinary, preferably timely and adapted to a level the pupils can understand and with which they can identify. The fact that these conventions have withstood the test of time may be because grammar is the one discipline among all the primary and lower secondary school disciplines which, despite considerable scientific development, has remained most constant during the past 100 years. (The differences Lesch refers to in German grammars (see page 201) primarily concern educational methods; otherwise he confirms Chervel's thesis on the constancy of the school subject (Chervel 1977). The same is true of Fossestøl 1987, Huot 1988 and Hertzberg 1990.)

The man who may have been the first to label such conventions rigid and artificial was not a researcher, although he apparently embarked on a brief career as a linguist before suddenly changing his mind. On several occasions, author Eugène Ionesco mentioned that the starting point for his absurd drama was the mechanical remoteness and contentlessness in school grammars. This connection is most clearly expressed in the drama *La Leçon* (1951), in which some of the teacher's monologues paraphrase vocabulary and structures from the grammars. In contrast, there is one rare example of deliberate employment of a quasi-literary solution intended to draw attention to and discuss the artificiality of such examples. Linguist Marianne Haslev published an introduction to syntax in which the protagonists in all the examples are animals (Haslev 1975).

Åke Pettersson has studied the selection and use of example words in popular school grammars (Pettersson 1987). The material involved the use of nouns, adjectives and verbs in three books for grades 4 and 6 in primary school. Pettersson found 243 different forms of nouns. After eliminating doubles and proper names, he was left with 170 common nouns. These were compared with the vocabulary used in a total of 955 essays written by 191 different pupils in grades 4 and 6. Eliminating doubles and proper names, that left 109 common nouns. The comparison clearly revealed that the vocabulary used in the grammars was more concrete than the pupils' vocabularies. The pupils' language abounded with abstracts, but there were few in the textbooks. The books' repeated use of "childish" and familiar names for animals and plants was especially striking. Words like tablecloth, kitten, pillow, cake, leaves and violets occurred only in the textbook material; so often, in fact, that Pettersson believes many pupils will receive the impression that this sphere of meaning is in itself a criterion for being a noun. While temporal and causal expressions occurred with remarkable frequency in the pupils' essays, they were seldom used in the textbooks. Pettersson also compared the two groups with a survey of the vocabulary used in adult newspaper language. The scope of the nouns used by the pupils was far more "adult" than the textbook language.

With certain reservations due to the modest scope of his investigation, Pettersson drew the following conclusions: Pupils are not allowed to see how words and word classes are parts of authentic texts; the perspective is that of the word list. They do not see the connection with their own language usage. The abstract/mental world of ideas is kept outside the realm of pupils of this age. The grammars distance themselves from the prose used outside the classroom.

One might then ask about the extent to which the negative observations made about grammars are applicable to the view of the world presented in textbooks on other subjects. One well-known example of distortion involves the math problems used in arithmetic books for generations. Some of them accidently foiled their own effectiveness as a tool: "If 11 men dig a ditch for 4.5 days, how many men would it take to dig the same ditch in 2 3/5 days?" Others turned the world upside-down by providing the logical answer and asking for a calculation that no one needed to calculate: "A clerk wrote 8 addresses in 5 minutes. How many addresses did he write in 1.5 hours?" Yet Grevholm, Nilsson and Bratt have demonstrated that this tradition still exists, through other varieties of unreality, in modern math books (Grevholm - Nilsson - Bratt 1988, pp. 272-88).

In theory, textbook authors may advocate vastly different approaches to the question of how one should represent the "world" and "life" in textbooks intended for particular age levels. In light of objectives such as molding attitudes, selection and individuality, which characterize the curricula of many countries today, it should be legitimate to write a chemistry textbook which is primarily an introduction to environmental protection. Using pollution as the general theme, an author could conceivably cover a considerable share of chemistry's most important topics, while relating the topics to the reader's everyday life.

Granted, no books that have followed that recipe have met with any measure of commercial success as yet. The most prevalent approach today is still based on the tradition of the broadest possible coverage of a subject, sub-divided into topic units, like in the grammars. Moreover, today's textbook authors still write texts intended to take account of grade level and neutrality. The majority of all textbook research conducted thus far encompasses one or more levels - in terms of subjects, grades and/or neutrality. Meantime, most of the negative textbook criticism, whether in the wake of the investigations or independent of them, charges that deference to so many different factors makes the text inaccessible because the language becomes "boring," "diluted" or "dead" (see Evensen 1986, page 183). In this context, the focus has generally been on the issue of neutrality, but several investigations discussed in this chapter show that in many cases educational adaptation has not had the intended effect. Åke Pettersson's study even indicates that deliberate attempts at educational adaptation may have an alienating effect, since we know too little and consequently assume the existence of children's language and a children's "world" - for ten to twelve year olds, for example - which does not exist at all. Of and by itself, adaptation to a particular level could suddenly become just as controversial as ideology, for example, were it not for the fact that the concept is probably already closely related to ideology.

Metadiscourse

Investigations and criticism in the form of debate have had ramifications. A great deal of public lip service has been paid to striving for personality and certain profiles in textbooks (Sanness 1987, California Board of Education 1988, Barth 1991). In this light, the question of the textbook author's own presence, i.e., of the books' *metadiscourse* gains importance.

Metadiscourse was discussed by Avon Crismore in an article entitled "The Rhetoric of Textbooks: Metadiscourse" (Crismore 1984). Crismore compared texts from nine textbooks in social studies with nine non-textbook adult texts in the same subjects (history, politics, geography and economics). The textbooks ranged from third to twelfth grade levels; the texts for adults were largely written for the general public; they included articles and excerpts from books. The starting point was "written authorial commentary (metadiscourse)". Crismore shows that research into the voice of the author has long traditions in literary research, but that it has not been investigated in textbooks (see de Castell, page 201). Crismore wants to "create a typology of metadiscourse based on the functions of language and rhetorical techniques, and then examine how it is used by writers of American Social Studies texts." (Crismore 1984, p. 282.)

Crismore defines metadiscourse as part of many, but not all, informative texts. There is a "contentless level" which consists of the author's entry into the text; of his explicit or implicit "discoursing about the discourse" (p. 280). This might involve factors such as comments about the progress or design of the text, personal views concerning the material, information about sources or direct petitions or appeals to the reader. Although one could divide these factors into a number of sub-categories, Crismore distinguishes between two main groups. The one is "informational", the other "attitudinal". The author subdivides the latter group into four sub-groups which may be exemplified as follows: Even more important than the reform was ... (assertion); This is an exaggeration, of course, but ... (emphasis); Perhaps hunger was the worst ... (reservation); Unfortunately, far too few turned out to vote ... (evaluation).

The occurrences of metadiscourse were measured automatically per 1,000-word text unit (beyond 1,000 words, the text lengths varied all the way up to 12,000 words). On the other hand, a review of the "presentation style and patterns of use", as well as the direct, personal manifestation of the author, called for the extensive use of quotations and a qualitative analysis.

One important, but rather unusual point concerning Crismore's choice of material was the way he distinguished between typical and atypical texts. Very popular textbook texts were typical, while little-used ones were atypical. Eight of the adult texts were typical in the sense that they were popular and one was atypical in the sense that it was scholarly and written for a special audience.

Crismore discovered significant differences between typical and atypical textbook texts. The former group used very little formal metadiscourse such as discussion of the book's objectives or an explanation of the plan and structure, while such metadiscourse was very common in the latter group (58 of a total of 82 such elements were found in two of the three atypical textbook texts). There was strong correlation between the atypical textbook texts and the ordinary adult texts insofar as it was common to explain and define the texts' plan of action, something which virtually never occurred in the typical textbooks. Crismore found similar patterns in summaries, or so-called "post-plans".

Might one find the same correlation in attitudinal metadiscourse? The investigation revealed that all four groups (see above) were used far more frequently in adult texts than in those intended for pupils. To the extent that such elements occurred in the textbooks, they occurred primarily in the atypical texts. One striking feature was that this type of text far more frequently used these tactics to try to establish a "we" relationship in the text. Crismore's conclusion is cited here because it suggests an answer to the question about the relationship between ordinary prose and textbook prose (see page 217):

Textbooks seem to use attitudinal metadiscourse to refer to concrete people or happenings in the primary discourse while non-textbooks use 'it to refer to abstract concepts as well as concrete phenomena. Another difference is the tendency of non-textbook writers to be present in text with a first person for expressing attitudinal metadiscourse while the textbooks prefer more distance and use second or third person. A third difference is the large amount of emphatics and hedges used by non-textbook writers to argue their points. The final difference is that textbook writers use simple evaluatives only (and very few of them) while non-textbook writers use both simple and complex evaluatives. (Crismore 1984, p. 295.)

Indirectly, this quotation raises the question of the justification for leaving out or cutting down on the use - in textbook prose - of a number of stylistic instruments that are important in ordinary prose.

According to Crismore, personal argumentative sequences with reference to abstracts are virtually never used in textbook prose. In other words, Crismore's investigation of metadiscourse confirms Åke Pettersson's discovery about the vocabulary of grammars: The absence or lack of abstraction is greater in the textbooks' "reality" than in the pupils' and/or the non-textbook "reality". An investigation mentioned by Woodward - Elliot - Nagel 1988 substantiates and puts some perspective on Crismore's view:

> Starting with the premise that textbook prose is dull and boring, the authors asked three groups - text linguists, college composition instructors, and editors of *Time-Life* - to rewrite a passage on the Vietnam War taken from a grade 11 history textbook. High school students recalled 40 % more of the passage rewritten by the *Time-Life* editors compared to minor gains for the other rewritten passages. (Graves - Slater 1986.)

Åke Pettersson's observations are limited to one area in one discipline of one subject. One might ask whether the question is not just as much one of type of language and type of abstraction as one of abstract - less abstract - not abstract. This last point was made by J.R. Martin of the University of Sydney (Martin 1988). Martin studied and described history and geography as two inherently separate linguistic expressions at both the university and the textbook level. The relationship between abstract academic discourse and pedagogic discourse presents a problem because the latter type of language, which Martin calls "secret English", has its own rules and constraints, of which few pupils and only some teachers are aware (see Tonjes, page 199). Nor is the solution as easy as ignoring textbooks and basing instruction on pupils' own personal experience, because "the danger of moving too far in this direction is that students are denied access to the major tools of the humanities and sciences; technicality and abstraction." (Martin 1988, p. 169.)

The problem is to explain the special nature of pedagogic discourse to teachers and pupils so that they can consciously work with the language used in textbooks and thus lay a solid foundation for the independent acquisition of knowledge implied in the curricula. Certain research results give us reason to assume that it can be very difficult to pass such insight on to pupils, particularly because they have different points of departure for reading the books at home - and at school. Some pupils already understand the textbooks' "ideational schemata"; while others do not understand it (Anderson - Armbruster 1984; see also page 198).

The abstract-concrete problem has been formulated even more dramatically by Danish researcher Sven Sødring Jensen, who writes in his doctoral dissertation that:

> By aspiring to a high level of abstraction, numerous persons, relationships and actions are put into short formula. By using an ordinary linguistic expression, one ensures that the formulas can be told to and read by the pupil. However, at the same time one finds that the explanation cannot be understood, i.e., acquired by the pupil. (Sødring Jensen 1978.)

Causal Explanations

Explanation is a key word, for both J.R. Martin ("... both understand and challenge explanations"; p. 171) and Sødring Jensen. Causal relationships play a very large part in history and social studies books. A few large-scale investigations have examined this situation.

All readers perceive new texts on the basis of their own personal qualifications for understanding, learning and retaining what they read. Such "reader's schema, or organized knowledge of the world" (Anderson - Armbruster 1984, p. 181), will vary considerably. Now the text also has its own schema, and the factor that determines how well the pupil will understand what is explained in the book will be the concurrence between the pupil's schema and the text's schema. Bonnie Armbruster and Thomas Anderson's investigation thus involves an entirely different text element from Avon Crismore's. Yet in principle, they are based on the same hypothesis: That linguistic and stylistic analyses of an element on the structural level can be highly indicative of the entire text's possibilities:

> (...) much of the content of the disciplines, or subject matter areas, can be formulated in a relatively small number of generic structures or generalized plots, each with its own set of content categories or types of information. These structures reflect typical patterns of thought or ways of conceptualizing the content of the subject-matter area. (Anderson - Armbruster 1984, p. 182.)

Armbruster and Anderson call such "generic structures" *frames*. The subject of history is largely based on explaining events in light of man's motives. Hence it is valid to speak of a psychologically-based frame. The authors refer to the so-called "story grammars". They are psycholinguistic models of common structures in stories which are easily understood and readily retained: Something happens to the protagonist which makes it necessary to undertake some action to achieve a goal, and there are very specific conventions regarding how people behave, problems are solved and goals are achieved. Anderson and Armbruster found that this model lent itself well for use as the main frame for history books; as a "goal-frame" consisting of the elements "plan", "action" and "outcome". They found that the texts contained a very limited number of superordinate goals such as conquering and keeping countries or power, maintaining order (history and politics), ensuring food, water and warmth (biology), using and distributing resources, and ensuring economic growth (economics/social science). Such frame-goals could be subdivided into many groups of elements which could be subdivided again. The authors discuss several such main frames and indicate, for example, the existence of a very specific "war-frame", whose rather inflexible development is followed in book after book.

The investigation itself was limited to the application of the goal-frame to explanatory descriptions of psychologically-based courses of event. The topic was the completion of the first railroad connection between east and west on the North American continent. The texts were taken from three different 5th grade books, each of which was the subject of four questions: Does the text explain its objective? Plan? Action? Outcome?

Only one of the three texts answered as many as three of the questions. The two others answered just one question each. Anderson and Armbruster also analyzed the answers in light of elementary linguistic rules for logical textual cohesion/logical connection, and found repeated contraventions which corroborated the negative result of the goal-frame's questions.

(Anderson and Armbruster are among the very few researchers who have tried to incorporate new insight into textbook writing. The year after they completed their investigation of textual structures, they presented an "ideal" chapter of a textbook, with a well-grounded, uniform, practicable internal plan, called "Americans Develop Plans for Government" (Anderson - Armbruster 1985). The chapter was evaluated by several researchers. The reactions of Gary M. Schumacher (Schumacher 1985) give some indication of the difficulties involved in evaluating even a scientifically prepared textbook text:

At the beginning of my comments I indicated that the process of designing an ideal text is analogous to computer simulation in that it forces us to translate concepts into an actual product. Now we need to consider this analogy more fully. In doing computer simulations, a simulation is not complete until we have run the program and determined how well it fits human performance. Similarly, there is an additional step which needs to be carried out in the design of texts - we need to have students use them and determine how well they work. Unfortunately this task presents an interesting problem - how do we measure how well they work? In the past our principal approach would have been to have students use the materials. We would then ascertain either how well they did on tests about the information (retention measures) or how much they liked them. As Schumacher and Waller have argued, however, outcome measures such as these provide limited information about the effectiveness of text design. Retention measures, for example, provide an especially narrow window through which to view the usefulness of text. In fact it can be convincingly argued that retention of the material should not be our major concern. (Schumacher 1985, p. 266.))

Other research has corroborated the impression of *argumentation* as an element of fundamental importance to the accessibility of textbook texts (Bamberger - Vanecek 1988; see page 192). Toulmin - Rieke - Janik 1979 used a model containing six "categories of argumentation" grouped according to logical function: "Thesis" (statement, conclusion), "reason" (material which makes the thesis relevant), "warrant" (justifies the connection between thesis and reason), "backing" (data that supports points under warrant), "modal qualifier" (defines and distinguishes), and "rebuttal" (reservations). Mauri Åhlberg (Åhlberg 1990) applied the model in an analysis of two Finnish biology texts for the lower secondary level. In the one text, which dealt with animal tissue, he found nine theses, six reasons, four warrants and one modal qualifier. In the second, which was an introductory *discussion* (to and for the pupil) of the question of why and how one works with biology, he found 24 theses and no other argumentational types of statements. Both texts were approximately 100 words long. (The investigation was based upon and confirmed observations in a study by M-L. Julkunen (1990).) Thus the unilateral dominance of theses may appear to confirm the randomness entailed in the construction of causal structures. R.W. Paul has undertaken laboratory analyses which indicate the same dominance of (unexplained) theses (Paul 1987). This means that pupils do not learn to argue. And if they don't learn to argue, they don't learn to distinguish between important and less important material. And if they can't make that distinction, it becomes more difficult to retain knowledge.

Like Anderson and Armbruster 1984, Staffan Selander (Selander 1988) studied causal explanations in history books in an effort to compare how different authors presented the same topic. He chose a number of radically different topics and analyzed, among other things, chapters from two books at the middle school level, one published in 1925 and one in 1975. Based on several detailed analyses of the selection of material, the style and the arrangement of the texts, Selander claims that although personal interests, contemporary trends and current curricula may provide some variation, it appears that textbook authors consistently seem to write books based on patterns established by their predecessors. Meanwhile, several other comparisons between the two books showed that it was arbitrary whether or not causes were brought into the presentation of individual events - an observation which would, in theory, probably have resulted in several 0's on Armbruster and Anderson's goal frame schema. Insofar as there were any causal explanations, Selander found religious and political motives to receive far more emphasis than economic motives, and he found that results were more often attributed to individual than to collective efforts.

Mauri Åhlberg has investigated what he calls "concept mapping" and "concept matrices" as tools for the analysis of the structure of textbook texts (Åhlberg 1990). In this context, we are dealing with conceptual or topical units which might comprise a word, a paragraph, or a chapter, and which are connected to other related or non-related concepts in many ways. Åhlberg refers to Staffan Selander, who writes that "Every sensory impression and every perception are transformed through a process of codification to a lasting memory, provided that they are incorporated into a network of conceptual connections" (Selander 1988, p. 128). A narrative text is in itself a concept, a narrative structure which in turn consists of other concepts arranged in various types of hierarchies. This is also true of cogitative texts, in which the concepts are used as the cornerstones of a presentation, but not in the same way as people or actions. According to Åhlberg, both text types often overlap and analyses of conceptual connections will give an indication of quality, especially if they are examined as part of an analysis that takes account of argumentation and content (Åhlberg 1990, p. 9). He refers *inter alia* to Starver and Bay, who analyzed "the conceptual structure and reasoning demand of elementary science texts at the primary level" (Starver - Bay 1989). Åhlberg, who, like Armbruster and Anderson calls the concept elements "nodes", has developed a method for producing a graphic representation of their role in the text, and he is working on the development of a system applicable to larger text units.

Åhlberg's colleague at the University of Joensuu, Marja-Liisa Julkunen, has conducted a large-scale investigation of conceptual relationships and concepts in Finnish textbooks for the lower secondary level and the first year of upper secondary school. Two hundred and twenty five paragraphs of approximately one hundred words were selected from 49 different books in history, religion, geography and biology. Julkunen found that the number of concepts per se was not necessarily any indication of accessibility, but that their cohesion was crucial. The most important connection from the concept world of the text to that of the pupil was assumed to be the pupils' experience at the lower levels. At the higher levels, on the other hand, the main connection comprised examples supported by illustrations and tables. The systematic processing and development of definitions was less common. Otherwise, Julkunen registered numerous contraventions and shortcomings in hierarchies and levels:

> When the text and concept analyses are compared, it becomes obvious that the analyzed textbooks do not enhance learning in the best possible way. The results suggest that the textbook writers do not use the rather simple linguistic devices that could make learning from texts easier. (Julkunen 1990, p. 19.)

It will always be difficult to label a text's structural elements because demarcation will have to be effected at several levels (theme, style, mood, composition). In any model, the most important aspects of every labelling attempt will involve, first of all, the question of how precisely the model describes the subject's and grade level's textbook text, second, the degree to which the description facilitates relating specific text patterns to specific subjects/plans/grade levels/authors/publishers, and third, whether it is these particular patterns - the variations and collocations in question - which best serve the objective regarding the book's accessibility.

Perspectives

These investigations are also mainly characterized by the more or less explicit desire to improve textbooks. To some extent, they are all descriptive *and* normative; some conclude with schemas that the readers themselves presumably can apply to test the quality of the books they use. Relatively speaking, this category has a far greater number of evaluation criteria than any other group.

The dominant constituent is the linguistic expression. As far as method is concerned, the majority of the investigations consist of book investigations based on assumptions about how the texts will work. These assumptions are in turn based largely on readability theories which first evolved in educational research during the 1950s and have since seemed to multiply exponentially. The title of readability researcher Mogens Jansen's English-language presentation of the topic in Denmark is indicative: *The Teaching of Reading without Really any Method* (Jansen - Jacobsen - Jensen 1978). Following the first investigations of what has come to be called the micro-level, vocabulary for instance (Sudmann 1978), in the course of the 1980s such research approached macro-levels such as literary genres (Gillham 1986), the authorial role (Crismore 1984), ideology (Selander 1988) or logical/educational structures (Åhlberg 1990). A corresponding expansion has occurred from textbook investigations conducted by reading teachers toward text analyses in all subjects; analyses conducted by experts in the subjects and/or experts in fields such as psychology, linguistics, education or philosophy. The trends have moved from the traditional, largely age-related requirements for the simplification of vocabulary and syntax toward an increasingly psycho- and sociolinguistic recognition of the scope of the problem of *communication* in the textbook texts.

Although it is possible to refer to macro-levels such as genres, the authorial role, logical structures and ideology, a survey would show that very little has been done in these fields in connection with accessibility. Nor have what might be called educational and methodological structures been examined anywhere near as extensively as linguistic structures. That is, they have hardly been investigated at all: How chronological should the contents of a history textbook be for a 10-year-old? How should natural science and social science be integrated in countries in which so-called knowledge subjects comprise a single curricular unit? What are the reasons for and the consequences of the fact that the amount of written text in mathematics books for grades 1 - 9 has increased considerably relative to the content of symbols?

Peter Weinbrenner summarizes his discussion of "Text Type, Text Structure and Text Clarity" (Laubig - Peters - Weinbrenner

1986, pp. 317-19), by referring to S.-O. Tergan's comprehensive survey of the field (Tergan 1983), and places the remaining problems into six categories:

- There is no generally accepted readability theory which can be applied to the learning effect.
- Thus far, investigations have almost exclusively quantified knowledge acquisition (What is retained?).
- "Superficial structure" has received a disproportionate amount of attention compared with "deep structure".
- Too much focus on the text has undermined necessary investigations into other aspects of the teacher's role and the classroom situation.
- The testing situations have been spurious ("laboratory situation").
- Sentence structure has dominated at the expense of the semantic structures (which Weinbrenner calls micro- and macro-structures, respectively).

No attempt will be made to evaluate the various readability theories in this survey. Several recent surveys not only review the theories, they also point out the need to apply psycholinguistic insight more systematically in connection with educational and not least popularization problems involving (individual) subjects:

> Simplified material can often be used in educational programs intended to train pupils in reading comprehension gradually and in a controlled manner. To select reading material of the simplified variety and then adapt it to the rest of an educational program, one must know how and the degree to which this reading material differs from authentic material, i.e., material which has not been simplified or revised for educational purposes. Only with this sort of insight does one have a sound basis for attempting to ensure further development in respect of the ability to read authentic texts, which is of course the ultimate goal for reading training in most long-term educational programs. (Simensen 1986, p. 1.)

The above quotation was taken from an investigation conducted by Aud Marit Simensen on people's intuition about text simplification: *Text Simplification. An Experiment.* The author provides a review of previous work done in this field and describes the models used for the investigations. Her own experiment is based on the desire to break down the barrier between form and content in readability studies. This work subscribes to the series of recent experiments intended to shed light on texts in more total communicative contexts (Källgeren - Sigurd - Westman 1977), and supports the view that it is possible to learn far more about how "a particular cognitive content can best be conveyed to particular groups of readers" (p. 104).

Ferdinand de Saussure's classical distinction between *langue* (meaning collectively developed, normalized language) and *parole* (meaning more individual or situation/function-specific language; see Dale 1960, p. 31) will, when applied to the genre of textbook texts, raise two types of questions. The one concerns the degree of normality in textbook texts' so-called ordinary prose. The other applies to the special nature of textbook prose, which at one and the same time is a manifestation of scholarship, popularization, educational philosophy, educational method and - possibly - of the author's personality.

Since textbook texts are written for school and educational purposes, it would be difficult to associate their "normality" exclusively with the descriptive ("Textbooks are written in neutral prose"). It would be equally difficult to tie their special characteristics exclusively to the normative ("Textbooks tell what is correct and democratic" (grammar/social science)). In a very special way, textbook texts are conveyors of information and attitudes. Perhaps one might even say that by virtue of their institutional authority, they neutralize norms in a language and within a context which really belongs only to the school. This dual nature is also reflected in the fuzziness of the questions posed in many investigations. A hypothetical example may provide a useful illustration. General questions may be posed in a way which may invite descriptive approaches (1): "How much of the text consists of a cogitative representation?" Detailed questions may be posed in a way which may invite descriptive approaches (2): "Which argumentational functions do the examples in the paragraph about foreign aid have?" General questions may be posed in a way which may invite evaluation (3): "How comprehensible are the cogitative segments of the text?" Detailed questions may be posed in a way which may invite evaluation (4): "How familiar are the examples used in the paragraphs about foreign aid?" If applied to authentic texts, such questions would quickly reveal that the text was more complex than the measurement system. Questions 1 and 2 invite quantitative measurement and the classification of a body of text which most probably consists of both descriptive and normative elements. Questions 3 and 4 are also in a borderland area; in formal terms, they belong among investigations based on registered observations. Moreover, the criterion of "advance insight", which may in itself be controversial (depending *inter alia* on the occurrence of the same topic other places in the same textbook), is built into the question. Such borderland cases are inevitable. As regards analyses that claim to be scientific in the orthodox sense of the word, this will impose constraints on fields of vision and possibilities. Thus if one wants to investigate the language or content of larger textual units, one encounters one inescapable question: Could such duality be discovered and discussed without a system that has enough latitude to allow subjectivity?

Several researchers have analyzed textbook language on the basis of specific assumptions about ordinary prose; assumptions which may or may not derive from general theories postulated by language and readability researchers. However, very few have ever written analyses which are holistic in the sense that they simultaneously relate linguistic analyses to patterns for evaluating ordinary prose, to discussions of the special nature of the relevant subject's content and to the textbook genre's extraordinarily large number of different premises. (Bamberger - Vanecek 1988, Ahier 1988, and especially Selander 1988 go quite far in this direction.) This is understandable in light of the requirements for such analyses devised by modern textual linguistics. Bernt Fossestøl, author of what might well be the 1980s most exhaustive international survey over this field of research, has shown how chosing the *entire* (textbook) text as a point of departure can uncover new connections (Fossestøl 1980).

One of Fossestøl's students, Norunn Askeland, compared 20 textbook texts in religion (Askeland 1984). She applied several methods; her analysis is divided into three parts: a LIX analysis, a syntactical analysis and an analysis of textual cohesion. Askeland concludes that:

> The LIX analysis and the syntactical analysis mainly showed that there were inherent stylistic differences between the textbooks and the texts. The analysis of textual cohesion was the first to expose the difference in degree of difficulty, and which provided a point of departure for a discussion of the relationship between syntax, semantics and degree of difficulty. The analysis of textual cohesion also illuminated the relationship between composition and textual cohesion.
>
> The analyses brought forth several examples in which form, content and communicative situation were inseparable. One must view instructive texts from the perspective of interaction. Texts in religion appear to function best when they are cohesive *and when the texts provide latitude for a dialogue with the reader, whether he is a teacher or a pupil.* (Askeland 1984; *my* emphasis.)

The preceding quotation offers a reminder of the one perspective which must be placed above all those mentioned above. I'm referring to Suzanne de Castell's contention that we must also examine the attitudes of teachers and pupils to the texts contained in the textbooks. She asserts that traditional comprehension studies will not change much until the textbook texts are rejuvenated as literary works: They are not lexical documents. They, in themselves, are interpretations of the world and must therefore also be interpreted, like pupils learn to do with fiction texts much earlier (de Castell 1990; see page 201). That perspective makes it natural to ask whether it is not new *approaches to problems* rather than new *methods* that are needed in the area of accessibility.

Based on such approaches, new investigations could progress in directions such as those Florence Davies suggests in her analysis of traditional criteria for textbook evaluation (Davies 1986). She contends that the point of departure for discussions and investigations has been marked by specific, fixed ideas about function, structure and use, and that this fact has biased the result:

> The language of a textbook, according to one view, can be regarded as impenetrable and jargonistic, or, according to another, as necessarily subject specific, and representative of a particular genre. (...) The potential of textbooks for presenting bias can be considered grounds for teachers to censor or censure them, or to use them to encourage pupils actively to evaluate the texts themselves. The use of textbooks can be passive or active. The adoption of one set of criteria can result in global criticisms of textbooks and a consequent retreat from print. *The adoption of the alternative set of criteria could result in a transformation in the use of textbooks, and the exploitation of a largely untapped potential.* (Davies 1986; *my* emphasis.)

Effects and Effectiveness

A textbook text can achieve specific effects by using simple textual and typographical techniques. Sophisticated equipment makes it possible to endow texts with even more visual appeal, thereby commanding attention and stimulating reader interest. The question of the extent to which extra-textual enhancements in themselves contribute to the effectiveness of a book as an educational tool, or whether such enhancements accentuate viewpoints and attitudes in the text, will not be treated here. Granted, for years the requirements of teachers and publishers in Western countries have made lavish extra-textual enhancements standard fare. Teachers and textbook authors in the former USSR are also interested in more enhancements (Sujew 1986). However, with the exception of a few major contributions, research on the relationship between extra-textual enhancements and effectiveness has been almost inversely proportional to the growth seen in the technical development of textbooks.

In both principle and practice, it is impossible to distinguish between a presentation's visual impact and its effectiveness. A book will achieve optimal effectiveness if the material between its covers is written and adapted in a way that allows most of the pupils, during the time available to them, with or without the guidance of a good teacher, to study the book and grasp the knowledge, understanding and skills specified in the curriculum, as measured by tests and examinations administered at different levels. (The definition of optimal effectiveness disregards factors related to organization of the teaching process and school day, which might have a negative effect on the unassailable starting point, the book itself.)

With such a broad definition of effectiveness, both *accessibility* and *effects* become subordinate factors, relatively speaking, as they do in ordinary language usage. A richly illustrated text written in an easily accessible style is not necessarily motivating, informative, skill-promoting or easy to remember, and thereby automatically effective as an educational tool. The concept of accessibility was narrowed down in the previous chapter and limited mainly to a question of vocabulary, style and structure. However, factors such as volume, arrangement, information-density and the text-picture correlation are also relevant to the question of effectiveness. One can turn aspects of language, style, and extra-textual enhancements into a number of measurable elements and make theoretically based statements about probable degrees of effectiveness. Such statements, however, are rare, and little research has been done in this field. One explanation for this is the versatility of the concept of effectiveness itself, another very obvious reason is the problem of methodology (see page 234).

Illustrations

"The impact of technologies both ancient and modern on children's learning is either negligible or unknown." This quotation from David R. Olson (Olson 1974) expresses deep-seated skepticism to automatically applying technological innovations to education. But the fact that textbooks may account for as much as fifty per cent of all books published on a worldwide basis, measured in the number of copies printed, is a result of skilled product development and marketing strategies. First Dewey (Dewey 1938) and later Freire (Freire 1970) pointed out that these commercial forces could eventually work against school policy and educational goals. Michael Apple and Susan Jungck have compared the electronic media challenge facing today's teachers to the situation of books 100 years ago (Apple - Jungck 1990). They maintain that teachers' working conditions in the 1990s are, in principal, quite similar to their conditions in 1890: Low status, modest wages, variable working conditions, time pressure, and curricula they feel unqualified to teach. Just as the time was ripe 100 years ago for demanding access to standardized textbooks for all grade levels, today teachers are demanding access to a good assortment of office equipment to allow them to satisfy the curricula. These demands did not come unanimously from all teachers then, nor do they now; in many schools in many countries, demands are being reduced to the need for updated textbooks. But teaching aids *are* available, whether in the form of books or new technology. However, this fact may be troublesome since many teachers feel that teaching aids might deprive them of some of their autonomy, regardless of the publishers' assurances to the contrary. It is likely that widespread skepticism to new technology and sophisticated equipment still exists. The attitude to illustrations is a case in point:

> It is odd to think, in an age when we can create and use pictures on a scale never before seen, that schools' attitude toward pictures has retreated into the scholastic Middle Ages. It is still applicable, as it was then, that "letters make one wise, but pictures make one foolish". Thus we have a blind school for the sighted. (Eklund - Hedman - Bergquist 1986, p. 5.)

The authors are board members of the Swedish Picture and Word Academy. Gert Z. Nordström, a professor at the Stockholm College of Arts, Crafts and Design, writes: "There is widespread albeit often concealed antagonism to pictures in society, and this is also evident in schools, education and teaching" (Nordström 1989, p. 159.)

These Swedish comments directly contradict the unambiguous results of all the research studies that have asked teachers what they look for when choosing new textbooks. The teachers all strongly emphasize the importance of good illustrations. (Evans 1987, O'Brien 1988, Woodward 1990.) However, this inconsistency might not be as clear-cut as it appears. What do teachers actually mean by *good* illustrations? Does it suffice that the pictures look like they might have an inspirational effect? Or do teachers know exactly what they're looking for and evaluate illustrations as independent teaching instruments? The ability to answer these questions requires insight into two areas. First, we must know whether/how the books' illustrations are used in the classroom. Second, we must know what educational potential lies in illustrations: Are opportunities lost in the "school for the blind"? Hardly any research has been done on the first point. (Christina Gustafsson's comprehensive use study (see page 385) demonstrates that the amount of time spent on the direct use of illustrations is minimal.) As regards the second point, both theory and research are lacking. François Richaudeau's introduction to the technology of textbook development includes a separate chapter treating the use of pictures, but with the exception of references to standard picture theories from readability researchers, he quotes only one study on the implications of using illustrations. Carried out in Nepal, the study presents evidence that artists' drawings are more inspiring as well as more informative than photographs. (Richaudeau 1986, pp. 176-77.)

In an article from 1991, Arthus Woodward describes the situation as follows:

> Perhaps most disturbing is the seeming irrelevance of research on illustrations to selectors and producers. To date, research seems to have had little impact and provided few guidelines for practical application. Indeed, the vast majority of research on illustration is undertaken without regard to actual textbooks or the population that will read them. (Woodward 1991, p. 18.)

The question of the instructional value of illustrations may to some extent be directed toward the *effect* per se: Are they inspirational? Such questions lead to new ones concerning circumstances independent of the books themselves: Is it true that pupils require extra-textual inspiration? To some extent, these questions concern *effectiveness*: What can one learn from illustrations in textbooks? As far as visual impact is concerned, extensive research will be required to find the answer. Many would also contend that this issue is largely academic - everyone likes a few pictures. In response, others would maintain that the question becomes less and less academic as the proportion of illustrations increases. Arthur Woodward studied the relationship between consecutive text and illustrations in two natural science series for grades one through six. In both series, illustrative material covered an average of more than 50 per cent of the pages. As expected, the proportion of illustrations was largest in the books for the lowest grades, but it was as high as 43 per cent (both series) in the fifth grade books (Woodward 1989).

The issue of effectiveness can be broken down into three parts, as Woodward did in a comparative study of the chapters about electricity in two sixth-grade textbooks. The study was cited in the article "Do Illustrations Serve an Instructional Purpose in U.S. Textbooks?". It treats the use of picture captions, the effectiveness of illustrations alone as educational instruments and the way in which teachers' manuals deal with the use of pictures (Woodward 1991, p. 10).

Five criteria were used to analyze picture captions: no text, identification of what is depicted, text that quotes from the consecutive text, text that supplements the consecutive text, and questions directed at the reader. While 74 per cent of the illustrations in the first book had captions, the comparable figure was only 47 per cent in the second. Further, it was found that a large proportion of the picture captions were either simple identifications or quotations/restatements of the consecutive text. The one book had no supplementary texts or questions at all. Woodward also examined the references between the consecutive text and the pictures. Direct references numbered well under 50 per cent both ways, in both books.

Four criteria were used to analyze the true effectiveness of illustrations alone as educational instruments: Illustrations with no demonstrable relevance to the content of the consecutive text, pictures of objects or subjects related to the text without being directly connected to it, pictures that exemplified the consecutive text, and pictures that supplemented the subject of the consecutive text with new information and new perspectives. Woodward found that the majority of the illustrations (75 and 86 per cent) were related to the text in one way or another, and could generally be placed in one of the first two groups. Only three illustrations in each book could be characterized as supplementary (fourth group).

Teachers' manuals were also examined. The first had 17 references to 20 of a total of 42 illustrations in the book; the second, four references to four of a total of 36 illustrations. Advice concerning the use of illustrations was limited to pointing out that the books had some illustrations. Woodward concludes that there is definite "evidence that illustrations are hastily assembled with little regard to their being closely related to the text" (p. 17). At the same time, he points out clear differences between the two books that were examined. Regarding the illustrations' captions, placement and relation to consecutive text, one of the books seemed at least to have an "illustrative strategy" (p. 15). In the other book, however, the illustrations were "generally instructionally ineffective". Woodward refers to another study which concludes that intuition, traditions and market factors decide the illustrative strategies of publishing houses (Houghton - Willows 1987).

The impression of inconsistency is strengthened by the results of other studies. Rune Pettersson interviewed picture editors and graphic designers in Swedish publishing houses and concluded that "(...) in practice, procurement time, accessibility and clarity are the most important factors for selecting illustrations" (Pettersson 1991, p. 142). He refers to investigations conducted in the United States and Canada and claims that the practical work of selecting illustrations is based on the same factors in foreign publications as it is in Sweden.

Pettersson's study is cited from his book *Pictures in Teaching Materials* (1991), a survey which examines and discusses research on the use of illustrations in textbooks. In addition to offering an introduction into basic illustrational theory, the survey provides an overview not only of the relatively few and scattered analyses that exist, but also of studies on how illustrations are used in teaching. On the whole, the book reinforces the tendencies pointed out in Woodward's article. Pettersson's summary of his own and others' research (pp. 69-70; pp. 93-126) indirectly confirms the claim that textbooks, in terms of their illustrations, are aptly described as existing in "a blind school for the sighted".

Effectiveness

Curricula and measurements in the form of grades and examinations are formal methods for regulating school content and setting standards. In principle, the most effective teaching aids are those which most quickly enable the majority of pupils to fulfill the requirements. Since a school's primary function is to help pupils fulfill educational goals regarding knowledge and skills, one might automatically assume that the field of textbook research would be dominated by studies measuring how the pupils use textbooks, and what and how much they learn from them. It turns out, however, that the extent of this type of research is very limited for a variety of reasons.

First, current governing mechanisms such as educational objectives and curricula are the result of years of political compromise. Trends toward teaching guides for individual subjects and local autonomy have increased the potential for different interpretations of textbooks, teaching and measurements. The "result" becomes a mutable concept. This will be increasingly true as the objective of individualized and differentiated teaching gains ground.

Second, a school is based on teaching *and* educating. As superordinate objectives (see page 159), attitudes are as important as knowledge and skills. This makes it impossible to measure teaching effectiveness as a single factor. The fact that the curricula in many countries maintain that the knowledge/skills/attitudes triumvirate should be embodied in each individual discipline makes the concept of effectiveness vague, and, to some, suspect. Debates about "schools for knowledge" as opposed to "schools for caretaking" can often be traced to underlying attitudes for or against such multi-faceted schools.

Third, in practice it is difficult to measure achievement, even on the basis of well-defined units. Such research would represent severe interference with the teaching, and be time-consuming and research intensive.

Fourth, it seems unnatural to measure the learning process as a result based solely on the merit of the textbook. It is a prevailing opinion that learning involves interaction between a book and a reader, and that the result depends upon the reader's qualifications and the way he makes use of them when he confronts the text:

It is not enough that certain materials and methods have proved effective with other individuals at other times. There must be a reason for thinking that they will function in generating an experience that has educative quality with particular individuals at a particular time. (Dewey 1938, p. 45.)

The tradition of measuring effectiveness has been most common in nations with specific ideological educational objectives, such as, for instance, the former USSR and GDR. Experiences from these nations are summarized in volume 60 of *Informationen zu Schulbuchfragen 1988* (see page 76). In an introductory article, Werner Jungk writes that studies took two directions in the 1980s. On the one hand, they steadily developed more refined ("verfeinerte") methods for measuring the degree to which specific structural elements in the books can improve learning. On the other, they became increasingly more engaged in studying individual investigations in relation to the complex totality of all teaching materials ("Gesamtkomplex aller Unterrichtsmaterialen") (Jungk 1988, pp. 18-19). Jungk points out that it is untenable that "bei der Analyse von Struktureelementen eines Schulbuches stehenzubleibed"; one must combine detail and totality, "the analytical view" with "the synthetical view". Jungk describes three essential levels ("Ebene") which individual analyses must always take into account. These are: the class and the classroom situation, the school and the teaching situation in general, and the prevailing situation in the nation and the international community (pp. 19-21).

The above is exemplified in a representative analysis made in the (former) East German tradition. Käte Nestler examined how the topic of the water cycle was presented in four different fourth-grade textbooks: one Hungarian, one East German, one West German and one "textbook" (with two texts) that was specially developed at the College of Education in Köthen-Halle (Nestler 1990). The books were used in separate classes. None of the five classes involved had previously been taught about the water cycle and their scholastic levels were about equal. All the pupils worked with the texts and then with the tests, without any teacher guidance. Nestler subsequently measured what the pupils had learned from the textbooks: "ihre Wirkung auf die kognitive Verarbeitung der textinhalte bei Schülern der Klasse 4". In the report she points out that in spite of the limitations of this type of "Wirkungsuntersuchung", research has shown that differences in the style and structure of textbook texts can result in differences in their effects on the learning process.

The primary aim of the study was not to compare the quality of the books, although it was clearly evident that the pupils learned more from some books than others, with one very important addition: No single book was "best" on all points. There were significant variations on a number of central points. Most important to Nestler was to identify the factors within the texts themselves that added to or detracted from the learning process, measured according to what the pupils learned from them. In all the texts her conclusions supported the tendency indicated by the few Western investigations made in the same field (see page 231): The use of examples in the texts – their "world" – and the selection and use of concepts and technical terms are decisive, in a negative way. More than fifty per cent of the pupils may experience difficulty understanding; many of them misunderstand/do not comprehend the material. (Studies by Nestler and other East German researchers are presented in volume 47 of *Informationen zu Schulbuchfragen* (1983).)

Nestler's study covers the relationship between book and pupil, but excludes the teacher. As was seen in the section on accessibility, in the Western world most investigations of this kind are purely book studies, often based to a greater or lesser extent on earlier research which might be based partly on text analyses and partly on fieldwork. For example when Harriet Tyson-Bernstein and Arthur Woodward wrote a critical article entitled "Why Students Aren't Learning Very Much from Textbooks" (Tyson-Bernstein - Woodward 1989), they referred to a number of studies and reports that support their assertion. But the article dealt primarily with a presumed ineffectiveness because there is a lack of widespread pupil observations and no tradition for the up-to-date systematization of such observations within the totality described by Jungk.

Workbook Questions and Pupils' Reading

A prime example of how a field of vision can be abruptly expanded and a perspective sharpened when first one sets out to observe pupils closely is Mason and Osborn's study of two "reading periods" in classes from the first to the sixth grade (Mason - Osborn 1982). The extensive use of workbooks persuaded the authors to study them too, in addition to the basic textbooks. As early as in 1979, using essentially traditional methods of literary analysis, Agnes Nobel concluded that the contemporary workbooks used in many subjects had to be ineffective since they were the result of "a mechanistic attitude toward teaching materials" (Nobel 1979, p. 61). Subsequent workbook research has uncovered weaknesses within the educational system itself and pointed out new problems (Moosbrugger 1985, Ginsburger-Vogel 1986, Osborn - Decker 1990). For example, a new perspective appears when Steffan Selander points out that the consecutive text in a certain history book shows clear signs of having been written and arranged to provide direct answers to the questions posed at the beginning and end of each chapter (Selander 1988, p. 76).

In 1991, Shepardson and Pizzini reported that:

> The fact that no difference was observed in the proportion of question levels among science disciplines suggests that students are uniformly exposed to low-level cognitive questions throughout their junior high school science education experience. The result is that students become accustomed to responding to low-level cognitive questions, and are limited in their comprehension of textual information. (Shepardson - Pizzini 1991, p. 680.)

Shepardson and Pizzini determined the cognitive level of questions in junior high school textbooks using an analysis scheme which classifies the cognitive level of questions as input ("Name the parts of the flower"), processing ("How are pine trees different from oak trees?"), and output ("What would be the best solution to our air pollution problems?"). Their starting point was that since comprehension of textual information involves extracting and integrating textual information with prior knowledge, an overabundance of input-level questions would inhibit the students' cognitive level of interaction with the textual information. Since they did find such an extensive use of low-level cognitive questions, they conclude that this "would appear to restrict text comprehension" by limiting the prior knowledge generated to interact with the textual information, by creating a low-level purpose for reading, and by reducing the integration of textual information with existing knowledge. (P. 680).

In terms of textbooks, the research into pupils' interest has been limited to the subject of reading training. Numerous investigations have been conducted to test the significance of content, text structure and illustration to the reading process, measured by different, often controversial methods (Jansen - Jacobsen - Jensen 1978). In terms of individual subjects, attempts at measurements are sporadic despite steadily growing evidence that textbooks are used in different ways in different subjects (Stodolsky 1988). Beverton's questionnaire based on *journals* from 116 pupils showed typical results concerning the amount and type of material that was read (see page 199), but could only evaluate learning effectiveness indirectly. A second, more qualitative, way to relate to the pupils' work is to interview them. Lauren A. Sosniak and Carole L. Perlman talked to 44 lower secondary pupils about teaching and textbooks in the subjects of mathematics, English and history (Sosniak - Perlman 1990). Apart from attesting to strong teacher-control and the extensive use of books in all subjects, based on the pupils' own accounts and comments, the authors conclude that:

(...) work with textbooks in the different subject matters suggests dramatically different potential for *empowering* students in their studies of the disciplines, for shaping classroom activity in such a way as to *engage* students intellectually and emotionally, and for *helping* students see connections between their school tasks and their life experiences. (Sosniak - Perlman 1990, p. 436.)

This investigation does not measure results either. However, like most of the other approaches mentioned in this chapter, it does uncover elements that should be included in more systematic measurements.

There are a few examples of more comprehensive approaches. While it is true that none of these measurements deals with material learned from figures or tables, both investigations take pupils as their point of departure.

The first looks at teaching and teaching materials in light of the pupils' living and working situation both in and outside school. Yngve Nordkvelle's study of social science instruction at a Norwegian upper secondary school concludes that textbooks form the backbone of teaching (Nordkvelle 1988, p. 94). Teaching material read at home and in school is the fundamental starting point for classroom discussions and group work. Should the text in the textbook conflict with the traditions of the subject in terms of curricula requirements and teachers' viewpoints, the traditions will win - competing, however, against media influence. This observation concerns one particular aspect of learning, namely, the effect of influence. In terms of the learning process as regards text and material for examinations, however, textbooks are virtually sovereign:

> (...) the first thing students look for in their notebooks when about to commence their homework is: What will be on tomorrow's test? Most students subscribe to the following view: The important thing is my ability to remember what is in the book, and the speed and clarity with which I write my answers. Participation in the classroom is something you do to keep your eyes open; you get good marks by doing well in the written tests. (...) It is vital to "cram" the selected pages, taking notes and memorizing the essentials. (Nordkvelle 1991, pp. 9-10.)

Nordkvelle's investigation is especially pertinent to the subject of Third World countries as they are treated in textbooks and in the classroom. A whole different subject entirely is the part textbooks play in ensuring the effectiveness of the teaching process in Third World countries. Certain studies, especially those commissioned by the World Bank, show that the poorer a country is, the stronger the correlation between access to/use of textbooks - more than of the availability of trained teachers - and school results. The more affluent a society, the more difficult it is to prove these direct correlations (Heyneman - Farrell - Sepulveda-Stuardo 1978, Farrell - Heyneman 1989).

The second study analyzes teaching and textbooks and the pupils' understanding of them and the subject. It is a thorough, comprehensive analysis based on educational philosophy. In his book *Spotlight on Science* (Sjøberg 1979), Svein Sjøberg reports on three investigations: The first analyzed the most commonly used seventh grade physics/chemistry textbook using a taxonomy of cognitive demand based on Piaget's theory regarding the stages of intellectual development. The second tested seventh graders' general ability, irrespective of subject boundaries, to think in *proportionality*, a central concept in many theories of cognitive development, as well as in quantitative descriptions of the natural sciences. The third investigation measured how much pupils had actually understood about key topics. Sjøberg summarizes his results as follows:

> The textbooks are primarily directed toward an understanding of the subject matter based on the assumption that students are at the formal operational stage. This, at least, is a consequence of the National Curriculum's lists of topics.
>
> The great majority of pupils are, however, at the concrete operational stage. They will therefore not be able to master the subject matter in the way the book intends.
>
> But pupils who *are* at the formal operational stage will also have problems. (...) In that case, since many of the new words are by no means justified in terms of the pupils' concrete world of experience, it must all seem quite meaningless. (Sjøberg 1978, pp. 140-41.)

One of Sjøberg's crucial points is the clear distinction between how much of a text pupils can show they have read and can repeat, and how much of the same text they actually understand. Of the research presented in this survey, Sjøberg's goes furthest in attempting to "measure" the fulfillment of more than one single or partial goal, in that he includes the book, the teacher, and the pupil. Like most of Allard and Sundblad's studies, reading and writing education researchers may, as has been common practice, analyze words in textbook texts and demonstrate that many key concepts in the context of the book are incomprehensible at the intended age level (Allard - Sundblad 1986, p. 27). Their conclusion is the same as Sjøberg's. One might say they treat the question of accessibility and effectiveness on a micro level, while Sjøberg works on a macro level - even though he lacks the dimension of "contemporary society" (See Jungk, page 228, and discussion on page 204).

Perspectives

The material from this group of investigations is too limited to make any attempt at systematization. There is a striking discrepancy between the importance of the textbooks' knowledge-imparting function and the extent to which the studies treat this function. Possible reasons for this have been discussed previously (see page 227); the methodological problems are especially obvious. The main problem is classification, which is related to the controversial nature of the concept of knowledge. Nevertheless, some classification is already present in the books. Authors and publishers compile them on the basis of their own ideas about what kind of text, which pictures and which structures best teach the pupils. Therefore, it should theoretically be possible to limit these categories and create measurement systems to accommodate them. However, this would presuppose access to virtually unlimited resources.

Klaus Lange has reasoned that methodological problems cannot justify omitting the perspective of the books' effect in textbook analyses: "The reference to the extensive difficulties involved in an empirical control of the hypotheses on effectiveness and influence does not justify precluding these premises." (Lange 1981, p. 17.) Some major theoretical studies have also been done in this field. The most important of these studies focus on the question of the textbooks' effectiveness in a way that also sheds light on other aspects of "books in use". They will therefore be presented here.

Theoreticians from such dissimilar political systems as the former GDR and Switzerland have examined the possibilities for an empirical check ("Überprüfung") of the knowledge-related influence of textbook material. The theoreticians are Manfred Baumann from the Wolfgang Ratke Hochschule in Köthen and

Yanouchka Oppel and Bernard Spreng at the Institut romand de recherche et de documentation pédagogiques in Neuchâtel. The two features they have in common are also seen in other work in this field. First, the relationship between books and pupils is extremely central (books and teachers dominate studies about control). Second, within all the different investigations this is the area in which the need for a more precise definition of the terms "textbook" and "teaching methods" is most strongly emphasized.

Manfred Baumann's analysis, "Methoden und Probleme der Schulbuchforschung im Überblick", offers proof of the need for this thoroughness with detail - but it must be carefully combined with a holistic perspective - for which Werner Jungk (see page 228) has also been searching:

> This survey was to show that a large number of different factors related to textbook use must be evaluated against one another in a holistic perspective in every individual analysis. (...) We are special in that we always work with textbook material. We must analyze this material as thoroughly as possible to discover what has to be processed by teachers and pupils, which requirements are posed by the textbook material and what actually elicits a particular effect. (Baumann 1983, p. 18.)

In accordance with this viewpoint, Baumann has devised a two-part model that organizes all measured and measurable dimensions either under "Teilgegenstandsbereiche" (individual fields) or "Verfahren" (methods of procedure). The former covers the textbooks, pupil knowledge, activities (of teachers and pupils) and forms of teaching. The latter consists of ways to describe these fields as well as ways to evaluate them. Baumann maintains that the combination of elements from the two groups will vary with each investigation, according to a precise definition of its objective. Baumann points out that the acquisition of knowledge, the teaching procedure and the motivation for learning will not automatically correlate if the objective is to study a particular form of effect, "die entscheidende Wirkungsrelation". He would like to see methods developed which would encompass both the cognitive and the emotional aspects of the process, and mentions the classification of different types of tasks, for example, as an example of as yet uncovered areas of research. This is necessary so that: "very specific effects can be registered and included in a control strategy or a uniform test of effects. Only then is it possible to compare *whether or not* positive effects can be registered." (Pp. 22-23.)

Baumann's requirement for separating and defining is also one of Bernard Spreng's premises (Spreng 1976). With other researchers at the Institut romand, he analyzed French-language textbooks from the same starting point that Sigurgeirsson used in Iceland (see page 180). He did this because curricula and the book stock were going to be updated. The Swiss did not make the same type of use-analyses as the Icelanders, but developed standard systems of analysis. Spreng insists that all facets of the concept "textbook" must be defined, and that the books' functions must be defined within a system of values in which the components are clearly limited in relation to one other. In his introduction he therefore discusses systems such as Bloom's taxonomy, a system of classification to which all other methods of educational evaluation should be able to adapt. ("(...) il est en fait difficile d'imaginer un comportement pédagogique qui n'entrerait pas dans cette classification"; p. 21.) Spreng places the individual functions in six main groups (knowledge, understanding, application, evaluation, elaboration and creation). As in all other systems, the triumvirate of knowledge/skills/attitudes recurs here. Spreng's main point is not originality in the classification per se, but the need - in every research situation - to adapt the classification to precise definitions of what a "textbook" is or should be in a given situation.

Spreng's colleague Yanouchka Oppel conducted a study that provided such a basis for a comprehensive description and evaluation of the books: "L'analyse des manuels scolaires. Elaboration d'une grille descriptive" (Oppel 1976). She analyzes the basic premises for the development of such descriptions and shows that textbook evaluation forms usually mix categories so uncritically that their results become unreliable. The model is flexible; it can be used to evaluate books in the classroom or as a point of departure for the definition of research tasks. It may be expanded or contracted and still provide a clear basis for deciding which overall or individual factors pertaining to society, school, education and books should be included or excluded in each case. The theory is similar to Baumann's: The object of the analysis (the book) must in each case be decided on the basis of the characteristics inherent in the book and the situation.

This model has been tested and modified but its perspective is consistently that of the textbook. Oppel's work does not treat the ways in which one might measure the conveyance of values, it simply points out and systematizes what one *can* look for - in the books. There is no "grille d'analyse" directly adapted to pupils' book use, nor is there any mention of knowledge acquisition. Yet indirectly, such a "grille d'analyse" does exist in many subjects and in most countries, particularly at higher levels, in the form of tests and examinations. First, the relationship between textbooks and examinations is among the book's *raisons d'être*; textbook critics would say it's their only *raison d'être*. Second, an examination can be used to measure what the books have or have not achieved. For example, there will be some pupils taking the examination who have not studied anything but the textbooks, just as there will be some who have not read them at all. The numerous correlations and possibilities for measurement opened up by this perspective have not been utilized, possibly because of methodological problems and/or more controversial issues concerning school policy. These measurements will have to be based on experimentation. Apart from the East German tradition (*Informationen zu Schulbuchfragen*, Volumes 47 and 60; see Nestler page 228), virtually no scientific testing has been done. Opposition to this might seem to be built into the system - there are rather strict limits to what school administrators/parents will accept of special evaluations of *their* children. The more an examination system is generally understood to be important to future careers, the more resistance there will be to experimentation that might impeach the influence of the very same system.

As previously mentioned, function categorization varies somewhat from theory to theory. As a rule, these differences are caused by the way the terms are used rather than by real contradictions. The position advocated by Baumann, Spreng and Oppel is also apparent in the surveys of West German theoreticians such as Hartmut Hacker and Manfred Laubig. Hacker separates the functions into six groups: "Repräsentationsfunktion, Steuerungsfunktion, Motivierungsfunktion, Differenzierungsfunktion, Übungs- und Kontrollfunktion" (Hacker 1980; pp. 14-27). Laubig refers to these categories and, to some extent, bases his own work on them. His report gathers them under the concept "Verwendungszusammenhang", to which he adds another concept: "Wirkungszusammenhang". Thus parallel approaches turn up in several groups (Laubig 1986, pp. 26-27). Some researchers make use of variations on the use-effect (Verwendung-Wirkung) dichotomy. However, as I have pointed out in this survey, the investigations have not been dominated by these functions, but by two others: Control and readability.

Chapter V

The Development of Textbooks

Introduction

In a lecture delivered when he was inaugurated into the Royal Academy of Letters, History and Antiquities in 1987, Swedish literary sociologist Lars Furuland analyzed a textbook that had dominated the market for several generations (Furuland 1987). It was the *Primary School Reader*, the literary "educator of the people" published in 1868, which virtually reigned supreme in Swedish schools until the turn of the century. Although it met some competition at that time, the work was nevertheless published in newer, ever larger editions up until 1938, in spite of having been subjected to strong criticism in both the previous and present century from cultural and political quarters, as well as censure by school personnel and well-known authors such as Ellen Key, August Bondeson and Herbert Tingsten.

Lars Furuland examined this criticism in light of comments from pupils and teachers who had used the book during the period under discussion.

He also explained how the book came into being and assumed its content: In 1862, history professor Fredrik Ferdinand Carlson was appointed Sweden's minister of education. Carlson was concerned about the school reader issue, so he supervised the editing of a new reader, which was compiled by a team of five men, all teachers in the higher grades. Their specialties were language, literature, history, forestry and physics. The reader was not a group effort in the ordinary sense. All decisions were made by Minister Carlson, who invariably had the last word on what should be included in each of the seven fields of knowledge comprising the comprehensive, universal work.

Furuland also described the physical development of the book, including the design of the cover, which had its own special history.

Lars Furuland then proceeded to outline and analyze the book's content:

> My task here is to give a brief account of the origin of this textbook, to examine its content, especially the choice of texts, to comment on the debate about the book, including the views of autodidacts [self-taught individuals who have used the book without supervision] and, finally, to attempt to explain precisely why the evergreen became the insignia and symbol of the reader. (p. 3.)

This statement - and Furuland's analysis - contain the elements of a rather process-oriented approach to textbook research which this chapter attempts to systematize into:

- Authors,
- Publishers, Authorities, Curricula and Teaching, and
- Production and The Market.

Authors

An author's contribution to a completed textbook may be seen as more or less significant, depending on how much importance one attaches to such elements as curricula, publishers, consultants and the school situation. The farther back we go in time, the easier it is to find examples of "great" textbook authors who dominated the market to such an extent that their names sometimes became synonymous with the subject itself. Yet no country can boast of having produced a literary history of textbooks, so portrayals of authors are rare although they are occasionally found in connection with discussions of well-known books. One exception is the biography of Joel Dorman Steele (Archibald 1900), who wrote history books. The "blatant" lack of attention paid to these authors elicited the following observation from the former head of the US Library of Congress, librarian, textbook writer and essayist Daniel J. Boorstin:

> Textbooks have a basic role in civilization and the role is peculiar in a number of ways. Perhaps one of the most interesting is the disproportion between the glamour and prestige of the authorship of textbooks and the significance of textbooks in the civilization. A greater disproportion than there is, perhaps, in any other kind of authorship. (...) To be a textbook writer is considered to be below the competence and status of many scholars. (Library of Congress 1981, p. IX.)

Hélène Huot studied publishers' catalogs for the year 1989 (Huot 1989). She ascertained that in some subjects Nathan listed only the book title and not the author's name. As a rule Magnard listed only the authors' surnames, and Hachette usually followed the same practice, surnames only, leaving out even the authors' first initials.

Boorstin and Huot describe the modern-day situation; author teams are many and author profiles few. "In the beginning" the situation was quite different:

> By the 1840s, we can already find individuals who made their fortunes by writing textbooks. In the classical field, the outstanding example is Thomas Kerchever Arnold, the author of a book on Latin Prose Composition which is still in use. Together with Kennedy's Latin Primer, this book lay at the centre of a dominant pattern of elite schooling well into the 20th century. Arnold produced dozens of books, many of which were either unauthorised translations from German books or collages, assembled from several sources. With Arnold and his rivals in the 1840s, in fact, we encounter another predictable facet of capitalist production and marketing; plagiarism. By this time, the text as well as the book was coming to be seen as a commodity, the property of its creator, and this decade is marked by a series of controversies in which authors accuse each other of theft and attempt to establish their own claims of priority. (Stray 1991, p. 4.)

Prior to Arnold, who was British, two American textbook authors experienced tremendous success in the USA. There were two best-selling reading textbooks in the United States during the late eighteenth and nineteenth centuries. The first was Noah Webster's spelling book, the second was a series entitled the McGuffey Readers, named after its original author. Jennifer Monaghan has explored the substantive role played by these authors in view of the commercial aspects of their textbooks and their relationship to the books' success (Monaghan 1991).

It is possible to reduce the significance of individual authors' contributions to textbooks for reasons which may in themselves provide some explanation for the low status of these writers. One may assume that a textbook will be marked by its author's attitudes and norms. Even so, isn't the author himself still a product of a collective consciousness, i.e., of the attitudes prevalent in a given society at a given time? It is often claimed that many voices can sometimes be heard in pieces of fiction as well. But a novelist is not bound in the same way by formal requirements regarding choice of subject matter, suitability for the given level, accuracy or neutrality. In textbooks, the collective consciousness is manifested as the sum of directives and statements made by others, and it places constraints on individual expression: "Even if it is not possible to separate the one consciousness from the other, it is important to point out that the consciousness of the text is something greater than that of the individual writer or publisher." (Thorson 1988, p. 126.) From that perspective, even textbooks are not solely purveyors of fact. It cannot be taken for granted that textbooks meet the standards for perspective and objectivity to which some of them aspire in their prefaces.

While this situation forms the basis for numerous ideological analyses, it also deserves to occupy a central position in an examination of the phenomenon of authorship. Who are the people behind authors' names; what are their backgrounds, how are they recruited, and what are their motives for writing such books? Who are the editors and consultants, both inside and outside the publishing houses, and how much do they influence the final texts? What traditions and interests have governed the author and/or his consultants?

There are two systematic discussions concerning the role of the author. Robert Bierstedt writes about "The Writers of Textbooks" in Cronbach's book from 1955, and Egil Børre Johnsen has included a chapter about authors in *Hidden Literature* (Johnsen 1989). Bierstedt emphasizes that the subject is unexplored territory. He bases the need for examining the question of who really writes textbooks on the main premise put forth in Cronbach's book: "If our conclusions are sound, the text can be improved further." (Cronbach 1955, p. 8.) Johnsen's point of departure is that of a textbook writer. He focuses on professional awareness and the professionalization process in particular. There are signs that this trend is evolving in certain countries; for example, both Norway and Sweden have separate trade unions for this category of writer. Except in connection with trade unions, it is difficult to find textbook authors categorized as a separate occupational group.

There are no public education courses designed especially for them and no special scholarships or prizes; textbook writing is not part of college or university syllabuses, nor does it receive much media attention. Johnsen examines the reasons why this is still true in most countries. He finds a correlation between low author status and increasing editorial participation in a progressively more product-oriented publishing world. However, Johnsen concludes that the changing situation in school and society will bring about a new attitude toward the work of writing schoolbooks - among writers, publishers, and the authorities. New curricula, mainly emphasizing cardinal goals aimed at stimulating local and regional (pupil) initiative, call for a new, holistic evaluation of "form, language and artistic content. Here we find the germ of a new occupational awareness and a more marked perception of textbook writing as a *profession*." (Johnsen 1989, p. 52.)

As early as in 1955, in his lengthy report entitled "The Publishing Process" (Schramm 1955), Wilbur Schramm claimed that:

It would be extremely hard if not impossible to find a group of 100 authors who have had an impact on the patterns of our text productions as great as that of the 100 leading educational editors in the publishing houses of this country.

Therefore, an important question is *who are the editors?* (P. 159.)

The fact that textbook writers are organized into trade unions opens up certain possibilities for investigations into the sociology of literature. In 1987 the Association of Norwegian Non-Fiction Writers (whose name has since been changed to the Norwegian Non-Fiction Writers' and Translators' Association) sent out a questionnaire to those members who write general non-fiction books and/or textbooks (just less than half the organization's members write textbooks only). Of the 731 who replied, most had full-time jobs in other fields. They had written a total of more than 4000 books, half of which were intended for use at various levels within the educational system. 13 percent of the authors were primary and secondary school teachers, but only four percent of those who had written books for use in the primary school were full-time primary school teachers in 1987. Three of four authors were men, and their average age was higher than that of fiction writers; most were between the ages of 40 and 55. More than 50 percent of the writers lived in the metropolitan Oslo area and nearly 20 percent of the others lived in other parts of southeastern Norway (Sjøberg 1987).

One would have to go all the way back to 1931 to find a more scientific attempt to describe textbook authors' professional backgrounds. At that time Herman G. Richey published the results of his investigation called "The Professional Status of Textbook Authors" (Richey 1931). Richey's premise was that textbooks represent the work of several persons ("for the most part, the results of evolutionary processes and not purely the creations of those who write them" (p. 67)). Nevertheless, he conceded that textbooks bore the stamp of individual writers ("are given character by the authors' conception of the purposes and nature of education" (p. 67)). Richey believed that a study which might possibly shed light on occupational groupings and institutional ties could therefore give some indication of the forces and interests that govern or are represented by the authors. Richey registered 1562 textbooks in the subjects of geometry, arithmetic, history and English, written by more than a thousand writers and published in the USA from 1876 to 1926. The publications were organized into five decades and grouped by subject. The authors were grouped according to their occupations. During the period as a whole, almost exactly 50 percent of the authors held teaching positions at levels ranging from the university to primary school; the others were either in school administration or no other occupation was found or reported (the last group comprised a total of 17 percent). This is quite different from the situation today, when the majority of the authors are full or part-time teachers. Another striking difference is that while only a small number of university teachers write schoolbooks today, this group dominated the field in the USA from 1876 to 1926, accounting for no less than 30 percent of textbook authors in the decade from 1917 to 1926.

The Norwegian Non-Fiction Writers' and Translators' Association took the initiative to conduct a thorough study dealing exclusively with textbook writers in 1990. Questionnaires were sent to 626 authors of primary and secondary school texts and responses were received from 361 of them. Behind the study lay acknowledgement of the fact that authorship is a complex process. The object of the questions was to chart the authors' assessment of central links in the writing process. The questionnaire consisted of three main parts: Authors' assessments of their collaboration with the publisher, of their relationship to consultants and of the correlation between textbook writing and teaching. On the basis of the questionnaires, ten writers were selected for a follow-up round based on personal interviews. The material from the study was processed at the University of Tromsø (Haavelsrud 1991). The results indicate that radical differences exist in initiation procedures and collaboration routines between authors and publishers. This is the case within individual publishing houses, from publisher to publisher and from author to author under otherwise identical conditions as regards subject and level. The authors were unanimous in their response to the question concerning which group they had in mind while writing - colleagues, teachers or pupils. Without exception, they answered pupils. There was somewhat less consensus about whether or not they considered teaching experience a prerequisite for writing textbooks, although the majority answered yes. One other striking result was that a clear majority felt there was considerable room for improvement before textbooks fulfilled their real potential as teaching media. The study also uncovered conspicuous dissatisfaction with much of the help provided by consultants. A remarkable discrepancy was noted in the amount of contact between authors and the various types of consultants. While specialists maintain on-going contact with authors more than 50 per cent of the time, less frequent contact is established with the consultants whose job it is to examine educational content, equality of status and language.

The modest incidence of literature on textbook writing may also be interpreted as an expression of how little emphasis researchers and textbook theoreticians have placed on the individual author's significance in the process. Quite a significant amount of research has been done on the language used in textbooks, but almost nothing has been done on methods of approach or how the texts have come about. The most important of the few contributions available stem from the USA. Two were published at 60 year intervals and, viewed together, they give a good picture of both the needs and possibilities in this field.

The first stands out due to its fresh approaches and enlightened conclusions. When the National Society for the Study of Education (NSSE) decided to devote their 1931 yearbook to textbooks, their intention was "to gather information about the methods and procedures which authors of textbooks in spelling, mathematics, reading, and the social studies designate as scientific." (NSSE Yearbook 1931, p. 27.) On the basis of a survey they conducted, Schorling and Edmonson tried to figure out how various textbook authors thought and worked. Their sources were the prefaces authors wrote to their textbooks, articles authors had written on their own fields and on education, the sources they listed in and in connection with their books, and teachers' manuals and other supplementary materials they might have written. The main objective was to investigate the claim that appeared in prefaces and advertisements throughout the 1920s, namely "the claim that scientific techniques had been systematically applied in creating the textbooks." (P. 27.) Based on the source material - i.e., the authorial sources mentioned above - which encompassed 246 titles, Schorling and Edmonson mapped out, subject by subject, the textbook writers' ideological backgrounds with special emphasis on their professional-scientific alignments. The results as regards the subject of social studies are representative for the entire study as far as the target group problem is concerned:

In the field of the social studies for the first six grades, some textbook writers recognize at least three problems: determination of content for a designated grade, adaptation of materials to the reading abilities of the children concerned, and provision for motivation and individual differences. *Apparently authors can secure slightly more objective help on the first of these problems than on the others.* (*My* emphasis.) (Schorling - Edmonson 1931, p. 55.)

According to the study, the most important reference materials used by textbook writers were other textbooks, children's books, curricula, specialist statements, research reports and psychology books. In addition, it turned out that "a few authors conduct personal investigations and experiments as a partial basis for their books" (p. 55). But the writers concluded that such activity "is in the pioneer stage, in which investigators are attempting to refine their techniques." (P. 55.)

The next time NSSE devoted an entire yearbook to the subject of textbooks was in 1990 (NSSE Yearbook 1990). There too, we find an article that deals with the role of authors: "Writing and Editing Textbooks" (Young 1990). The odd thing here is that hardly any research findings at all were produced during the 60-year interval between the two yearbooks. Nonetheless, the report is interesting as an account of an alternative to the survey-type of investigation. The author describes the revision and publication of a new edition of a biology text, which was first published in 1921 under the title *Biology for Beginners*. In 1978 it had 60 percent of the American market, and plans were made to revise and reissue it as *Modern Biology*. Work on the new 1981 edition took three years, and editor Jean Young gives a detailed account of its progress. Based on her description and the editor's general experience, certain conclusions are drawn about the role of the author. Young feels that the influence textbook writers exert on the form and content of their books differs significantly depending on subject and level. It appears an author's influence is directly proportional to the book's level of specialization and complexity. In 1947 James Otto became co-author of *Biology for Beginners*. He then proceeded to set a trend for other publishers' biology books which lasted for more than 40 years: "Few authors enjoy this kind of influence today. But those chosen for a specific educational slant largely determine what is in textbooks." (P. 75.) Viewed as a whole, Young's case is an account of a process whereby authors appear to have something between a primary and a secondary role:

> At Holt (the publishers), the science textbook authors were given ample opportunity to provide feedback on galleys sent to them for approval. However, editors have the last word because they are updated on feedback from customers, are aware of how

much and what can go into the book, get feedback from consultants, and are responsible to meet the bound book date. One author complained bitterly about "the short, choppy" sentences of the 1978 edition of MB. But, the editor had purposely rewritten the sentences to comply with demands from customers for a lower reading level. (Young 1990, p. 76.)

In one of her sharp criticisms of the publishing trade, Harriet Tyson-Bernstein goes so far as to assert that personal authorship is often no more than an illusion, even when an author's name appears on the cover. She refers to a review of Professor Clarence Ver Steeg's well-known history book *American Spirit*, where Robert Nisbet writes that:

"(...) neither Professor Ver Steeg nor his four teacher-consultants wrote the book. Every sign suggests it was assembled by anonymous word processors - human as well as mechanical - working ingloriously in the recesses of the publishing factory." (Tyson-Bernstein 1988, p. 197.)

Hélène Huot claims that publishing houses try to recruit authors primarily from among high-ranking school administrators; a conspicuous number of books are written by *inspecteurs généraux* or *inspecteurs départementaux* (Huot 1989, pp. 56-62).

There are also a few cases in which the development of textbooks has been placed in a somewhat less commercial and more scholarly context.

The first of these is particularly interesting in that it concerns the question of authorship. Henriette S. Verduin-Muller, a faculty member at the Geography Institute at the State University of Utrecht, has written an account of a textbook project in geography: "The Textbook: A Knowledge Product" (Verduin-Muller 1990). Her basic premise is that such radical changes take place when scientific knowledge is translated into educational (textual) knowledge that the textbook author's objectives and aspirations, as stated in the preface, are often put to shame. The books are knowledge products and they exist in their own world. If we want to examine that, it's not sufficient to analyse texts on a linguistic level, books on a technical level or user situations on an educational level. We must also determine how the books came into being. Indeed, an understanding of precisely that process may be considered indispensable for selecting the correct method:

> Finally, exploring the fundamental features of the process of constructing knowledge products, including textbooks, also implies in principle making methodologies available for textbook analysis. In other words, discovering the growth process also means getting a grip on the reverse process, namely that of analysis. (Verduin-Muller 1990, p. 13.)

Verduin-Muller asserts that the moment one deals with the textbook as a knowledge *product*, it becomes necessary to know and evaluate the production process that lies behind it. This has consequences for those who are going to write and develop the books; "product-directed thinking and production-directed thinking will go hand in hand once the right conditions are established" (p. 6). This train of thought lies behind a project led by one of Verduin-Muller's colleagues, Frances Slater: *People and Environments, Issues and Enquiries* (Slater 1986). Slater, a member of staff at the Faculty of Education at the University of London, instructs future teachers in how to teach geography. A publishing house asked her to select experts to write a geography book for upper-secondary school, "focusing on current developments in society and in geographical education. (...) The textbook manuscript emerged therefore as a network of closely interlocking subject-content and learning activities." (P. 9.) The unusual aspect of this approach was that it was not a publisher's editor but a university-affiliated teachers' training specialist who was in charge.

Verduin-Muller also points out that while countless manuals have been written on the art of writing well, the deluge of books "says nothing as to the recognition of the necessity to combine the art of writing and a knowledge of the subject in hand." (P. 4.) There are also books that give exhaustive presentations of the technical side of textbook production. The most recently published (as of December 1992) is François Richaudeau's *Manuel de typographie et de mise en page* (Richaudeau 1989). The book is based on the idea that authorship and book production can take place at one and the same desk today. Such books have been published in other countries as well. Typically, Young's article (see above, page 250) contains no references to literature that deals with the text as a literary problem. On the other hand, the author does refer to standard works such as David H. Jonassen's two-volume opus, *The Technology of Text* (1982).

In line with Verduin-Muller's view, there is probably support for the claim that no thorough study has ever been made of the relationship between knowledge and literature/book in the school's or the individual subject's popularization process. However, certain manuals go quite far in that direction. One example is Leif Becker Jensen's book, *Out of the Ivory Tower* from 1987. Becker Jensen teaches "Communication and Information" at the University Center of Roskilde. In 1988 he taught a graduating class in which some of the students submitted a manuscript for a geography textbook as their thesis.

One of the few examples of an author's own case history is Ludwig Helbig's "Identitätsprobleme eines Schulbuchmachers" (Helbig 1979). Helbig, a professor of political science in Ludwigsburg, wrote a social studies text which he felt became a shuttlecock in shifting political winds. In a strongly polemical article he rails about the randomness of the evaluation process: The book was included on lists of recommended titles one year but disappeared the next after elections brought about change of local government. When he set about looking for a pattern in the changes that had taken place over a period of several years, however, he found no correlation with party politics at either the local or the Bundesländer level. What he did find was inconsistencies in recommendations from different schoolbook commissions, in reviews in professional journals and in user reactions. The three groups - Schulbuchzensoren, Rezensenten and Der vorletzte Endeverbraucher (that is, the teacher) - are, according to Helbig, victims of what he calls *Ausgewogenheit*:

Motto: "Let what you say be simply 'Yes' or 'No'; anything more than this comes from evil." (From the Sermon on the Mount, Matthew 5:37.) Counter-motto (for someone writing a political science textbook): "Let what you say be simply 'Perhaps' or 'Maybe'." And even that is not AUSGEWOGEN. (*Ausgewogen* = 'equable', 'well thought-through', 'balanced', 'objective'. (Etc.))

(...)

I used to think there was one *Ausgewogenheit* for the CDU party and another for the SPD party, but it turns out that neither of the two Bundesländer where these parties have their respective strongholds, i.e., Rheinland-Pfalzen and Hessen, want anything to do with me. That is not always the case, however, a number of other CDU Länder and SPD Länder haven't rejected me at all. Here I am, I can do no more. (Helbig 1979, pp. 97 and 100.)

Helbig's confession indirectly highlights two relationships. First, his thoughts and feelings say something about why the possibilities for recruiting textbook writers are limited. Second, the article is a reminder that no systematic investigations have ever been made to examine either the theoretical basis for or the practice of the various approval systems.

A parallel to Helbig's disclosure may be found in the USA, where history book writer H. W. Bragdon gives a systematic account of the compromises and changes he had to make during the process of manuscript revision: "Ninth Edition Adventures with a Textbook" (Bragdon 1978).

There is also a most comprehensive collection of American articles which bears a title that points in the direction of (technical) text revision: *Designing Usable Texts* (Duffy - Waller 1985). The book contains two articles about the role of the author which are based on approaches not mentioned above. In the first, Elizabeth Orna contends that most textbooks authors complicate the textbook development process and make it more expensive (Orna 1985), while the other article outlines a training program for textbook writers (Felker - Redish - Peterson 1985).

Like many others, Patricia Wright (Wright 1985) contends (in the same book) that the publisher often has the final word on the texts, but Wright looks at this role in a new light: New production techniques are simplifying the transformation of text from manuscript to book, and that, she asserts, may diminish the role of the publisher. David R. Olson (Olson 1985) maintains that schoolbook texts create an illusion of autonomy, authority and objectivity. The illusion is based on tradition and technique more than personality. The rationale underlying Duffy and Waller's book is that a new theoretical foundation is required if the books - possibly - are to appeal to readers personally and directly: "(...) we lack a common language for discussing functional text." (Preface, p. XIV.)

In other words, little research has been done on textbook authors. Our lack of progress may have something to do with the attitude commonly adopted with respect to textbooks and textbook writers. Low status is a factor that occurs repeatedly in the articles of a more personal nature written by textbook authors themselves (Hellern 1988, Johnsen 1988). In one such article, Victor Hellern writes:

> Today's curricula usually contain such broad formulations, or teaching guides as they are called, that textbook writers and publishers actually enjoy great freedom. The problem is that only a few avail themselves of this freedom or have enough imagination to move off in new directions. (Hellern 1988, p. 32.)

Insofar as Hellern is right, one might ask whether it might not be worthwhile to investigate the reasons for this passivity. In 1983 the AFEF (Association Française des Enseignants de Français) organized a round-table debate on the subject. The proceedings were printed in the organization's journal (*Le Français Aujourd'hui* 70/1983), where one of the country's best-known textbook authors, Alain Pagès, gives a definition of something called "Autonomie du discours pédagogique." He is searching for a concept to prove that what appears in textbooks is something other than and more than popularized simplifications. It is not "un discours scientifique au rabais", and the author is not "un auteur d'articles qui simplifie ses connaissances". On the contrary, the writer is - or ought to aspire to be - one who brings *his* message in his own language and that of the genre: "Il est quelqu'un qui tend vers un message autonome et original". (Pagès 1983, p. 18.)

Such a self-description kindles expectations of an authorial role with higher status. But since the role of the textbook author remains strongly linked to other parts of the production process, "authorship" remains a question of the publisher's role as well.

Authors and Publishers

Frank A. Jensen (Jensen 1931) sent a questionnaire to 36 major US textbook publishers and received replies from 33 of them. The answers were "of such general character that they cannot be reported in tabular form, but typical replies are quoted as evidence for conclusions reached" (p. 80). The answers to the question of how the publishers obtained manuscripts showed first of all that they themselves took the initiative, usually through a network of regular contacts in the school system. Secondly, it was such personal contacts that resulted in books; an average of only five percent of the manuscripts submitted by "outsiders" were accepted. Jensen doesn't mention the number of unsolicited manuscripts compared to the number of recruited ones, but all the replies cited indicate a fair number. Yet it did not appear that publishers wanted to accept them for publication: "Practically no manuscripts submitted to our editorial department are accepted. We usually find the author we think likely to produce the type of textbook we want and then work with him in planning the book and in working it out." (P. 85.)

The responses to the question of to what extent and/or how manuscripts were revised by the publishing houses varied somewhat from one publisher to the next and may indicate different practices. In a few unusual cases manuscripts were not revised, but authors usually made changes as advised. Sometimes other authors were assigned the job of rewriting a text. Nearly all the replies indicated that the publishers' suggestions for revision were perceived as constructive criticism. In-house revision was a regular routine in one of the biggest companies, which replied:

> Most successful textbooks are made by publishers' editors and not by the authors. Ninety percent of all manuscripts that come into the publisher's office have to be rewritten from a to z. Either the author does this according to specifications agreed

upon with the publisher's editor, or the editor does it, or they both work together. The publisher's viewpoint is a national one; the author's viewpoint as a rule is a more or less local one. Textbooks have to be made to suit the needs of all the states. (Jensen 1931, p. 89.)

Jensen also inquired about "experimental editions", that is, the extent to which publishers produced sample texts for testing in selected classes with a view to further development. All the publishing houses answered the question, but: "It does not seem to be the general practice to print experimental editions to try in the schoolroom. Most publishers assume that the author has tried his technique and content in the classroom before putting his material into manuscript form." (P. 91.)

Jensen's observations concerning publishers' author recruitment, manuscript editing and experimental activities are more than 60 years old. No subsequent studies have been made to indicate any change in these practices. That does not necessarily mean that the situation is unaltered or little changed - we simply lack research. In the meantime, Jensen's observations were corroborated by the findings of Olson 1985, Wright 1985 and Young 1990. M. Brammer gives a comparable account in the article "Textbook Publishing" (Brammer 1967), in which he feels justified in claiming that editors and publishers are both the originators and the authors of textbooks. All these studies pertain to the USA, but the survey conducted by the Norwegian Non-Fiction Writers' and Translators' Association in 1990 (Haavelsrud 1991) indicates similar results in Norway on the same points.

Presumably, the strong publishing house tradition offers a partial explanation as to why most literature on the development of textbooks primarily focuses on the publishers' role, usually as it relates to the authorities, teachers and the market more than to writers. But there is probably another explanation as well: Most of the literature referred to here stems perforce from the academic community. Broadly speaking, such groups have traditionally combined a certain faith in the professional integrity of public regulatory mechanisms such as schools, curriculum plans and teachers, with a correspondingly strong skepticism toward developmental endeavors originating in the commercial sector.

The actual development of a text - the writing, rewriting and editing - is probably that aspect of textbook production as a whole which has received the least amount of attention in relation to the work it involves. The scanty research done so far offers very little basis for considering the opportunities and possibilities in the area. In consequence, I have chosen to add to this discussion a section which incorporates perspectives drawn from the field of fiction-writing.

Textbook Authorship from the Perspective of Fiction

The author-publisher issue has not occupied a very central position in literary research either. Nevertheless, it has traditionally held a certain place in literary history, and the increasing interest shown in the sociology of literature in recent years appears to be reinforcing this position. Drawing an analogy with the work of fiction writers might provide grounds for a closer scrutiny of several aspects of the situation pertaining to textbooks.

Of course, there are certain similarities. Publishers often contribute appreciably to the completion of fiction manuscripts. Independent consultants and the authors's "own" editor can influence and revise what the author has written to a significant degree. Fiction projects sometimes require a publisher to make a larger investment in terms of time and scope than textbook projects. On the other hand, we are dealing with a type of literature essentially comprising intellectual products which have not been solicited by the publishers. In principle, such products rarely get anywhere unless they display originality right from the outset. Although this point of view may be valid for a great deal of fiction, it certainly doesn't apply to the entire spectrum. The boundary lines are fuzzy: What about popular young people's series or crime series that regularly feature the same heroes? Such cases bear a strong resemblance to textbook publication. The publishers ask the authors to produce more of the same. The writing staff may be changed or replaced while Knut Gribb (hero of a popular Norwegian private investigator series) or, for that matter, an introductory course in chemistry, endures. A cynical extension of the parallel might then postulate that just as publishers give crime readers what they want, textbook editors take care to give their series a single, uniform profile for the following reason: "We give teachers what they want based on what we already know they want." A number of article writers contend that publishers have no option but to think this way, not least to protect their profits. The publishing house staff members who reply to such criticism usually say that teachers are a very conservative professional group. But we know too little about this point as yet; it involves not least the question of how books reach schools and how they are selected.

Language studies are of particular interest in this context as the field covers both poetry and prose. What is the ratio between fiction and non-fiction? What does each contribute to the effectiveness of foreign language-learning? How are they combined in mother-tongue language studies? Why do some publishers produce anthologies where each genre is put into a separate volume, while others combine many genres into one book? Literature anthologies for the upper secondary level show a striking divergence between 19th and 20th century books: The former contain a significantly stronger element of non-fiction prose. More recently, a distinction has emerged between anthologies for academic and vocational courses: The latter contain a noticeably stronger element of non-fiction. Why? It is not unreasonable to assume that the distribution of genres, and the way they are grouped, may be seen as ideological and educational expressions which, like the texts they incorporate, can mold pupils' perception of the relationship between language and reality.

As regards how the topic of school is dealt with in adult fiction, the attitudes expressed there must be seen as a reflection of some reality (Johnsen 1989a). I will now present some fiction texts which, although written by adult authors, also say something about *pupils'* reactions to textbooks. It is virtually impossible to find written pupil evaluations of textbooks in other contexts. Some of the texts discussed here may also provide examples of more complex authorial roles than those ordinarily associated with textbooks. The classic textbook depiction, insofar as it exists, consists of a declaration of love for particular books. This may be a vivid history book, such as when Martin A. Hansen allows the protagonist in his short story *Agerhønen* (1947) to get through some difficult times thanks to Nordahl Rolfsen's *World History for the Young* (1903). Martin A. Hansen subsequently re-addresses the same book and the same theme in an essay with the provocative title "The World Novel" (1956). The type of book most often applauded, however, is the reader, as it usually provides a longed-for counterbalance to factual studies. Thomas Mann opens his introduction to a special edition of Adalbert von Schamissor's classical story *Peter Schlemihl* with such praise. Typical for this type of expression is the way in which Mann emphasizes enjoyment and safety; reading was "not dangerous and almost a pleasure". Another typical feature, for Thomas Mann and his contemporaries, that is, was belief in the literary canon as an *educational criterion*: "(...) and although any comrade who proved uninterested or awkward here (i.e. in reading) could excel in any other special field, he was still perceived as an uncultivated being" (Mann 1935, p. 145).

Anyone attempting to register instances of textbook descriptions in fiction would probably discover a preponderance of negative attitudes. The most convincing example, and perhaps the best known today, involved a feature film that swept across the USA and Europe in 1990. It was Peter Weir's dramatization of Tom Schulman's story, *Dead Poets Society* (1989). One of the film's main themes is poetry and prose juxtaposed as two clearly separate modes of life. The setting is a school called Saint Andrew's, located somewhere in the USA, and the year is 1959. A new teacher, armed with poetry and experience of life, challenges the stifling conformity of the school. The contrast is illustrated by a scene where he tells everyone in the class to tear up the pages of their literary history books. Afterwards, the pupils leave the school building to go outside and read Keats aloud.

Although it is more difficult to find depictions that are complimentary to textbooks in general, they do exist. English poet and novelist Roy Fuller wrote a classic school novel, *The Ruined Boys*, published in 1959, the year in which Peter Weir's film is set. The protagonist is a new pupil at a public school called Seafolde

House. The author allows him to overcome the insecurity of being new through learning and books. The traditional school novel conflict between syllabus-cramming teachers/books and unwilling pupils is turned around; the main theme is the joy and strength that can be discovered through learning:

> As Gerald accumulated his new form's textbooks in his desk and on the shelf by it, he was seized with a vague but intense excitement, as though within his grasp was some key to happy existence, and he perceived that even in the most unlikely places there resided a mysterious fascination. He saw, for instance, that the last chapter of the algebra was on the Binomial Theorem, and the words struck him like the half-familiar words "Gobi Desert"might strike a traveller who against all expectations is in fact about to start off on an expedition to Central Asia.
> (...)
> In spite of the fears that had beset him as he made the change, he soon found that the work of the new form was not beyond his powers, and quite quickly *he could look back on last term as the owner of an electric train remembers his clockwork mouse.*
> (*My* emphasis; Fuller 1959, p. 92 in the 1987 edition.)

Even in light of the fact that we are dealing with the reality of a novel here, we would be too hasty if we failed to stop and ask what kind of school books were capable of evoking feelings like this in the 1950s. It is also necessary to know the circumstances surrounding Gerald's enthusiasm. Roy Fuller doesn't seem to allow his character to take refuge in books, since the protagonist eventually finds a place in school society. Nor is the school represented as idyllic, i.e., as a place where a love of books is acquired as part of the package; the teachers are neither great heroes nor great villains. The books, the textbooks, become the focal point in the life of a pupil with quite unexceptional gifts and a highly ordinary thirst for knowledge. Granted, we are dealing with fiction, but at least Fuller's novel demonstrates that a so-called realistic and strongly autobiographical story can deal with the concept of textbook authorship having moral and educational value. As the quotation shows, this train of thought couples mysticism and fantasy on one hand and factual knowledge on the other. In other words, the same kind of books that impede young people's development in Tom Schulman's story become instruments to break down barriers in Fuller's.

Roy Fuller's depiction can be seen as a literary hypothesis about textbooks' potential for combining vision and reality. In the world of reality there is at least one example of a particularly successful experiment which can be cited in support of such a hypothesis. I'm referring to Selma Lagerlöf's schoolbook about the Swedish nation and people, *Nils Holgersson's Wonderful Journey Through Sweden* from 1906. In his monograph about the book, Gunnar Ahlströhm writes about this combination in the chapter called "Schoolbooks and Poetry". The book owes its success to the fact that "knowledge acquires the wings of poetry" and accompanies the reader as a trustworthy guide on a journey through a world full of wonders. However, this "wonderful" world is no imaginary fantasy landscape - it *is* the kingdom of Sweden. Portrayals of events and scenes pour forth as though streaming from an "inexhaustible wellspring of imagination". (Ahlströhm 1942, p. 221.)

Selma Lagerlöf's book is the most internationally known of those in the tradition of "tales of lands and peoples". It was directly inspired by Nordahl Rolfsen's Norwegian readers and has roots and parallels in books such as Fénelon's *Les aventures de Télémaque*, Walter Scott's *Tales of a Grandfather* and Topelius' *Book about Our Country*. One French forerunner was the reader that affected the entire Third Republic - Bruno's *Le tour de France par deux enfants*.

One other series of tales was probably used in school as much as Bruno's during the same period: Alsace writers Erckmann and Chatrian's historical and geographical accounts for children and young people (*L'Ami Fritz* (1864); *Histoire d'un Conscrit de 1813* (1864)). The authorship was a symbiosis which at one and the same time demonstrated and combined various approaches to the task of writing "with a moral". In a biography subtitled *Le trait d'union* (The Hyphen), Jean-Pierre Rioux describes his view of the ideal educational "team":

One cannot count on dividing assignments as Erckmann once

described: "He (Chatrian) relieved me of all the problems which could get in the way of my writing." If one studies his correspondence and essays carefully, one will arrive at more subtle conclusions. L. Schoumacker has expressed it thus: "The idea always came from Erckmann alone; but it was developed by Erckmann and Chatrian jointly, then written by Erckmann alone, with subsequent editing together with Chatrian, before the latter took over responsibility for the further progress." (...) He (Erckmann) constructs scenes and plots. He then sends the drafts by letter or describes them directly to Chatrian, who makes suggestions for changes in both form and content. This interaction goes on continuously; chapters are revised at Erckmann's home almost daily. (Rioux 1989, p. 107.)

One might say that in the case of Erckmann-Chatrian, the combination of the fanciful and the down-to-earth was somehow transferred to the plane of authorship. Characteristic of their books, as of *Nils Holgersson's Wonderful Journey Through Sweden*, is the total confluence of fiction and non-fiction. This phenomenon should offer a useful point of departure for more thorough reviews of the fiction/non-fiction issue, on philosophical as well as educational grounds: To what degree ought or can the view that every depiction of reality must involve selection and interpretation have an impact on the writing of textbooks in general knowledge subjects and languages at the primary and lower-secondary level, for example, or perhaps even at higher levels?

The Argentine/French author Julio Cortázar has offered his own answer to such questions. He argues that all information should in principle be accessible to children who read. The only prerequisite is that the material be presented in an atmosphere expressive of a love of life; of faith and joy. In his book *Libro de Manuel* (Cortázar 1973), the author relates how the adults (family and friends) in a group of revolutionary socialists try to arrange the life of a boy named Manuel. They fail to find any suitable school books, so they comment on the texts found in the every day world around them, addressing themselves to Manuel. In this way *Libro de Manuel* becomes both a documentary novel and a recipe for textbooks (manuel(o) means textbook in French and Spanish). The main objective is not the conveyance of knowledge alone, but also that which curricula would call the "conveyance of values", and Cortázar's critics call "indoctrination". The text moves in a rather fixed direction; the boy is supposed to read himself to a faith in life and develop "the urge to love and play, and the need for a worthy life on earth not dominated by elbows and dollars." (Cortázar 1974, pp. 8-9.) Such a statement of objectives would hardly be found in any country's curriculum guidelines. But the reality contained in the statement doesn't deviate much from the goals that underlie such guidelines. The anomaly arises when Cortázar, in his capacity as a linguistically and philosophically trained writer, uses new words to describe the new reality around him, whereas the textbooks continue to use the old words.

Cortázar's textbook took shape almost overnight within a circle of family and friends. It became a kind of manifestation of the educational possibilities of the extended intellectual family. Yet even if we disregard the personal aspect of the development of such a book, it is clear that no production, distribution or consumer apparatus anywhere would approve a textbook designed according to Cortázar's pattern today. However, that certainly doesn't mean that his model or, for that matter, the other models of a more literary nature that have been mentioned previously, need remain untried in the field of author/publisher collaboration. Experimentation in this area probably never became more comprehensive than it was in Jensen's 1931 investigation because we still know too little about the consequences of such solutions.

Perspectives

There is something stereotyped and rigid about the few investigations and the modest number of articles in this field. The literature has dealt with authors' backgrounds and/or their relationship to publishing houses. The term background generally refers to a run-down on the authors' educational and professional qualifications, more than to their sex, age or place of residence. As regards authors' relationships to publishing houses, it is natural to compare the studies with the investigations that examine the question of textbook-centered versus teacher-centered teaching. As mentioned elsewhere, it is sometimes tempting to believe that such investigations are motivated by the desire to expose teacher dependence (see page 177). In the same way, the prevailing view in the literature on textbook authors is that they have become increasingly more dependent on and at the mercy of powerful publishers' editors (exceptions from this attitude may be found in Cronbach 1955 and Pagès 1983). There are very few studies of obvious topics such as the process of textbook writing, the relationship between one or several authors or the relationship between an author's name and book distribution. Facts from such fields might provide sufficient grounds for comparative quality studies, for example.

The distribution of different procedures and materials within such a modest body of literature is an interesting topic. The most common approach is the use of questionnaires, which has dominated the field for generations (Richey 1931, Haavelsrud 1991). The questionnaires have occasionally been combined with interviews (Haavelsrud 1991). There are also several detailed case stories (Bragdon 1978, Helbig 1979, Moffett 1988, Young 1990), which provide useful material for shedding light on authors' independence of approval systems and/or publishing houses. Prefaces written by authors are still another source, if possible, in combination with any articles in which the authors may have commented on their backgrounds or objectives (Schorling - Edmonson 1931). One objection concerns the fact that it is quite possible to write a preface that states specific objectives without those same objectives ever being fulfilled in the book. When supplemented by other analyses, the prefaces may directly or indirectly provide signals about attitudes and personalities, thus elucidating the metadiscourse used in the books, for example (Crismore 1984; see page 205). One might compare the situation to that of church records, which list nothing except who has been *registered* as parents, while this narrowing to the purely formal facts does not prevent geneological research.

Such reports and independent articles have usually been written in essay form. One essay which is outstanding for both its scope and depth is Robert Bierstedt's contribution to Cronbach 1955. It involves an analysis undertaken by a sociologist. Bierstedt bases his essay on theory rather than on any special collection of data. He draws up the framework for a social science-oriented analysis of textbook authorship written from the perspective of the entire literary institution more than a generation before this same phenomenon became a key word in the world of literary research. His summary is cited in the present context because it underlines the complexity inherent in an analysis of the authorial role and because it says something about how constructive it might prove to be to take this particular approach as a point of departure for examining the whole:

> We have noticed several social and economic factors which determine the selection of textbook writers. We have attended also to the cultural influences, of both a situational and an ideological character, which enter into the transmission of a culture, by way of the textbook, from one generation to the next through the institution of education. Some of these factors are too profound and some of them are too subtle for any analysis short of that supplied by a sociology of knowledge. Others, like the influence of national allegiances, have been treated in many competent studies, and are matters of continuing concern to statesmen and educators and authors alike. Some, finally, are unique, and these appear because the authors of textbooks occupy unique statuses in a society. (Bierstedt 1955, p. 128.)

Publishers, Authorities, Curricula and Teaching

First of all, the development of a textbook presupposes the production of text. In physical terms, this work is directly related to writing and responding to writing. As pointed out earlier, there are few investigations of or reports on exactly how this process works.

Second, the development of a textbook entails that text production is constantly influenced by given external parameters that dictate the objectives and potential of the final product: School systems, curricula and publishing house practices. The term "the development of textbooks" is used in a third sense as well. In many countries today, the external parameters are flexible enough to allow and even encourage "development" in the sense of innovation. (Walker 1991.)

The point at issue is how personal, institutional and traditional interests influence development. Different forces will exert different influences at different times during the development process. For example, curricula will most likely exert more influence than the publisher in the early stages of the process, although this situation will gradually shift.

Another issue is that of stability. The school situation, curricula and publisher policy may remain stable for quite some time. Yet schools and plans can change in the face of shifting political and educational winds which do not necessarily coincide. Publishing house policy and practice will also be influenced by factors such as market conditions and approval schemes. These influences need not be synchronized with other influences. On the other hand, generally weak local and national economies that affect school budgets will most likely influence both the school situation and publishing policy. We see this situation in a number of countries in the early 1990s.

These problems are hard to examine due to their scope and complexity. One might well ask whether there is any point in studying the development of textbooks - or of any particular textbook - in light of isolated factors such as author, curricula and publisher, since they are all related to one another. The situation is complex because each factor influences the others, based on its own input factors which vary from group to group. The school system and its courses, levels, class sizes, teacher competency, number of periods and examinations are all fixed entities. Teachers, however, exercise considerable latitude. Curricula are to be respected and followed, but their influence merely as teaching guides for individual subjects is expanding steadily. Some people contend that publishers' books exert more influence than plans and teachers. Still, the use of textbooks is not obligatory. It all boils down to the fact that from concept to desk, books are developed and chosen by people who interpret guidelines. It is therefore interesting to know whether any studies have investigated the following questions: Are there historical patterns which show the relationship of these elements to one another? Are there any traditions of interpretation that prevail despite formal changes in the system? If so, do theory and practice differ to the same extent in all the groups?

Few studies have been conducted in this area, but the number of articles written on the subject may indicate that the field is deserving of study. Articles of this type are occasionally written by teachers or authors, but more often by parents or publishers, although researchers sometimes attempt to put pieces together to form a pattern. Some of the contributions from the researchers provide sufficient material to comprise building blocks, although the foundation may still be lacking.

Publishers

As mentioned, the number of articles written by publishers is greater than the corresponding number of contributions written by textbook authors. Opinions of this type are often published when a public debate arises about a particular textbook. Publishers wrote a number of articles in the wake of Frances FitzGerald's criticism of American publishers' single-minded quest for profits (see page 98). As a typical example, I have selected a lecture delivered by John H. Williamson, president of the Silver Burdett Company, to the 1979 textbook conference held by the Library of Congress (Williamson 1981). The lecture was entitled "Textbook Publishing: Facts and Myths." An inventory of the "myths" on which Williamson based his lecture gives indirect insight into the forces at work in the relationship between publisher and system. I will not delve any further into the "facts" that Williamson cites to dispel what he calls myths. They are presented in abbreviated form in parentheses below each point. My primary intention has been to register areas in which we should learn more about how forces work with and/or against one another:

1   The textbook industry is enormous. (Not at all; total gross annual sales to school systems in the USA are ca. USD 700 million. The Xerox Corporation alone has a turnover of 8 times as much.)

2   Schools spend a lot of money on textbooks. (No; an average of 0.75 % of a school's budget is used to buy textbooks.)

3   Textbook publishers have large profit margins. (No; the average corresponds to a normal savings account interest rate.)

4   Publishers are exclusively motivated by profit. (The market is limited and specialized and must therefore be served on its own terms. Consequently, textbook publishing personnel are therefore often recruited from the school system.)

5   Textbook publishers refuse to print inexpensive unbound editions. (Experience shows that schools don't want books that wear out quickly.)

6 Unbound editions are much cheaper than bound. (The price difference is minimal.)

7 Publishing personnel without any real teaching experience write the books, while sales personnel determine the contents. (Content, level, and design are determined by the author and publisher in cooperation. The opinion of the sales department is taken into consideration; sometimes it is accepted, other times rejected.)

8 Publishers have a broad network of contacts in schools and can control what happens in the classroom. (Publishers must find their way through a maze of educational bureaucracy before finally arriving in the classroom. A textbook's influence is in the hands of the teacher.)

9 Textbooks are one of society's most powerful political instruments. (History shows that legislators, planners and lobbyists have been frustrated in their efforts to control development through textbooks.) (Williamson 1981, pp. 38-39.)

Readily available statistics will most likely bear out the facts and views Williamson presents in the two first points of his entries. The situation is more obscure as regards the latter parts, however, and his claims are more debatable. Yet the point here is not to switch back and forth between "fact" and "myth", but to demonstrate how decisive a publisher's role must necessarily be in the life of a textbook from its inception to the student's desk. This key role is double insofar as the publisher is the sender, receiver and intermediary between sender and receiver, all at the same time. A publishing house receives regulations, curricula, manuscripts, consultant evaluations, teacher responses and sales statistics, and it publishes books. At the same time, a publisher acts as an intermediary between the various parts of the school system because its editors have to interpret plans, directives and needs in light of their interaction with authors and teachers. This interpretation finds its way to the end-user in the school system through textbooks.

It is not uncommon to find textbook editors who have taught school, written textbooks and been actively involved with teaching plans and consultancy work for publishers and/or the authorities. In this way they serve "their own interests" to some extent by creating values based on educational ideals, and they serve the publishing company's interests to some extent by generating financial values.

This predicament is discussed in Michael W. Apple's lengthy essay "The Political Economy of Text Publishing" (Apple 1984). The author also refers to a more comprehensive study made in the early 1980s (Coser - Kadushin - Powell 1982), which concludes that most executive positions are held by men, that few editors apply for these positions because of any special interest in education, and that nearly 75% of them started in sales or marketing. All these points can probably be challenged when looking at Norwegian publishing in the 1990s. With regard to American publishing traditions, however, Apple concludes that chief editors:

> will be predominantly male, thereby reproducing patriarchal relations within the firm itself. Second, their general background will complement the existing market structure that dominates text production. Financial capital, short-term perspectives, and high profit margins will be seen as major goals. A substantial cultural vision or the concerns associated with strategies based on symbolic capital will necessarily take a backseat, where they exist at all. (P. 313)

Apple's distinction between financial and symbolic capital stems from Frenchman Pierre Bourdieu's theory on the reproduction of knowledge in school and culture. Apple uses this distinction to differentiate between the main types of publishers. Publishers motivated by financial capital think in terms of short-term profits; publishers seeking primarily to accumulate symbolic capital have long-term goals. Profits are equally important to the second group, but it will tend to allow more latitude for experimentation and risk-taking.

Apple points out that this kind of distinction is theoretical and implies a gross over-simplification of the facts. The production and sale of books are primarily influenced by the financial capital motive, but also by a number of conditions that in addition will vary from one publisher to the next, regardless of type (see Goldstein, page 306). There is:

> a whole array of differences concerning the kind of technology that is employed by the press, the bureaucratic and organizational structures that coordinate and control the day-to-day work of the company, and the different risks and monetary and marketing policies of each. Each also refers to important differences in relations with authors in time scheduling and, ultimately, in what counts as "success". *Behind the commodity, the book, thus stands a whole set of human relations.* (P. 310; *my* emphasis.)

There is another argument that also appears to support Apple's view. Textbooks are based on formalized guidelines. The subject per se, government policy and the curricula provide frameworks that span the range from proposal to directive. B. Cooper investigated changes over time in the subject of mathematics, using textbooks as his main source of material (Cooper 1984). He concluded that change could be explained only through an awareness of the many professional, political, educational and cultural interests in play at any given time. Based on this, he constructed a model for analyzing changes in school subjects. Textbooks play a central role as integral parts of a system in which all parts must be seen in relation to one other. The main function of the textbook is to lead the student into a paradigm. Here Cooper builds further on Kuhn's scientific theories. Different elements of the subject represent different interests and at any given time some of these will stand in opposition to others, as will be evident in the textbooks:

> During periods of scientific normalcy, the textbooks may vary in degree of difficulty and emphasis, but not in substance. During periods of scientific revolution, on the other hand, new textbooks are written, based on new substance. In contrast,

Cooper is of the opinion that subgroups with conflicting views are the status quo in the subject. He also believes that representatives of the subject at university level have little opportunity to influence the subject as taught in school. The school subject's teachers will pursue their own interests in designing the school subject. Many user groups will also be interested in the subject as taught in school and in the design of the textbooks. One must therefore be aware of the simultaneous existence of manifold perspectives and interests if one is to shed light on subject-related changes in textbooks. (Engelsen 1990, p. 171.)

Cooper's point of view, as well as Apple's, would imply that publishers wanting to succeed in the market do not venture into "innovations" without taking care that the books first of all preserve this *status quo* of each subject. Critics claiming that the textbook tradition is one very constant demonstration of such a compromise, with incorporation as an issue stronger than that of change (Johnsen 1989), have been able to argue not least from the material supplied by investigations and practice of approval systems.

Approval

Some countries have no official approval scheme. Although others have such schemes, the rules and their enforcement vary. It is difficult to show any pattern in or reason for the differences. For example, Norway and Finland have such schemes; Denmark and Sweden do not. In a small country such as Iceland, and in a totalitarian system such as the former GDR, where the state produced all the textbooks, production implies approval. About half the states in the USA practice some form of approval scheme - but that doesn't mean the other states exercise no censorship. The same dichotomy exists in Switzerland. All the German *Länder* have approval schemes, but the rules differ significantly. France has an official approval scheme, but its practice is quite liberal. Great Britain and the Netherlands have no such systems, while there are very well-developed approval schemes in Austria and Japan.

The information above covers the countries about which I was able to find information. A preliminary survey prepared by the Institute for Textbook Research in Vienna is especially thorough in its coverage of German-speaking areas (Bamberger 1992). The tendency in recent years has moved toward reduction or discontinuation. Sweden discontinued approval in 1991. Finland is considering a new development system to replace post-production approval. Norway's scheme will either be discontinued or re-vamped in 1993. Austria is currently (December 1992) considering various alternatives.)

Besides the publisher, the senders and receivers in the textbook process include the authors (in part), (school) authorities, and teachers/students. There can be no talk of double roles here as there may be in the case of editors. In most countries, authorities indirectly disclaim any responsibility for processing "feedback" because their approval schemes operate in advance. Teachers and students are certainly free to send feedback to publishers, although they rarely take the initiative to do so. When they do, however, the feedback rarely has anything to do with the *development* of textbooks.

The publisher's role as intermediary is reinforced in a number of countries in that the publisher also supervises the contact between the approval authorities and the authors. In Norway, the editor appoints an adviser, who is in turn assisted by officially appointed consultants in matters regarding language, methodology and equal status between the sexes. In time, editors usually build up a good rapport with the members of the specialist boards who mediate the contact. This promotes textbook approval consensus, which often endures and influences new curricula.

The most pressing argument in favor of approval schemes is the need for quality assurance, especially in relation to school legislation and curricula.

The oft-heard arguments against approval schemes fall into two categories: The scheme is viewed as an offshoot of autocratic/totalitarian regimes which have outlived themselves and the scheme works against teacher freedom and textbook development.

The most complete survey of the pros and cons connected with the most common forms of approval may be found in "NOU 1978:

26: Teaching Materials in Schools and Adult Education." Many solicited comments are included, and the committee in charge of the report evaluates each point in detail. The conclusion begins thus:

> The above cites a number of opinions on the investigation, evaluation and potential approval of teaching materials. They differ radically as regards what is considered to be the goal of such activity and what the effects - or side-effects - are or may be. The various bodies' evaluations have differed at different times but have also differed from each other at the same point in time. Many of the opinions solicited have pointed out factors that favor a particular solution - without drawing conclusions. (NOU 1978: 26, p. 220.)

The committee's own final conclusion reflects this uncertainty. A majority of five were in favor of suspending the scheme; a minority of three wanted a "greatly reformed textbook approval scheme" (p. 223). The politicians went with the minority, and in 1984 a new set of textbook approval rules were enacted. They did not, however, represent any great reform.

There is one very comprehensive Norwegian study based on material of this sort, Bjarne Bjørndal's study of textbook didactics (Bjørndal 1982). As a part of his study, the author requested the National Council for Primary and Lower Secondary Education's permission to review a significant number of textbook evaluations. Bjørndal and his associates went through a total of 182 consultant evaluations of textbooks' educational relevance/didactics since the 1970s. The subjects dealt with were Norwegian, natural science, social studies, mathematics and religion. They found the investigations were mainly, if not entirely, related to subject matter, not educational theory. On the one hand, they found a lack of central evaluation criteria, while on the other they criticized the lack of consistency practiced in connection with the criteria that were employed. Inconsistency is present when one main objective (for example, subject content) is emphasized at the expense of others (for example, didactic and/or linguistic levels). It is possible to interpret the results of Bjørndal's study as an expression of an educational policy position (the "knowledge school" as opposed to the "work school"). If this is the case, it is most likely due to the fact that we tend to fractionalize investigations into main elements such as language, subject matter, equal status between the sexes and educational theory. This type of fractionalization is also common in other systems. One critic in the USA is the renowned readability and textbook researcher Jeanne S. Chall. She investigated the development of one series of readers over a period of 35 years (Chall 1977), looking at it in relation to studies that showed a sinking tendency in the level of student knowledge acquisition. One of her conclusions was that although picture counts, readability tests, and other such measures may yield important data, textbooks have a total character that cannot be measured by their separate parts alone. From this point of view, the question is whether, in cognitive and scientific terms, evaluation systems like Norway's are not more "atomistic" than "holistic" in their approach. If so, practice and theory are out of harmony. For the time being, however, no other studies exist to illuminate the question.

Alain Choppin has made a thorough historical study of the freedom of choice and the approval of French textbooks (Choppin 1986-87). The authorities sought to centralize control during two periods; in the century following the revolution of 1789 and from 1940 to 1945. Since WW II the country has kept to a system that was originally established in 1881: Teachers in primary and lower secondary schools are free to choose books after consulting among themselves, then their booklists are sent to the county authorities (le département) for largely pro forma approval. At the upper secondary level, teachers choose freely after consulting among themselves. More recent debate in France about the choice of textbooks revolves around two issues, both of which only partially pertain to the question of approval. First, who pays for schoolbooks at the primary and lower secondary levels? (Up until 1977, the local municipalities paid; since then the national government has footed the bill.) Second, what does the term "textbook" actually entail? (The development of education technology has come a long way in French cities. More general secondary literature, so-called "livres parascolaires", is also gaining ground and seems to be blurring the distinction between traditional textbooks and other genres - see page 307.)

There is a considerable amount of American literature available on the subject of textbook approval, most of it in the form of articles. The earliest article is probably also the most lengthy one. It is W.L. Coffey's survey of textbook approval in the USA as it was organized in 1931 (Coffey 1931):

> Every state in the union, as this chapter discloses, has passed textbook laws. Several states have placed the control of textbooks in the hands of boards with little restriction. The majority of the states, however, have placed more or less limitation upon the rights of officers who have been given authority to determine adoption, sale, and the use of textbooks. (P. 249.)

Coffey does not discuss the control scheme as an ideological instrument, but his survey covers vast fields. Since it is extremely detailed and since there may be considerable variation from state to state, Coffey's survey probably offers the most comprehensive overview available of the different reasons for and forms of statutory regulations, along with a look at the vastly different ways of administrating control. It demonstrates indirectly, for example, differences in approach (state/region/local government) and the choice of persons/groups to conduct the investigations which must clearly spring from different attitudes toward educational objectives.

A survey of this type may serve as the basis for further study. One example is Tulley and Farr's analysis of the laws in 22 states (Tulley - Farr 1985). Another is the same authors' contribution to a special issue of *Book Research Quarterly* which deals with textbook approval (1/2 1985). The latter article discusses the relationship between approval and quality enhancement. All in all, the authors find a preponderance of negative correlations as regards this point, as does another prominent article published by W. Fox in "The Boston Globe" that same year. Fox argues that publishers will neither update nor improve textbooks as long as the existing textbook approval schemes prevail. In his view, approval systems act as free insurance.

Some American studies have investigated how approval committees work. D.A. Powell grouped the factors influencing such committees into five categories: the members' political affiliation, the publishers' commitment, pilot schemes, the committees' work procedures and the members' educational orientation (Powell 1985). Building in part on this study, a group of researchers at the Center for the Study of Reading at the University of Illinois compiled a guidebook for members of approval committees on how to evaluate textbooks (Dole - Rogers - Osborn 1987). It was tested against controls in four different states. The results were largely dependent upon the committee's leadership, the general interest level, the time available and the supplementary guidance provided.

A comparable picture of epidemic randomness has been drawn by J. Dan Marshall, who investigated the approval system used in Texas (Marshall 1991). As regards the significance of *the constellation of persons* involved in the approval process, he found that "we are rather late in discovering our professional ignorance of the phenomena surrounding textbook selection and adoption." (Marshall 1991, p. 74.)

It will always be possible to some extent to describe the financial and political framework that dictates textbook parameters. It is harder to discern the motives of those who will ultimately be making the decisions. This is difficult not only at the complex level of the individual teacher, but also higher up in the system. Government ministries, departments and sub-committees have developed a number of democratic mechanisms to promote change as well as to preserve the status quo, depending for the most part on the level of commitment among the bureaucrats/bureaucracy involved. *One* such mechanism is the delegation of authority, which often involves long-term processes which may delay decisions. The mechanisms often demand perseverance and resources, and may therefore favor those who already *are* and *have* (Langfeldt 1991).

Another recent U.S. study surveys the current situation and indicates that things may not have changed much since Coffey wrote his article in 1931. James R. Squire (Squire 1985) shows that in 1984, 22 US states practiced the adoption of textbooks on a state-wide basis and that the same states accounted for nearly 50 % of publisher revenues. It is remarkable that with the exception of one state, all 22 states are located in the southwest, southeast and western United States. Otherwise, "the basic list of adoption states has not changed over the past two decades, although certain changes in state practices have occurred" (p.13).

One of Squire's main points is that non-state control is by no means equivalent to free choice. He says:

> But if nonadoption, or so-called open territory states, account for 52.67% of industry revenue, the procedures for screening and selecting do not differ markedly from those followed in state adoptions. Most of the large cities in "open territory" have established systematic procedures for reviewing textbooks on a rotating sequence. (Squire 1985, p. 13.)

American articles typically deal with the problem of textbook approval in conjunction with two other factors, i.e., market and publisher. This is particularly relevant to the theme of this chapter insofar as markets are ideology-oriented and publishers are the bearers of ideology. (See pages 271 and 304.)

A retrospective study written in the form often referred to as a case story is a very special approach. The few existing examples are all typically polemical. One of them, however, is particularly remarkable in its scope, thoroughness and exceptional combination of autobiographical and quasi-scientific methodology: James Moffett's *Storm in the Mountains: A Case Study of Censorship, Conflict, and Consciousness* (Moffett 1988).

Moffett wrote the book in response to a controversy that is considered to have been the most violent and extensive textbook protest action in the history of the United States. It took place in Kanawha County, West Virginia, during the 1974-75 school year and it involved English literature textbooks printed by a number of major publishing houses. In his book *Censors in the Classroom* Edward B. Jenkinson describes the same controversy, as well as other censorship attempts east and west of the Mississippi (Jenkinson 1979).) Moffett edited a series called *Interaction*, which was severely criticized. More than 10 years later, he wrote an account of what actually happened, partly in an effort to give his own version (which he emphasizes) and partly "to explain how this case may illuminate phenomena bigger today than then" (Preface, p.x). His account covers interviews with the leaders of the protest action as well as an analysis of the objections to the literary texts. This he based in the main on a 500-page report from the Board of Education, that is, the board of approval where the controversy was played out. In addition, the author attempts to give a socio-psychological interpretation of the causes underlying the protest action. An outside reader might describe the anthology as "open" and "liberal" and the protesters as fundamentalist fanatics when it came to certain issues like religion and sex.

The book was reviewed in an issue of *The American Journal of Education*. The reviewer, George Hillocks Jr., played a key role in the investigations that followed in the wake of the controversy, which involved personal conflict, defamation and so on. He points out that Moffett had not interviewed the main leader, had not availed himself of the taped records of the meetings, and had made no attempt to investigate "the protesters' objections, which might have allowed an understanding of the religious and philosophical assumptions underlying them" (Hillocks 1991, p. 269). For Hillocks, the case was more a disclosure of deep conflicts in the United States between fundamentalist Christian ideology and what he calls "secular humanism", than a story of some intolerant parents' need to curb progressive innovators.

The story of *Storm in the Mountains* is a new and perhaps prophetic version of the conflicts related to history book revision. The case could also have been discussed in the chapter on ideological studies, but is incorporated here because it relates to the philosophy of textbook development. The point of departure was to some extent paradoxical. *Interaction* was a particularly ambitious literary project for the Houghton Mifflin Publishing Company. It included tapes, films, games, activity cards and anthologies. Moffett, known in the United States and Scandinavia as a pioneer in the field of process-oriented composition training, was an early critic of mother tongue textbooks (Moffett 1968). When he accepted the job of editing *Interaction*, it was partly because it enabled him to meet the enemy on its own territory. The series was intended to liberate students from textbook material by offering so much information that anyone could orient himself "in a rich variety of materials not produced especially for schools" (Moffett 1988, p. 214). In short, one might say that he wished to realize the idea of the individualized multi-media approach in a single series for a single school subject. In this sense this was, in financial terms, a bold idea even for the affluent society from which it originated. Its objectives and solutions may thus be perceived as a rare example of textbook development as a research project per se. When the series was launched, the president of the Houghton Mifflin Company announced that the series was "the largest program of school materials ever done till then" (p. 4). Little insight was gained into the series' potential or effects because the protest action against it was so effective. Nonetheless, this literary series (*Interaction*) and its biography (*Storm in the Mountains*), separately and perhaps especially together, comprise something so unique as an attempt to capture the pulse of a particular time and climate based on the "textbook world." The commercial results and/or interpretational controversies (Hillock versus Moffett) do not prevent this story from providing an important perspective on methodology. In particular, it raises the issue of whether it is possible to find methodologies that can relate research studies of an ideological nature, for example, more closely to a realistic user situation while the books are being developed and launched.

Approval and the Textbook Concept

The example of *les parascolaires* (see page 307) shows how school policy can affect publishers' operations - in intended and unintended ways - and, similarly, how publishers' solutions may come to influence teaching. If this influence acts in the "wrong" direction, school authorities can intervene by effecting new measures. Yet certain requirements must be met if those measures are to be effective. The most important ones are related to the textbook concept and the explicit or implicit definitions which, for example, exempt books from/commit them to an approval scheme or do/do not require the purchase of a full class set.

It cannot be said that the textbook concept has been subject to any official re-assessment or upgrading consonant with media development in western countries, although the need for this is apparent in a number of contexts. In his report on Norwegian written culture in an educational perspective, Eiliv Vinje calls for a revision of the textbook concept:

> The school system has undergone a development that provides ample opportunity for examining the traditional textbook concept. But this is where we find a paradox that is a little disturbing and a little discomforting. In light of the development outlined above, it is amazing to see how constant the textbook concept has remained. It hasn't changed since the war, despite the rapid development of the school. (Vinje 1990, p. 216.)

Kåre Skadberg has explained how the Norwegian Language Council works when it examines the language used in textbooks (Skadberg 1987). The quotation below reveals the uncertainty that prevails about the concept. It also indirectly reveals the randomness caused by the lack of clarity:

> Supplementary and complementary books of various types have flooded the market. Workbooks, theme booklets, reference books, exercise books and AV aids have thus gained a far more dominant role in the classroom situation. It is now actually possible for teachers to teach without using one *main* (*my* emphasis) textbook in a subject.
>
> It hasn't been considered feasible or desirable to establish a public approval scheme that would cover all published and unpublished teaching material, like the Language Council has advocated. *It has been decided to limit the approval scheme to the (most) important textbooks.* (Skadberg 1987, p. 131; *my* emphasis.)

Skadberg also points out that the growing quantity of exercise books and supplements must of necessity lead the council - not least due to capacity problems - to exclude from scrutiny the manuscripts for pamphlets produced in large print runs. Consequently, publishing houses send few such manuscripts to the council for approval. This "incompleteness" is also a sign of inconsistency, at least if one presumes that the texts in the exercise books and the other supplements convey knowledge and influence pupils in somewhat the same way as the texts in approved textbooks. We don't know much about this last aspect, as little research has been done on methods of use or the time spent on supplementary literature.

At first glance, it seems obvious that the significance of this would differ from subject to subject (Pöggeler 1985). In a comprehensive study of supplements and workbooks in several subjects, Jean Osborn and Karen Decker nonetheless ask whether there isn't a "workbook genre" across traditional subject boundaries (Osborn - Decker 1990). Studies like this, which target workbooks as an independent type of textbook, can be counted on one hand. Perhaps the most comprehensive of them is from Austria. Marina Moosbrugger studied the exercises in textbooks at 1st and 3rd grade levels. She demonstrated first of all that the number of exercises has increased so rapidly that many "textbooks" now bear a strong resemblance to "exercise books". Second, she found a clear pattern in the relationship between curricula and exercises. The correspondence was poor at several levels, especially as regards degree of difficulty. Moosbrugger drew a conclusion from this, upon which she has based a development program:

> The discrepancy between curricular requirements and their fulfillment, e.g., their manifestation in the form of textbooks, leads one to assume that the criteria used to check the correlation between curricula and textbooks took little, if any, account of the exercises. It would therefore be worthwhile to apply criteria that also took the exercises into account before approving the books. When designing new textbooks, it is possible to avoid the problems due to entrenchment in traditions by using an interdisciplinary forum consisting of representatives from research, didactics, educational science and the school. (Moosbrugger 1985, p. 127.)

There is a distinct disparity between researchers' interest in basal texts on the one hand, and supplementary literature on the other, viewed in light of the role distribution between the two types of books in the classroom. In Norwegian primary and lower secondary schools, arithmetic exercise books functioned as basal texts far into the latter half of this century. A stir was created in 1959 when Helga Stene presented an analysis of sex-role patterns in an exercise book in arithmetic. The book contained 540 exercises, of which almost 200 involved persons of a particular sex. Of those 200, only four involved female protagonists. (Stene 1981.) Theoretically, an approval committee responsible for equality between the sexes need not intervene in this case on purely formal grounds, because the book was an exercise book. In other words, the system is vulnerable in a real as well as in a formal sense. If we assume that books of the "parascolaires" type will gain general, universal acceptance, the authorities in the different countries would find it difficult to intervene rapidly - even if they wanted to. First, the use of approved textbooks is not mandatory. Second, the right to copy and reproduce texts is in the process of being sanctioned by law in most countries. And third, there are a number of countries that don't have national approval schemes. In practice, in the near future, market development will therefore probably be equally contingent on two other conditions, i.e., the needs and wishes of those who select the books, and municipal and state finances.

Goldstein 1978, Neumann 1989, Huot 1989, Apple 1990, and Apple - Christian Smith 1991 are among the few individual authors who have tried to present more holistic analyses of the political aspects of textbook production and the market. Like NSSE's collection of articles on the same topic (NSSE 1990), they all express the view that publishers' practices and policies from the 1970s and 1980s did not serve the objectives for educational innovation which were concurrently incorporated into curricula and implemented *inter alia* through changes in teacher education and school structure. (Goldstein proposes government subsidization of publishing houses' development work.)

One potential field of study might be the posing of questions that would confirm or reject such a view. With regard to major publishing houses with extensive programs: What percentage of the profits from the textbook section is spent on other departments?

What percentage of the profits goes to polishing and revising existing series, and what percentage is spent on the development of major new series? How much of the innovation budget is spent on the writing of single, independent books, and how much goes to series or packages aimed at several grades/levels/subjects/functions?

We can only conjecture about the degree to which the answers to such questions directly stimulate publishers' willingness or ability to modernize. Perhaps we need approaches that - regardless of publisher policy - place the industry within a perspective that also sheds light on conditions they themselves can neither keep track of nor control.

Curricula and Teaching

Publishing houses play a more modest role in respect of curricula and teaching. Generally speaking, curricular planning committees have been dominated by practicing teachers. The research community has rarely been represented on these committees in Norway, for instance. As mentioned earlier, frequent contact with the expert councils probably allows publishers some opportunity for influencing the approval process, but they have no influence on the development and revision of curricula. Several countries have rules, implicit or explicit, stating that neither publishing houses nor authors may serve as members of curricular planning committees. However, these rules may vary somewhat in practice. Over the past decade there have been marginal attempts at drawing publishers into curricular planning. Such cooperation has been established at the national level in the Netherlands, and a similar scheme is now (1992) being considered by a committee appointed by Norway's National Council for Upper Secondary Education. Such initiatives may be motivated by politics or finances; in Norway the measure is attributable *inter alia* to the need for textbooks in many new subjects that attract few students.

It was not until the 1970s that an extended definition of education saw a breakthrough in curricula for primary, lower and upper secondary schools in the Nordic countries. According to the extended definition, teaching and learning were also to encompass attitudes and skills. The atomistic view of knowledge, whereby subjects were fractionalized into sub-topics and pupils were encouraged to regurgitate memorized fractions on command, has been replaced by a holistic view which emphasizes the ability to grasp relationships. Process training has been elevated to the same level as knowledge; it has become important to observe, classify, measure, collect, experiment, analyze, interpret and evaluate. This view is underpinned by an educational, democratic and theoretical school of thought whereby it is just as important to find an approach to a subject that captures the imagination and promotes understanding, as it is to review all the disciplines in the same subject. Accordingly, the interpretation of the general, overall curricular guidelines has to play a key part in educational planning and book development.

The first research done in the field of teaching guides - textbooks in the Nordic countries was reported in Sweden in the latter half of the 1970s. Among the most important of these investigations were Ulf P. Lundgren's studies in curricular theory (Lundgren 1977, 1989). Like several of his colleagues (Svingby 1985, Englund 1986), Lundgren made a systematic study of curricula as *one aspect of a highly complex teaching system*. He believed that analyses of educational processes had somehow to be tied to:

> a general theory of education and its function in society. The final point is most essential. The internal functions and effects of education cannot be explained without relating them to a basic theory of education and society. This theory must, then, be built on an explanatory model which specifies the determinants of the teaching process. (Lundgren 1977, p. 31.)

The question is who should decide what the curricula should include and, not necessarily dependent on that, what pupils will ultimately learn. The answer depends on factors other than legislation and curricula. Does curricular content really exert any significant degree of influence on the pupils, compared with what American researchers have chosen to call "the hidden curriculum" - that is, the entire social context surrounding the teaching of a subject (Giroux - Penna 1978)?

To analyze the "whole", Gunilla Svingby developed a model which takes historical, social, national and local conditions into account (Svingby 1978, p. 51). It is obvious that the curriculum-textbook relationship is just one of many interactions in this context, and that publishing houses cannot automatically be assumed to wield a great deal of influence, even though many textbooks are sold and used. The point at issue is still whether or not this connection, which actually grows "looser" in a system based on teaching guides, may enhance the influence of publishers and textbooks. All available investigations from the 1980s indicate that teachers largely follow the teaching plans incorporated into the textbooks. It does not appear, however, that the innovative thoughts embodied in the new curricula have led to any immediate renunciation of textbooks. On the contrary, it looks as though textbooks have reinforced their position in step with the decline of regular syllabi records. A shift in focus from book/publisher curricula interpretation to teacher/pupil interpretation will probably call for long-term changes in teacher education as well (see Ball - Feiman-Nemser 1988, p. 73), unless, hypothetically, such change could be brought about by means of the textbooks themselves.

This issue must be viewed in connection with still another. Political considerations play a part in the appointment of regulatory committees. This implies that traditional statements of objectives - especially in new times with an expanded definition of education - will reflect some of the important ideological contradictions seen in society. Their character of *compromise* makes interpretation more difficult. Gunilla Svingby points this out in one of her works:

> The officially stated objectives do not express unambiguous, consistent intentions, but are full of contradictions themselves, (...) which makes it possible to explain the objectives in terms of interpretations that lead back to one ideology or another. (...) In this way, conflicts and contradictions will be hidden at the official level, and the resolution of the problems (which are in reality ideological contradictions) will be left to practice, where the prevailing tradition in the system will have ample opportunity to interpret and adapt the objective in a way which conserves it. (Svingby 1977; here quoted from Englund 1982, p. 42.)

Svingby's results were confirmed and to some extent supplemented by Britt Ulstrup Engelsen in a subsequent investigation concerning the relationship between curricula and the teaching of literature at the lower secondary level (Engelsen 1988). Engelsen compared the treatment of subject matter in debates and in the curricula. She found that noticeable changes occurred every time a view from a debate on literary philosophy was incorporated into curricular documents. To some extent, however, major new topics were toned down and re-interpreted to make them less controversial and to some extent they were slotted into different contexts. Still, there was a pattern: All the different views *were* incorporated into the curricula. This was accomplished by incorporating controversial points into statements of compromise that could certainly give the appearance of agreement, but which were open to different interpretations. Engelsen's observation supports those of Michael W. Apple and Allan Luke.

Insofar as such an observation is valid for other subjects and levels, it would add to the importance assigned to the publishers' role as interpreter. At the same time, it would diminish the control exerted by curricula, coinciding with the views derived from theoretical curricular research in the course of the past decade (Engelsen 1990, p. 64).

This brings us to yet another salient point: The extent to which a publisher evaluates the curricula in light of the so-called hidden curriculum - the big new classes, the mobility inherent in society and school structure, the shifting trends in leisure time and homework, and the competition from economic pressures exerted by the youth culture outside the school. Viewed in this way, there can be no doubt that the hidden curriculum is also included in the curricula, which attach importance *inter alia* to individual and local differentiation. To what extent do publishers find it expedient to reveal and exploit this part of the curriculum and of a (formerly more or less rather hidden) tradition? The same question may be posed in an historical perspective based on the results of several investigations which show that some works published by a single publisher and a single author have undergone nothing but volume-related changes during a decade of changing curricula and school structures (Damerow 1980, Woodward 1987).

The questions posed above deal primarily with the development of textbooks. As of today, we lack investigations that could build bridges to the considerably larger body of knowledge we have about textbooks in use. However, it is very important to note that the publishing houses are, of necessity, the principal players in this process. The textbook industry and its products are inextricably linked to school structure and traditions.

Although there is a lack of research, there is a wealth of polemical literature on publishers and textbooks. This is particularly true in the USA, where the market potential is tremendous, provided, that is, that the publishers manage to coordinate state and regional requirements concerning the continued strong need for a national superstructure (Westbury 1990, p. 8). In principle, the same situation applies to a number of other western countries as well, albeit on a smaller scale. In this type of literature it is possible to distinguish between three common, somewhat conflicting, basic attitudes toward the role of publishing houses. All are represented in NSSE's 89th Yearbook (NSSE 1990), and will be summarized briefly here.

Ian Westbury, a professor of curriculum studies, criticizes the US publishing industry when he calls it "a faithful reflection of the system, i.e., the market that it serves and the larger contents in which it works." (Westbury 1990, p. 18.) The system contains built-in obstacles that impede development, including a "legal framework" (approval schemes, etc.), research funding problems, publishers' development procedures, servility to the market, constraints and apathy from the school's decision-making bodies, and a lack of contact between research and insight on the one hand, and practice on the other. The books are not good enough because the system is not good enough:

> *To charge one part of the system with lacking something that the system as a whole lacks is an unwarranted projection of the problems of the whole onto that part.* (P. 19; *my* emphasis.)

In the same book, publishers James Squire and Richard Morgan give an account of what they call standard procedure in the publishing houses' development of textbooks (Squire - Morgan

1990). The requirements include "a basic rationale prepared in advance" (p. 115). It contains a detailed plan of both "the philosophy of the instructional design" and "key instructional features". Such project descriptions are usually produced through the collaborative efforts of "senior authors" and "senior editors". Together, they hire "professional and scholarly leaders on projects of this kind and just as regularly listen to their advice." (P. 115.) Squire and Morgan also appear to testify to the existence of the link between theory and practice that Westbury was looking for: "But always the successful publisher checks the advice secured from academicians against the attitudes of school practitioners." (P. 115.)

Jean Young, an experienced teacher and editor, has written a description (Young 1990) of the publishing houses' situation which may capture the most salient features of the descriptions by Westbury and Squire/Morgan:

> (...) I can understand the constraints under which publishers operate. Particularly, it seems that publishers have to sit on a fence between being too innovative and not being innovative enough. To the extent they are convinced that an innovation will be accepted by teachers, they will be purveyors of educational innovations. (P. 83.)

The last quotations serve to remind us that teachers' selection criteria and use of textbooks in practice - or at least assumptions about these practices - have, in a manner of speaking, a retroactive effect on some of the development processes in the publishing houses.

Perspectives

The section on curricula and teaching points out how people, institutions and traditions work together and how they work against one another. In the preceding section, these factors were grouped into publishers, authorities, curricula and teaching. The role of the publisher clearly dominates the literature. The publishing house is where all the threads are drawn together. Opinions about the major part played by the publisher are often initially negative, possibly due to scholarly skepticism of commercial development. Notwithstanding, we recognize the same principal problem here as in the literature on the role of the textbook author and the role of the teacher: Who controls textbook development? State and local governing boards, schools, authors and publishing houses are all sources of material for shedding light on this issue. Yet it is unlikely that any country has routines for saving or systematizing such material, any more than they have traditions of performing routine scientific analyses of it. It would be difficult to use the material, formally or otherwise. This may be connected to "closed" approval procedures, no public access to the statements of consultants, conflicts of principle that indicate personal conflicts, the innate nature of competition between publishing houses and business secrets. The USA has encouraged the production of a wide range of polemical articles on these topics. On the other hand, there are very few textbook-based studies that relate school content to factors such as curricula/authorities/publishers. In terms of traditional educational research, curricular analyses and studies of the school system's organization are comprehensive undertakings, frequently entailing methodological, structural and political assessments. In that context, the subject matter and the way in which it is presented in the textbooks, seem to be of little interest.

The phenomenon of approval is very special. Depending on its form and function, an approval system may provide texts with direction, either political or propaganda-related. If such an approval system comprises many elements (as in Norway: language, subject matter, equal status, methodology), is centralized and has long, stable traditions in a country, it could potentially result in absolute educational-ideological concepts which might delay or prevent the transfer of new objectives from new curricula to new textbooks. A kind of consensus might arise concerning textbook customs and use, a *meta-ideology* which steers all decisions in one particular direction and becomes a system within or superordinate to the main system rather than an integral part *of* it (Johnsen 1989). However, there has been far more criticism of the way in which approval schemes are practiced than of their existence as such.

Anyone wishing to explore the relationship between law, politics and pedagogics within a state control system will have to distinguish between "after" and "before"; between the main part of the work that involves how investigators reach the decision "approved" or "rejected" on the one hand, and the main part of the work that authors and publishers perform to satisfy the requirements of the system on the other. During the 1980s there was a shift in public approval work in Sweden. Researchers began to investigate the books in existence and their use in order to gain new insight that might improve the quality of subsequent books. This sort of investigation would be "prophylactic", i.e., it would be development. (In 1991, however, the approval system was abolished in Sweden; see page 273.) There is a certain hidden logic behind this. In all countries with approval schemes, the justification - at least officially - has been the desire to improve quality. In countries with less ambitious or no traditions of textbook research, the milieu surrounding the approval scheme has probably been the only place other than in the publishing houses where textbooks have been systematically discussed and evaluated. Formally speaking, the scheme is the only official guarantee that any account is taken of recent research and new educational ideas. Consequently, the secretariats of the expert councils and their consultants are in a peculiar way the only forum for "textbook research".

The lack of research may also be related to the problem of methods. It may appear as though text analysis traditions derived from the revision of history books have not only been applied to other areas uncritically, but that they have formed such a strong school of thought that the initiative disappears as soon as one moves outside the book pages and on to a process such as writing or manuscript revision. Yet this explanation is not completely acceptable. Some research tasks stand out, as they could be performed within the parameters of the book. One example might be to perform comparative analyses of books in countries with and without approval schemes, another to compare books produced in totalitarian countries by government publishing houses with books produced through free market forces by various publishers in the west. One might also examine the contents of the books and venture explanations concerning the spiritual and political climate that may have determined their content (Jacobmeyer 1986). Notwithstanding, it should be self-evident that a text does not provide sufficient grounds for gauging how those who interpret, define and transfer knowledge and values through educational texts think, govern and are governed. Categories such as editorial work, comments from consultants or the composition of curricular committees cannot be measured in a text in itself. They are part of the processes which, due to a lack of traditions such as observation, filing or registering, can only be examined on an ongoing basis - if circumstances permit. (Investigations of how texts in the same book have changed over time are in the gray zone; see Cooper 1984 and Young 1990, page 272 and page 250.)

Perhaps the problem is the categorization itself. The division into publishers, school systems, and teaching used in this survey is by no means arbitrary; it coincides with the way in which the material is organized in the literature on the topic (see, for example, Woodward - Elliott 1990). The divisions are so broad that one might ask whether researchers have been scared away by the sheer bulk of material: The slim chances of reaching a definite, reliable result actually make this material more suitable for essays as well. The dilemma is reflected in the procedure followed in the few studies that have tried to capture the whole (Bjørndal 1982, Apple 1984, Woodward 1987, Cody 1990, Haavelsrud 1991).

No one has conducted a research-based, combined book *and* system analysis which might shed light on the totality of the textbook development process. But is it at all possible to capture the totality by applying limited, inexpensive approaches? For practical reasons, the answer must be no if one wants to do this *as a post-publication* process. On the other hand, it should be possible to keep a diary of the entire process, given that one could coordinate the work among all the implicated groups.

There is one example of an experiment that goes quite far in that direction, i.e., the development of the Atlantic Curriculum Project of several editions of *Science Plus*, a textbook series for science teaching in the lower secondary grades. Charles P. McFadden reported on the development of the program because "the struggle which the authors waged to maintain editorial control and the problematic relationships that emerged between curriculum design and materials development are probably very instructive about what happens in more typical cases." (McFadden 1992, p. 71.) The author presents a number of recommendations to sum up his experience. Two of them clearly point toward the principles of contemporaneousness and coordination mentioned in the chapter of this book entitled *Conclusion*:

> Curriculum development projects should include a suitably lengthy informal stage, one without time-limited contracts and obligations to produce curriculum plans and materials. This stage should be used for formative evaluation, professional development, experimental curriculum design, and supportive materials development, including classroom testing.
>
> Curriculum design and curriculum materials development are mutual tasks that should be united in curriculum development projects; both the design and the materials should be tested together. This presupposes a curriculum decision-making process that is supportive of such a procedure. This process might take the form of either limiting the decision making to the selection of such curricula or establishing a collaboration between the curriculum decision makers and the curriculum materials developers. (McFadden 1992, pp. 83-84.)

In a discussion of theory, Gerd Stein writes about how certain parameters contribute to making the textbook into a political medium (Stein 1977). One of these parameters is an approval system (the other three are revision, distribution/access and market), although approval is not the parameter that draws the most attention. This is probably because textbook analyses are usually pedagogically motivated. Any analyses of approval practices, on the other hand, will have political implications right from the start. As a field of research, this topic will be more suspect than "non-political" educational aspects, for example. As far as the question of approval as an expression of ideology is concerned, many critical questions still await clarification: How can one justify approval from an ideological and/or school policy perspective? How feasible is the idea of a public investigation which is intended to ensure objectivity in schoolbooks seen in the light of recent cognitive and scientific theory? Do any general, implicit censorship bodies operate outside established approval systems? If so, do they exist in countries both with and without approval systems?

Production and the Market

In the preceding section, the word "production" was chiefly used in the sense of text production. In this section, "production" will refer to work the publishers do to set, print and publish a book. The process is comprehensive and involves factors such as format, number of pages, binding, paper quality, (number of) colors, layout, choice of raw materials and printer, time frame - and the market. In this context, the term "market" refers to those who select and purchase textbooks; primarily teachers, schools and pupils/parents in primary and lower and upper secondary schools.

There are analyses that try to place the entire process in context, but they are generally quite old (with the exception of Huot 1989 and Choppin 1992; see page 307 and page 150). The main one is Wilbur Schramm's "The Publishing Process" (Schramm 1955), which discusses finances, technical production and competition, and evaluates the interaction between publishers, authors and marketing departments. Schramm uncovered patterns which some claim will still apply:

> Text materials, like any other mass communication, must abide by the laws of copyright, libel, decency, and sedition. Beyond that, restrictions imposed upon the content of the text are largely the product of informal pressures operating through the freedom of the consumer to reject what he does not like or through the pressures of special-interest groups on consumers and producers. (P. 131.)

Scramm's work was supplemented by a somewhat later contribution: M. Brammer's article "Textbook Publishing"

(Brammer 1967). The author studied the connection between the writing, appearance and purchase of textbooks and claimed that publishers' editors and publishers are the real authors of textbooks.

With these exceptions, the literature on production and the market deals with *parts* of the field. The links in the process may be examined from historical, technical, financial, political or consumer-related perspectives. This survey arranges the material into four approaches whose boundaries are somewhat fluid: Historical, technical-financial, political and consumer-related.

Historical Approach

From this perspective, the history of textbooks is the history of publishing. In non-authoritarian countries, this will involve the history of publishing houses that have published other books and those that are exclusively textbook publishers. It will also involve the history of *large* publishing houses. A few publishers account for the majority of publications. In a draft of a work on French publishing history, Alain Choppin (Choppin 1990) uses textbooks in the subject of Greek to illustrate this point. From 1789 to 1986, 1004 titles were published by a total of 227 publishers. However, 120 of the houses published just one title and more than half the titles were actually published by just six houses. Choppin has arrived at comparable figures for textbooks in Latin and Italian. These figures would probably hold true for other subjects as well, and it is likely that the same patterns would be found in other countries.

Thus the question is whether and/or how textbook history figures in official publishing house histories. Most large publishing houses that have existed for more than 50 years have probably published commemorative books. Such company histories are beyond the scope of the present survey, but examples from a country where such material is available, i.e., Norway, point to trends in the historical development which may shed light on the problems of today.

The four largest publishing houses in Norway are Aschehoug, Cappelen, Gyldendal and the Scandinavian University Press. The first celebrated its 100th anniversary in 1972, the second its 150th anniversary in 1979. University librarian Harald L. Tveterås was commissioned to write the commemorative histories of both publishing houses (Tveterås 1972, 1979). The subject of textbooks take up 10 of 383 pages in the history of Aschehoug and 85 of 477 pages in the history of Cappelen. There is no apparent reason for the under-representation or for the substantial difference between the two publishing houses (Johnsen 1989). The difference must be interpreted as an expression of modest, but varying degrees of historical awareness about the textbook publishing activities of the individual publishing house.

In two contexts Tveterås shows what close ties there can be between the authorities and publishing houses in a small country which is totally dominated by a public school system. The very foundation of some publishers' existence is ensured by their contracts to publish public documents such as statutes and curricula. At the same time, reforms within the school system have had a major impact on the production of textbooks:

> In many countries school reforms intervene less in an individual's freedom of choice because society possesses the breadth and strength to accept a variety of educational solutions. In a country such as ours, a controversial school reform will have far more significant consequences because there will be no alternatives. There are few private schools and, although those schools may be partially funded by state and local government subsidies, many people will see them as isolated minimum variants compared with the powerful, monochromatic public school system. (Tveterås 1979, p. 166.)

If we were to replace "private schools" with *small publishing houses* and "public school system" with *2-3 major publishing houses*, we have drawn a picture of something which, at least up until the 1980s, was virtually a monopoly situation in Norwegian textbook production.

No one has ever investigated what guarantee small, manageable conditions and a democratic form of government actually provide for competition and variation. At the national level, this issue is high on the current agenda of many small countries because their major publishing houses are being controlled by fewer owners. In Norway, for example, three of the above-mentioned publishing houses are part of the same Norwegian ownership consortium; while the fourth is part of a Swedish-owned system. The issue also gains significance in light of the growing internationalization seen in the development of teaching materials for the Third World (see page 303).

In volume IV of *Histoire de l'Edition Française*, Alain Choppin has compiled a survey of the publication history of French textbooks (Choppin 1986-87). Choppin distinguishes between three main development stages. From the 1880s, when books were first required in primary and lower secondary schools, until the 1920s, textbook production was largely analogous with the production of ordinary non-fiction books.

The 1930s saw the advent of "La révolution des manuels". Publishers accepted the challenge posed by illustrated magazines and journals, mainly by increasing the number of illustrations used in textbooks. Moreover, the illustrations were to be produced by well-known artists. This trend continued for several decades. It was, however, determined more by external competitive factors than by school reforms.

The *real* revolution took place in the 1960s. New educational ideas were incorporated into school reforms which, in conjunction with technical innovations and increasing affluence, set luxurious new standards for textbooks. This in turn entailed shared responsibility for production; we see the development of teamwork, where "création" and "fabrication" blend together. All the technical niceties and extra-textual enhancements were designed to present the material to pupils in a way that conformed to curricular objectives concerning independent activities and understanding. Yet these efforts did not correspond to one market requirement: "(...) the teachers who choose the books can hardly assess their quality without using them. Thus external criteria ("critères externes") such as typography and illustrations are most determinative for their selection." (P. 302.) During the early half of the century, teachers had to distinguish between and select books mainly on the basis of text; later it became possible to select them more on the basis of appearance, quite independent of text.

Technical – Financial Approach

Estimates of production costs and lists of editions, impressions and textbook sales are, in principle, public information in European countries and US states. A review of such material might reveal how much emphasis each publishing house has assigned to each subject at each level in the various steps of the process, measured in terms of money. In a broad, general historical perspective, such investigations might tell us something about the development of what might be called the written culture of the school. Detailed comparisons of two publications on the same subject, published by different publishers, would furnish information for the debate on (or lack of debate on) variation and diversity in the total stock of textbooks.

It is difficult to find examples of any such comparisons performed outside the industry. Internal comparisons are, for good reason, hard to obtain. In Norway there are general publishing industry surveys and deficiency reports conducted in the 1980s by publishing houses and/or by the government, which indicate textbook consumption and document financial needs (Report No. 23 1982-1983 to the Storting; Deficiency Committee's Report 1985; Egeland 1986). Such surveys exist in other countries as well; one of the more exhaustive is the Swedish market survey undertaken in 1987-1988 (Ds 1988: 22/23; see page 384).

It has proven very difficult to interpret such documents in a way that might lead to a plan of action on which political consensus could be reached. One important reason for this is that no one really has a full overview of all the possibilities offered by information technology. It is especially important to note that a decentralized school system, combined with different levels of financial resources at the municipal and county levels, could reinforce the very differences that regulations and curricula are trying to eliminate:

> If we look at school Norway as a whole, there is a danger that we might, at the end of the 1980s, see growing differences in educational opportunities from class to class and school to school, with regard to computer technology. This refers not to

computer courses or the like, but to the use of computer technology in general, in accordance with the curricula. The curricula are the same for everyone, but there the similarity ends. (Røsvik 1990, p. 20.)

In this respect, the stage is set for a revolution not only in the school system, where one might conceive of each teacher/pupil as a producer of teaching material, supplemented by the school library, but also on the production end: How should the publishing houses react? Neither they nor the school can rely on studies of a trend in progress. Yet there is no shortage of opinions. A narrow national and broad international contribution may also help put the situation in perspective:

In 1988 two post-graduate students at the Norwegian College of Advanced Technology in Trondheim published a thesis on the textbook business (Tiller - Nordahl 1988). They contended that Norwegian publishing houses were not up to date with their technology and that they could benefit substantially from upgrading their production systems. Their proposals for technical solutions were motivated by a general decline in appropriations for teaching materials: "Maybe the best textbook should have everything; a wealth of visual aids and good, comprehensible text. But in our opinion, schools have been placed in a no-win situation, where they have to decide between books with expensive extra-textual enhancements and thereby few books, or *good enough* books, but enough of them." (P. 130-131.) They describe the "textbook of tomorrow" as being in black and white, with simple straight-glued joints, A4 format, 100 - 250 pages long, with the simplest possible lay-out.

This view is no less interesting when compared with different countries' actual expenditures on teaching materials, mainly books, per pupil in primary and lower secondary schools. Stephen Paul Heyneman of the World Bank has prepared a comparison of annual expenditures in a number of countries, measured in dollars. In 1984, Bolivia spent USD 0.80 per pupil, Spain approximately USD 40, Hungary approximately USD 90, the USA and Japan approximately USD 250 and the Scandinavian countries USD 300 or more.

The results of this study were recapitulated in a seminar report from the World Bank: *Textbooks in the Developing World* (Farrell - Heyneman 1989). The same publication contains a contribution from three representatives of EDUCONSULT, a development center in Geneva (Fernig - McDougal - Ohlman 1989). They place the possibilities of information technology in a global perspective, based on the following problem/title: "Will Textbooks be Replaced by New Information Technologies?" The authors introduce their article with what western countries might perceive as a rather derogatory comparison that places textbooks in a broad economic context:

> To put the matter baldly, two main problems occur with textbooks: either they are available and teachers rely too much on them - teachers teach the textbooks despite training to the contrary - or as often happens in developing countries, textbooks are in too short supply to be of much value. (P. 197.)

The authors give no definite answer to the question of how the educational gap can be closed or to whether new technology will serve such a trend. On the other hand, they point out that education needs a "fuller exchange of information", combined with "results of research, evaluations of existing software and courseware, and specification for their development." (P. 205.)

One factor that is often ignored when discussing textbook use, as opposed to technical development and the media revolution in the school, is that for nearly a generation textbooks themselves have embodied results and examples of advanced technology. Tiller and Nordahl assert that in the 1980s, the textbook publication costs of ordinary Norwegian publishing houses frequently accounted for as much as 40 per cent of the book shop price ("Total publishing costs comprise the costs of technical production, the manuscript and binding or stitching/stapling costs of the entire impression." (P. 66.)). Richaudeau's introduction to the topic (Richaudeau 1986) indicates that the process is expensive. While there are clear indications that extra-textual enhancements such as colors and illustrations make users anticipate educational advantages, to date no studies have been made of the correspondence between extra-textual enhancements and degree of learning.

Stephen Paul Heyneman believes that the issue of textbooks versus other teaching media should be superseded by another question. In a global perspective, it will be more important to ask where each country can get its books produced cheapest. Electronics and technology have opened up possibilities for joint productions across national borders and for specialization in a global/local perspective, that is, the production of so-called local teaching material need not depend on owning production equipment: "Many small nations (Sierra Leone is an example) have successfully combined local development and production of general primary texts with adaption of foreign texts for more specialized subjects with small readerships at higher schooling levels." (Heyneman 1989, p. 9.)

In the sporadic debates for and against the use of textbooks at all, elements such as volume and enhancements are recurring arguments from the "no" side. Typical of this criticism is Michel Barré's book from 1983: *L'aventure documentaire. Une alternative aux manuels scolaires.* The author views the question *inter alia* in a philosophical-ecological context. Teachers are dissatisfied with the books, so they turn to the copying machine. Yet they still continue to use the textbooks. The result is unwarranted paper consumption, a "massacre des forêts" (p. 22). According to Barré, there are other ways to use literature, ways that can be justified both ecologically and educationally, such as, for example, school libraries and modern electronic media.

A more profound consideration of the relationship between extra-textual enhancements and educational objectives may be found in Arthur Woodward's analysis "Do Illustrations Serve an Instructional Purpose in U.S. Textbooks?" (Woodward 1991-93). The author refers to investigations that concur fully about what teachers want: Textbooks should be richly illustrated. Further, he refers to measurements indicating that social science textbooks at the lower secondary level sometimes have more illustrations than text. Woodward also raises the question of the qualifications of teachers, i.e., the most important group of textbook selectors. This in turn brings us to the question of teachers' qualifications, which is discussed in the section on Consumer Approach (p. 309).

Political Approach

In all the western countries mentioned in this survey, we find a mixture of private and public sector involvement in textbook publishing. Despite sporadic proposals for and attempts to set up state publishing houses, the private houses are still publishing textbooks. Public funds are used to purchase the books at the primary and lower secondary levels and, in some countries, at the upper secondary level as well.

In its own way, the textbook as a product is thus part of the mixed economy typical of these countries. Textbooks are industrial commodities sold on a market dictated by public and private interests. They are considered a necessary part of teaching. They are in demand and they command a price. They are subject to requirements based on the needs of the buyers. Many publishers compete with one another in the west. Their textbooks vary in physical and educational quality. In terms of such criteria, textbooks are at the mercy of the ordinary principles of a market economy.

Still, the authorities also exercise considerable influence on this market. First of all, laws, regulations and curricula, most clearly manifested through more or less formalized approval systems, make it possible to control the content of the books. Second, the authorities can regulate the market through appropriations which may be either discontinued/reduced or increased/elevated to subsidies, for example.

Peter H. Neumann has investigated this system in France, (West) Germany, Great Britain and the USA (Neumann 1989). He arrived at six major questions which were asked in each of the countries - the gist of the responses is given following each question:

1 What system is used for education and book procurement?
(Compulsory basic education, national/local book purchasing.)

2 Compared with other media, what part do textbooks play in the school today?
(The teachers' unequivocal response was that the books are just as important as ever; however, sales do not substantiate

this fully. Computers are considered at least as effective as books in certain subjects.)

3 To what degree are textbooks an expression of national or other political interests?
(Great Britain has exercised less syllabus control and more local autonomy than the other countries. But there, too, it is becoming increasingly difficult for publishing houses to base themselves on sufficiently widespread political or professional consensus to ensure large markets. First, because the local perspective is gaining ground in curricula and schools. And second, because: "Consensus has become more difficult to achieve following the social, scientific, and technical revolutions of the last decades." (P. 116.))

4 Who approves the books, and how are they selected?
(About the USA, see page 279. Only (West) Germany practices advance approval. France and Great Britain employ no approval schemes. Very little funding for the purchase of books comes from the national government, most of it derives from municipal sources. Irrespective of country, variations in municipal economy and practice will therefore lead to differences in the range and availability of books.)

5 What role does the textbook industry play? How free is competition; how good are the textbooks?
(Textbook production is the financial backbone of many publishing houses that publish other, more speculative types of publications. Still, the market is sensitive. Changes in curricula, school structure and the classes themselves may result in sharp shifts between competing publishers. The effects of financial uncertainty or downswings show up rapidly on school budgets. In 1980, book budgets on the whole were cut in all the countries investigated. The industry has no trade organizations that wield influence comparable to the teachers' unions, for example. None of the four countries were able to cite examples of regular or organized evaluations of textbook quality in the form of reviews or public

documents.)

6 What cooperation exists among the countries investigated, and
    between developed and developing countries, in the field of
    textbook development?
    (The field of textbooks is politically sensitive in an
    international context. An unwritten law states that every
    nation should develop its own textbook literature. However,
    plagiarism abounds, and exchanges, sale of rights, adaptation
    and translation between developed countries, especially in the
    natural sciences and foreign languages, are commonplace in
    the industry. In general, developing countries have not made
    much progress; Latin America and Africa comprise a market
    for publishers in the USA, Great Britain and France. Their
    involvement is partly commercial, partly non-commercial.)

P. Goldstein wrote a book on textbook production in 1978:
Changing the American Schoolbook: Law, Politics and Technology.
He, too, points out the unpredictability of the forces at work behind
the production of textbooks. He asserts that the status quo and
repetition are a common policy pattern among major publishing
houses. This is true even of fields such as locally/regionally
adapted texts and in areas involving new/untested teaching
methods. According to Goldstein, this lack of innovation is
ascribable to causes other than commercial publishing interests
alone. The regulatory system is deficient because it offers little
protection against the copying of even the most meticulously
developed innovations. State and regional authorities have
traditionally been in favor of spending some of their school budgets
on innovation, but this attitude does not include innovation in
textbooks. However, on this point the textbook market is no
different from other types of consumer markets; it demands
novelty. In the 1970s the answer for the publishing houses was
"modernization", which mainly involved investing money in further
extra-textual enhancements.

   Goldstein's idea was picked up and developed further in one
rather outstanding publication written in the 1980s. Hélène Huot's
book from 1989, *Dans la jungle des manuels scolaires*, is based on

a holistic analysis of publishing house production and policy from the viewpoint of society. Formerly an upper secondary school teacher, Huot is now a professor of linguistics at the Université de Paris VII. She has edited the *Bulletin d'information sur les manuels scolaires* since 1986. The journal is published three to four times a year and it contains reviews of new textbooks for primary, lower secondary and upper secondary schools. Huot's editorial work aroused her interest in the part publishing houses play in book development, so she undertook an investigation of publishing houses and schoolbook production in France. One of the most central topics in her book involves a phenomenon that sheds light on several aspects of production, namely, "les parascolaires".

In the 1980s, the market for lower secondary school textbooks in France bore witness to a government resolution enacted in 1977. The law, which is still in force, states that the school shall provide pupils with textbooks and any accompanying workbooks. Earlier, this applied to primary school as well. Lower secondary schools were subject to an additional provision, however: No set of books could be renewed or discarded for at least four school years. Today teachers still choose the books, but their choices take place within budget quotas set by the state and municipality.

For publishers, the ramifications of the act meant a narrowing of the market in respect of "les collèges". Nevertheless, they arrived at a solution that boosted sales as well as revenues. They developed a type of book called "livres parascolaires", which the schools are not obligated to buy: Glossaries, sample examination questions and keys, study guides with the syllabus in key word form, introductions to study techniques, school editions of works of fiction. Obviously, these types of books were not new. The innovative idea was the shift in marketing strategy: Publishing houses intensified their efforts to sell the books to parents, and their strategy paid off thanks to growing skepticism about the effectiveness of the school system (in the 1980s, the school issue was one of the main planks in the political platform of the non-socialist opposition to Mitterrand's government). At least one innovation was developed at that time, however: A new genre in the field of "parascolaires", namely "les cahiers de vacances". These "vacation books" contain summaries of the past year's syllabus and introduce new material for the coming year to provide a "smooth transition" into the autumn. The vacation books turned out to be best-sellers. The first publishing house on this market, Hachette, grossed one-third of its 1988 textbook revenues from the sale of "les parascolaires". Vacation book earnings accounted for half of that one-third (Huot 1989, p. 98).

Books of the "parascolaires" type sell very well not least because of their price - and possibly also because of their appearance. Parents find it easier to buy booklets at a price of not more than NOK 40 - 50. The booklets are easy to produce; they are generally printed in black and white and, with their simple extra-textual enhancements and modest number of pages, they seem less formidable than ordinary textbooks. Hence a new situation has arisen, shaking up the traditional textbook concept and entailing ramifications far outside the textbook market alone. At least three questions demand attention in this context:

Shouldn't the success of such cheap black/white pamphlets lead the authorities, publishers, teachers and researchers to re-discuss and re-evaluate the textbook concept? If it turns out that a growing number of pupils manage well without the typical thick, heavy, lavishly enhanced, expensive textbooks of the 1970s and 1980s, isn't the stage set and the market ripe for a new type of books more in line with the views of Tiller and Nordahl (see page 301), for example?

If brief study guides and supplementary materials such as "les parascolaires" were eventually to supplant textbooks, what professional and educational consequences could this change have?

What does the strong, easily-won popularity of "les parascolaires" say about the utility and quality of the books that dominated the market in the 1980s? This last question might also be posed in such a way as to place more emphasis on the textbooks' dependence on their surroundings: How high are the professional and educational ambitions in a system which is - possibly - prepared to abandon the principle of a broad, comprehensive presentation for the principles of the "bare essentials"?

Consumer Approach

In principle, there are three systems for book selection:

The *mandatory use* of certain titles may be seen in totalitarian states, where a (state) publishing house may have a monopoly or where the state may select particular titles if there are several works to choose from. One might also contend that such mandatory use exists in western democracies that practice approval schemes. However, no one is required to use textbooks, and there are usually several competing titles on the market. Yet if consensus and practice say that books are to be used, if the curricula are so comprehensive and teacher education so deficient that books are viewed as an educational necessity, and if it is true that books published by different publishing houses are essentially the same, then the choice among different publishers is illusory (Johnsen 1989). This actually places constraints on the users and makes the market stable.

The term *advisory* may be used to describe the attitude and practice that dominate western countries - except that the expression has to include weak as well as strong degrees of control.

Although pupils at the upper secondary level pay for their own books in most countries, the selection of books is usually undertaken by teachers. Their freedom of choice is not total, however, as there are a number of limiting factors. Influence exerted by the school principal, the teachers' council, the section and the parents, as well as the general financial situation of the school in question, the size of the school and the chances for selling the books second-hand - all these conditions will exert varying degrees of influence on the choice of textbooks and result in very different choices from one school to the next. In any event, it is clear that teachers play a key role in the process.

This applies to primary and lower secondary school as well, although the situation there is more complex. The books are purchased with taxpayers' money, so the schools can lend out the books and replace them when they are worn out and/or out of date. Sweden is the most progressive country in this sense, as the Ministry of Education wants to order the municipalities to ensure that primary and lower secondary school pupils are allowed to keep their textbooks in core subjects (Government Proposition 1988/89:4). The division of financial responsibility between state and local governments is a crucial point in Sweden and in other countries. Most countries have municipal or regional bodies which - always within the parameters of specific budget quotas - are at least theoretically in a position to influence and in some cases even alter the proposals made by teachers and schools. The exercise of influence prior to and during the book selection process is difficult to unmask. There are examples of interventions instituted by school boards, commissions or pressure groups from outside the system to change selections that have been made (Cody 1989, Moffett 1988), but they are rare. The reasons cited for any such changes have usually involved criticism of ideological points, occasionally criticism of the subject matter and, exceptionally, pedagogical objections.

Total freedom would mean that individual teachers could choose literature independently, free from the influence of colleagues, school administrators, parents, finances, publishers' information and lists - based on their own educational ideas and/or evaluations of pupils' needs and possibilities. In light of the above, this kind of book selection is unlikely ever to be anything but a theoretical model.

Teachers' Background and their Use of Books

The preceding point brings us to teachers' educational qualifications for evaluating and using textbooks.

There are two conditions in particular that tend to accentuate the issue of textbook knowledge in teacher education. One is the books' continued dominant position in teaching (see page 176), the other is the sustained criticism of the books' contents and of their educational and linguistic quality (see page 185).

Provided it is true that many books are in widespread circulation despite the fact that they suffer from significant deficiencies, then we must question whether this is symptomatic of a fundamental shortcoming in teacher education: Are new graduates less capable of making independent educational and professional decisions than they should be? Also, there is the question of whether or not textbook knowledge has the status of an element or a separate discipline in teacher education.

As to the first question, of the many investigations conducted in this field, few of them have taken textbooks into account. It is also unlikely that textbook knowledge comprises a separate, formal discipline in any country's teacher education plans. On the other hand, familiarity with teaching aids and, not least, the personal ability to select and preferably develop teaching aids is often *referred to* as being valuable and worthwhile.

Moreover, teachers often say they find textbook selection difficult, especially since they often do not discover the good and bad points of textbooks until after they have actually used them. Yet several investigations show that once a textbook is selected, it often remains in use, and it may even have a competitive edge when due for replacement - even though it may not have been considered satisfactory. Such a tendency is probably reinforced by the fact that the number of books available in core subjects even in small western nations is now so large that it has become virtually impossible to keep abreast of all of them (see the section on Jansen 1969, page 382).

It must be interpreted as a sign of the absence or lack of textbook knowledge in teacher education programs that textbook selection is scarcely mentioned in educational literature. However, there is one American investigation that is comprehensive enough to deserve mention in this context.

 Ball and Feiman-Nemser reported on their study in an article in *Curriculum Inquiry*: "Using Textbooks and Teachers' Guides: A Dilemma for Beginning Teachers and Teachers Educators" (Ball - Feiman-Nemser 1988). Based on the situation discussed above, they posed three questions:

1 What did teacher education students learn about textbooks and syllabus planning?

2 How did teacher education students view topics such as the use of textbooks and syllabus planning once they completed their educations?

3 How did they use textbooks and teachers' guides when they were doing their student teaching?

The investigation was conducted over a two-year period (1982-84). Six students were followed through their basic teacher education courses. They attended two different education programs with considerable "structural and ideological differences" (the one focused on the teaching role, the other on the learning role). The six students, all female, were volunteers. Two had half-grown children. As to their academic records, they spanned the full range of performance levels.

Ball and Feiman-Nemser registered how the students were taught and their reactions to what they learned. The material consisted of notes and tape recordings of classes and conversations. The results were unequivocal for all students in both groups. They may be summed up as follows:

> Although the student teachers were enrolled in two different teacher education programs, all of them developed the impression that if they wanted to be good teachers, they should avoid following textbooks and relying on teachers' guides. They believed that good teaching means creating your own lessons and materials instead. These ideas proved difficult to act on during student teaching when the student teachers worked in classrooms where textbooks formed the core of instruction and they confronted the fact that they were beginning teachers lacking knowledge, skill and experience. (Ball - Feiman-Nemser 1988, p. 401.)

Ball and Feiman-Nemser attach great importance to observations of the relationship between subject matter and educational ideology. They feel justified in saying that teachers educators and the programs' educational direction dominated to such an extent that "neither program pursued a critique of the subject matter content" (p. 414). The teachers assumed a certain level of subject insight among the students, who were given the impression that *their* knowledge and ideas were better suited as a point of departure than the textbooks' (p. 414). In practice, the students' dilemma unfolded as follows:

> In spite of what they had been taught in their courses, the student teachers in both programs ended up using textbook programs to teach reading, math, science, and social studies. Some student teachers felt pressed to maintain the established classroom practice. Others were simply overwhelmed by the responsibility of teaching for the entire day, and resorted to textbooks as a reasonable way to manage, or at least survive, the demands. (P. 415.)

Ball and Feiman-Nemser's demonstration of this dilemma - or perhaps it should be called this vicious circle - amplifies Vigander's view that anyone who wants to change something in the system has to begin with the beginners (see page 87). Further, Ball and Feiman-Nemser demonstrate the need for more information about the relationship between teachers' knowledge of subject matter and that of the books, in light of curricula, education and the teaching situation.

The investigation substantiates the claim that established teachers are, and that newly educated teachers become, textbook users. This is supported by a French study which measured teachers' attitudes toward textbooks. The study, probably the most comprehensive of its kind, was to some extent the result of increasing pressures on school budgets. Compulsory schooling was introduced for everyone up to the age of 15-16 in the 1970s. Up to then, pupils had gotten their schoolbooks for free in primary school, but now that system had to be expanded to include the lower secondary level. Representatives of the state and local governments - who were footing the bill - argued in favor of fewer, thinner schoolbooks. Publishers, authors and many parents and teachers feared government-run production and mounted a counter-campaign under the slogan "Non à l'enseignement au rabais" (No discount education). The discussion eventually degenerated into a debate for and against the use of textbooks, and in 1980 the ministry decided to ask a group of researchers at the Institut National de Recherche Pédagogique to investigate teachers' attitudes toward schoolbooks (Tournier - Navarro 1985).

A total of 2,282 questionnaires were completed by the same number of teachers, divided among 124 lower secondary schools and 38 upper secondary schools. The sample of schools was drawn with an eye to encompassing variations in numerous areas. The choice of teachers and questions was based on five main variables: The different subjects/age of pupils/age of teachers/sex of teachers/ education of teachers. The questionnaires were very comprehensive. Statistical and mathematical experts took part in planning the questions and processing the responses.

The answers may be summarized as follows: Practically all the teachers viewed textbooks as an asset - most of them described textbooks as indispensable. Yet at both the lower and upper secondary school levels, teachers emphasized that the books were something *they* themselves controlled the use of; the books were tools, not commandments etched in stone. It was possible to demonstrate clear differences related to subject, level and teachers' education, but sex and age did not appear particularly significant. The main trend was that books were used more frequently in the humanities than in the natural sciences, and that independence of the book increased in direct proportion to the level being taught and the education of the teacher.

Two comprehensive American investigations point in the same direction as the INRP report. In a poll conducted by the National Assessment of Educational Progress for Reading (Lapointe 1986), nine of ten primary and lower secondary school teachers responded that they were satisfied with the aids available for teaching reading and writing. According to another poll, conducted by the Educational Products Information Exchange Institute among 600 teachers, some 80 per cent of the respondents replied that they would use their current books again in classes comparable to those they had at the time (EPIE 1977). Yet another investigation was very clear in its conclusion. In 1976, the US National Science Foundation took the initiative to conduct several investigations on classroom instruction in natural science, mathematics and social studies. An analysis of teachers' attitudes toward social studies books concluded: "Teachers tend not only to rely on, but to believe in, the textbooks as the source of knowledge. Textbooks are not seen as support materials, but as the central instrument of instruction by most social studies teachers." (Shaver - Davis - Helburn 1979, p. 150.)

A Norwegian study conducted in the 1970s may provide certain grounds for making assumptions about how books are selected for the schools. The Oppland County director of schools wanted to know how teachers selected books, so Oppland Regional College carried out a project over a two-year period (Oppland Regional College, 1978). Their questionnaire was distributed to schools in 24 municipalities; approximately one-half of the schools responded. The two most important sources of information were other teachers and advertisements or courses sponsored by publishing houses. There was a great deal of uncertainty about who it was that selected the books at the individual school. A majority believed the school board was responsible for selection, while 20 per cent believed the individual school itself was responsible for the final selection. In several cases, there were different answers to the question from within one and the same municipality.

As regards teachers' own initiative, the investigation from Oppland showed that the testing of new teaching materials was often limited to teachers over the age of 40. This may imply that experience is required before a teacher feels the necessary confidence in relation to the books. However, this investigation is now 15 years old. It stems from an era when teachers' awareness of a personal, more "closed" responsibility for and control of teaching was probably still very strong. Today, development and testing are a formal part of the school's cooperation pattern. One cannot therefore assume that the answers to the questions about the use of new books would have the same distribution now as they had a generation ago. At the same time, it is possible that generational differences are now less significant than the differences between individual, more consistent types of teachers. This question was discussed by Lee J. Cronbach in an article entitled "The Text in Use" (Cronbach 1955), in which he distinguishes between three main levels of instruction and discusses the question of which type of teacher the books are/should be primarily written for (see page 181).

The view that textbooks work best when they can expeditiously be adapted to the teacher's style - and not vice versa - has been further developed in Zahorik 1990 (see page 175). A recent Norwegian study has been done in the same area. Sigrun Aaneby examined teachers' choices of natural science textbooks at six upper secondary schools in the Oslo area (Aaneby 1991). Her material consisted of recorded interviews and conversations. The author takes a close look at the various teachers' educations, backgrounds and working situations. Significant differences in these areas result in vastly different degrees of awareness of and preparation for the selection and use of textbooks - only slightly more than half the teachers had read the prefaces of the books they were using. (According to Aaneby, this is understandable; the prefaces really say very little about the thought processes underlying the books.) Aaneby also analyzed the selection situation at the individual school before looking at the features of the books that the teachers found important, e.g., the author's professional background and the books' extra-textual enhancements (use of illustrations and colors):

> The teachers who are most satisfied with their selections do not find the textbook controlling ("I use my old educational ideas with the new book"). Those who experience the textbook as controlling, do not necessarily find that to be a problem ("It's a wonderful challenge"), although some teachers do find it a problem ("I was influenced far more than I realized." "Following the book makes one a poorer teacher."). (...) The key to successful textbook selection lies in finding textbooks that suit the teacher's educational ideas, so the teacher doesn't have to adapt to the book.
>
> In conclusion, I asked the teachers to say whether they feel a need for guidance in connection with textbook selection by asking this question: "Is there a need for assistance from other, independent, neutral bodies to help evaluate textbooks?"
>
> The responses I got indicate that there are divided opinions about this. Yet it is striking to note that those who are least satisfied with their own textbook selection are among the ones most pleased by the prospects of some kind of assistance. Those who are satisfied, on the other hand, believe such assistance to be unnecessary ("We have the expertise ourselves."). (Aaneby

1991, p. 10.)

Tentatively, Aaneby proffers the following answer to the question of good textbook selection: "The teacher who selects a textbook that has qualities which lead her to feel that the book works well in the classroom has made a good selection" (p. 2). Aaneby concludes by writing that "a good teacher-textbook relationship must be based on the textbook suiting the teacher, not on the teacher adapting to the textbook" (p. 11).

This view of the teacher-textbook relationship still leaves one question unanswered. If the teacher practices an instructional method which is not successful - is it possible to exert a positive influence on this method through (better) books? In other words and in a larger perspective: Can textbooks improve schooling?

Teachers' Guides

Teachers' guides should give certain indications of how textbook authors and publishers view the interaction between textbooks, pupils and teachers. Such guides have scarcely been studied. Teachers' guides are not encompassed by approval schemes in some countries that practice such schemes - Norway, for example. The few major studies made of such books have vastly different points of departure. Ulrich Schubert has used teachers' guides and teachers' manuals in local history and topography to study the development of the subject from 1918 - 1965 (Schubert 1987). In the USA, Arthur Woodward believed that teachers' guides could provide certain indications about teachers' independence in relation to textbooks. He has analyzed teachers' guides for textbooks from the 1920s to the 1970s (Woodward 1986). Woodward finds a clear tendency away from more general discussions of problems and strategies and toward detailed descriptions of classroom instruction:

> In the case of the modern reading basal, it is notable that, in contrast to earlier materials, the role of the teacher is that of a manager of lessons, questions, and activities. Because recently published basals and teachers' guides attempt to meet every eventuality and need, teachers are given little discretion as to

what can happen in a classroom. (Woodward 1990, p. 188.)

Teachers' guides are designed to accommodate as many needs as possible. They cannot justifiably be viewed as indirect descriptions of one teacher level or another. Yet when analyzed over the course of time, as in Woodward's study, at least they give an indication of the trend in *opinion* about what most teachers need. One might claim that the genre "guides" has been overlooked for far too long, consisting mainly of "hit and miss" attempts, so the guides produced during the past decades cover and express needs that have existed for a long time. Insofar as such a claim is justified, it is difficult to draw any definite conclusions from Woodward's investigation about degree of textbook independence then and now. Generally speaking, the question of how much can be learned from teachers' guides will depend on one's view of the publisher-teacher relationship. The more convinced one is that publishers do everything in their power to satisfy dominating, thoroughly analyzed teachers' needs, the more reliable teachers' guides will be as testimony not only of publishers' views of the teachers' independence, but also of actual conditions. The question will then concern the extent to which one can talk about thoroughly analyzed teachers' needs at all. Since such analyses are rare, the question should rather be: What needs have teachers expressed to the publishers, which teachers express these needs and which forums provide venues for such feedback?

The grounds for asking these questions were derived indirectly from an investigation referred to by Hélène Huot (Huot 1989). In 1984-85, a national school commission investigated teachers' relationships to textbooks in seven French "départements". They used questionnaires, and the results corroborated the trend demonstrated in the INRP investigation (see page 313). The study concentrated on finding out how teachers select textbooks. It turned out that approximately 70 per cent of the teachers select the books themselves, but that they take the school's traditions into account. Less than half of all participants felt they had sufficient information to undertake such a selection. Three of four answered in the affirmative when asked whether they were in favor of a body that could provide information which was as systematic, regular and neutral as possible. If this degree of uncertainty is indicative of teachers in general, there is even more reason to ask what the information the other way, from the teachers to the publishers, that is, actually consists of.

A systematic analysis of the publishers' sales brochures and advertisements would probably give a good indication of what publishers see as teachers' most important needs. D. Anderson analyzed publishing houses' "launching" language, finding it to comprise a deliberate sales rhetoric which was also incorporated into the textbooks; the wording, arrangement and typography may give a first impression of renewal and practical advantages which do not actually exist (Anderson 1981). Perhaps analyses of this type should be combined with investigations of teachers' own assessments of the needs depicted in the advertisements. Theoretically, it should be possible to analyze the entire flow of information between producers and consumers, then to let these results form the basis for incorporating an information system into the school system itself, which takes account of the time teachers spend studying. A large part of the framework for such a program has already been set up by Hélène Huot in her analysis of French publishing houses' information systems (Huot 1989). The analysis sets the stage for a type of textbook information based on a combination of registration and reviews (Huot 1990).

It is possible to define "teachers' guides" in purely physical terms; they include printed booklets bearing the name teachers' guides and are produced for teachers only. There are also other types of printed teachers' guides which are separate from the curricula. It is possible to talk about a "hidden teachers' guide" in the textbooks. One issue that remains open and has hardly ever been investigated is that of the degree to which problems/ assignments and other supplementary materials in the books are intended to be used on the teacher's initiative. Authors and publishers will contend that this must be up to the discretion of the individual teacher. However, it has been shown that parts of textbooks may be at a formal level that excludes the pupil without any typographical or other indication that these pages are intended for the *teacher* (Gillham 1986). This inherent uncertainty may be sensed in the prefaces to textbooks. Textbooks from the 1970s,

1980s and 1990s demonstrate all three of the main variations of addressee solutions found in different countries: There are prefaces written directly and exclusively to the pupil, prefaces written directly to the teacher alone and prefaces clearly addressed to both parties and/or which leave one in doubt as to the identity of the intended addressee.

On rare occasions, attempts have been made to register and work with pupils' attitudes toward and wishes concerning textbooks (see page 182). Yet there is no documentation that views or wishes from pupils have played any part in textbook selection.

Lists of textbook evaluation criteria have been and still are produced by researchers, publishers, teachers' groups and students. It would no doubt be extremely difficult to find examples of any such lists that have been accepted as a constant template for systematic use at the national or local level by teachers' groups or school committees.

The very few examples of major projects which try to establish a procedure for more systematic evaluation of textbook quality do not come from publishing houses. One recent example in the Nordic countries is *A Textbook on Textbooks* (LFF 1991); a book produced by the textbook writers' trade association in Sweden. In 1988, the Institut National de Recherche Pédagogique in Paris published *Des manuels pour apprendre* (*Textbooks to Learn From*). Both titles tend toward evaluative theories and cite some analytical examples. The most recent and also the most comprehensive work, however, is Alains Choppin's *Les Manuels Scolaires* from 1992 (see page 150).

Perspectives

This chapter has distinguished between four different approaches: Historical, technical-financial, political and consumer-related.

As regards the *historical* approach, the work being conducted at the Institut National de Recherche Pédagogique in Paris is the only example of a broad, scientific registration of the history of textbook publishing which cuts across the lines between traditional publishing house histories. No one can dispute the thoroughness of this work, which may well become a model for work in other countries (see page 358). In an unsigned review of the project's first subject lists (textbooks in Greek and Latin), however, the method of presentation was criticized. The books in each subject are ordered chronologically and alphabetically by author's name. According to the reviewer, this is by no means ideal if the objective is to:

> (...) support historical research on subjects and disciplines, which is far more important and pressing than statistical studies. Anyone interested in the history of particular subjects needs to be able to distinguish among different levels (primary and lower secondary, upper secondary, short/long, classical/modern, etc.), and among different types of textbooks (grammars, anthologies, exercise books, dictionaries, etc.). Naturally, it is also important to be familiar with prolific authors, but not with publication dates, author names and book types, all mixed up together. Of course, it is possible to design lists of levels and book types based on the registers at the back. But these refer to numbers in the chronological list, so such an approach would call for time-consuming, tedious efforts. (*Manuels scolaires* 10/1988, p. 40.)

This criticism reveals a certain conflict between educational and historical priorities. The conflict is not limited to the historical approach; it also appears in several other areas when attempts are made to strike a balance between theoretical and applied research. It is evident, for example, in the researcher-publisher relationship. This cannot accurately be called a conflict, of course, since it is not manifest. It is rather a lack of contact and information. The problem stems from a lack of basic discussion about the purpose of investigating what one investigates. In the example from INRP, the reviewer maintains that it is not enough to state that one wishes to pave the way for textbook research, one must also identify the type of research.

Technical-financial and *political* approaches to research tasks are addressed indirectly in John H. Williamson's list of "facts" and "myths" in the publishing industry (see page 269). Publishing statistics, estimates, budgets and accounts from individual publishing houses are to some extent accessible and they *could* provide a basis for analyses. However, such analyses also presuppose clearly defined objectives. But who shall define them - and in which direction - as long as knowledge of and viewpoints on the ultimate goal, i.e., the textbooks' functions and methods of use, are as limited and uncertain as research indicates? This makes it difficult to argue in favor of one technical-financial solution or another without relating the material and methods to a convincing, well-grounded idea of what kind of books one wants to see produced, distributed and used. This comes to light clearly in Tiller and Nordahl 1989, and in the investigation conducted by Norway's State Textbook Committee (Ulvik 1991). The latter study aimed at registering user reactions to a special type of book which in itself comprised a technical-financial experiment. So-called *dual language* editions (60 per cent bokmål (Dano-Norwegian) and 40 per cent nynorsk (New Norwegian)) were published to save money so that linguistic minority groups could be ensured access to books. The investigation found significantly less correlation than expected between language policy background and book evaluations. Ulvik's study shows how literary quality and pupils' perceptions of it are superordinate to the politically motivated, structural and technical-financial factors which *were to be* measured.

A number of investigations deal with coverage; e.g., how the individual school, municipality or region is supplied with (approved) textbooks. A Swedish investigation, Ds 1988:22, has been mentioned as being especially thorough. One characteristic feature of this study and of other similar studies is that their basic attitude toward textbooks is positive - in contrast to many other types of studies. Consistent with the principles of western mixed economies, such investigations are often the result of cooperation between publishing houses and municipalities, such as, for instance, when municipalities take part in polls organized by publishers (The Norwegian Publishers Association 1991). Strictly speaking, however, it is amazing that such investigations take place and are followed up at a point in time when the curricula have been calling for minimal textbook use and maximal production by teachers themselves for years. It is also remarkable that such studies can trigger "rescue operations" on the part of the State if they reveal significant needs or biases (Johnsen 1989).

These examples underline the need for a thorough clarification, first and foremost, of the question of which holistic perspective one is trying to place technical-financial and publishing policy conditions into, not least in relation to problems and experiences from other areas, including books in use.

As to *consumer-related* approaches, the main question is how teachers select textbooks. This has rarely been investigated by direct observation, as was the case in Ball and Feiman-Nemser 1988. The study must be given credence because it was based on classroom observations, logs and notes from the respondents and interviews. In addition, it was conducted over a two-year period. On the other hand, no more than six students/teachers took part in the project and they were all female (see page 312).

Although the investigation conducted by Ball and Feiman-Nemser in this field is somewhat exceptional, it can be placed in the tradition in which the objective is to find out how independent and controlling teachers are in relation to textbooks. There is far more information available from the numerous investigations in which teachers themselves describe their attitudes to textbooks by completing questionnaires. Examples from the USA, France and Norway have revealed a general tendency for the majority of teachers to want and use books, but they want books adapted to *their* way of teaching. The results of such surveys are not unequivocal, however. For example, conflicting conclusions have been drawn about the connection between teaching experience and the degree of teacher control when using textbooks (see page 171). At the same time, several comprehensive classroom studies indicate very different teachers' attitudes and ways of using textbooks than the surveys based on questionnaires might indicate.

If it is true that teachers are extremely dependent on textbooks in their teaching, it is remarkable that teachers' guides are not formalized as a regular part of teacher education and that they have so rarely been analyzed as major sources of knowledge about prevailing educational philosophies.

Another open question is which of Cronbach's teacher types textbooks are written for (see page 181). In principle, today's textbooks are not written for teachers. When completing a questionnaire sent out in 1991 by the Norwegian Non-Fiction

Writers' and Translators' Association, most Norwegian textbook authors responded that they write for the pupils (Haavelsrud 1991). It is paradoxical that we nevertheless know more about teachers than pupils as textbook users. Cronbach 1955 contains an analysis by Willard B. Spalding: "The Selection and Distribution of Printed Materials". Spalding points to stability and stagnation as a pattern in the production, sales and selection processes. He concludes that change and development are contingent on theoretical discussions and clarifications. There can be no improvement without scientifically-tested theories about what good textbooks are. Spalding explains the consequences of a lack of theory as follows:

> It seems probable that the absence of tested theory about the good text leads to or perpetuates five conditions.
>
> First, it leads to political decisions about who shall advise in the selection of books. If there were tested theory, then persons could be trained as experts in the use of theory. (...)
>
> Second, it leads to the selling of books rather than to their selection. Again, if tested theory were used by experts in each school system, the needs of the local schools, the problems of the local culture, the ability of the local children, the skill of the local teachers, and similar items could be brought to bear upon the problem of selecting material. (...)
>
> Third, it leads to diversity in the procedures for selection. The absence of theory makes it impossible to train people to select books well. (...)
>
> Fourth, it perpetuates the lack of training in selection and use of texts which is so characteristic of colleges of education and teachers' colleges today. (...)
>
> Fifth, it perpetuates the role of the band wagon, the selection of books solely because many other persons have chosen them. (...) The need for security when making difficult decisions will undoubtedly keep the band wagon rolling until a tested theory can be developed and persons trained to use it. When this happens, they will feel secure in doing what they know they can do well, and the band wagon will have fewer riders. (Spalding 1955, pp. 181-82.)

Chapter VI

Conclusion

Summary

Up to the 1970s, the field was dominated by a few traditions (history book revision and historical content analyses) and by individual and composite works published at long intervals (NSSE Yearbook 1931, Cronbach 1955, Dance 1960, Elson 1964, Schüddekopf 1966, Andolf 1972). Production subsequently increased steadily, and by the 1980s the literature included articles, essays and research reports containing analyses of the development, production, use and content of textbooks. The situation as of 1993 is that textbook research has been formalized in some countries (e.g., Austria, Germany, Japan and Sweden), where separate institutes have been established for textbook research. In other countries, certain universities conduct textbook research. National and international networks are also under development (e.g., AERA-SIG in the USA, an international UNESCO-Braunschweig network, PARADIGM in the UK, and PEXU in the Nordic countries).

The results thus far may be summed up as follows:

Little research has been done on the writing, development and distribution of textbooks. Most of the literature consists of articles criticizing either the approval systems or the role of the publisher (chapter V).

Book use has received slightly more attention, but so far the primary focus has been on textbook analyses based on readability theories rather than on classroom surveys. The results are conclusive on several points: Textbooks have been and continue to be the most widely-used teaching aid. Although it is hard to pinpoint exactly how textbooks are used in the classroom, it is clear that practices vary considerably. The way in which pupils read and use textbooks has not yet been studied adequately, but existing reports tell of poor accessibility and questionable effectiveness (chapter IV).

Content analyses have dominated textbook research. They have primarily been ideological in nature, aimed at improving textbooks' faculty for instilling tolerance and international understanding. Recent research in the fields of philosophy, education and linguistics has helped broaden the general field of vision. Today research looks not only at the selection and distribution of material in textbooks, it also tries to examine their content in light of their form and use. Results deriving from this research should indicate that it is time to reconsider several features of the textbook genre, whose textual form has remained largely unchanged for the past few decades (chapters II and III).

Researchers have employed a wide variety of different methods, ranging from impressionistic-polemical analyses to precise, mathematical-statistical surveys. In the studies emphasizing scientific methods, researchers have encountered one or more of the following problems: How to distinguish between development, use and content; how, in view of the interdisciplinary nature of the textbook, to establish criteria for the division of emphasis between subject content, pedagogy, didactics and literature; how to deal with the constraints ensuing from traditional limitations and commitment to methods used in the social sciences; how to distinguish between the descriptive and the normative in one's own publication/report. Considering the wide variety of methods used, it appears we have learned the most from the studies that have given the most meticulous explanation of their intentions in relation to the categorization of their material.

Many studies have lacked an overall perspective. In addition, ambiguous attitudes toward the production and use of textbooks are found in publishing houses and schools. Such ambiguity may be considered both a cause and an effect of the fact that the total research-book development-teaching cycle has not previously been analyzed as a potential area for improving not only the books, but also the school. Such work is contingent upon maintaining an overall perspective over the part textbooks play both in school and in society. This issue is discussed under the heading *A View of*

Textbooks. In addition, I argue for more attention to be paid to the textbook as a literary genre (*The Interpretability of Textbooks*). Finally, certain methodological principles must be adjusted to coincide with an overall perspective. They are discussed under *A View of Approaches* and illustrated in *A View of Research Tasks*.

A View of Textbooks

A textbook is neither just subject content, nor pedagogy, nor literature, nor information, nor morals nor politics. It is the freebooter of public information, operating in the gray zone between community and home, science and propaganda, special subject and general education, adult and child.

In recent decades, certain aspects of social development have heightened the significance of this multi-faceted role. The advent of electronic communications has made linguistic ability a key concept in education, working life and life in general. Expertise is often largely a question of being conversant with the LSP (language for special purposes) of a particular field. The vocabularies used in most of the school's theoretical and practical subjects may be considered variants of the mother-tongue. Language mastery has become essential in view of our daily contact with printed and electronic texts. In addition, the media revolution is steadily raising the minimum level of linguistic insight required of everyone who wants to gain understanding and, with understanding, the self-confidence and desire to take an active part in the community.

At the same time, the disjointed, entertainment-oriented waves of information flooding the leisure-time market may jeopardize children's self-images and perception of the world instead of manifesting coherence and stimulating their will to live. School is the only place where children still gather together under one roof to read and analyze texts of any length. In that sense, school may be viewed as the last guarantee of equal development opportunities. Yet this is true only to the extent that the school uses texts that are physically and linguistically accessible enough to be read, understood and used by the majority of pupils. Failure on this point will create marked social divisions between an articulate, active minority and a linguistically impoverished, passive majority.

A basic tenet of the modern school system is that teaching should be centered on the local environment and the individual. Shared national characteristics also become more highly appreciated during a time marked by rapid internationalization. At the same time, pressure on and from other nations is something of value. The old questions from classic history book revision reassert themselves with renewed relevance: How should textbooks depict the home, the region, the nation and the world?

New and complex demands on teachers have reinforced the position of the textbook. During times marked by teaching staff uncertainty and great mobility among families, this literature, more than any other element of knowledge dissemination, comprises the very essence of the contract between children and society.

The problem facing us today is as follows: On the one hand the standards for general qualifications are being raised, while on the other the dynamics at work in today's society are impeding the development of precisely the same qualifications. The result is a paradox in respect of all our ideas about education (Jensen 1991, p. 5). We strive for effectiveness and expertise, but we cannot press requirements for qualifications any further in a theoretical direction unless the evolutionary pattern is holistic and general. Without a broad base, the whole system will break down; people won't want to take part if they don't recognize the system's relevance. Thus the challenge facing those who make textbooks is to write books that guarantee academic progression *and* general education. This presupposes processes of a different nature from those discussed in the chapter of this book called *The Development of Textbooks*. We must build new textbook experiences that are open to an infinite variety of perspectives. We must replace our pensive perusing with active processing. The textbooks themselves must pave the way for other activities which are more open and less predictable - activities which, paradoxically, are dependent on textbooks for development. This might mean they would have to incorporate some sort of "fifth column" texts that contravene their own traditions. Perhaps we can envision a genre that discusses a subject while teaching it to children and young people; a genre open to - even demanding - interpretation and independent study.

The ideal textbook might therefore be summed up as follows:

- In every subject, it would use ordinary language and language for special purposes in a way that would inspire in the majority of pupils the desire to read and use such language;

- In every subject, it would describe individuals, nature and society in a way that would give the majority of pupils insight into and interest in connections which many would otherwise find hard to discover on their own, outside the school environment.

The Interpretability of Textbooks

Several investigations have drawn attention to the decline in reading motivation that takes place during the transition from primary to lower secondary level (Beverton 1986, Perera 1986, Sosniak-Perlman 1990, de Castell 1990). Concurrent with this transition, there is a change in the kind of reading material pupils are given. Expository prose gains a strong position, reducing pupils' exposure to fiction and other more literary texts. At the same time, increasing emphasis is nevertheless placed on literary comprehension and analysis, areas in which most language teachers (mother-tongue and foreign) have received training. It would be difficult, however, to point to any corresponding interpretation or analysis of all the new documentary literature which views the material as a literary product expressive of a mode of thought. This situation may be attributed to factors related to 1) history, 2) the philosophy of science, 3) pedagogy and 4) production.

1. Historically speaking, the ancient Greeks were the fathers of Western science and technology, which are based on logical analyses of nature and society. An exacting, sharp language based on mathematics demands registration, definition and systematization. Children learn in school that life can be managed by ordering it into conceptual systems. A logical analysis of the classifiable phenomena which comprise reality seems to be inherent in the nature of man; we are pre-programmed, so to speak. However, language, including ordinary prose, is studded with images and symbols. Pupils are also expected to deal with these phenomena in school. But this rather more diffuse, creative way of writing and thinking is supposed to be taught them through fine literature and aesthetic subjects. We tend to overlook the fact that

the ostensibly strict scientific tradition is replete with images and symbols, with highly interpretable "paradigms". This is true of textbooks as well. In fact, many textbook titles suggest that the books present comprehensive coverage of a subject, which must perforce entail a philosophy of the subject, life or the world (*From Word to Statement, Biology, Our Own Language, Our Society*). Nonetheless, many people still view ordinary textbook prose as being identical with indisputable fact, i.e., they are unable to separate the veracity of the language from the veracity of the facts described by the language (see page 126).

2. With regard to the philosophy of science, in the non-aesthetic disciplines, the ideal of objectivity has traditionally dominated not only research institutions, but also the school (see page 134). This means that textbooks have - errouneously - been viewed as objective conveyors of fact. Fiction, on the other hand, has been preeminent as the interpreter of the world, so it has been considered natural to view fiction as a challenge on which one must take a position. (I've chosen to disregard the tradition that prevailed in primary schools far into the twentieth century, involving the rote memorization of moralistic fiction (see page 173).)

3. This, in turn, has an impact on education. Investigations concerning use clearly indicate that textbooks are predominantly used as reference books and as study guides to prepare for examinations. Although not formally or officially stated anywhere, in practice, the general attitude is that textbooks exist in order to be regurgitated on command (see page 232).

4. Today, textbooks are mass-produced and not unique (Johnsen 1989, Trotzig 1989, Woodward 1990). Very few comparative studies show any significant differences in methods or general approaches among competing books for the same level. In any event, the widespread belief that the books are alike will not promote any initiative to treat the school's documentary literature as something requiring interpretation (see page 201).

It is now time to consider the question of *textbooks as interpretable expressions* from all angles. First of all, it is related to the development of general scientific theory in the humanities (see Gordon, Kjørup and Lunden, page 343). Second, it is ascribable to the advent of new scientific concepts and modes of thought in the field of literature. Four key terms in this context are: analyses of language usage, the question of genre, the reader-book relationship and the relationship between the school's objectives and educational texts in light of linguistic theory.

In many countries analyses of language usage now supplement traditional literary analyses. In Norway, for example, literary analyses of prose texts in school were unheard of before the mid-1970s, when they enjoyed a breakthrough in the subject of Norwegian. This general trend was to some extent related to political currents in the wake of the 1968 movement, gaining ground as it became accepted that "language is power"; i.e., it was acknowledged that so-called non-fiction literature could be biased and subjective. It would be unnatural if such a realization did not have repercussions on one of the most common varieties of non-fiction literature besides newspapers, namely the textbook.

The question of genre is also partially a result of the recognition of non-fiction prose as interpretive, and therefore interpretable. Parallel to process-oriented composition training, which experienced a definitive breakthrough in the USA in the early 1980s and has now become popular in Europe as well, pupils have become more conscious of genre. This has caused more attention to be focused on textbook genres. Should textbooks consist exclusively of non-fiction prose, like reference books? The question may be considered from different angles. One approach is that taken by Myers, who investigated the use of dialogue in educational texts over a relatively long period of time (Myers 1990). He ascertained that dialogue is a very common literary form which is rapidly gaining even more ground in our century. He contends that the form neither reduces the "realism" of a presentation nor the authority of a text (see Olson, page 173). Mauri Åhlberg (Åhlberg 1991) points out that the monologue-dialogue ratio has rarely been used as an approach to investigations of educational discourse (the latter referring to both oral and written text). Other examples of ideas involving the comprehensiveness of genres in educational texts have been put forth in Harold Rosen's *The Importance of Story* (1985), Kieran Egan's *Teaching as Story Telling* (1986), Herdis Toft's *Story Flora.*

On the Didactic Function of the Story (1990), and Eiliv Vinje's *Stories and Composition Training* (1990). Gilbert T. Sewall of the American Textbook Council coined the motto *Rededicate the textbook to the text:*

> Textbook reform efforts should concentrate on enlivening passages, making them less impersonal and providing more human drama. Textbook historiography should abandon readability formulas that can dumb material down. In fact, it should welcome complex sentences and challenging vocabulary, where appropriate, as such writing can expand both comprehension of the subject and appreciation of literature. (Sewall 1987, p. 74.)

The most comprehensive discussion of this topic may be found in Gillham 1986 (see page 199).

The reader-book relationship has only lately been given much attention, even by readability specialists. Rosenblatt 1978 and Fisch 1980 represented a breakthrough. The former pointed out that no text is complete until it has been read, and that there must of necessity be several ways to read all texts since they are used by people with vastly different backgrounds, even if they are the same age. The latter goes a step further and claims that groups of reading and interpretation patterns emerge which are determined more by society than by individuals. Suzanne de Castell has pointed out the significance of such viewpoints in discussing the relationship between the authority of the teacher and that of the textbook. She herself believes that "For all the educational value and justification such critical theories might have for teachers' practice, however, outside the English class, most student textbooks are likely to remain 'beyond criticism'." (De Castell 1990, p. 78.) De Castell claims that as long as the receptive and regurgitative attitude toward textbooks remains unchanged in the classroom, textbooks will also remain unchanged.

Textual linguist Mauri Åhlberg's analyses of text structures (see page 212) may be viewed as an argument in favor of the same view. In a more recent work (Åhlberg 1991), the author concludes that good learning may require pupils and teachers to adopt the same searching attitude toward the text/world as the scientist assumes:

> Probably the best way to learn deeply would be to make learning more like solving problems of real life, similar to investigations, and small scale cooperative research projects. Concept mapping and argumentation analysis could be used as flexible tools also in that kind of teaching and learning. (Åhlberg 1991, p. 43.)

This view is supported by John Ahier, who argues that textbook analyses have overlooked possible opportunities for and ways of using books. In a chapter of Ahier 1988 called "The Text and the Child", the author charges that "approaches to textbooks have never established the particular nature of such books except with regard to their use by children" (p. 41). Like others who have addressed the topic, he denies that there is any "universal method of 'reading' all texts, or a universal standpoint for all contexts from which all texts can be read." (P. 41.) Probably the closest anyone can come to such a universal standpoint in research would literally be to insist on coordination between intention and category (see page 345).

Such coordination would imply a view of the textbook as an object of research - and the pupil as a researcher - also in the classroom (Björnsson 1967; see page 190). Historian Kåre Lunden has indirectly justified such a view on the basis of the need to rescue reading motivation in an age in which "loaded" material is made "worth-less" and thereby insignificant in the textbooks (see page 134). In that context, it is important to note that Thomas S. Kuhn used *natural science* textbooks as his starting point when he presented his theories on paradigm changes. This took place before that oft quoted book, *The Structure of Scientific Revolutions*, was published in 1962 (Kuhn 1962). He presented the view in a collection of articles (Kuhn 1962a), in which he writes that researchers are not the only occupational group to borrow standards and methods from the instruction of others. Sometimes these elements are borrowed at a very early point in time:

Perhaps the most striking feature of scientific education is that, to an extent quite unknown in other creative fields, it is conducted through textbooks, works written especially for students. Until he is ready, or very nearly ready, to begin his own dissertation, the student of chemistry, physics, astronomy, geology, or biology is seldom either asked to attempt trial research projects or exposed to the immediate products of research done by others - to, that is, the professional communications that scientists write for their peers. Collections of "source reading" play a negligible role in *scientific* education. Nor is the science student encouraged to read the historical classics of his field - works in which he might encounter other ways of regarding the questions discussed in his text, but in which he would also meet problems, concepts, and standards of solution that his future profession had long-since discarded and replaced. (Kuhn 1962, p. 350.)

Still, there is certainly no active consensus aimed at realizing the standpoint of the reader as researcher. Although such an approach would undoubtedly be consistent with the spirit of more recent curricula, it is extremely rare to come across textbook prefaces like this one (for a 5th grade textbook):

This textbook is not in itself history. Nor is it in itself geography. It is only one of millions of books written on these subjects. And the books are written by different people who in turn have read what others have read and written.

Imagine a stage so deep that no one can see where it ends. That is *history*. And the stage is placed in a setting so vast that no one can see all of it. That is *geography*.

In front of it all hangs a curtain that stretches all the way to heaven. No one can remove the curtain. But it is possible to pull it aside a wee bit and get a glimpse. This textbook is just such a glimpse. (Johnsen 1992, p. 5.)

Viewing textbook texts as interpretable expressions would represent something of a revolution for most teachers and pupils, as evidenced clearly by the few investigations based on surveys of pupils' opinions (Sosniak 1990). Staffan Selander (Selander 1990; see page 80) has defined the textbook as a genre and asked whether the books, such as they are, can really be considered worthy of interpretation:

> The textbooks are not written by the great minds of humanity although we do in these texts find traces of a cultural world. Nor does it seem very meaningful trying to detect the author's purpose with the text although there is an institutionally determined purpose. (...) The reader cannot choose any kind of "frame" (to frame a text is to read the text out of a specific perspective: a novel can be read as a biography or as a fantasy, as a true story or as a fictitious story, etc.) and thus construct any possible meaning out of the texts in the textbook, simply because the framing is already at hand. *It is also to be read as a true representation of the outside world, as objective, necessary and real.* (Selander 1990, p. 147, *my* emphasis.)

I have added emphasis to the last sentence. The claim made there may be assessed on two levels. First, does it cover the prevailing attitudes and, second, if so, is one of the textbook's main tasks to influence such attitudes?

As I see it, the answer to both questions is yes. Anyone who aims at change such as that mentioned above must ask what should come first: a change in the attitude of those who write the books or of those who use them? Should the book come first and change the teaching, or does teaching have to be revolutionized first? Where does textbook research fit into the picture? Ian Westbury has stressed that one single link should not be blamed for the breakdown of a system comprised of weak links (Westbury 1982, see page 289). This survey has revealed a clear tendency for textbook research to focus too unilaterally on individual links in the system. Based on this, contemporaneousness and coordination, as attempted by Verduin-Muller (see page 251), must be the optimal solution for anyone wanting to see change.

A View of Approaches

Different textbook investigations use the word "method" in vastly different senses. It has been used as a synonym for scale (e.g., use of time) and as a unit of measurement (e.g., number of pages). The word has also been used to refer to the type of source material used (e.g., statistics). Further, it has been used to describe the practical procedures employed (e.g., interviews or classroom observation). Finally, it has been used to refer to the mode of analysis, where it is common to distinguish between quantitative and qualitative.

The complex textbook, teaching and knowledge concept per se (see page 157) entails that every practical study will include several of these factors, or possibly just one of them which will thereby become so comprehensive that it will have to be divided into smaller, independent units. In addition, neither "textbook", "teaching" nor "knowledge" are factors which will remain static from subject to subject or from level to level. Separately, they may be dissected and classified into groups. Such groups may resemble each other in two parallel investigations, but that doesn't necessarily mean they've been given the same designation. Conversely, the same designation may be used to refer to several different phenomena. The survey has shown that there are a multitude of possible combinations and variations. The sections entitled *Perspectives* include all the following factors, to the extent they were available in each individual case:

- Intention of the investigation,
- Categorization,
- Material,
- Mode of analysis.

A consistent effort has been made to systematize the investigations according to what has invariably been called *approaches*. In this presentation the term refers to intention as well as categories, based on the rationale that categories are selected and determined on the basis of the intention and that the categories themselves may influence the intention. This standpoint calls for a more precise definition of the term *categorization*, which in its broadest sense refers to the process, use or production-related aspects of the textbook phenomenon in question. The most comprehensive theoretical system of categorization for textbook analyses was devised by Peter Weinbrenner, who uses 25 overlapping categories, ordered according to the following five "Dimensionen": "Wissenschaftstheorie / Design / Fachwissenschaft / Fachdidaktik / Facherzeihungswissenschaft". In turn, these "Dimensionen", or factors, fall into a single higher category: they are parts of a "produktorientierten, wirtschafts- und sozialwissenschaftlichen Schulbuchforschung" (Weinbrenner 1986a, p. 327). One example of a broad and open form of categorization may be seen in Olsson 1986. In the 1980s, *culture* became a central, highly controversial field of research. Olsson harmonizes a relatively new concept (cultural perception) in another subject (geography), as it is developed in textbooks (language and pictures), with the curricula (school history and politics) and the science of history.

However, the term *categorization* is most often used in a very restricted sense, as exemplified in DsU 1980: 4 (see page 385), where the discussion of method states that "to conduct a meaningful discussion, one must somehow reduce the data, i.e. one must categorize" (p. 28). The same source contends that categorization must satisfy two criteria: Categories must be "mutually exclusive" and they must be "so well-defined that anyone will be able to repeat the classification or establish new categories of his own." However, the source also states that the content of the categories will generally be controversial, often due to superficial disagreement. The most important point is not the categories in themselves. It is "not until they are applied to a problem, that one can judge the quality." (P. 28.)

Liberal, open categorization usually combines an inter-disciplinary perspective and a broad outlook with corresponding limitations on verifiability and scientific character. The more narrow the categorization, the greater the reliability - and the greater the corresponding reduction in perspective. The formulations expounded in DsU 1980:4 are representative of the efforts to comply with traditional, social science research ideals rather than of attempts to seek out new models based on the attributes of the textbook. The more narrowly defined the category - for example the ability of the pupils in a given class at a given level to find synonyms for a given number of foreign words in a particular book - the greater the apparent chance to achieve "tenable" results in the sense that they can be tested and proven to have a high degree of reliability and validity (Holsti 1969, Holter 1990). Such limitations may satisfy certain requirements as regards objectivity, but they are worthless if they haven't been thoroughly correlated with an equally precise statement of intention for the project of which they are part. The overwhelming majority of textbook analyses that claim to be scientific invest a great deal of methodological preparation in detailing exactly what they will and will not investigate. It usually turns out that this work has no reasonable correlate in the justification for making the investigation or in its objective. Hence the relationship between a precisely defined intention and the choice of categories and units of measurement remains obscure or poorly clarified.

This problem has been placed within a frame of scientific theory by historian Kåre Lunden (Lunden 1990). Lunden's analysis applies to textbooks, not to textbook research. However, his criticism of the books necessitates an answer to the question of how authors view textbooks. Indirectly, the study eventually reveals a strong correlation between the problems of the textbook writer, the teacher and the textbook researcher as regards attitudes and procedures. This fact has also been a recurrent theme in this survey. The same complexity that faces teachers when they set up evaluation criteria for "a good textbook" confronts the textbook researcher when he sets out to define his task.

Lunden criticizes the history and social studies textbooks used in Norway in the past few decades as being "worth-less" in every sense of the word, saying there are no more attitudes left in them to uncover. To Lunden, this situation is symptomatic of a cultural crisis. It may be interpreted as a more or less involuntary perversion of the natural sciences' ideal of objectivity. In an effort to justify his claim, Lunden discusses the relationship between the natural sciences and the humanities. The two fields explore different types of objects; the scholar's objects (ideas, actions, institutions) are man-made and thus serve a purpose - "the end constitutes the object" (p. 222). From this, Lunden draws the following conclusion about methodological approaches in the humanities:

> The humanities have a special object, and are in a special situation, which, as I see it, means that the humanist, when identifying a meaningful phenomenon, is dependent on building on his own, inner experience of sense or meaning. As far as I can see, this does not entail that the fundamental method - the identification of phenomena as belonging to general classes - can be unlike the scientific. *But it may entail that the results - the identifications - in the humanities are particularly uncertain, and in a special way relatively subjective.* (Lunden 1990, p. 229; *my* emphasis.)

Then member of the National Humanities Research Council Søren Kjørup wrote a preface to Jørgen Møller's analysis of Danish history books (Møller 1983): "The Humanities in Research and Communication." Like Kåre Lunden, he emphasizes the intrinsic nature of and prerequisites for humanities research: "(...) not merely the creation of new knowledge, but also the creation of new points of view, new interpretations." (P. 11.) At the most profound level, this is the same premise which more or less consciously underlies Cronbach's image of the researcher as poet, or of the support expressed by Gordon and Antonietti for the analogy as a guideline (see below). Lee J. Cronbach writes that a theory may be compared to a poem: "Its function is to create out of a mass of fact or impression an epitome which gives the sense of the whole"; theory *may* be removed from fact as Shakespeare's *Henry V* is from the docu-ments that originated during that monarch's reign (Cronbach 1955, p. 61). The determination and use of theory will inevitably entail interpretations which play some things up and others down.

Regardless of the argumentative weight we might attach to Cronbach's comparison, the example says something about the effect of analogies. More than a generation after Cronbach, David Gordon wrote about "a new, rather exciting perspective that has developed in the social sciences: understanding social life through analogies derived from the humanities rather than from the natural sciences" (Gordon 1988, p. 426). Such a perspective changes the scientific mode of thought; society is viewed less as a systematic organism than as "a serious game, a sidewalk drama, or a behavioral text" (Geertz 1980, p. 168). Gordon refers to Paul Ricoeur's theories concerning the school's hidden curriculum (Ricoeur 1981) and adopts Geertz' standpoint to use one phenomenon/analogy as the main expression for school and education: Text. School is a text. Gordon attempts to illustrate how such a paramount, analogical perspective can pave the way for a new understanding of - in casu - "educational phenomena".

Analogies are often useful in trying to discover new points of view: "Basically, the development of a new theory in the scientific disciplines has been and will continue to be relatively frequently justified by an analogy to an entirely different field of study." (Antonietti 1991, p. 111.) An analogy can pave the way for new interpretations of all the facts at hand - "facts" which, in new contexts, may be subject to change. Naturally, the analogy may also be used as a methodological starting point without precluding tried and proven systems of evaluation.

Of interest here is the demand for versality in Marxist scientific theory, as developed by the Frankfurt school and Habermas ("das Erkenntnis leitende Interesse"). A program is acceptable only when it does not destroy "(...) den forschungslogischen Zusammenhang zwischen Erkenntnisinteressen, wissenschaftlichen Fragestellungen, Untersuchungsmethoden und Interpretationen der Ergebnisse." (Klafki 1978; here quoted from Schubert 1987, p. 38.) Yet this versatility is not contingent upon having a Marxist outlook; it may be required and applied without its purpose necessarily being emancipatory, for example. Nor is it particularly new (Kuhn 1962; see page 337). Cronbach and McMurray outlined the same perspective in their 1955 work. More than 20 years later Peter Meyers presented a similar program in his basic introduction to different analytical methods (Meyers 1976). He sums up his introduction in six "Grundregeln für zukünftige Schulbuchanalysen" (pp. 68-69). His primary assertion is worded as follows in points 1 and 2:

> Every textbook analysis should start with a thorough discussion of goals and the purpose of the work. This is even more important since it has been demonstrated that the method selected is strongly influenced by the objective. The writer of a textbook analysis must be fully aware of the relevance of his objective. (...) Investigations without clearly delimited categories fall outside the realm of any discussion. (Meyers 1976, p. 68.)

It is also the "particularly uncertain" (Lunden) aspect of the humanities' identifications that constitutes my own justification for insisting that a close connection be made between intention and category. It is not sufficient for an author to state that he has examined an account of this or that trade at one place or another during this or that period of time in these or those social studies books, and that the job was commissioned by a particular trade association. Nor is it sufficient for the author to state that he is in some way biased, e.g., that his investigation is based on the assumption that the trade is underrepresented or that a description of it is somehow distorted. The author must also indicate why it is relevant to shed light on this point in particular, and justify his choice of categories systematically to coincide with such an account. A broad, readily quantifiable factor like the number of lines of text dealing directly with the trade in question, or a narrower category like business administration, are meaningless unless meticulously related to the aim of the investigation.

The viewpoint concerning the connection between intention and category does not preclude the fact that categories will necessarily develop from vastly different points of departure. They may spring from registration and source material, from didactical points, or from social debate. Theoretically speaking, the number of starting points is legion. The most important point is that the categorization is accurate and obvious in light of the intention and the identification, which may – or should – emerge "in a special way relatively subjective" (Lunden).

A View of Research Tasks

I now return to the statement that "textbooks are hopeless no matter how you approach them" (see Johansson, page 158). Another analogy might be useful in this context. I have chosen one from the world of children's toys. There is, undoubtedly, something *kaleidoscopic* about the nature of textbook content and textbook use. (A kaleidoscope is a tubular device containing mirrors and small bits of colored glass. The child looks through a peephole at one end and the backlighted colors on the other end form new patterns each time the tube is turned.) Like the bits of colored glass, the majority of written texts in the school are being studied within rather closed walls (the textbooks). But don't teachers wield some influence? Yes, in the sense that they occasionally make small adjustments to the mirrors from the outside, adjustments which cause but minor changes in the constellations formed by the pages.

As the texts on these pages are sustained inside the system, they don't change with the passage of time. Some would reject this analogy on the grounds that new books flow into the system all the time. On the other hand, the comparison may still be valid because the renewal has been no stronger than that it might be compared to the somewhat arbitrary light conditions (political, educational and methodological currents), which simply affect the quality of the same old figures. The main rule is that the laws of nature within the walls are stronger than the forces on the outside. These laws, this textbook language, form their own *Kaleidoscopia* which is the school's own and, some would say, infinitely unrevisable text, eclipsing the authority of curricula, teachers and books. In that perspective, true change might be obtained only or primarily from the inside by blowing up the kaleidoscope.

It is possible to stretch the analogy far enough to accommodate pupils as well. A child does not make a sharp distinction between himself and what he sees. The child who looks at the glass bits or reads the books is both an onlooker and a participant in the apparatus/system. The analogy becomes somewhat misleading at this point. A child at play twists and shakes the kaleidoscope, following his own rhythm to decide for himself when to change the pattern. Many would contend that pupils do not always enjoy the same freedom in the school kaleidoscope.

A textbook researcher revisiting his childhood can no longer be both an observer and a participant. Granted, he may relive reading situations and be moved by memories of first experiences, but during the second round of reading he is an outsider, an observer of both child and school. Influenced by adult philosophies of education, he will try to penetrate his children's - not his own childhood's - schooling and reading. To do so, he needs a systematic point of view; a method or, if you will, another kaleidoscope that can be placed around the school's own kaleidoscopes to reveal the patterns in *their* hodgepodge of books. In this sense, the kaleidoscope becomes a reflection of both object and method.

The researcher encounters at least one important limitation. He must choose among different procedures which are all imperfect. His most drastic recourses are, on the one hand, to shake the apparatus hard and often ("impressionistic") and, on the other, to hold the kaleidoscope in a fixed position, frozen on particular constellations for certain periods of time, with certain bits in focus and the light just so ("scientific"). The most reassuring course of action, and the preferred one, has been not to upset the research kaleidoscope too much. Educational literature abounds with descriptions of "captured moments". But as for the school kaleidoscope, isn't it always in motion? Although it may move slowly, without major shake-ups, isn't it nevertheless perpetually in motion? Texts, readers and venues change. It also turns out that even if the same methods are applied to the factors in a number of investigations, no two investigations will ever have identical constellations - any more than two kaleidoscope images will ever be completely identical.

The crucial point would be one of *simultaneity*: Textbook

research must become less of an "after the event"-activity and more of an integrated part of the development and use of textbooks. The requirements should be based on the realization that the goal constitutes the object. Textbook research will not command broad, general interest until it is synchronized with development and use. This is consistent with the distinctive qualities inherent in textbooks as processes, instruments and products. Textbook research is research into the transmission of knowledge. Like the interdisciplinary factor, this brand of distinctive quality should warrant this research. We should not assume that the primary goal of current international textbook research is to eliminate any interpretations which could be perceived as being biased. Some would claim it is more important to fight functional illiteracy; to produce readily-comprehensible books which teach pupils knowledge of subjects as well as independence. This is hardly the case for most textbook readers today. If textbook research is to lead to any improvement, the planning and performance of every research project should be accompanied by developmental and information work that, in one way or another, implicates all involved parties in a more open form of educational culture:

- Those who determine message and content: Professional and research communities at colleges and universities, political bodies, school-related legislation and curricula;
- Those who produce and distribute the books: Authors, editors, designers, consultants and marketing experts;
- Those who evaluate and select books: School boards, teachers' councils, individual teachers;
- Those who use the books: Pupils, teachers, parents.

Conducting research and disseminating information about it are two sides of the same coin. Anyone wishing to learn more about the reasons for the poor dissemination of textbook knowledge must also investigate the choice of program and procedures used by those who have done the research. Which professional groups have taken part in planning such investigations? At the university? At the school book publishers? At school? Which system is used to communicate views and results within the textbook research community while the researchers themselves are busy collecting and processing material? Which teachers get the opportunity to contribute their experiences before the results are printed in a journal they may never read? Which pupils ever hear about it?

Every research project ought to begin by stating the type of interdisciplinary approach selected for the study in question, then be conducted accordingly. Further, no investigation, even if it is directly associated with only one of the links in the textbook chain, should overlook any of the other links. Research results must be exchanged, processed and developed in a continuous cycle of researchers - syllabus planners - authors - publishers - teachers - pupils. Results must not be brought in from the outside as more or less random precipitates of the indisputable facts ultimately left intact after an isolated investigation. The textbook should represent both a research object and a research result.

The principle regarding the coordination of many links is, in turn, a result of the fact that textbook research still lacks a platform in the world of science. Such recognition is essential if the field is to gain status and develop further. The solution must be to ascertain an overall definition of the discipline which takes ample account of its interdisciplinary nature. Such an open outlook should also enable researchers to ask the right questions and thus choose the most useful tasks.

Chapter VII

Appendix:
Registration as a Basis for Analysis

Problems

The number of textbook titles to be examined need not be especially large before the registration process begins to present problems. The term "textbook" is in itself complex and fluid. In countries with approval schemes, for example, one has to decide whether the register is to include non-approved textbooks. Norway's approval system has never covered study aids and workbooks unless they are parts of complete works, yet many of these books have played an important role in teaching. Looking back on the past, although many textbooks have probably been reviewed and approved, some of them may no longer be available today. A given title may be available in one edition but be out of print in an extensively revised and perhaps more widely used edition. The problem *edition/impression/author/title* manifests itself in several ways when one sets about registering or classifying textbooks from an historical perspective. Many textbooks have been issued in several editions and impressions; moreover, they may have changed title, contents and author profile in the process. According to Beckson and Ganz (1990), the term *edition* refers to the total number of copies of a work printed from a single set of type (new editions implying that changes or revisions have been made in the original typesetting), and the term *impression* refers to the total number of copies printed at one time while the type or plates are in the press (new impressions implying that the same type or plates are used for a reprinting). But this distinction is not consistently observed in all countries. In some cases it can also be difficult to obtain complete information about the number of editions/impressions. Some may be out of print, and practice may vary between numbering successive editions on one hand and merely giving the total number of copies printed on the other.

Eva Bjørkvold and Frøydis Hertzberg (Bjørkvold - Hertzberg 1976), who studied Norwegian grammar textbooks published between 1816 and 1973, narrowed the field partly by choosing representative samples of the grammars published in many editions/impressions, i.e., grammars which had a long life span, and partly by using formal criteria - for example a change of title or author where information about editions/impressions was lacking or unclear. In this way they collocated a pool of primary source material consisting of 133 different grammars, while their total sample comprised 188 different editions/impressions. Their presentation was based on a purely practical solution. Regardless of the designation on the colophon page or elsewhere in the books, they use the term edition consistently, unless special considerations call for more precision (p. 14).

When the term edition is used to designate a genre, as in school editions (of, for example, Ludvig Holberg's comedies), there are even more sets of editions to keep track of. Which edition of the work is the school edition based on? Has the school edition been subject to extensive revision and, if so, has this been indicated with a new *edition* designation on the colophon page? Leif Longum has written an article on his examination of 86 school editions of Norwegian authors (Longum 1987) without touching on this last question. He uses edition consistently about an individual selection's title and impression consistently for all new reissues, i.e., a best seller is "a work printed in 10 impressions or more" (p. 67). Like Bjørkvold and Hertzberg, he includes the years for the first and last numbered impressions.

There is an important distinction between registering the publications of textbooks on the one hand, and trying to register their distribution on the other. The latter area is the most difficult to survey. Even if all the publishers made their sales figures available, it would only be possible to draw approximate conclusions about the life cycle of books. *Second-hand books* and *class sets* are two key words in this context.

For most studies, a thorough clarification of the relationship between objectives and methods on one hand, and the selection process on the other will be more important than the degree of comprehensiveness. This may be illustrated by the three criteria that Tyler Kepner (Kepner 1935, see page 44) used as the basis for his study of the development of geography and history books:

> (...) no effort will be made to list all titles. Rather an attempt will be made to select (1) those textbooks, which by reason of the large number of editions in which they were printed, were obviously influential books, (2) those in United States history, for example, in which the author had also established himself as a writer in other historical fields, and (3) those which merit attention for their special characteristics, though probably not widely used. (P. 144.)

The first criterion dominates major historical studies, while both the last two criteria, and the combination of all three, are unusual in such studies.

Sources

The usual sources are national archives, university libraries, educational libraries and national bibliographies. Experience has shown, however, that even all these taken together cannot be assumed to offer complete information in the areas mentioned above, at any rate not in the Nordic countries. This is first of all because the system of classification will vary over a long period of time and, second, because entries on file cards are not always systematically and/or completely updated. Information may also be provided by publishing houses, insofar as they are still in existence. The largest Norwegian publishers have some data on file about sales and printings. The practice varies from in-depth systematic listings in anniversary catalogs to rather more scanty records. A common tendency is for such records to be more carefully and systematically maintained the further back we go in time. For example, several major publishers find it more difficult to locate information from the period 1960-80 than from 1920-60.

The same tendency may be seen in the filing practices of the educational councils, relevant in this context because they have administered approval schemes and/or made various general and specific statements about textbooks in a number of countries. Norway is a good example because the tradition dates back to July 24, 1885, when the very first provisions concerning the authorization of textbooks were issued by the Ministry. They were followed the next year by a circular making authorization contingent upon books following the orthographic rules adopted in 1885. In the 1890s, several directives were issued requiring upper secondary school principals to list the titles of the textbooks used by their schools in the schools' annual reports. This practice was followed until 1916. In the first decade of the 1900s, the Ministry was very conscientious about distributing evaluations of new textbooks for primary and secondary schools, based on the books' contents and educational merits. As the number of titles increased and as the approval scheme, which officially dates back to the Compulsory Education Act of 1889, was further developed, the Ministry and the educational councils were reduced merely to publishing lists of titles in bulletins and annual reports. From 1955, such reviews for primary and secondary schools were made public and published sporadically in a gazette called "The Norwegian School", which existed for 30 years. The Ministry and the publishing houses tried several catalog schemes in an effort to provide up-to-date, yearly printed information about all available approved textbook literature for primary and secondary schools, but it became increasingly difficult to keep track of the flood of books produced in the 1970s and 1980s. One example is the *1992 Catalog of Teaching Materials for the Upper Secondary School (Læremiddelkatalogen for den videregående skole 1992)*. It is 430 pages long and includes roughly 5000 titles. A reference list of entries arranged by subject runs to more than 600 words; a summary of the various courses of study in this type of school fills 22 pages. At present (February, 1993), the Norwegian Publishers' Association and the publishers' central distribution company, Forlagssentralen A/S, are trying to incorporate all titles used in primary and secondary schools in a new computerized database system.

In Sweden, Swedish textbooks were registered in the Swedish National Bibliography until 1976. Since then, new titles have been entered in LIBRIS, a communal database for the country's research libraries. In Denmark, the National Center for Educational Materials published comprehensive catalogs as well as some smaller ones covering individual subjects every year in the 1980s. However, the National Center was closed down in 1990.

One major source of information about textbooks in use is the schools themselves. Bound annual reports for the two decades just before and after the turn of the century exist for a score of secondary schools in Norway. They are housed at the Norwegian

Educational Library in Oslo and they contain meticulous lists of the material covered in every subject. As previously noted, the tradition of annual reports was kept up until 1916. In the inter-war years, most upper secondary schools had teachers keep records of which readers and textbooks they used and what they covered during the year. Few of these records have survived; a survey conducted in 1990 on the subject of Norwegian elicited positive responses and relatively complete lists from only one third of the upper secondary schools polled in Norway (Johnsen 1992a). The system more or less disintegrated during the 1970s and 80s, when it was replaced by prescribed reading lists for final year pupils. There is no rule saying that these lists have to be kept on file. The tendency to *forget* is underlined here because it should be seen in connection with a question that is discussed elsewhere: At any given time, how much attention do subjects/textbooks themselves pay to what has gone on before (Kuhn 1962, see page 338)?

A register which goes back approximately a hundred years from 1990, and which is based on all the material available from all of the sources named above, will on the one hand hardly risk overlooking textbooks that have been used, even to a very limited extent. On the other hand, such an approach is no guarantee that absolutely every title, and certainly not every edition or impression, will be included on the list.

The sole objective of an investigation may be to achieve the most complete and detailed survey possible. Such an objective need not only be based on the satisfaction derived from compiling a definitive compendium. Another argument for such thoroughness is that the existence of such material can provide an incentive for new research. The most striking example of this is the project "Emmanuelle" at the Institut National de Recherche Pédagogique in Paris (Choppin - Decouche-Beauchais 1988; Choppin - Rodriguez 1989). Every textbook published after 1789 for every level and subject in primary and secondary school is registered in a database, with information about titles, authors, publishers, educational level and edition/impression. In addition, all the information in the database is indexed under 43 different key words or fields ("champs"), for example, illustrator/printer/library (information about where the book is available)/discipline/approval.

There are two ways of accessing the data; either on line access (as for all multi-criteria data bases): 43 variable names or fields can be combined thanks to boolean operators, and - or - not; or through the publication of comprehensive catalogs, discipline by discipline.

The project is based on all the kinds of sources mentioned above. It is very useful to have access to "Bibliographie de la France", a journal published weekly since 1811, which lists all new editions of books - including textbooks. But even that is incomplete and deficient. The head of the project, Alain Choppin, gives an account of all the sources for French school book research in an article in Thérèse Charmasson's basic text for and about school history research (Charmasson 1986).

In 1991 the Emmanuelle material comprised over 80,000 titles. The results up to that time in four subjects (Latin, Greek, Italian and German) were published in book form. The study, started in 1979, will run for several more years. The software is now developed to the point where it can be adapted for use with other languages. (See page 394.) The justification for financing such a large apparatus was and is that the material has significance for new research. The primary goal is to achieve the greatest possible degree of comprehensiveness.

When we look at studies dealing with a large number of titles, we see that there are several avenues of approach, not all of which place the same emphasis on accuracy or completeness. It would be natural to assume that approaches vary depending on the objectives of the various studies. However, it appears that such immediately obvious correlations do not always exist. The following survey presents analyses based on large amounts of data that have been organized according to the attention paid to the selection and registration of titles; that is, the more an analysis focuses on this problem, the farther down on the list it will come, as a rule. The content and form of the analyses will only be discussed and evaluated here to the extent that they shed light on the correlation between registration and objective. In the main the presentation will observe the order Norwegian - Nordic - other countries.

Comprehensiveness and Scholarship

There is not necessarily any correlation between the level of formal scholarship and the level of justification for the selection and registration of titles. Here I have used a doctoral dissertation, a study done by an institute and a master's thesis to illustrate this point.

Karin Tarschys' doctoral dissertation on mother tongue instruction in Sweden's secondary schools at the end of the 19th and beginning of the 20th century (Tarschys 1955) is based on a large corpus of source material, a fraction of which consists of textbooks and anthologies. The primary source material consists of official documents and scholarly and popular literature about the development of the school system. It is against this background that she looks at the teaching of Swedish as a mother tongue. From the preface it is evident that Tarschys has not seen it as her main task to deduce literary canon from her material, although that might have been possible within the framework of such a comprehensive survey. Her work is first and foremost an investigation of the literature read by teachers and researchers, not that read by pupils. It would be unreasonable to demand a textbook bibliography under these circumstances. On the other hand, Tarschys does not directly address the possibilities that textbooks offer for saying something about one of her main themes, namely the attitude taken toward the school and society during different periods of time. Other studies of a similar nature may reflect very different viewpoints. In *A History of English Language Teaching* (Howatt 1984), A.P.R. Howatt uses textbooks as his primary source material and goes so far as to include short biographies of several of the authors.

Bjarne Bjørndal's study of textbook didactics (Bjørndal 1982) is a less comprehensive study with a lower level of scholarly ambition than Tarschys' investigation. Bjørndal's investigation focuses on a wide selection of textbooks. The author has examined development trends in Norwegian textbook literature "from about 1950 to 1981." The primary aim of his survey is to "highlight the interaction between newer didactic ideas, such as those expressed during the international educational debate of the 1960s and 1970s, and the trends currently developing in textbook literature in Norway and certain other countries." (Preface p. 1.) Bjørndal examines most of the theoretical subjects taught in primary school and includes books from all grade levels. The textbooks are indexed alphabetically by author at the end of the report, comprising 169 titles in all (pp. 195-209). In some cases the number of the impression is given after the title, in others, the number of the edition, and in still other cases, only the year of publication. Sometimes several editions are listed. There is no indication as to what system, if any, was employed to order this information, nor is there any discussion of the classification or selection criteria employed. Nothing is said about the degree to which the author regards the survey as comprehensive. The books are evaluated collectively, and each is anonymous within its particular subject area.

The author himself calls attention to the limitations inherent in this approach:

We feel the need to guard ourselves by emphasizing that the conclusions set forth will of necessity be the result of our subjective evaluation. It is thus not unlikely that others would evaluate the registered phenomena differently. This does not necessarily preclude this kind of evaluation from having some significance for textbook writers, publishers, teachers and others who are required to form an opinion about the didactic element in textbooks. (P. 99.)

These explicit reservations about subjectivity and limited usefulness make it unreasonable to demand a more thorough bibliography. The work does, however, raise a few questions regarding the problem of registration. For example, if there are major differences between the books on a particular subject in the area under investigation, isn't it important to know something about their distribution, i.e., how many, when and where? What if one textbook/one system has dominated the market, as was the case in general knowledge subjects and to some degree in Norwegian as well, during the period under investigation? Wouldn't such information be highly relevant to the stated goal of helping textbook writers, publishers and teachers?

Øystein Eek has written a master's thesis on what has been written about literary history in Norwegian upper secondary textbooks and encyclopedias during the period from 1840 to 1950 (Eek 1982). The material covers approximately fifty literary histories and a list of references to a dozen different encyclopedias. The literary histories, which received far more extensive treatment in Eek's presentation than the encyclopedia texts, have been published in many different editions and impressions. To the extent that information about this was available in the Norwegian National Bibliography, from the Norwegian Education Library, or from the publishers, Eek has included it in his bibliography. He has thereby provided a reliable record of the pattern of distribution within the time period and a relatively reliable reference as regards the extent of distribution (sales figures are not provided). This is important since Eek's study of educational and popular literary history writing establishes historical viewpoints. In addition, the thoroughness of the survey will save time and effort for others who might wish to work with the subject.

Essay Writing

The fact that an investigation does not explain the registration criteria employed or does not try to be exhaustive is not a problem per se. The problem arises when the author tries to draw general conclusions.

Historian Marc Ferro (Ferro 1986) has written a book about how history is handed down from adults to children all over the world ("à travers le monde entier"; subtitle). The source material consists of films, fiction, and popular and scholarly literature about history teaching, as well as textbooks from four continents. Ferro's presentation has no academic pretensions. What he writes in the preface, however, is quite fitting for the relatively modest, but nonetheless important, tradition of larger studies of the same type from other authors in other countries. It is important because it deals with books that have attracted public attention and had an impact:

> The project is so gigantic, so megalomanic, that I must acknowledge and justify all inadequacy.
> (...)
> Still, I have not given up the race. On the contrary, what I have given up is the thought of making every chapter into a little dissertation. A whole lifetime would not be adequate for that; it's as hopeless a problem as trying to square a circle. Before I could get to the end, I would have to begin again, with a new generation of books, films and perhaps new, as yet unknown products. (Pp. 11-12.)

Ferro gives the year and place of publication for the textbooks he has used, but he explains neither the criteria for nor the system of selection. The presentation remains true to its main thought, which is to show the complex background for how nations acquire their different images of one another.

Another French author, linguist Dominique Maingueneau, does the same thing in his analysis of French textbooks during the Third Republic (Maingueneau 1979). He reviews a classic reader (Bruno 1877) and a large number of textbooks in language, history, philosophy and geography in order to show how the textbooks individually and collectively describe not only the society and the time in which they were written, but also the school they were written for ("...le discours que tiennent les manuels, l'école sur le "monde' (dans tous les sens) constitue en profondeur un discours sur l'école elle-même." (P. XV.)). The account is organized thematically in chapters like "L'Algérie", "Le peuple français", "Le désert", "La mère patrie" and "Les bienfaits de la civilisation". As with Ferro, there is no outline for or systematization of the selections. The titles are presented exclusively, and quite randomly, in the form of footnotes.

The approach has been characterized as "impressionistic" (Togeby 1978), based on another work which also follows a distinct train of thought: Herbert Tingsten's study of ideology in textbooks, particularly those for history, geography and religion, published in a number of countries (France, Italy, Germany, the USA, Austria and Sweden) during the past century (Tingsten 1969). But Tingsten provides no systematic overview either. The dust jacket of the Norwegian edition describes the work as "a very comprehensive, dedicated and scholarly study." But that description does not hold up when measured against the standards of academic reliability and validity that would commonly be required in connection with content analyses of the type Tingsten has engaged in here.

Although Frances FitzGerald (FitzGerald 1979) shares Tingsten's ideological starting point, she is also very concerned with demonstrating how commercial interests play a part in determining the content and viewpoints of textbooks. Yet she does not explain how textbooks included in the study are selected either. Her only form of systematization is a bibliography where textbooks are listed together with other titles under the heading "United States History Texts", chronologically arranged in five different time periods.

Besides "impressionistic", the writings of authors like Ferro, Maingueneau, Tingsten and FitzGerald can also be characterized as essays. They are included in a survey of textbook studies because, first, they deal with a large corpus of material, second, they represent central approaches to the study of textbooks and, third, these titles, with the exception of Maingueneau, have become best sellers which have had a profound impact on the public's perception of the nature and significance of textbooks.

Several surveys of textbook research have tended to omit inquiries written *con amore*, accounts which primarily aim at describing educational developments, content and culture-building endeavors in textbook literature. One early example is Clifton Johnson's richly illustrated journey through American textbook literature of the 18th and 19th centuries (Johnson 1904; new edition 1963). His point of departure for writing the book was very nostalgic at the turn of the century:

> The contrast between the dainty picture books that are provided to entice the school children of the present along the paths of knowledge, and the sparsely illustrated volumes conned by the little folk of two or three generations ago, is very great; and yet the old books seemed beautiful to the children then, and the charm all comes back when a person of middle age or beyond happens on one of these humble friends of his youth. What an aroma of the far-gone days of childhood hovers in the yellow pages! (P. XVII.)

Johnson handles the material with the same freedom as, for example, Ferro and Tingsten, but he provides rather more detailed information about which institutions in which states, which individuals, which book dealers and so forth he has consulted. Among his sources is The Henry Barnard Collection, which boasts a virtually complete collection of the textbook titles used in the USA prior to 1850.

Studies based on one particular book collection are rare. John A. Nietz' *Old Textbooks*, which looks at American school books from colonial times to the year 1900, is a good example, however (Nietz 1961). The author himself collected the books, which comprised over 8,000 volumes when he began to write about them. He was motivated by the thought that "An analysis of the school textbooks used in the past reveals a truer history of what was taught in the earliest schools than does a study of past educational theories alone." (P. 1.)

Carpenter's American textbook history (Carpenter 1963) begins in the 1700s and continues up to modern times, but its main emphasis is on the 19th century. Like Marc Ferro and Karin Tarschys, Carpenter has compiled a bibliography dominated not by textbook titles, but by books about school and cultural development. He is as free as Johnson in his presentation, but whereas Johnson delights in highlighting pages of text and illustrations, Carpenter is more concerned with textbook writers and the history of publishing houses. He also stresses the development of the subject American language and literature, although without specifying any survey of titles or direct selection criteria: "No attempt has been made to present a comprehensive bibliographical treatment of the subject, (...) It is hoped that no outstandingly important texts or classes of texts have been inadvertently omitted." (Pp. 7–8.)

Historical Investigations

Readers

The standard work in historical textbook research in the USA is Ruth Miller Elson's study of American textbooks in the nineteenth century (Elson 1964). She scrutinized more than 1,000 of "the most popular textbooks used in the first eight years of schooling, since high school was not then a normal part of the education of most Americans (...)" (p. VIII). This work distinguishes itself with an unusual thoroughness in the references, except that it contains no information about how the titles were obtained. They are arranged chronologically in five subject groups: primers, readers, and geography, history and arithmetic books. Only one date is given for each title (the year of the first edition), and the authors' and publishers' names are included. Every title has a code number, and the author uses the codes, with page references to each individual book, in the form of footnotes in the body of the text. These footnotes cover an average of one-fifth of every page. When she writes, for example, about descriptions of Columbus, the number of source references on a single page runs to over thirty (p. 190). Although the situation is hypothetical, this means that a reader with access to the books could check every single reference.

Readers dominate Elson's investigation and several of the others mentioned previously, as well as the many historically oriented surveys and analyses in German. Two of the newer standard works are Heinz Tischer's and Hermann Helmers' descriptions of the history of the reader in German primary school (Tischer 1969, Helmers 1970). The former covers the time up to the mid-1800s and, generally speaking, the latter covers the period 1650-1967. A comparison of the two approaches shows that registration and selection can have a significant impact on the final evaluation and results. Helmers' method is discussed on page 92; he is selective and uses angles of approach based on didactics and cultural history. He sets up different perspectives and arrives at different conclusions from Tischer, who stops at around 1850. This is not because there were too many titles. In contrast to Helmers, Tischer claims that up to that time readers had undergone constant development and renewal as agents of social criticism. According to Tischer, the topical portion of their educational function subsequently disappeared from textbooks which, in spite of changes in text selection and equipment, no longer undergo any real development, but remain locked in the role of the conveyor of traditions.

The decisive criterion for Tischer is originality, based on the conflict between tradition and renewal. His primary aim has been to investigate what happens to the "old" in the books which he and/or his predecessors regard as "new." Tischer refers to three major studies as the foundation for his own work, pointing out that they have each had their own way of dealing with large corpora. One has tried to register and describe everything, but singled out a few titles for more detailed analysis (Fechner 1879); a second has also selected a few titles, which make up the entire corpus (Krumbach 1894 and 1896); and a third used many titles that are evaluated separately according to an extremely fragmented system of categorization. (Bünger 1899.)

The best known German study of the reader's history in schools of higher education was written by Peter-Martin Roeder (Roeder 1961). He registers more than 100 titles from 1700 up to the present day and includes a list of secondary literature covering even more titles. In his introduction, Roeder remarks on the lack of previous work relating to reading books for the higher grades, asserting that distribution has been difficult to ascertain. He claims that the development of reading books in the 18th and 19th centuries varied considerably in different parts of Germany, but he does not have enough material to document the claim. Nevertheless, Roeder shares Tischer's view that, generally speaking, readers became more alike in the latter half of the 19th century, a factor which justified highly discerning selection procedures.

It is notable that Tischer's three leading references all deal with the previous century. The bibliographies in large-scale historical surveys by other researchers (Carpenter 1963, Elson 1964, Choppin 1977) may also suggest that comprehensive registrations/analyses with historical aims were more common in the second half of the last century than in our own times.

Germany has an exhaustive production of studies, books and articles on readers. Dieter Marenbach has put forward a number of theories on the reason for this in an analysis of readers from the 1970s (Marenbach 1980). Until well into our century, readers were also the most important *subject* texts. Most adults have more positive associations with this first school book than with others. Readers can be used more independently of the teacher, and they tend to promote reading more than most textbooks. Of all the printed materials used by schools, readers have traditionally been considered the most important transmitters of values.

The bibliography for Marenbach's article refers to 23 readers and to 51 different books and articles about the subject. This phenomenon, i.e., that there are more references to theoretical studies than to primary sources, is not limited to German literature on the subject. It is also internationally common in studies on the general history of literature, for instance. Yet in the case of readers, where the quantity of material in German is so enormous, the discrepancy is striking.

Reference is also made to Marenbach's article in this context because it demonstrates how difficult it is to systematize the literature on the topic. Including subtitles, the 51 references discuss historical as well as educational, didactic, methodological, psychological, ethnographic and political approaches - which may overlap in individual titles or through several titles.

Grammar Books

Apart from the Emmanuelle project, French textbook researchers cannot point to as many large-scale surveys as their German colleagues can. One investigation that does indicate problems and discuss boundaries is André Chervel's analysis of French school grammars during the past two hundred years (Chervel 1977). He demonstrates the size of the corpus by giving a complete listing of the grammar titles published in the course of a single year, 1840. Most are school grammars, and there are a total of 34 titles. Altogether, he registered 2500 titles used in the 1800s, most of which were designed for use in schools. He has built upon a large survey by Jean-Claude Chevalier (Chevalier 1968), who, after analyzing grammars up to 1750, writes that "a systematic registration of all these titles is beyond the reach of a single person." (Chervel, p. 29.) In a note discussing the selection, Chervel describes his own method for sifting through the large body of material:

> I had to be satisfied with a typical selection. This was actually self-evident. The material is, from book to book, characterized by repetitions ("caractère éminemment répétitif"); plagiarism appears constantly among textbook authors. In my historical survey I have tried to register and date all editions that represent changes or innovative thinking, but this will always be an approximation which more detailed research could modify. On the other hand, I feel that repeated observations of the same phenomena within given time frames will be sufficient to place the advent of new trends or schools of thought within a definite period. (P. 29.)

Further, Chervel points out the problem that all textbook researchers run into and which appears to increase in direct proportion to the size of the corpus: Ideally, the complex function of textbooks and the overlapping nature of school subjects ought to be supplemented by other views. What about related subjects like grammars in Greek, Latin and modern foreign languages? What about language books which include far more than just grammar? What of the distinction/connection between the renewal of grammar theory on the one hand, and the renewal in the textbooks' educational methodology on the other? How do they compare with grammars in neighboring countries - with the same or a different language - during the same periods?

Anthologies

In many countries the twentieth century saw more widespread distribution of selected texts, or anthologies, which expanded the selection of readers available to children and young people. It is difficult to summarize anthologies because they have so many authors and so many kinds of contributions. This is particularly true of the registration of modern anthologies compiled after WW II, because so many have been made and they are so comprehensive. Still, the Nordic countries have made a few studies that attempt to systematize large corpora of anthology material.

For a variety of reasons, Torben Frische's investigation of the reading of literature in the Danish upper secondary school from 1910 to 1971 (Frische 1977) focuses on individual works. The author points out that individual works dominate syllabi in terms of the number of pages, and that the sources (syllabus records and yearbooks) give more reliable information about principal works than about individual texts contained in or separate from anthologies.

Frische's work is subtitled "The Promotion of Cultural Literacy in Grammar Schools as Illustrated by a Statistical Investigation of the Texts used to Teach Literature". The scope of the information obtained, the discussion of the texts' selection and use, and the overall tabular presentation is the most thorough model covering the use of historical material from the individual schools available in the Nordic countries. Frische uses information from the syllabi of a total of 1,470 final-year classes during the period in question. This results in a total of 21,870 pupils, who studied 73,877 principal works included in 177 different titles.

The existence of such a large corpus combined with his own special angle of approach created certain problems for Frische, something which indirectly raises the question of what is ultimately more important, the registration or the analysis. About this he writes:

> But now that this material, which I am using for a special purpose, has been sought for other purposes and, as I also pointed out in the introduction, will be available for further use,

I see no particular reason to let my report be governed by the exclusive use I have made of it in this dissertation. (P. 38.)

One Nordic anthology study that is remarkably thorough is Staffan Björck's survey and analysis of Swedish poetry anthologies from 1730 to 1983 (Björck 1984). Björck examines nearly 400 titles but does not include school anthologies. However, the work covers many principle viewpoints about the anthology as a genre, and it is mentioned here not least because of its comprehensive list of titles. The catalog, prepared by librarian Sylvia Törnkvist, contains all the standard bibliographical information about the editor, year, impression, revisions, number of pages and, in addition, individual treatment of the authors and contents in the form of short personal comments. In addition to this, every title is marked with symbols that give information about the way in which the anthology in question was organized. Viewed together, the symbols represent a register which not only expands the normal scope of registration, but goes a long way toward forming a pattern to describe anthologies as a genre. A total of ten such categories are used, reiterated here in the form of key words, as in the book (the symbols are not given). The key words:

- indicate that the anthology is limited to a particular area;
- that the publisher has attempted to make a representative selection that covers the material fully;
- that the selection is rather personal, subjective; there are many fuzzy areas between the extremes, but most anthologies are arranged either chron(ologically), alph(abetically) or them(atically);
- indicate that elementary data on the authors has been provided;
- indicate that detailed information about the authors has been provided;
- indicate that poem sources have been provided;
- indicate that other bibliographical information has been provided;
- indicate an artistic lay-out made solely for the work in question;

- indicate photographic illustrations;
- indicate a portrait of the author irrespective of the technical execution.

Mother Tongue Language and Literature Books

Ian Michael's book, *The Teaching of English* (Michael 1987) is a standard work both in this group of books and in general. Textbooks in English language and literature comprise most of the material used in a study of mother tongue instruction throughout three centuries, from approximately 1570 to 1870. Michael had a dual purpose. He wanted to refute the assertion that the subject of English was "a relatively recent addition to the curriculum" (p. 1), and he wanted to show what a significant corpus textbooks in particular comprise as far back as the 16th century. The result is a bibliography of 2,708 titles (of which 183 are American); of these about 70 per cent were consulted and used directly in the analysis.

Nevertheless, in his introduction Michael writes that his registration and analysis are only a beginning; he is undertaking a "tentative quantitative analysis" of the material and has had to use "marginal judgments about what is relevant" (p. 6). Michael's definition of textbooks is very broad. It covers books used by pupils at school, books which are read aloud in class as part of schoolwork, books used by teachers and parents for guidance and handbooks/instruction manuals. Categorization represents a major problem. The author has managed to limit the categories to a total of ten, but he emphasizes that the category transitions are often fluid. Categorization is more difficult in literary than in language disciplines. Each category has a code which is listed after the year in the bibliography. The ten categories are listed here to illustrate the problem:

1	S	Spelling, excluding orthographical reform; dictation; elementary punctuation; exercises in false spelling.
2	RE	Elementary reading.
	RA	Anthologies; single-author texts; readers not in series;

copybooks.

RH   Books primarily for home reading but perhaps used in school.

RS   Readers in series.

3   P   Performance; elocutionary and dramatic texts; pronunciation; memory.

4   B   *Belles lettres*; rhetoric; criticism; prosody; history of literature.

5   G   Grammar; exercises in false syntax; advanced punctuation.

6   La   Language; vocabulary; orthographical reform; etymology; history of the English language.

    D   Dictionaries used in school.

7   Ex   Written expression; oral expression when distinguished from performance; debate.

8   C   Compendia.

9   Ed   Educational texts relating to English teaching.

10   Lo   Logic: texts likely to have been used in school.

(Michael 1987, p. 9.)

Like Bjørkvold and Hertzberg (see page 354), Michael does not distinguish between edition and impression, but chooses the same solution from practical necessity: "The term 'edition' is used here for all printings and is not distinguished from 'impression'." (P. 386.) Sources are given for the books that have been located. Not found and not analyzed books are included in the survey if they are "potentially significant works" (p. 386). The number of pages in a book is noted only if it is conspicuous for being particularly high or low. The publisher is only listed when the information serves to distinguish between similar-sounding titles.

In the article "Aspects of Textbook Research" (Michael 1990), the author has summarized his experiences, principles and desires in this way:

Some implications for research

(i) The decision whether or not to treat a publication as a textbook will have to be made for each work separately. Criteria will include: author's explicit or implied intentions; publisher's advertisements; publishing history; use made of the book; price; tone of the book (instructional, explanatory, moralistic).

(ii) The publishing history of a book provides the best factual basis for an assessment of its influence.

(iii) We need bibliographical studies of important textbooks, including the identification of editions which contained significant changes.

(iv) We need to collect available and seek out fresh, information about the location of copies. Textbooks are not often cataloged by the libraries which hold them.

(v) It would be useful to collect biographical, autobiographical and fictional references to particular textbooks (Cobbett as a young soldier learning Lowth's grammar by heart).

Only when we have a far wider range of factual information will it be possible to bring the evidence of textbooks to bear on aspects of social and political history which they could illuminate. (Michael 1990, p. 7.)

History and Geography Books

Textbooks make up the main corpus of material for the two largest Nordic studies of the development of history teaching. Göran Andolf has written a dissertation on the period from 1820 to 1965 in the Swedish upper secondary school (Andolf 1972), and Jørgen Møller has written about Danish upper secondary school teaching over the past 100 years, with emphasis on the years after 1930 (Møller 1983).

Göran Andolf's survey of Swedish textbooks through 150 years is based on the most thorough registration of history books carried out in Nordic textbook research up to the present time. In a separate chapter entitled "The Textbook Stock", Andolf gives an account of the limitations and possibilities inherent in the work of compiling a survey. A comprehensive filing system is not necessarily a guarantee for exhaustiveness in the sense of encompassing all published titles. Already in 1817 Lorenzo Hammarsköld published a "directory" of all the textbooks published in Sweden up to that time. Hammarsköld's work was based on the yearly summaries from book printers, but some of these summaries proved to be incomplete. Beginning in 1817, these efforts were systematized by the so-called "textbook audits" which, up to 1843, listed 77 textbooks in Swedish and 107 in history. It has since come to light that nine titles were missing from that survey. In contrast, the registration which was continued until 1868 by the "textbook commission" is believed to be entirely reliable. From 1877 to 1910, textbook surveys were carried out centrally as a part of the work of Sweden's Official Statistics. This registration was very accurate for the first three years; then it was decided to make surveys every tenth year rather than annually. It was deemed unlikely that a new title would come on the market and then completely disappear from it in just ten short years.

The question of comprehensiveness is also relevant to the type and amount of information given about each book. Where such key questions as grade level and distribution are concerned, the sources are inadequate. The two sources mentioned above (the audits and the commissions) include books with subtitles such as "For the School and the Home" and "For Ladies and Young People". It is not known whether these were regarded and/or used as textbooks. The audits refer to yearly reports from school principals, but repeatedly point out that such reports were often very summary.

In 1856 it was decided that all schools should issue annual reports including information about the textbooks they used. Andolf writes that from 1859 to 1961 yearly reports were printed from "nearly all upper secondary schools" (p. 118). The textbooks are as a rule listed there, although often only by title and possibly one author's surname.

The National Textbook Committee was established in 1938 and, as a result, lists of all approved textbooks were made from 1940 to 1955. Since then booklists have been published regularly in "News from the National Board of Education".

Andolf concludes the survey of his possibilities with the

following summation:

> We have no complete list of all the books used in upper
> secondary schools from 1821 to 1843, but we know more about
> the period from 1876 to 1910. We know which books the
> schools have had to choose from since 1940, but not which were
> actually chosen. This is of little consequence for the general
> history book used in upper secondary schools, since there was
> usually just one textbook and its successors to choose from until
> 1954. It is hard to say whether, and if so, to what extent, non-
> approved textbooks were used in the classroom. It is unlikely
> that an examination of the annual reports would help clarify the
> situation. (Pp. 119-120.)

On the basis of the source material up to 1910, Andolf has set up
a table showing how frequently the books were used. He too uses
spot checks for every decade, with a few minor exceptions and one
major one: From 1930 to 1957 the selection was so limited and the
changes so small that a closer examination was superfluous. The
table shows how many upper secondary schools used the textbooks
that were available in 1844, 1860, 1870, and so on up to 1961. The
table gives a conclusive basis for determining which titles
dominated during the period.

It is not clear, however, whether individual schools used more
than one title, something which according to Andolf himself (p.
129) is the rule after about 1940. Nor does the table say anything
about which editions were used; the author consistently refers to
the year of the first printing.

As regards book size, Andolf uses a system for converting to
standard pages (p. 131). The system involves converting the text of
each book into 2000-character pages, and it offers a highly reliable
way of comparing books. The fact that Andolf has counted
illustrations as ordinary text presents more of a problem.

There are certain limitations in Andolf's selection. Teaching and
textbooks in national (Swedish) history are not included in the
study. And "Books which are never or only rarely used in upper
secondary schools are not discussed, nor are readers." (P. 117.)

Jørgen Møller (Møller 1983) deals with history instruction in the upper secondary school from 1900 to 1972. His point of departure is partly the desire to investigate the view of society and the world presented in the classroom and partly to look more closely at the relationship between history as a scholarly discipline and as a school subject. His presentation is based on three groups of sources: public documents ("formalia"), textbooks, and historical source material. Counting a 55-page tabular survey of the distribution of the books, the discussion of textbooks comprises 150 of the book's 261 pages.

Altogether, the textbooks cover 26 versions of world history and 6 versions of Nordic history. The books are presented consecutively one by one, and accurate information is provided about editions, years of publication, and changes in authorship. The schools' programs and annual reports are listed as sources. Møller has registered distribution and use throughout the period, based on steadily decreasing intervals as changes began to occur more quickly and the number of titles increased (1900/1920/1930/1940/ 1950/1955/1960/1963/1966/1969/1972). In 1900, 31 schools were investigated, in 1972, the number was 106. The selection of schools aimed at achieving a cross-section of sizes, types and locations. In this way the author has produced a picture of the distribution and life span of every title throughout the entire period.

Another study of history books, Staffan Selander's *Textbook Knowledge* (Selander 1988), lists 42 textbook titles as the basis for the analysis. In contrast, Selander provides no information about the books but the name of the author, the grade level and the year of first publication. His point of departure and his methods are totally different from Andolf's and Møller's. Selander wants to investigate "how knowledge has been structured and how it can be understood and explained through a pedagogical text analysis." (P. 9.) He selects two topics - the French revolution and Sweden's years as a major power. He then looks closely at the presentation of the topics, mainly in two books, but with examples from and references to the rest of his material. He offers no initial detailed explanation as regards the temporal or geographical distribution of the books. On the one hand, Selander can refer to past research in this area, and one might also say that his reasoning becomes apparent as his discussion progresses. On the other hand, one might ask whether more detailed groundwork would actually have changed the validity or nature of the analysis.

Lena Olsson has studied the view of culture presented in Swedish geography books used in lower and upper secondary schools from 1870 to 1985 (Olsson 1986). Like Göran Andolf and Jørgen Møller, she has compiled a large corpus, well over 50 titles if one includes editions for different grades. Like Andolf she has discovered a great deal about distribution with the help of the documents from the audits and commissions from 1876 to 1910. Olsson's study includes a thorough accounting of sources, publication years and editions (pp. 76-83). Distribution is the operative factor in this statement from her presentation:

> "The question of which textbooks ought to be included in my study cannot, however, be divorced from the underlying assumption that the contents of teaching materials also influence the teachers and pupils who use them. *The consequence of that assumption is that the textbooks used more frequently in the schools ought to form the basis for the analysis (my* emphasis)." (P. 13.)

This may be viewed in conjunction with Olsson's point of departure, which is distinguished from Andolf's, Tarschys' and Møller's on one side, and Selander's on the other. The first three attempt to use their corpora to capture a whole teaching tradition. Selander is intentionally selective because his goal calls for a detailed analysis, partly based on language, of what it takes to create an educational knowledge-bearing text in the subject of history. Like Andolf and Møller, Olsson analyzes the contents of the books. But she is selective in two ways: Her topic is limited to the view of culture presented in the books, and her choice of material is determined by the distribution of the books. Her study is based on two assumptions: that textbooks have a strong influence, and that this influence is both quantitative and cumulative. Such assumptions are also presented by Andolf and Møller, but they do not accept the consequences of them to the same degree. Torben Frische stands at the other end of this scale (Frische 1977). In his case one might be justified in claiming that the registration itself, including the discussion of and attempt to achieve a completely representative cross-section, is a major issue. But if so, it is one of several major issues. It is important to establish that during the 1970-1971 school year, 32 of 100 Danish upper secondary school pupils read *Erasmus Montanus*. But it is also important to know that one of 100 read *Peer Gynt*. Minimal representation, or absence, may say something in itself. In addition we learn, for example, that each of these two works are grouped under two different types of literature; "critical neo-humanism" and "dialectical idealization". Compared with other empirical material, this information achieves perspective.

Raymond Humbert's commemorative book about the French revolution (Humbert 1989) offers a combination of documentation and analysis, although it is more impressionistic in its avenue of approach. The author sees the revolution as it must have appeared to French pupils from books published between 1881 and 1936. Since he places a great deal of emphasis on illustrations, availability and technical quality played an important part in Humbert's choice of titles.

Alongside the strong tradition of reader research, there is another tradition that has been prominent in German textbook research. Its center is still located at its point of origin, in Braunschweig, where the Georg Eckert Institute for International Textbook Research was founded in 1951. The objective was to advance peace and understanding among nations by examining history and geography textbooks in various countries, with particular emphasis on how each presents its own country and other nations. Naturally, national groups selected the books from their respective countries, and they chose widely distributed books which were currently in use at the time. More important than an historical survey (of the textbooks) and comprehensive registration was a close reading of the most commonly used texts about their own and other countries.

Otto-Ernst Schüddekopf summarized the experience gained from the work, which was conducted at the institute in Braunschweig and elsewhere, primarily under the direction of the Council of Europe (Schüddekopf 1967). Schüddekopf does not discuss the problem of registration and selection. However, in one place he quotes a statement from one of the multilateral discussion meetings: "The trouble with textbooks is that with rare exceptions they are all alike." (Eugene N. Anderson; p. 150.) Indirectly, this may be part of the reason why the problem of selection is avoided in so many discussions of the subject, i.e., there may be some sort of unofficial consensus that if you know one, you know them all. If so, this has not been stated explicitly by those who have actually undertaken the work of examining large quantities of books in a given subject.

The survey presented thus far in this chapter has given a certain impression of the growth of early textbook research. The field began to expand during the interim between the world wars and experienced a strong surge in the first decade after WWII. However, this in no way implies that textbook registration and analyses were non-existent before well into the 20th century. Significant, if relatively exceptional, studies were conducted very early in the century. One well-known example is W. Lietzmann's work on the teaching of mathematics in upper secondary schools in Prussia from 1880 to 1906 (Lietzmann 1909). Among other things, the author examines Kambly's *Elementary Mathematics*, a textbook first published in 1850, which had sold over 850,000 copies by the turn of the century.

Investigations of Contemporary Literature

There are two particularly thorough, non-historical Nordic surveys that deal with larger groups of textbooks evaluated in their entirety (in contrast to linguistic analyses, for example, which might be based on text samples from an even greater number of titles). The first is Mogens Jansen's registration and analysis of Danish readers for the first through the seventh school years (Jansen 1969), and the second is the Swedish Ministry of Education's Report from the Teaching Media Survey (Ds 1988:22-24).

Mogens Jansen's survey covers all the books in use in Danish primary and lower secondary schools in 1966, a matter of more than 20 different series of textbooks, several of which consist of more than a dozen titles for various grades and levels.

The registration was invariably carried out by two groups working independently of one another. The combined result is first and foremost a comprehensive bibliographical survey in the traditional sense. In addition, it is a work which, through practical examples, demonstrates problems and solutions for those who wish to use the registration as a basis for content and genre analyses. The object has not been to go so far as to evaluate the subject content and methodology in the books, but to "investigate whether, by registering the subject matter in readers, and perhaps to some extent follow up by a reader analysis, one might find some interesting starting points for registering teaching activities defined on the basis of subject matter. This did not prove possible through these registrations, although in the process one skimmed a number of subject areas, and worked in a rather detailed fashion with others." (P. 12). Examples of registration fields that were studied closely are ways of categorizing material, ways of calculating standard page sizes and ways of differentiating between original (what is new or reworked for the textbook) and old material.

In a series of annotated tables, Jansen shows how such a comprehensive registration can be used for analyses based on a number of different approaches, e.g., studies of authors' canons, of the relationship between the material in readers and that in textbooks for other subjects, of genre and of guides and handbooks. In addition, Jansen discusses the problem of measuring texts in historical and geographical perspectives. In this context, the study emphasizes the ratio of Danish to non-Danish material. The results are presented in a figure which compares different countries using a scale on which the average number of pages devoted to Danish material is valued at 1, and in which country size has been taken into account. Not unexpectedly, Denmark fills a greater portion of the map than Europe, Asia and Africa combined. This figure has since turned up in textbook studies from other countries.

In an introductory chapter, "Collected descriptions of textbooks" (pp. 13-16), Jansen gives a brief survey of earlier literature on the topic. Firstly, he contends that little has been written about it, at any rate in the Nordic countries. And secondly, he points out that any attention devoted to the topic at all has more frequently been occasioned by literary, essayistic or polemical texts than by textbook analyses:

"The transition from rather emotional debates such as those mentioned here to a far more measured, controlled debate can scarcely be accomplished without initiating registrations and analyses, which may serve as a - sometimes disturbingly pedestrian - control of otherwise well-formulated views." (P. 16.)

In closing, Jansen examines the possibilities for using the study as the basis for evaluating the quality of readers. He dismisses such a possibility on the grounds that such an evaluation "only really has meaning when undertaken within the framework of the individual school by the individual teacher in one specific class and with a view to that class's individual pupils." (P. 265.) Jansen points out that the systematization of all the books available in one discipline would ensure reliability in the choice of books; a choice "that is otherwise very difficult for the individual teacher and scarcely possible for the entire teaching staff of a school." (P. 13.) This point of view provided the primary motivation for a more comprehensive registration and systematization carried out by one of Jansen's co-workers: Danish composition books for use in grades 8 - 10 (Christiansen 1985).

In 1987 Sweden's Ministry of Education was assigned the task of "surveying the teaching material situation in the school" (Ds 1988:23, p. 7). The results were published the following year in the form of a three-volume report (Ds 1988:22, Ds 1988:23, Ds 1988:24). Volume 2 (School books 2 - 400 primary and lower secondary school classes) is an account of a registration carried out in a nationwide selection of municipalities, schools and classes in cooperation with Sweden Statistics.

The municipalities were chosen and the results processed through the use of advanced mathematical statistical theory. The objective was to obtain data that was so representative that the responses from the 376 classes in 138 schools from a total of 40 municipalities could give results that were valid for the country as a whole in all the areas investigated. The municipalities were divided into five types (urban centers, service centers, industrial centers, sparsely populated areas and average municipalities.) In processing the statistics, the income levels, political situations and immigrant populations of the individual municipalities were also taken into consideration.

On the one hand, the point was to measure the conditions surrounding the use of textbooks (finances, purchasing practices, library situation) and, on the other, to look at the way in which textbooks are used (on their own, or as supplemented or supplementary materials). As regards registration, the study is quite unique in its thoroughness. The first of 40 tables gives a detailed summary of all the titles, in every subject and at every level, in use in the 138 schools in the course of the 1987-1988 school year. In addition, the percentage of occurrence of every title in the various classes has been calculated, at the same time as the study projects the same percentage estimates for the nation as a whole.

Because the target was contemporary, because the initiative

came from the school authorities (so that the municipalities followed up) and because five employees at Sweden Statistics were available to help, this registration from the 1987-88 school year represents a new development. It is also innovative in that it registers both titles and use. Moreover, it verifies observations made in a number of areas by studies from other time periods based upon assumptions drawn from circulation and sales figures alone: First of all, despite the tremendous selection of textbooks from which to choose today, a few titles dominate in every subject. And second, textbooks play - at any rate measured in terms of time consumption - a major role in the teaching of most subjects.

The Swedish Ministry of Education commissioned a number of other textbook studies prior to this one. The first examined production conditions in the textbook market (Ds U 1978:12, Ds U 1978:13) and was based on a registration that formed a thick catalog of books currently in use at the time. Another investigation looked at teaching material coverage in different municipalities (Ds U 1978:14).

Still another Swedish study was entitled *The Function of Teaching Materials in Instruction* (Ds U 1980:4, Ds U 1980:5). The objective, and thus also the registration, were entirely different from the 1987-1988 study. The mandate was "to study the extent to which teaching materials control instruction and the conditions under which such control can be avoided or reduced." (Ds U 1980:4, p 1.) An examination was made of selected subjects and how they were taught, based partly on observing classes and partly on interviews. The sample of schools and municipalities was far more modest than in the 1987-88 study, and there were so few textbooks in some subjects that the references to them could be contained in a single footnote. Nor was any systematic distinction made between different types of textbooks, for example basic texts and workbooks. The tables list textbooks under the heading of "printed text material", in contrast to other types of teaching aids, such as radio programs or stenciled hand-outs. In subjects with a larger selection of textbooks, such as Swedish, booklists were made, including titles only. No indication was given of when the books were published or how widely distributed they were. This is not unusual since all such information is available in the study from 1978. On the other hand, it is evident that in the subject of Swedish, for example, the individual school used different Swedish books, representing the following types of textbooks: readers, reading skills, workbooks, basic texts, fact books, keys, penmanship, guides, wordlists, experience, expressions. Reports were made on 24 of a total of 29 "observations" (1 observation = One 40-minute class). The reports concurred with the summaries for the other subjects investigated, i.e., that the use of "printed text material" occupied an average of half the teaching time. The study evaluated the control effect of such material on the basis of five categories: methods, material selection, language, ideology and learning effect. One question that arises concerns the degree to which one can draw any conclusions in these areas - about "ideology", for example - without a registration of the use of "printed text materials" that systematically differentiates between, e.g., wordlists and passages on literary history in a basic text. The study also distinguishes between two other levels: "Information-bearing supplementary materials" and "non-information-bearing supplementary materials". In the first group, there is a further division between "central teaching materials" (which include "printed text materials") and "other supplementary materials". It may appear that the books - which may primarily have been the main point of departure - receive less attention as genres and isolated variations as the study probes deeper into the manifold, complex process that a classroom teaching hour is. The group's research work develops almost of natural necessity from a relatively product-oriented starting point toward a more process-oriented position. This also brings to light a problem discussed rarely if at all in textbook studies from the 1960s and 1970s, that is, the question of how broad to make the definition of the concept "textbook".

Up to 1989/90, the registration of textbooks in Germany was a problem due to the boundary between East and West. Many West German titles were not known or available to the people in East Germany who might have wished to examine them. Such examinations were undertaken in East Germany, although on a very modest scale and undertaken mainly for their deterrent effect. They were comparative studies of an ideological nature, a fact that did not prevent East Germany from also conducting extremely advanced theoretical textbook research (*Schulbuchgestaltung in der DDR* 1984). In West Germany, the registration of East German books was simple because in the East most subjects in primary and lower secondary school had only one textbook. The authors were always multiple and unknown; the title pages often indicated no more than "Autorenkollektiv". Textbooks in history for the first six grades, *Geschichte 5-10*, were examined by West Germany's Reinhard Sprenger in an article about the two Germanies in 1977 (Sprenger 1977). In the reference to volume 10, Sprenger makes the following note: "*Geschichte 10* - different authors, who are presented with all the titles - Volk und Wissen, Volkseigener Verlag, Berlin 1973." Sprenger is no less dismissive of the picture of Germany presented in books from the East than East German analysts are to the representation in the West. By way of introduction (p. 82), Sprenger questions the point of analyzing a textbook that has a monopoly in a particular subject. He refutes the validity of such an analysis, contending that a selection of several competing titles ("plurality") is a condition for what he calls the conveyance of true history. In this context he draws attention to the multiplicity of West German titles. Yet he never questions whether having a wide selection of titles guarantees the presentation of more than one version of history. This has been pointed out by several people who have abandoned the exhaustive registration of large corpora, claiming that the books are all alike in content and attitudes. (See pages 272 and 380.)

One problem with the usual type of registrations that include more than alphabetical lists of titles is restricting the number of classification categories. There are surprisingly few examples of the use of text or pages from the textbooks themselves to clarify or justify the categorization, such as Mogens Jansen did (Jansen 1969). In his presentation, facsimiles of textbook pages are not chance illustrations, but part of the registration.

Another example of how material can be physically integrated into a study/registration is the large composite volume *Politik im Schulbuch* (Pöggeler 1985), in which nine different researchers analyze primers, religion books, arithmetic books, biology books, song books and history books. Both the titles and the descriptions in all the articles are arranged in historical periods: Empire (1871-1918), Weimar Republic (1918-1933), National Socialism (1933-1945), Federal Republic of Germany (FRG) and German Democratic Republic (GDR) (1945-1980). This is a tightly-packed volume in which the average article length is 30 pages. Nonetheless, each article is accompanied by a large number of pages consisting of facsimiles from the textbooks. In addition, the bibliography provides accurate information about the edition used, including the year of publication.

No collective or systematic explanation has been given for the selection of the reproduced primary material within the parameter given (politics). The source is given: The books come from Germany's third or fourth largest collection of textbooks, the "Pöggeler Collection" in Aachen. Even though some of the authors have also used other sources, the project had to forgo any claim to comprehensiveness. The goal was originally to carry out a "Gesamtuntersuchung" (collective investigation) to be published in five volumes.

Perspectives

The survey above has mainly focused on studies that register and treat a substantial number of textbook titles, of which the majority in one way or another have been incorporated into analyses, where they exist. The primary aim of these investigations has been one of the following:

- To achieve the most complete survey, diachronous or synchronous, of the stock of books, and perhaps in addition to draw up lines for further research (Jansen 1969, Frische 1977, Choppin 1989),
- to give a general survey of a school subject's content and development over a longer period of time (Tarschys 1955, Andolf 1972, Møller 1983, Michael 1987),
- to give a general survey of an academic discipline's content and development over a longer period of time (Bjørkvold - Hertzberg 1976, Chervel 1977),
- to map the specific characteristics and development of a particular textbook genre, especially readers (Tischer 1969, Helmers 1970),
- to elucidate specific aspects of textbook content in accordance with paramount goals of a political nature (Georg Eckert Institute 1951, Pöggeler 1985),
- to evaluate all or the greatest possible number of books in the existing stock of textbooks in light of general, overall pedagogical-didactic goals (Bjørndal 1982),
- to elucidate the textbook situation in light of overall goals of educational politics (Sweden: Ds U 1978-1979, 1980; Ds 1988).

The problem of method in connection with registration has first and foremost been of a practical-economic nature. It has been a question of time, resources and availability of sources. As a rule, all registrations will of necessity be marked by limitations in one or more of these areas. No matter how methodically one works or how bountiful the resources at hand, a shortage of source material will set limits. This is true not only of historical investigations, but also of contemporary surveys made since textbooks came into mass production. In addition the problem of response represents a major difficulty in most studies.

The objective of the study must dictate the stringency of the demands for comprehensiveness and accuracy in listing authors' names, publication dates, book types, impressions, editions or sales figures. Thus the problem of registration becomes at least as much a question of selection and reasons for the selection, based on previous registrations, if any, as of the systematization of known and new-found titles.

Insofar as the relationship between objective on the one hand and thoroughness of registration on the other is concerned, the survey reveals great variation in solutions from author to author. Some examples demonstrate that this variety is not necessarily determined by differences in approach at all. At one extreme we find Tingsten 1969, who draws very general conclusions about nationalism in European school books without attempting to disguise that his sample is random. Lars Furuland has written an article in which he points out that Tingsten's inaccuracy goes extremely far in places:

> One important source is given as the *Reader for Primary School*; no more exact references are given. In the first part of the chapter "the line of religious propaganda" is illustrated with striking examples of children's beliefs about God, not least about fear of punishment from the hand of God. Only one of the ten or so quoted texts is taken, as nearly as I could find out, from Carlson's reader (editions 1-7). (Furuland 1988, p. 8.)

The method of registration and the specification of titles is also limited in Bjørndal 1982. As with Tingsten, however, this is not necessarily a mistake; the author emphasizes that the work is chiefly a subjective interpretation undertaken with the intention of helping to improve the books. The material was meant to provide a foundation for discussing the didactic condition of the entire book stock (see page 275). The situation is nevertheless different from Tingsten's case. Bjørndal's report is written on the basis of a school research project carried out in an educational research center. One hundred and thirty-three books were analyzed without any explanation of their selection and without the inclusion of quotations or specific references. In other words, the system is the exact opposite of that which Elson 1969 used in the examination of 1000 titles where every quotation and reference was identified by edition and page. This is unacceptable based on standard practice and the methodological requirements applied to such studies. However, as an experiment and an attempt to go in new directions, it is interesting. It looks as though the researchers dared to take the leap into subjective approximation because their goal was so patently practical. If so, this is a dubious justification at best. In one of the subjects, Norwegian, the selection was limited to readers. But to what extent can the study's point of view about readers' didactic function benefit textbooks in Norwegian as long as Norwegian is a subject in which the inherent integration of language and literature is one of the primary goals?

The modest degree of registration in Tarschys 1955 is a consequence of the author's placing more emphasis on sources other than textbooks for the history of mother tongue instruction. Even though the subject matter and didactic viewpoints as expressed in the books receive considerable attention, the author does not explain her sample, nor does she address the question of how representative it is. Textbook passages are brought in as illustrations, especially of (diverging) professional opinions. They become symptomatic of attitudes more than expressions of the tenor of the schools. With the greatest respect for the breadth of documentation as regards shifting professional views, it might be claimed that Tarschys' attitude toward the registration of textbooks - in an historical presentation of mother tongue instruction - is nonchalant insofar it says nothing about selection or priorities. Furthermore, the thesis was written in 1955, i.e., at a juncture in time when the stock of textbooks was undoubtedly far more surveyable than ten or fifteen years later.

A jump from the studies mentioned above to those which come closest to exhaustiveness also reveals different patterns. Such virtual exhaustiveness can be achieved at the expense of something else; it can take time and attention away from the central issue. It may boil down to a question of whether meticulous registration work is always equally necessary; whether it serves a purpose, beyond its use as a scholarly "alibi". In Frische 1977, the author points out that the registration of the primary works used in 1,470 graduating classes is unnecessarily lengthy in relation to the analysis, and explains the discrepancy quite simply as the need for an overview (p. 175).

In his historical analysis of the development of the subject of mother-tongue instruction in Great Britain (Michael 1987), Ian Michael used the extensive registration in itself as an argument for the hypothesis, i.e., that such a widely taught discipline did exist. With Bjørkvold and Hertzberg 1976, the correspondence between registration and selection was also methodically functional. In spite of this, there is, as the authors also point out, an element of self-contradiction in the delimitation. It is expressed in the title (*School Grammars*); how does one distinguish between subject content and educational content in classifying titles that do not state any specific target group?

Andolf 1972 emphasizes the same sources as Tarschys (public documents, polemical literature, scholarly literature). The difference is that Andolf uses textbooks in addition as his primary source. Painstakingly accurate registration work thus becomes one of the pre-conditions for delivering what the title (*Teaching*) promises.

Kepner 1935 stands apart. Not only does he emphasize the conclusions that can be drawn from an analysis of books that were not widely distributed, in clear contradiction to Olsson 1986, for example. By attaching special importance to books written by authors established in other contexts as well, he also differentiates between types of author. This broadens his perspective and has probably had an effect on his results (see page 355).

The possibilities for comprehensiveness increase when the registering is contemporary, at any rate if the area/country is not too large. Jansen 1969 and Ds 1988 are examples of two types of virtually complete surveys of book stocks at a given time, motivated by research and school policy considerations respectively. In the first case the survey was virtually exhaustive because several groups were able to work in parallel and thereby serve as reciprocal controls. In the other case the guarantee lay in the mathematical-statistical methods and a large government polling system.

Like other literature, textbooks have genre characteristics that can vary synchronously and diachronously. It almost seems an unwritten rule that such characteristics not form part of the registration. The exceptions are Göran Andolf, Staffan Björck, Mogens Jansen and Ian Michael, who all included some information about genre. The omission of this aspect must be considered open to discussion. A demonstration of diversification and variation - or of one-sidedness - will be of importance, among other things, for the discussion of the view that all the books are "the same".

One recurring problem is the question of the possibility of and methods for a more global registration than any undertaken to date. In 1990 the National Psychological- Educational Library in Sweden published a report on the availability of textbooks from other countries as the foundation for research (Hansson 1990). The report states that the library has over 100,000 textbooks, of which approximately 25,000 are foreign. The report concludes with a proposal for a permanent arrangement for the purchase of foreign textbooks in core subjects for an annual sum of approximately 100,000 Swedish crowns. No comparable arrangement has been either established or proposed in the other Nordic countries.

The fact that certain countries (such as France; see page 358) have come far, particularly in the field of historical studies, therefore supports the contention that this must have at least as much to do with the assignment of cultural policy priorities and strong literary traditions as with methodological inroads. Granted, the technological developments of the past few decades have expanded the choice of registration methods. But other countries with the same access to electronics have not availed themselves of the possibilities to the same degree.

Theoretically, the possibility for computerized registration should enhance our chances of gaining insight into our own times. Such endeavors are taking place not only nationally, but internationally. Pivotal institutions are The European Documentation and Information System for Education (the EUDISED database) at the Council of Europe in Strasbourg, the Georg Eckert Institute in Braunschweig, the National Institute for Educational Research in Paris, and the International Educational Library in Budapest. However, the two-fold problem remains the same. We lack the capacity and routines that would automatically bring new editions into the system and make the material known and conveniently available to those who need it. The Emmanuelle system in Paris has probably come furthest. But even when technical conditions are favorable, language and media policy complications cause problems for the transfer of systems across national borders. The ideal, total survey based on continuous, automatic exchanges of information is more a problem of cultural policy and communication than one of machine capacity.

Chapter VIII

References

The titles of French and German works have not been translated. Titles of Nordic works are referred to in the original language followed by a translation, the latter corresponding to the title used in the text proper.

The titles of works published as books, as well as the titles of periodicals, journals and newspapers, are in italics. An exception is made for the original titles of Nordic books. I have chosen to do this in order to distinguish more easily between the original text and a non-existent translation as far as major Nordic works are concerned. Unless originally written in English, none of the Nordic books are available in English translation. (Selma Lagerlöf's *Nils Holgersson's Wonderful Journey Through Sweden* is the only exception.)

The titles of published articles are put in quotation marks, with sources (collection of articles, periodical) cited. Quotation marks are also being used for unpublished manuscripts, theses, reports, and papers, with reference to place of origin. The distinction between "manuscript" and "paper" is a practical one: "Manuscripts" have been put at my disposal by the courtesy of the authors; "papers" have been copied and presented, partly as lectures, at conferences. Further, all "manuscripts" are in my possession, while some of the "papers" referred to are known to me only through the reading of other authors' presentation of them.

Most of the papers referred to as having been presented at the Georg-Eckert-Institut, are available in English, French and German. The titles of Nordic works belonging to the group of articles, reports, manuscripts, and papers are translated into English in parenthesis, following the original title, whereas references to institutions and places of publication are indicated as in the original language. The reason for this is partly my wish to remind the reader that these translations are non-existent and partly that those wishing to acquire the documents may do so by making inquiries through local institutions in the countries of origin.

In the case of works with more than one author, the authors are listed in alphabetical order unless the names are arranged differently in the relevant publication.

If two or more editions of a particular title have been published, I shall be referring to the one most recent. In the rare cases where contextual points differ in the various editions, references are made to year of publication for all editions concerned. Some references are made to exceptionally long-lived textbooks, e.g. Munch, P.: Verdenshistorie. *(A History of the World.)* København 1907–1967.

Ahier, John: *Industry, Children and the Nation. An Analysis of National Identity in School Textbooks.* London 1988.
Ahlström, Gunnar: Den underbara resan. En bok om Selma Lagerlöfs Nils Holgersson. *(The Wonderful Journey. A Book about Selma Lagerlöf's Nils Holgersson.)* Malmö 1942.
Allard, Birgita, Bo Sundblad: När vi läser och skriver... *(As We Read and Write ...)* Stockholm 1986.
Altbach, Philip G., Gail P. Kelly: *Textbooks in the Third World. Policy, Content and Context.* New York 1988.
Alverman, D.: "Teacher-Student Mediation of Content Area Texts." In: *Theory into Practice* No. 27 1989.
Anderberg, Thomas: "Några aspekter på behandlingen av demokratifrågor i läromedel. En pilotundersökning och en studie i undersökningsmetodik." ("Some Aspects of the Treatment of Questions of Democracy in Text Materials. A Pilot Study and a Study of Investigatory Methods.") Skolöverstyrelsen. Stockholm 1981.
Anderson, D.: *Evaluating Curriculum Proposals: A Critical Guide.* London 1981.

Anderson, Richard C., Jean Osborn, Robert J. Tierney, (eds.): *Learning to Read in American Schools: Basal Readers and Content Texts.* New York 1981. (NB: All quotations are from proof sheet.)

Anderson, Thomas H., Bonnie B. Armbruster: "Content Area Textbooks." In: Anderson, Richard C., Jean Osborn, Robert J.Tierney (eds.): *Learning to Read in American Schools: Basal Readers and Content Texts.* New York 1981. (NB: All quotations are from proof sheet.)

Andolf, Göran: "Att mäta läroböcker." ("To measure textbooks.") In: *Historisk Tidskrift* No. 1, Stockholm 1971.

Andolf, Göran: Historien på gymnasiet. Undervisning och läroböcker 1820–1965. *(History in Upper Secodary Schools. Teaching and Textbooks 1820–1965.)* Uppsala 1972.

Angvik, Magne: "Skolebokanalyse som tema for lærerutdanning og forskning." ("Textbook Analysis as a Topic for Teachers' Education and Research.") In: *Norsk Pedagogisk Tidsskrift* No. 10, Oslo 1982.

Angvik, Magne: "Lokal- und Regionalgeschichte in Norwegischen Geschichtslehrbüchern." In: *Dortmunder Arbeiten zur Schulgeschichte und zur historischen Didaktik* No. 8 1985.

Antonietti, Allessandro: "Die Nutzung von Analogien beim Induktiven Denken." In: *Juventa. Unterrichtswissenschaft. Zeitchrift für Lernforschung* 2 Vj. 1991.

Anyon, Jean: "Ideology and United States History Textbooks." In: *Harvard Educational Review* 49:3, 1979.

Apple, Michael W.: "The Political Economy of Text Publishing." In: *Educational Theory* 34:4, 1984.

Apple, Michael W., Susan Jungck: "You Don't Have to Be a Teacher to Teach This Unit: Teaching, Technology, and Gender in the Classroom." In: *American Educational Research Journal* 27:2, 1990.

Apple, Michael W.: "The Text and Cultural Politics." In: Willinsky, John, Deanne Bogdan (eds.): *Embattled Books. Journal of Educational Thougt* 24:3A, Calgary 1990.

Apple, Michael W., Linda K. Christian-Smith: "The Politics of the Textbook." In: Apple, Michael W., Linda K. Christian-Smith(eds.): *The Politics of the Textbook.* London/New York 1991.

Applebee, Arthur N.: *Tradition and Reform in the Teaching of English. A History.* Urbana 1974.

Applebee, Arthur N.: "A Study of High School Literature Anthologies." Report Series 1.5. University of Albany, New York 1991.

Archibald, G.: *Joel Dorman Steele.* New York 1900.

Armbruster, Bonnie B., Thomas H. Anderson: "Structures of Explanations in History Textbooks or So What if Governor Stanford Missed the

Spike and Hit the Rail?" In: *Journal of Curriculum Studies* 16:2, 1984.

Armbruster, Bonnie B., Thomas H. Anderson: "Producing "Considerate" Expository Text: or Easy Reading is Damned Hard Writing." In: *Journal of Curriculum Studies* 17:3, 1985.

Arons, Stephen: "Lessons in Law and Conscience: Legal Aspects of Textbook Adoption and Censorship." In: De Castell, Suzanne, Allan Luke, Carmen Luke (eds.): *Language, Authority and Criticism.* London/New York/Philadelphia 1989.

Askeland, Norunn: "Læreboka som samhandling." ("The Textbook as Interaction.") Universitetet i Oslo 1984.

Atlantisch Onderwijs Paper VII: "NATO in History and Civics Textbooks. An International Survey With US, West German, UK, Belgian and Dutch Contributions." Atlantische Commissie, Haag 1990.

Autorenkollektiv: *Schulbuchgestaltung in der DDR.* Volk und Wissen Volkseigener Verlag. Berlin 1984.

Bagley, William C.: "The Textbook and Methods of Teaching." In: *The Thirtieth Yearbook of the NSSE. Part II.* Bloomington 1931.

Baker, Elizabeth W.: "The Development of Elementary English Language Textbooks in the United States." In: *Contributions to Education* No. 45, Nashville 1929.

Bakkemoen et al.: Fremad og aldri glemme. *(Onward and Never Forget.)* Oslo 1974.

Baldersheim, Harald, Jan Tvedt: Korrektiv til Andenæs, Aukrust og Hauge: Samfunnskunnskap for gymnaset. *(Corrective to Andenæs, Aukrust and Hauge: Social Science in Upper Secondary Schools.)* PAX KORREKTIV. Oslo 1970.

Ball, Deborah Loewenberg, Sharon Feiman-Nemser: "Using Textbooks and Teachers' Guides: A Dilemma for Beginning Teachers and Teacher Educators." In: *Curriculum Inquiry* 18:4, 1988.

Bamberger, Richard, Erich Vanecek: *Lesen, Verstehen, Lernen – Schreiben. Die Schwierigkeitsstufen von Texten in Deutscher Sprache.* Frankfurt am Main 1984.

Bamberger, Richard, Erich Vanecek: "Zur Lesbarkeit und Lernbarkeit von Schulbüchern." Institut für Schulbuchforschung. Wien 1988.

Bamberger, Richard: "Schulbuchforschung – eine weltweite Aufgabe." In: *Zeitschrift Unesco-Austria.* Wien 1990.

Bamberger, Richard: "Die Schulbuchbegutachtung in verschiedenen Ländern." Manuscript. Institut für Schulbuchforschung. Wien 1992.

Bark, Joachim, Dietger Pforte: *Die deutschsprachige Anthologie 1–2.*

Frankfurt am Main 1970.

Barré, Michel: *L'aventure documentaire. Une alternative aux manuels scolaires.* Paris 1983.

Barth, Roland S.: "Restructuring Schools: Some Questions for Teachers and Principals." In: *Phi Delta Kappan* 73:2, 1991.

Barthes, Roland: *Image – Music – Text.* New York 1977.

Baumann, Manfred: "Methoden und Probleme der Schulbuchforschung im Überblick." In: *Informationen zu Schulbuchfragen* No. 47 1983.

Beck, Isabel L.: "Developing Comprehension: The Impact of the Directed Reading Lesson." In: Anderson, Richard C., Jean Osborn, Robert J. Tierney (eds.): *Learning to Read in American Schools: Basal Readers and Content Texts.* New York 1981. (NB: All quotations are from proof sheet.)

Beckson, Karl, Arthur Ganz: *Literary Terms. A Dictionary.* London 1990.

Berelson, Bernard: *Content Analysis in Communication Research.* Glencoe 1952.

Berger, Peter, Thomas Luckmann: *The Social Construction of Reality: A Treatise in the Sociology of Knowledge.* New York 1966.

Berghahn, Volker R., Hanna Schissler (eds.): *Perceptions of History. An Analysis of School Textbooks.* Oxford/New York/ Hamburg 1987.

Bernstein, Basil: *Class, Codes and Control.* London 1971.

Beverton, Sue: "Going into Secondary School Reading." In: Gillham, Bruce (ed.): *The Language of School Subjects.* London 1986.

Bierstedt, Robert: "The Writers of Textbooks." In: Cronbach, Lee J.(ed.): *Text Materials in Modern Education.* Urbana 1955.

Biraimah, Karen L.: "Knowledge Control in Developing Countries: A Comparative Study of Togolese and Thai English Language Textbooks." Manuscript/Lecture. CIES Conference, University of Pittsburgh 1991.

Björck, Staffan: Svenska Språkets Skönheter. Om den lyriska antologin i Sverige – dess historia och former. *(Beauties of the Swedish Language. On the History and Forms of Poem Anthologies in Sweden.)* Stockholm 1984.

Bjørklid, Brynjulf, Tore Pryser: "Fremad og aldri glemme." ("Onward and Never Forget.") In: *Vinduet* No. 1 1975.

Bjørkvold, Eva, Frøydis Hertzberg: "Norsk skolegrammatikk. Tradisjon og nytenkning." ("School grammars in Norway. Tradition and reform.") Universitetet i Oslo 1976.

Bjørndal, Bjarne: Om lærebøker. *(On textbooks.)* Oslo 1967.

Bjørndal, Bjarne: "Et studium i lærebøkenes didaktikk." ("A Study on the Didactics of Textbooks.") Universitetet i Oslo 1982.

Björnsson, Carl-Hugo, Ragnar Dahlkvist, Anna-Maja Edstam, Ragnar Jarne: Språk och ordförråd i räkneläror. Experimentella studier kring några räkneläror. *(Language and Vocabulary in Math Textbooks. Experimental Studies Based on Some Arithmetic Books.)* Stockholm 1967.

Bonilauri, Bernard: *La désinformation scolaire. Essai sur les manuels d'enseignement.* Paris 1983.

Boorstin, Daniel J.: "Introduction." In: Cole, John Y., Thomas G. Sticht (eds.): *The Textbook in American Society.* Washington DC 1981.

Booth: "A Modern World History Course and the Thinking of Adolescent Pupils." In: *Educational Review* 32:3, 1980.

Bourdillon, Hilary (ed.): *History and Social Studies - Methodologies of Textbook Analysis.* Amsterdam 1992.

Bragdon, H.W.: "Dilemmas of a textbook writer." In: *Social Education* No. 33 1969.

Bragdon, H.W.: "Ninth edition adventures with a textbook." In: *Independent School* 37 (3), 1978.

Brammer, M.: "Textbook Publishing." In: Grannis, C.B. (ed.): *What happens in Textbook Publishing.* New York 1967.

Brink, Lars: Gymnasiets litterära kanon. Urval och värderingar i läromedel 1910–1945. *(The Literary Canon of Upper Secondary Schools. Selections and Values in Schoolbooks 1910-1945.)* Uppsala 1992.

Bromsjö, Birger: Samhällskunskap som skolämne. *(Social Sciences as a School Subject.)* Stockholm 1965.

Bruno, G.: *Le Tour de France par Deux Enfants.* Paris 1877.

Bulletin d'informations sur les manuels scolaires: See Huot, Helene.

Bünger, Friedrich: *Entwicklungsgeschichte des Volksschullesebuchs.* Leipzig 1899.

California Board of Education: "History-Social Science Framework for California Public Schools Kindergarten Through Grade Twelve." Preliminary edition. Sacramento 1988.

Carpenter, Charles: *History of American Schoolbooks.* Philadelphia 1963.

Caspard, P., F. Huguet: "Les Mémoires de maîtrise en histoire de l'éducation (1968–1979)." In: *Histoire de l'Éducation* No. 5 1979.

Caspard, Pierre: "De l'horrible danger d'une analyse superficielle des manuels scolaires." In: *Histoire de l'Education* No. 24 1984.

Catalog of Teaching Materials for the Upper Secondary School (Læremiddelkatalogen for den videregående skole 1992).

Chall, Jeanne S., Sue Conrad, Susan Harris-Sharples: *An Analysis of Textbooks in Relation to Declining SAT Scores.* Princeton NJ, 1977.

Charmasson, Thérèse (ed.): *L'Histoire de l'Enseignement, XIXe– XXe Siècles. Guide du Chercheur.* Institut National de Recherce Pédagogique. Paris 1986.

Chervel, André: *Histoire de la grammaire scolaire ... et il fallut apprendre à écrire à tous les petits Français.* Paris 1977.

Chevalier, Jean-Claude: *Histoire de la Syntaxe. Naissance de la notion de complément dans la grammaire francaise (1530–1750).* Genève 1968.

Choppin, Alain: "L'histoire des manuels scolaires: Une approche globale." In: *Histoire de l'Education,* décembre 1980. Paris 1980.

Choppin, Alain: "Le livre scolaire." In: *Histoire de l'Édition Francaise.* Tome IV. Paris 1986–87.

Choppin, Alain, Marie Anne Decouche-Beauchais, Fabiola Rodriguez: "Guide du Producteur de la Banque Emmanuelle." Institut National de Recherche Pédagogique. Paris 1988–89.

Choppin, Alain: "L'Histoire de l'Édition Scolaire en France." Manuscript. Paris 1990.

Choppin, Alain: *Les Manuels Scolaires: Histoire et Actualité.* Paris 1992.

Christiansen, Kurt Dahl et al.: Danskbøgerne i folkeskolen – et debatoplæg. *(Primary School Textbooks – an Invitation for Debate.)* Odense 1978.

Christiansen, Torben Bergmann: "Skriftlig dansk-bøger for 8.-10. klasse." ("Writing Skills Books – Danish – for Forms 8–10.") Danmarks Pædagogiske Institut, København 1985.

Clark, Christopher M.: "Real Lessons from Imaginary Teachers." In: *Journal of Curriculum Studies* 23:5, 1991.

Cody, Caroline: "The Politics of Textbook Publishing, Adoption, and Use." In: Elliott, David L. and Arthur Woodward (eds.): *Textbooks and Schooling in the United States.* Chicago 1990.

Coffey, W.L.: "Standards for Evaluating Proposed Textbook Legislation." In: *The Thirtieth Yearbook of the NSSE. Part II.* Bloomington 1931.

Cole, John Y., Thomas G. Sticht (eds.): *The Textbook in American Society.* Washington DC 1981.

Cooper, B.: "On Explaining Change in School Subjects." In: Goodson, I.F., S.J. Ball (eds.): *Defining the Curriculum. Histories and Ethnographies.* London 1984.

Cortázar, Julio: *Libro de Manuel.* Buenos Aires 1973.

Cortázar, Julio: *Livre de Manuel.* Paris 1974.

Coser, Lewis, Charles Kadushin, Walter Powell: *Books: The Culture and Commerce of Publishing.* New York 1982.

Crismore, Avon: "The Rhetoric of Textbooks: Metadiscourse." In: *Journal of Curriculum Studies* 16:3, 1984.

Cronbach, Lee J. (ed.): *Text Materials in Modern Education. A Comprehensive Theory and Platform for Research.* Urbana 1955.

Cronbach, Lee J.: "The Learning Process and Text Specifications." In: Cronbach, Lee J. (ed.): *Text Materials in Modern Education.* Urbana 1955.

Cronbach, Lee J.: "The Text in Use." In: Cronbach, Lee J. (ed.): *Text Materials in Modern Education.* Urbana 1955.

Dale, Johs. A.: Pierre Guiraud: Stilistikk. Omsett og tilrettelagd av Johs. A. Dale. *(Pierre Guiraud: Stylistics. Translated and adapted by Johs. A. Dale.)* Oslo 1960.

Damerow, Peter: "Concepts of Geometry in German Textbooks. Comparative Studies of Mathematics Curricula: Change and Stability 1960–1980." Institut für Didaktik der Mathematik, Bielefeld 1980.

Dance, E. H.: *History the Betrayer. A Study in Bias.* London 1960.

Danielson, Sylvia: Läroboksspråk. En undersökning av språket i vissa läroböcker för högstadium och gymnasium. *(Textbook Language. An Investigation of the Language in some Textbooks for Secondary and Upper Secondary School.)* Umeå 1975.

Danielsson, Annica: Tre antologier – tre verkligheter. En undersökning av gymnasiets litteraturförmedling 1945–1975. *(Three Anthologies – Three Worlds. An Investigation of the Teaching of Literature in Upper Secondary Schools 1945–1975.)* Lund 1988.

Darras, Francine, Isabelle Delcambre: "Savoirs, Textes et Discours: Comment ça se joue dans les manuels?" In: *Le Français Aujourd'hui* No. 74 1986.

Davies, Florence: "The Function of the Textbook in Sciences and the Humanities." In: Gillham, Bruce (ed.): *The Language of School Subjects.* London 1986.

De Castell, Suzanne, Carmen Luke, Allan Luke: "Beyond Criticism: The Authority of the School Textbook." In: De Castell, Suzanne, Allan Luke, Carmen Luke (eds.): *Language, Authority and Criticism. Readings on the School Textbook.* London/New York/Philadelphia 1989.

De Castell, Suzanne: "Teaching the Textbook: Teacher/Text Authority and the Problem of Interpretation." In: *Linguistics and Education* No. 2 1990.

Decroux-Masson, Annie: *Papa lit, maman coud.* Paris 1979.

"Deficiency Committee's Report." Oslo 1985. See: Kirke- og undervisningsdepartementet.

Den norske Forleggerforening: "Lærebokundersøkelsen i grunnskolen." ("The Textbook Investigation in Primary Schools.") Oslo 1991.

Dewey, John: *Experience and Education.* New York 1938.

Dole, Janice A., Theresa Rogers, Jean Osborn: "Improving the Selection of Basal Reading Programs: A Report of the Textbook Adoption Guidelines Project." In: *The Elementary School Journal* 87:3, 1987.

Donsky, B. von B.: "Trends in Elementary Writing Instruction, 1900–1959." In: *Language Arts* No. 61 1984.

Dooley, M.C.: "The Relationship between Arithmetic Research and the Content of Arithmetic Textbooks: 1900–1957." In: *The Arithmetic Teacher* No. 7 1960.

Ds U 1978:12–13: Läromedelsmarknaden – Produktions- och konkurrensförhållanden. *(The Textbook Market – Conditions for Production and Competition.)* Stockholm 1978.

Ds U 1978:14: Samhällets kostnader för inköp av läromedel samt lek- och arbetsmaterial. *(Public Expenses Covering Teaching Materials and Other Material for Playing and Working Activities.)* Stockholm 1978.

Ds U 1980:4–5: Läromedlens funktion i undervisningen. En rapport från utredningen om läromedelsmarknaden. *(The Function of Text Materials in Class. A Report from the Investigation of the Textbook Market.)* Stockholm 1980.

Ds 1988:22–24: (See: Rönström, Thomas.)

Duffy, Thomas M., Robert Waller (eds.): *Designing Usable Texts.* Orlando 1985.

Duneton, Claude, Jean-Pierre Pagliano: *Anti-manuel de français.* Paris 1978.

Eek, Øystein: "Kulturarv på formel – elementær litteraturhistorieskrivning i gymnaslærebøker og konversasjonsleksika i Norge fra 1840-årene til 1950-årene, med særlig vekt på Harald Beyers forfatterskap." ("Cultural Heritage as a Formula – the Writing of Elementary History of Literature for Upper Secondary Schools and in Encyclopedias in Norway from the 1840s and up to the 1950s, with Particular Emphasis on the Authorship of Harald Beyer.") Universitetet i Oslo 1982.

Egeland, Kjølv, Kristian Ottosen: "Foreløpig utkast til stortingsmelding om faglitteraturens situasjon." ("Draft of a White Paper on the Conditions for Non-Fiction Literature in Norway.") Kulturdepartementet, Oslo 1986.

Egeland, Marianne: "Lærebokmangler og -behov innenfor høyere utdanning." ("Lack of and Need for Textbooks in Colleges and Universities.") Lærebokutvalget for høyere utdanning, Oslo 1989.

Egerland, Herbert: "Lehrtextgestaltung in deutschsprachigen Schulbüchern (16. bis 18. Jahrhundert)." In: *Aus dem wissenschaftlichen Leben der Pädagogischen Hochschule "N. K. Krupskaja" Halle-Köthen* No. 5

1990.
Eklund, S., H. Hedman, L. Bergquist: "En blindskola för seende." ("A Blind School for the Sighted.") In: *Dagens Nyheter* 9.04. 1986.
Ellington, L.: "Blacks and Hispanics in High School Economic Texts." In: *Social Education* No. 50 1986.
Elliott, David L., Kathleen Carter Nagel, Arthur Woodward: "Do Textbooks Belong in Elementary Social Studies?" In: *Educational Leadership* No. 42 1985.
Elliott, David L.: "Textbooks and the Curriculum in the Postwar Area, 1950–1980." In: *NSSE Yearbook 1990. Part I.* Chicago 1990.
Elson, Ruth Miller: *Guardians of Tradition. American Schoolbooks of the Nineteenth Century.* Nebraska 1964.
EMMANUELLE: *Collection Emmanuelle. Les manuels scolaires en France de 1789 à nos jours. Répertoires. Catalogues.* Institut National de Recherche Pédagogique. Paris 1991.
Eng, Helga: Abstrakte begreper i barnets tanke og tale. *(Abstract Concepts in Childrens' Thougts and Speech.)* Oslo 1912.
Engelsen, Britt Ulstrup: "Litteraturdidaktiske strømninger i en planrevisjonstid. Del I–III." ("Didactics of Literature; Tendencies in a Period of Curricula Reforms. Report I–III.") Universitetet i Oslo 1988.
Engelsen, Britt Ulstrup: "Norskfaget i videregående skole: Litteraturdidaktisk vektlegging. Rapport I. ("The Teaching of Norwegian in Upper Secondary School: The Didactics of Literature. Report 1.") Universitetet i Oslo 1990.
Engeseth, John: "Fysikkundervisning i realgymnaset 1875–1933." ("The Teaching of Physics in Upper Secondary Scools 1875–1933.") Universitetet i Oslo 1984.
Englund, Boel: "Litteraturen i gymnasieskolan på 1920- och 1980-talet." ("Literature in Upper Secondary Schools in the 1920s and the 1980s.") In: Malmgren, Gun, Jan Thavenius (eds.): Svenskämnet i förvandling. Historiska perspektiv – aktuella utmaningar. *(Swedish as a Mother Tongue, a Subject in Change. Historical Perspectives – New Challenges.)* Lund 1991.
Englund, Tomas: "Samhällsorienteringens innehåll (läromedel och undervisning) – determinanter för innehållet och deras tolkning." ("Contents of Social Sciences (Teaching Materials and Teaching) – Determinants of Contents and their Interpretation.") Göteborgs universitet 1981.
Englund, Tomas: "Samhällsorienteringens innehåll." ("The Contents of Social Sciences.") In: Lundgren, Ulf P., Gunilla Svingby, Erik Wallin (eds.): Läroplaner och läromedel. En konferensrapport. *(Curricula and*

Teaching Materials. A Conference Report.) Stockholm 1982.

Englund, Tomas: "Om samhörighet och konflikt. En temagranskning av politiksynen i läromedel i samhällskunskap samt några didaktiska anteckningar om skolans medborgerliga och politiska fostran." ("On Solidarity and Conflict – An Investigation of Political Attitudes in Educational Materials for Social Science as well as some Didactic Observations about how Schools Encourage Civic and Political Awareness.") Statens Institut för Läromedel, Stockholm 1984.

Englund, Tomas: "Samhällsorientering och medborgarfostran i svensk skola under 1900-talet." ("Social Science and Civics in Sweden in the 20th century.") Uppsala 1986.

EPIE (Educational Products Information Exchange Institute): "Report on a National Study of the Nature and Quality of Instructional Materials Most Used by Teachers and Learners." Report No 76. New York 1977.

Eraut, Michael et al.: "The Analysis of Curriculum Materials." University of Sussex 1975.

Evans, M.A., C. Watson, D, M. Willows (eds.): "A Naturalistic Inquiry into Illustrations in Instructional Textbooks." In: Houghton, H.A., D.M. Willows: *The Psychology of Illustrations (2). Instructional Issues.* New York 1987.

Evensen, Lars Sigfred: "Den vet best hvor sko(l)en trykker..." ("Those who know best where the School (the Shoe) Pinches...") Universitetet i Trondheim 1986.

Farrell, Joseph P., Stephen P. Heyneman: *Textbooks in the Developing World. Economic and Educational Choices.* The World Bank. Washington DC 1989.

Fauvel, John, Ian Michael, Chris Stray, John Wilkes: "The Colloquium on Textbooks, Schools and Society." (Introduction of the Paradigm Network.) Chris Stray, Dept of Sociology, University College. Swansea 1990.

Fechner, Heinrich: "Die Geschichte des Volksschullesebuchs." In: Kehr, Carl (ed.): *Geschichte der Methodik des deutschen Volksschulunterrichts.* Band 2. Gotha 1879.

Felker, Daniel B., Janice C. Redish, Jane Peterson: "Training Authors for Informative Documents." In: Duffy, Thomas M., Robert Waller (eds.): *Designing Usable Texts.* Orlando 1985.

Fernig, L.R., J.F. McDougal, Herbert Ohlman: "Will Textbooks Be Replaced by New Information Technologies?" In: Farrell, Joseph P., Stephen P. Heyneman (eds.): *Textbooks in the Developing World.*

Economic and Educational Choices. The World Bank. Washington DC 1989.

Ferro, Marc: *Comment on raconte l'histoire aux enfants à travers le monde entier.* Paris 1986.

Fisch, S.: *Is There a Text in This Class? The Authority of Interpretive Communities.* Cambridge 1980.

FitzGerald, Frances: *America Revised. History Schoolbooks in the Twentieth Century.* Boston 1979.

Fleming, D.B., R.J. Nurse: "Vietnam Revised: Are our Textbooks Changing?" In: *Social Education* No. 46 1982.

Fossestøl, Bernt: Tekst og tekststruktur. Veier og mål i tekstlingvistikken. *(Text and Text Structure. Paths and Goals in Text Linguistics.)* Oslo 1980.

Fossestøl, Bernt: Norske grammatikker på 1800-tallet. *(Norwegian Grammars in the 19th Century.)* Oslo 1987.

Fox, T.H:, R.D. Hess: *An Analysis of Social Conflict in Social Studies Textbooks.* US Department of Health, Education, and Welfare. Washington DC 1972.

Fox, W.: "Textbook Publishing is Profitable but Controlled." In: *The Boston Globe* 1.12. 1985.

Freeman, Donald, Andrew Porter: "Does the Content of Classroom Instruction match the Content of Textbooks?" Manuscript. AERA Meeting, New Orleans 1988.

Freire, Paulo: Pedagogik för förtryckta. *(Education for the Oppressed.)* Stockholm 1970.

Frische, Torben: Dansk litteratur i gymnasiet 1910–71. *(Danish Literature in Upper Secondary School 1910–71.)* København 1977.

Fritzsche, Karl Peter: "Kommen wir nicht ohne Vorurteile aus?" In: *Internationale Schulbuchforschung* No. 4, Braunschweig 1989.

Fritzsche, Karl Peter: "Auf der Suche nach einer neuen Sprache: Schulbücher in der DDR." In: *Sprach - Report* No. 4 1990.

Fröchling, Jürgen: "Die mittelalterliche Stadt im deutschen Schulbuch von 1871 bis 1971." In: *Zur Sache Schulbuch.* Band 10. Kastellaun 1978.

Fuller, Roy: *The Ruined Boys.* London 1959.

Furuland, Lars: "'Lyssna till den granens susning...'. Om en läsebok som folkuppfostrare." ("'Listen to the Whispering of the Spruce...'. On a Primer as Educator of the People.") In: *Kungl. Vitterhets Historie och Antikvitets Akademiens Årsbok.* Stockholm 1987.

Gabler, Mel, Norma Gabler: "Mind Control Through Textbooks." In: *Phi Delta Kappan* 64:2, 1982.

Garcia, J., D.E. Tanner: "The Portrayal of Black Americans in U.S. History Textbooks." In: *The Social Studies* No. 76 1985.

Gattermann, Brigitte, Andrea Gintenstorfer: "Das Europabild im Schulbuch. Zum Europabegriff in den österreichischen Geschichts- und Geographiebüchern der 8. Schulstufe." Institut für Schulbuchforschung. Wien 1991.

Geertz, Clifford: "Blurred genres: The Refiguration of Social Thought." In: *The American Scholar* 49:2, 1980.

Georg-Eckert-Institut Für Internationale Schulbuchforschung:*Verzeichnis der Publikationen.* Stand: Juni 1990. Frankfurt 1990.

Georg-Eckert-Institut Für Internationale Schulbuchforschung: "Textbook Research under the Influence of Global Changes and International Crises (1988–1991)." Paper. Unesco International Expert Meeting. Griffith University, Australia 1991.

Gerot, Linda, Jane Oldenburg, Theo Van Leeuwen: "Language and Socialisation: Home and School. Proceedings from the Working Conference on Language in Education." Macquarie University, Sydney 1986.

Gilbert, Rob: "Text Analysis and Ideology Critique of Curricular Content." In: De Castell, Suzanne, Allan Luke, Carmen Luke (eds.): *Language, Authority and Criticism.* London/New York/Philadelphia 1989.

Gillham, Bruce (ed.): *The Language of School Subjects.* London 1986.

Gillham, Bruce: "Equal Opportunity and the Language of School Subjects." In: Gillham, Bruce (ed.): *The Language of School Subjects.* London 1986.

Ginsburger-Vogel, Yvette: *Les élèves face aux questions. Le statut des questions dans le discours didactique.* In: *Le Français Aujourd'hui* No. 74 1986.

Giroux, H., A. Penna: "Social Education in the Classroom: the Dynamics of the Hidden Curriculum." In: *Theory and Research in Social Education* 7:1, 1978.

Glinz, Hans: "Der Sprachunterricht im engeren Sinne oder Sprachlehre und Sprachkunde." In: *Handbuch des Deutschunterrichts I.* Emsdetten 1969.

Goldstein, P.: *Changing the American Schoolbook: Law, Politics, and Technology.* Lexington 1978.

Goodman, G., N. Homma, T. Najita, J.M. Becker: "The Japan/United States Textbook Project: Perceptions in the Textbooks in each Country about the History of the Other." In: *The History Teacher* No. 16 1983.

Gordon, David: "Education as Text: The Varieties of Educational Hiddenness." In: *Curriculum Inquiry* 18:4, 1988.

Gould, C.: "The Readability of School Biology Texts." In: *Journal of*

Biological Education 11:4, 1977.

Government Printing Office/National Commission on Excellence in Education: *A Nation at Risk: The Imperative for Educational Reform.* Washington DC 1983.

Graf, Dittmar: *Begriffstermen im Biologieunterricht der Sekundarstufe 1.* Frankfurt am Main 1989.

Gravem, Finn H.: "Vurdering av læremidler for bruk i undervisning. Begrepsdrøfting, vurderings- og kriterieproblematikk." ("Evaluation of Teaching Materials. Discussion of Concepts and of Criteria for Evaluation.") Universitetet i Oslo. (U.å.; year of issue not indicated.)

Graves, D.H.: "Language Arts Textbooks: A Writing Process Evaluation." In: *Language Arts* No. 54 1977.

Graves, M.F., W.H.Slater: "Could Textbooks Be Better Written and Would It Make a Difference?" In: *American Educator* 10:1, 1986.

Grevholm, Barbro, Margita Nilsson, Helge Bratt: "Läroböcker i matematik." ("Math Textbooks.") In: Rönström, Thomas (ed.): Skolböcker 1–3. *(Schoolbooks 1–3.)* Ds 1988:22–24. Stockholm 1988.

Griffen, W., J. Marciano: "Vietnam, the Textbook Version." In: *Social Science Record* No. 17 1980.

Grønlie, Tore: "Hvordan vurderer vi lærebøker i historie?" ("How do We Evaluate History Textbooks?") In: "Rapport fra NFFs seminar for lærebokforfattere på Leangkollen." (Seminar Report; The Norwegian Non-Fiction Writers' and Translators' Association) Oslo 1987.

Gullberg, A., A. Lind: "U-länder i läroböcker." ("Developing Countries in Textbooks.") Pedagogiska Institutionen, Rapport 3. Stockholms universitet 1969.

Gustafsson, Christina: "Läromedlens funktion i undervisningen – Rädovisning av förstudier." ("The Function of Teaching Materials in Class – some Preliminary Studies.") Manuscript. Stockholm 1978.

Gustafsson, Christina: Läromedlens funktion i undervisningen. *(The Function of Teaching Materials in Class.)* Ds U 1980:4. Stockholm 1980.

Gustafsson, Christina: "Läromedlens styrande funktion i undervisningen. En empirisk studie." ("The Influence of Teaching Materials in Class. An Empirical Study.") In: Lundgren, Ulf P., Gunilla Svingby, Erik Wallin (eds.): "Läroplaner och läromedel. En konferensrapport." ("Curricula and Teaching Materials. A Conference Report.") Högskolan för lärarutbildning, Stockholm 1982.

Guttentag, Marcia, Helen Bray: *Undoing Sex Stereotypes. Research and Resources for Educators.* New York 1976.

Gödde-Baumann, Beate (ed.): *Schul(buch)arbeit für Europa. IfS-Aktivitäten und Erfahrungen.* IfS-Spectrum. Sonderausgabe, Duisburg Juni 1987.

Hacker, Hartmut: "Didaktische Funktionen des Mediums Schulbuch." In: Hacker, Hartmut (ed.): *Das Schulbuch. Funktion und Verwendung im Unterricht.* Bad Heilbrunn 1980.

Hadenius, Stig, Claes-Olof Olsson: "Historieböckerna i det nye gymnasiet." ("The History Textbooks in the New Upper Secondary School." In: *Historisk tidskrift* No. 1, Stockholm 1971.

Hahn, C.L., G. Blankenship: "Women and Economic Textbooks." In: *Theory and Research in Social Education* 11:3, 1981.

Halliday, M.A.K.: *Explorations in the Functions of Language.* London 1973.

Hansen, Martin A.: "Verdensromanen." ("The World Novel.") In: Hansen, Martin A.: Midsommerkrans. *(Midsummer Wreath.)* København 1956.

Hansson, Krister: "Utländska läroböcker. En rapport om tillgång till och behov av läroböcker från andra länder som grund för läroboksforskning." ("Foreign Textbooks. A Report on Access to and Need for Textbooks from other Countries as a Condition for Textbook Research.") Statens Psykologisk-Pedagogiska Bibliotek, Stockholm 1990.

Harbo, Sigmund: "Objektivitetsgransking av lærebøker." ("Objectivity in Textbooks.") In: NOU 1978:26: Læremidler i skole og voksenopplæring. *(Teaching Materials in Schools and Adult Education.)* Oslo 1978.

Harrison, C.: *Readability in the Classroom.* Cambridge 1980.

Harvey, R., D. Kerslake, H. Shuard, M. Torbe: *Language Teaching and Learning: Mathematics.* London 1982.

Haslev, Marianne: Setningsanalyse og beslektede emner i syntaks. *(Sentence Analysis and Related Syntactic Themes.)* Oslo 1975.

Hasubek, P.: *Das deutsche Lesebuch in der Zeit des Nationalsozialismus. Ein Beitrag zur Literaturpädagogik zwischen 1933 und 1945.* Hannover 1972.

Heather, P.: *Reading Habits of 13–15 Year Olds.* C.R.U.S. British Library Service, London 1981.

Heide, Hjørdis: "Kjønnsroller i familie og samfunn i lærebøkene." ("Sexual Stereotypes in Family and Society in the Textbooks.") In: Koritzinsky, Theo (ed.): Samfunnsfag og påvirkning. *(Social Sciences and Influence.)* Oslo 1977.

Heinssen, J.: *Das Lesebuch als politisches Führungsmittel. Ein Beitrag zur Publizistik im Dritten Reich.* Minden 1964.

Helbig, Ludwig: "Identitätsprobleme eines Schulbuchmachers." In: Stein,

Gerd (ed.): *Schulbuchschelte. Politikum und Herausforderung.* Stuttgart 1979.

Helgheim, Johannes: Allmugeskolen i byane. *(The Common Primary Schools in the Cities.)* Oslo 1981.

Hellern, Victor: "Læreboka – den egentlige kulturbærer." ("Textbooks – Real Guardians of Culture.") In: Johnsen, Egil Børre, Åse Enerstvedt (eds.): En bok for sakens skyld. *(A Book for the Sake of the Case.)* Oslo 1988.

Hellesnes, Jon: Sosialisering og teknokrati. *(Socialization and Technocracy.)* Oslo 1975.

Helmers, Hermann: *Geschichte des deutschen Lesebuchs in Grundzügen.* Stuttgart 1970.

Henriksen, Turid: "Fremmedspråkpedagogikk, lærebøker og samfunn. Historisk utvikling av lærebøker i fransk i den norske skole." ("The Didactics of Foreign Language Teaching, Textbooks and Society. Historical Development of Textbooks in French in Norwegian Schools." Universitetet i Oslo 1989.

Herrick, V.E.: "The Concept of Curriculum Design." In: Herrick, V.E., R.E. Tyler (eds.): *Toward Improved Curriculum Theory.* Chicago 1950.

Hertzberg, Frøydis: " '– og denne Videnskab har man kaldet Grammatiken'. Tre studier i skolegrammatikkens historie." (" '– and this Science has been named Grammar'. Three Studies in the History of School Grammars.") Universitetet i Oslo 1990.

Heyman, Ingrid: "Textanalys av läroböcker om mat och matlagning inom vårdutbildningen." ("An Analysis of Textbooks on Food and Cooking in Nurses' Education.") In: *SPOV* No. 7, Härnösand 1989.

Heyneman, Stephen P., Joseph Farrell, Manuel Sepulveda-Stuardo: *Textbooks and Achievement: What we Know.* The World Bank. Washington DC 1978.

Hillocks, George Jr.: "Storm in the Mountains: A Case Study of Censorship, Conflict, and Consciousness." (Book Review.) In: *American Journal of Education* No. 21 1991.

Hinchman, K.: "The Textbook and Those Content Area Teachers." In: *Reading Research and Instruction* No. 26 1987.

Hinrichs, Ernst: "Absolutismus im Schulgeschichtsbuch." In: *Internationale Schulbuchforschung* No. 3, Braunschweig 1986.

Hinrichs, Ernst (ed.): *Regionalität. Der "kleine Raum" als Problem der internationalen Schulbuchforschung.* Schriftenreihe des Georg-Eckert-Instituts. Band 64, Frankfurt 1990.

Hirsch, E.D.Jr.: *Cultural Literacy. What Every American Needs To Know.* Boston 1987.

Holm et al.: Omkring os 4. (Arbeidsbok.) *(Around Us 4.)* (Ancillary Book.) København 1986.

Holsti, Ole R.: *Content Analysis for the Social Sciences and Humanities.* Reading, Massachusetts 1969.

Holter, Harriet, Ragnvald Kalleberg (eds.): Kvalitative metoder i samfunnsforskningen. *(Qualitative Methods in Social Science Research.)* Oslo 1990.

Holtz, H. (ed.): *Education and the American Dream.* New York 1989.

Houghton, H.A., D.M. Willows (eds.): *The Psychology of Illustration.* Volume 2. New York 1987.

Howatt, A.P.R.: *A History of English Language Teaching.* Oxford 1984.

Humbert, Raymond: *1789–1989. Il était une fois la Révolution: les manuels scolaires racontent.* Paris 1989.

Huot, Hélène (ed.): *Bulletin d'informations sur les manuels scolaires.* Revue trimestrielle. Société pour l'Information sur les Manuels Scolaires. Université de Paris VII. 1986-.

Huot, Hélène: *Et voilà pourquoi ils ne savent pas lire.* Paris 1988.

Huot, Hélène: *Dans la jungle des manuels scolaires.* Paris 1989.

Huot, Hélène, Francis Corblin: *Guide des manuels scolaires.* (1: Collège; 2: Lycée.) Paris 1990.

Hvenekilde, Anne: "Steiner for brød. 'Lettlest' o-fag for grunnskolen." ("Stones instead of Bread. 'Easy Readers' for the Content Areas.") In: *Norsklæreren* No. 3 1983.

Hvenekilde, Anne: "Nærblikk på o-fags-tekster." ("Focus on Content Area Texts.") In: *Norsklæreren* No. 3 1986.

Haavelsrud, Magnus (ed.): Indoktrinering eller politisering? *(Indoctrination or politicization?)* Oslo 1979.

Haavelsrud, Magnus: "Samspill om kunnskap." *("Promoting Knowledge Together.")* Universitetet i Tromsø 1991.

Informationen zu Schulbuchfragen. Heft 47: Beiträge zu Methoden der Schulbuchforschung. Manuscriptdruck. Volk und Wissen Volkseigener Verlag, Berlin 1983.

Informationen zu Schulbuchfragen. Heft 60: Bewährungsanalysen von Schulbüchern – Gedanken, Meinungen, Positionen. Manuscriptdruck. Volk und Wissen Volkseigener Verlag, Berlin 1988.

Ingham, J.: *Books and Reading Development.* London 1982.

INRP (Institut National de Recherche Pédagogique): *Des manuels pour apprendre. Rencontres Pédagogiques* No. 23 1988.

Jacobmeyer, Wolfgang (ed.): *Deutschlandbild und Deutsche Frage in den historischen, geographischen und sozialwissenschaftlichen Unterrichts-*

werken der Bundesrepublik Deutschland und der Deutschen Demokratischen Republik von 1949 bis in die 80er Jahre. Schriftenreihe des Georg-Eckert-Instituts. Band 43. Braunschweig 1986.

Janis, J.: "Textbook Revisions in the Sixties." In: *Teachers College Record* No. 72 1972.

Jansen, Mogens: Danske læsebøger 1.-7. skoleår. I: Registrering og analyse. *(Danish Readers One through Seven. I: Registration and Analysis.)* Danmarks pædagogiske institut. København 1969.

Jansen, Mogens, Bo Jacobsen, Poul Erik Jensen: *The Teaching of Reading without Really any Method. (An Analysis of Reading Instruction in Denmark.)* København 1978.

Jenkinson, Edward B.: *Censors in the Classroom. The Mind Benders.* London/Amsterdam 1979.

Jensen, Frank A.: "The Selection of Manuscripts by Publishers."In: *The Thirtieth Yearbook of the NSSE. Part II.* Bloomington 1931.

Jensen, Johan Fjord: "Dannelsen og de pædagogiske frirum." ("Education and Educational Liberty.") In: *Dansk Noter* No. 4 1991. Dansklærerforeningen. København 1991.

Jensen, Leif Becker: Ud af elfenbenstårnet. *(Out of the Ivory Tower.)* København 1987.

Jensen, P. O.: Orienteringsundervisning i 9.-10. klasse. *(History and Social Sciences Nine through Ten.)* Danmarks Pædagogiske Institut. København 1975.

Jensen, P. O.: Orienteringsundervisning i 3.-6. klasse. *(History and Social Sciences Three through Six.)* Danmarks Pædagogiske Institut. København 1977.

Johansson, Martin: "Den omöjliga läroboken." ("The Impossible Text Book.") In: Rönström, Thomas (ed.): Skolböcker 1–3. *(Schoolbooks 1–3.)* Ds 1988:22–24. Stockholm 1988.

Johnsen, Egil Børre: "Begynnelsen på en selvtillit." ("Building up Self-confidence.") In: Johnsen, Egil Børre, Åse Enerstvedt (eds.): En bok for sakens skyld. *(A Book for the Sake of the Case.)* Oslo 1988.

Johnsen, Egil Børre: Den skjulte litteraturen. *(Hidden Literature.)* Oslo 1989.

Johnsen, Egil Børre: "Læreren som litteratur." ("Teachers as Literature.") In: Jordell, Karl Øyvind, Per Olaf Aamodt (eds.): Læreren – fra kall til lønnskamp. *(Teachers – from Vocation to Trade Unionism.)* Oslo 1989a.

Johnsen, Egil Børre: Verden. *(The World.)* Oslo 1992.

Johnsen, Egil Børre: "Det tredje språket." ("The Third Language.") Manuscript. His 1992a.

oror5reason555

Johnson, Clifton: *Old-Time Schools and School-Books.* New York 1904.

Jonassen, David H.: *The Technology of Text 1–2.* New Jersey 1982.

Jones, Nick: "On Anthologies." In: *The Use of English* No. 3 1983.

Jones, Nick: "Anthologies and 'English Literature'". In: *The Use of English* No. 1 1984.

Jules, Didacus: "Building Democracy: Content and Ideology in Grenadian Educational Texts, 1979 – 1983." In: Apple, Michael W., Linda K. Christian-Smith (eds.): *The Politics of The Textbook.* London/New York 1991.

Julkunen, Marja-Liisa: "Textbooks in Concept Acquisition." Manuscript. Pexu Conference, Härnösand 1990.

Jungk, Werner: "Bewährungsanalysen zu Schulbüchern – zu theoretischen und methodologischen Grundlagen, Ergebnissen und weiterführende Fragestellungen." In: *Informationen zu Schulbuchfragen.* Heft 60, Berlin 1988.

Jørstad, Arvid: "Språkbruk og holdningar. Ein studie av utvalde kapittel i tre lærebøker i samfunnskunnskap for ungdomsskolen." ("Language Usage and Attitudes. A Study of Selected Chapters From Three Social Science High School Textbooks.") In: Ryen, Else, Kari Kjenndalen (eds.): Språkbruk og holdninger i grunnskolen. *(Language Use and Attitudes in Primary Schools.)* Oslo 1979.

Kamala, Rajoo, Margaret Rogers: "Global Education Content and Approaches in Four Major Elementary Social Studies Textbook Series." Manuscript. CIES Conference, University of Pittsburgh 1991.

Kane, R.B., M.A. Byrne, M.A. Hater: *Helping Children Read Mathematics.* New York 1974.

Karabétian, Stéphane: *Théories et Pratiques des Grammaires.*Paris 1988.

Kelly, Ernece B. (ed.): *Searching for America.* National Council of Teachers of English. Urbana 1972.

Kelly, Louis G.: *25 Centuries of Language Teaching.* Rowley, Massachusetts 1969.

Kepner, Tyler: "The Influence of Textbooks upon Method." In: *Yearbook of the National Council for the Social Studies. Fifth yearbook.* Philadelphia 1935.

Kirke- og undervisningsdepartementet: "Mangelutredningen. Innstilling fra arbeidsgruppen oppnevnt for å kartlegge mangelområder når det gjelder lærebokdekningen i grunnskolen og den videregående skole." ("Report on Subject Areas Lacking Textbooks in Primary and Secondary Schools.") Oslo 1985.

Kittang, Atle, Per Meldahl, Hans H. Skei: Om litteraturhistorieskriving.

Perspektiv på litteraturhistoriografiens vilkår og utvikling i europeisk og norsk sammenheng. *(On the Writing of Histories of Literature. Perspecitves on the Conditions and Development of Literary History in Europe and in Norway.)* Øvre Ervik 1983.

Kjørup, Søren: "Humaniora i forskning og formidling." ("The Humanities in Research and Teaching.") In: Møller, Jørgen: Historieundervisning i gymnasiet gennem de sidste 100 år. *(History Teaching in Upper Secondary Schools during the past 100 Years.)* København 1983.

Klafki, Wolfgang: "Ideologiekritik." In: Roth, Leo (ed.): *Methoden erziehungswissenschaftlicher Forschung.* Stuttgart 1978.

Klauss, Barbara, Günther Brilla: "Politik in Biologiebüchern."In: Pöggeler, Franz (ed.): *Politik im Schulbuch.* Bonn 1985.

Koritzinsky, Theo: "Samfunnsfag i skolen – didaktisk oversikt." ("Social Sciences in Schools, a Didactic Survey.") In: Koritzinsky, Theo (ed.): Samfunnsfag og påvirkning. *(Social Sciences and Influence.)* Oslo 1977.

Krumbach, Carl Julius: *Geschichte und Kritik der deutschen Schullesebücher.* Leipzig 1894 (B.1), 1896 (B.2).

Kubanek, Angelika: "Die dritte Welt im Englischlehrbuch der Bundesrepublik Deutschland." In: *Internationale Schulbuchforschung* No. 4, Frankfurt 1989.

Kuhn, Thomas S.: "The Functions of Dogma in Scientific Research." Paper 1962a; quotation from: Crombie, A. C. (ed.): *Scientific Research.* London 1963.

Kuhn, Thomas S.: *The Structure of Scientific Revolutions.* Chicago 1962.

Kwong, Julia: "Curriculum in Action: Mathematics in China's Elementary Schools." In: Altbach, Philip G., Gail P. Kelly (eds.): *Textbooks in the Third World. Policy, Content and Context.* New York 1988.

Kühnl, R. (ed.): *Geschichte und Ideologie. Kritische Analyse bundesdeutscher Geschichtsbücher.* Reinbek 1973.

Källgren, G., B. Sigurd, M. Westman: Tre experiment med text. *(Three Experiments with Texts.)* Stockholm 1977.

Lagerlöf, Selma: Nils Holgerssons underbara resa genom Sverige. *(Nils Holgersson's Wonderful Journey Through Sweden.)* Stockholm 1906.

Lange, Klaus: "Methodologie und Methoden sozialwissenschaftlicher Unterrichtsmedienforschung." In: *Internationale Schulbuchforschung* No. 1, Braunschweig 1981.

Langenbucher, Wolfgang, Claudia Mast: "Wie man mit Lesebüchern Wahlkampf macht." In: Stein, Gerd (ed.): *Schulbuch-Schelte als*

Politikum und Herausforderung wissenschaftlicher Schulbucharbeit. Stuttgart 1979.

Langfeldt, Liv: "80-årenes kamp om knappe ressurser ved UiO." ("Struggles due to Scarcity of Funds at the University of Oslo during the 80s.") In: *Forskningspolitikk* No. 4 1991.

Lapointe, Archie: "The State of Instruction in Reading and Writing in US Elementary Schools." In: *Phi Delta Kappan* No. 68 1986.

Laubig, Manfred: "Verwendungs- und Wirkungszusammenhang." In: Laubig, Manfred, Heidrun Peters, Peter Weinbrenner: "Methoden der Schulbuchanalyse." Universität Bielefeld 1986.

Leonardsen, Dag: "Om kriterier for vurdering av lærebøker." ("On Criteria for Evaluating Textbooks.") In: Haavelsrud, Magnus (ed.): Indoktrinering eller politisering? *(Indoctrination or Politicization?)* Oslo 1979.

Lesch, Hans-Wolfgang: "Das Problem der wissenschaftlichen Bezugsgrammatiken für Sprachbücher in den Bundesländern der alten BRD, oder: Warum Deutschlehrer Linguisten sein müssen." Manuscript. Hochschule Halle-Köthen Conference 1990.

LFF (Läromedelsförfattarnas Förening/Association of Swedish Textbook Writers): Lärobok om läroböcker. *(A Textbook on Textbooks.)* Uppsala 1991.

Library of Congress: *The Textbook in American Society.* (See: Cole, John Y., Thomas G. Sticht)

Lietzmann, W.: "Stoff und Methode im Mathematischen Unterricht der Norddeutschen Hoheren Schulen." In: *Internationale Mathematische Unterrichtskommission. B.1.* Leipzig 1909.

Lilienthal, Jutta: *Praxis der Literaturvermittlung. Der pädagogische Apparat französischer literarischer Schulausgaben.* Frankfurt 1974.

Logan, W.C., R.L. Needham: "What Elementary School Social Studies Textbooks Tell about the Vietnam War." In: *The Social Studies* No. 76 1985.

Longum, Leif: "Gjennom templets port... . Norske skoleutgaver og litteraturundervisningen 1900–1970." ("Through the Gate of the Temple... . School Editions and the Teaching of Literature 1900–1970.") In: *Norsk Litterær Årbok.* Oslo 1987.

Lorentzen, Svein: "Ungdomsskolens samfunnsfag – intensjon og realitet." ("Social Sciences in Lower Secondary Schools – Intentions and Reality.") Oslo 1984.

Lorentzen, Svein: "Det nasjonale i grunnskolens historiebøker – et selvbilde i forandring." ("The Nation in History Textbooks for the Primary School – a Portrait of a Changing Identity.") In: Knut Jordheim

(ed.): *Skolen. Årbok for norsk skolehistorie.* Oslo 1988.
Ludwig, Otto: *Der Schulaufsatz. Seine Geschichte in Deutschland.* Berlin 1988.
Luke, Allan: "The Secular World: Catholic Reconstruction of Dick and Jane." In: Apple, Michael W., Linda K. Christian-Smith (eds.): *The Politics of The Textbook.* London/New York 1991.
Lund, Erik: "En ny generasjon lærebøker i historie." ("A New Generation of History Textbooks.") In: *Historiekontakten* No. 2, Oslo 1990.
Lunden, Kåre: "Verdi-lause lærebøker." ("Worth-less Textbooks.") In: *Syn og Segn* No. 3, Oslo 1990.
Lundgren, Ulf P.: *Model Analysis of Pedagogical Processes.* Lund 1977.
Lundgren, Ulf P.: Att organisera omvärlden. En introduktion till läroplansteori. *(Organizing the World. An Introduction to Curriculum Theory.)* Stockholm 1989.
Lunzer, E., K. Gardner: *The Effective Use of Reading.* London 1979.
Lunzer, E., K. Gardner: *Learning From the Written Word.* Edinburgh 1984.
Læremiddelkatalogen for den videregående skole 1992. *(Catalog of Teaching Materials for the Upper Secondary School 1992.)* Forlagssentralen. Oslo 1992.
Lærum, Ole Didrik: "Faglitteratur og kunnskapseksplosjon." ("Non-Fiction Literature and Knowledge Explosion.") Lecture. NFF (Norwegian Non-Fiction Writers' and Translators' Association Conference), Oslo 1991.

MacGinitie, H. Walter: "Readability as a Solution Adds to the Problem." In: Anderson, Richard C., Jean Osborn, Robert J. Tierney (eds.): *Learning to Read in American Schools: Basal Readers and Content Texts.* New York 1981. (NB: All quotations are from proof sheet.)
Maingueneau, Dominique: *Les livres d'école de la République 1870–1914. (Discours et idéologie.)* Paris 1979.
Manuels Scolaires: *Bulletin d'Information.* (Ed.: La Société pour l'Information sur les Manuels Scolaires et les Moyens d'Enseignement.) No. 10, Paris 1988.
Mann, Thomas: *Leiden und Grösse der Meister.* Fischer-Bücherei 1935.
Marenbach, Dieter: "Das Lesebuch." In: Hacker, Hartmut (ed.): *Das Schulbuch. Funktion und Verwendung im Unterricht.* Bad Heilbrunn 1980.
Marienfeld, Wolfgang: "Schulbuchanalyse und Schulbuchrevision: Zur Methodenproblematik." In: *Internationales Jahrbuch des Georg-Eckert-Instituts.* Band 17, Braunschweig 1976.
Marland, Michael: "The Language of School." In: Marland, Michael (ed.):

Language Across the Curriculum. London 1982.

Marland, Michael (ed.): *Language Across the Curriculum.* London 1982.

Marshall, J. Dan: "With a Little Help from Some Friends: Publishers, Protesters, and Texas Textbook Decisions." In: Apple, Michael W., Linda K. Christian-Smith (eds.): *The Politics of The Textbook.* London/New York 1991.

Martin, J.R.: "Secret English: Discourse Technology in a Junior Secondary School." In: Gerot, Linda, Jane Oldenburg, Theo van Leeuwen (eds.): "Language and Socialization: Home and School." Macquarie University, Sidney 1988.

Martinsson, Bengt-Göran: Tradition och betydelse. *(Tradition and Meaning.)* Linköping 1989.

Mason, J., J. Osborn: "When do Children Begin 'Reading to Learn'? A Survey of Classroom Reading Instruction Practices in Grades Two through Five." Technical Report No. 261. Urbana 1982.

Mbuyi, Dennis: "Language and Texts in Africa." In: Altbach, Philip G., Gail P. Kelly (eds.): *Textbooks in the Third World. Policy, Content and Context.* New York 1988.

McCullough, Constance M.: "Preparation of Textbooks in the Mother Tongue. A Guide for Those Who Write and Those Who Evaluate Textbooks in Any Language." National Institute of Education. New Dehli/Delaware 1974.

McFadden, Charles P.: "Author-Publisher-Educator Relationships and Curriculum Reform." In: *Journal of Curriculum Studies* 24:1, 1992.

Meldahl, Per: "Om norske litteraturhistorier." ("On Books on the History of Norwegian Literature.") In: Kittang, Atle, Per Meldahl, Hans H. Skei: Om litteraturhistorieskriving. Perspektiv på litteratur-historiografiens vilkår og utvikling i europeisk og norsk sammenheng. *(On the Writing of Histories of Literature. Perspecitves on the Conditions and Development of Literary History in Europe and in Norway.)* Øvre Ervik 1983.

Metcalf, Fay D.: "The Treatment of NATO and the Atlantic Alliance in Textbooks in the United States." In: "Atlantisch Onderwijs Paper VII": "NATO in History and Civics Textbooks. An International Survey With US, West German, UK, Belgian and Dutch Contributions." Atlantische Commissie. Haag 1990.

Meyendorf, Gerhard: "Zur Geschichte der Schulbücher für den Chemie-unterricht der allgemeinbildenden Oberschule." In: *Informationen zu Schulbuchfragen.* Heft 61, Berlin 1989.

Meyer, J.W.: "The Effects of Education as an Institution." In: *American Journal of Sociology* 83:1, 1977.

Meyers, Peter: "Zur Problematik der Analyse von Schulgeschichtsbüchern." In: *Geschichte in Wissenschaft und Unterricht* 24:12, 1973.

Meyers, Peter: "Methoden zur Analyse historish-politischer Schulbücher." In: *Zur Sache Schulbuch.* Band 5. Kastellaun 1976.

Michael, Ian: "The Historical Study of English as a Subject; a Preliminary Inquiry into some Questions of Method." In: *History of Education* 8:3, 1979.

Michael, Ian: *The Teaching of English. From the Sixteenth Century to 1870.* Cambridge 1987.

Michael, Ian: "Aspects of Textbook Research." In: *Paradigm* No.2 1990.

Mikk, Jaan: "Computerized Readability Analysis of Textbooks of English. In: *Haridus* No. 6 1990. (Authorized translation; see: Tartu Ülikooli Toimetised.

Minnich, Harvey C.: *William Holmes McGuffey and His Readers.* New York 1936.

Moffett, James: *Teaching the Universe of Discourse.* Boston 1968.

Moffett, James: *Storm in the Mountains: A Case Study of Censorship, Conflict, and Consciousness.* Carbondale 1988.

Mok, Ineke: "Anti-Racism and Textbooks: An Evaluation of Geography and History for Secondary Education." Translation by Willy Aerdenburg. University of Amsterdam 1990.

Monaghan, Jennifer: "The Textbook as a Commercial Enterprise: The Involvement of Noah Webster and William Holmes McGuffey in the Promotion of Their Reading Textbooks." In: *Paragdigm* No. 6, Cambridge 1991.

Moosbrugger, Marina: "Das Niveau der Aufgaben in Lehrbüchern." In: *Unterrichtswissenschaft* No. 2 1985.

Munch, P.: Verdenshistorie. *(A History of the World.)* København 1907–1967.

Mukherjee, Hene, Ahmed Khairiah: "The Quest for National Unity: Language Text Books in Malaysia." In: Altbach, Philip G., Gail P. Kelly (eds.): *Textbooks in the Third World. Policy, Content and Context.* New York 1988.

Myers, Greg: "Fictional Forms and Science Textbooks." In: *Paradigm* No. 4, Cambridge 1990.

Mølgaard, John: "Skolebogen – et redskab i kampen for et levende demokrati." ("The Textbook – a Tool for Promoting Living Democracy.") In: *Information* 7.07. 1978.

Møller, Jørgen: Historieundervisning i gymnasiet gennem de sidste 100 år. *(The Teaching of History in Upper Secondary Scool for the last 100 years.)* København 1983.

Nestler, Käte: "Unterschiedliche sprachliche Gestaltung des gleichen Lehrtextinhalts ('Kreislauf des Wassers') in Heimatkundelehrbüchern der DDR, BRD und Ungarns und Ihre Wirk-ung auf die kognitive Verarbeitung der Textinhalte bei Schülern der Klasse 4." Manuscript. Halle-Köthen Conference 1990.

Neumann, Peter H.: "Publishing for Schools in the Federal Republic of Germany, France, the United Kingdom, and the United States." In: Farrell, Joseph P., Stephen P. Heyneman (eds.): *Textbooks in the Developing World. Economic and Educational Choices.* The World Bank. Washington DC 1989.

Nicholson, A.R.: "Mathematics and Language." In: *Mathematics in School* 6:5, 1977.

Nietz, John A.: *Old Textbooks.* Pittsburgh 1961.

Nobel, Agnes: Boken i skolan. En analys med särskild inriktning på bibliotekets funktion i grundskolan. *(The Book in School. An Analysis with Particular Emphasis on the Function of School Libraries.)* Stockholm 1979.

Nora, Pierre: "Ernest Lavisse, son rôle dans la formation du sentiment national." In: *Revue historique,* Juillet-Sept. 1962.

Nordkvelle, Yngve: "Bilder av utviklingsland i norske lærebøker. En undersøkelse av lærebøker for samfunnsfag, videregående skole, allmennfaglig studieretning." ("Portraits of Developing Countries in Norwegian Textbooks. An Investigation of Social Studies Textbooks in the Upper Secondary School.") Universitetet i Oslo 1986.

Nordkvelle, Yngve: "Bilder av utviklingsland i norske lærebøker. En undersøkelse av lærebøker for samfunnsfag i ungdomsskolen." ("Portraits of Developing Countries in Norwegian Textbooks. An Investigation of Social Studies Textbooks in the Lower Secondary School.") Universitetet i Oslo 1987.

Nordkvelle, Yngve: "Bildet av utviklingsland i undervisningen. Gåtvik videregående skole." ("The Image of Developing Countries in Education. Gåtvik Upper Secondary School.") Universitetet i Oslo 1988.

Nordkvelle, Yngve 1991: Letter 14.02. 1991.

Nordström, Gert Z.: Bilden i det postmoderna samhället. *(Pictures in Post-Modern Society.)* Stockholm 1989.

NOU 1978:26: "Læremidler i skole og voksenopplæring." ("Teaching Materials in School and Adult Education.") Oslo 1978.

NSSE Yearbook 1931: *Part II. The Textbook in American Education.* Prepared by the Society's Committee on the Textbook. Edited by Guy Montrose Whipple. Bloomington 1931.

NSSE Yearbook 1990: *Part I. Textbooks and Schooling in the United States.* Edited by David L. Elliott and Arthur Woodward. Chicago 1990.

Oberle, Kathleen: "Paradigm Wars: Who's Fighting; Who's Winning?" In: *The Alberta Journal of Research* 37:1, 1991.

O'Brien, S.: "The Reshaping of History. Marketers vs. Authors." In: *Curriculum Review* 28:1, 1988.

Odden, Svein Erik: "Norske lærebøker – en kritikk og noen forslag." ("Norwegian Textbooks – Criticism and Suggestions.") In: Tingsten, Herbert: Gud og fedrelandet. *(God and the Fatherland.)* Norwegian version by Svein Erik Odden. Oslo 1970.

Okonkwo, Chuka Eze: "Language and the Content of School Texts: The Nigerian Experience." In: Altbach, Philip G., Gail P. Kelly (eds.): *Textbooks in the Third World. Policy, Content and Context.* New York 1988.

Olson, David R., J.S. Bruner: "Learning Through Experience and Learning Through Media." In: Olson, David R. (ed.): *Media and Symbols.* NSSE Yearbook. Chicago 1974.

Olson, David R.: "From Utterance to Text: The Bias of Language in Speech and Writing." In: *Harvard Educational Review* No. 47 1977.

Olson, David R.: "On the Designing and Understanding of Written Texts." In: Duffy, T.M., R. Waller (eds.): *Designing Usable Texts.* Orlando 1985.

Olson, David R.: "On the Language and Authority of Textbooks." In: De Castell, Suzanne, Allan Luke, Carmen Luke (eds.): *Language, Authority and Criticism. Readings on the School Textbook.* London/New York/Philadelphia 1989.

Olson, David R.: "Sources of Authority in the Language of the School: A Response to 'Beyond Criticism'." In: De Castell, Suzanne, Allan Luke, Carmen Luke (eds.): *Language, Authority and Criticism. Readings on the School Textbook.* London/New York/Philadelphia 1989.

Olsson, Lena: Kulturkunskap i förändring. Kultursynen i svenska geografiläroböcker 1870–1985. *(Culture in Flux. Cultural Attitudes in Swedish Geography Textbooks 1870–1985.)* Lund 1986.

Ong, W.J.: *Ramism and the Decay of Dialogue.* Cambridge 1958.

Oppel, Yanouchka: "L'Analyse des Manuels Scolaires. Élaboration d'une Grille Descriptive." Institut Romand de Recherche et de Documentation Pédagogiques. Neuchâtel 1976.

Oppland Regional College: "Rapport fra lærebokprosjektet 1977/78. Forkortet versjon." ("Report from the Textbook Project 1977/78.

Abridged Version.") Oppland Distriktshøgskole, Lillehammer 1978.

Orna, Elizabeth: "The Author: Help or Stumbling Block on the Road to Designing Usable Texts?" In: Duffy, Thomas M., Robert Waller (eds.) *Designing Usable Texts.* Orlando 1985.

Osborn, Jean: "The Purposes, Uses and Contents of Workbooks and Some Guidelines for Publishers." In: Anderson, Richard C., Jean Osborn, Robert J. Tierney (eds.): *Learning to Read in American Schools: Basal Readers and Content Texts.* New York 1981. (NB: All quotations are from proof sheet.)

Osborn, Jean, Karen Decker: "Ancillary Materials, What's Out There?" Reading Research and Education Center. Urbana-Champaign 1990.

Outline of Japan Textbook Center. Japan Textbook Center, Tokyo 1991.

Overesch, Manfred: "Der Zeitraum von 1945 bis 1955 im deutschsprachigen Schulbuch (Österreich, Schweiz, Bundesrepublik Deutschlands und DDR)." In: *Das Schulbuch: Analyse – Kritik – Konstruktion. Zur Sache Schulbuch.* Band 10. Kastellaun 1978.

Pagès, Alain: (Participation in:) "Grandeur et servitude des auteurs de manuels. Table ronde". In: *Le Français Aujourd'hui* No. 70, Paris 1983.

Pallin, Johan Rudolf: Lärobok i nya tidens historia för elementarläroverkens högre klasser. *(Textbook in Contemporary History for Upper Secondary Schools.)* Stockholm 1878–1925.

Palm, Göran: Indoktrineringen i Sverige. *(The Indoctrination in Sweden.)* Stockholm 1968.

Paradigm: See Fauvel, John.

Parker, William Riley: "Where Do English Departments Come From?" In: *College English* 28:5, 1967.

Paul, R.W.: "Dialogical Thinking: Critical Thought Essential to the Acquisition of Rational Knowledge and Passions." In: Baron, J.B., R.J. Sternberg (eds.): *Teaching Thinking Skills.* New York 1987.

PAX KORREKTIV 1–4. (Series criticizing Norwegian Social Science Textbooks.) Oslo 1970–1971.

Perera, Katharine: "The Assessment of Linguistic Difficulty in Reading Material." In: *Educational Review* 32:2, 1980.

Perera, Katharine: "Some Linguistic Difficulties in School Texts." In: Gillham, Bruce (ed.): *The Language of School Subjects.* London 1986.

Pettersson, Rune: Bilder i läromedel. *(Pictures in Teaching Materials.)* Institutet för Infologi. Tullinge 1991.

Pettersson, Åke: "Bärbara substantiv. Om läroböckernas exempel." ("The 'Most Important' Nouns. The Example set by Textbooks." In: Ulf

Telemann (ed.): Grammatik på villovägar. *(Grammar Getting Lost.)* Stockholm 1987.

Platzack, Christer: Språket och läsbarheten. *(Language and Readability.)* Lund 1974.

Pons, Anne: *Le tour de France par Camille et Paul, deux enfants d'aujourd'hui, 1–2.* Paris 1978–79.

Powell, D.A.: "Selection of Reading Textbooks at the District Level: Is this a Rational Process?" In: *Book Research Quarterly* 1:3, 1985.

Pöggeler, Franz (ed.): *Politik im Schulbuch.* Bonn 1985.

Quéréel, Patrice: *Au feu les manuels. L'Idéologie dans les Manuels de Lecture à l'École Élémentaire.* Paris 1982.

"Rapport fra lærebokprosjektet 1976/77/78." ("Report on a textbook research project.") Oppland distriktshøgskole. Lillehammer 1978.

Regeringens Proposition 1988/89:4: Skolans utveckling och styrning. *(Development and Control of Schools.)* Stockholm 1989.

Reints, A., N.A.J. Lagerweij (eds.): "Om de kwaliteit van het leermiddel." ("On the Quality of Teaching Materials.") Tilburg/ Zwijsen 1989.

Reich, Brigitte: *Erziehung zur Völkerverständigung und zum Frieden.* Frankfurt am Main 1989.

Reising, Russell J.: *The Unusable Past. Theory and the Study of American Literature.* New York 1986.

Report to the Storting No. 23 1982–83: "On Textbooks." Oslo 1983.

Reynolds, C.J.: "Textbooks and Immigrants." In: *Phi Delta Kappan* No. 33 1952.

Richaudeau, François: *Conception et production des manuels scolaires. Guide pratique.* Paris 1986.

Richaudeau, François: *Manuel de Typographie et de Mise en Page.* Paris 1989.

Richey, Herman G.: "The Professional Status of Textbook Authors." In: *The Thirtieth Yearbook of the NSSE. Part II.* Bloomington 1931.

Richmond, J.: "What Do 87 Girls Read?" In: *The English Magazine* 1979.

Ricoeur, Paul: "The Model of the Text: Meaningful Action Considered as Text." In: Thompson, J.B. (ed.): *Hermeneutics and the Human Sciences.* Cambridge 1981.

Ringnes, Vivi: "Naturfagspråket." ("The Language of Science Subjects.") In: Horsfjord, Vidar (ed.): "Naturfagundervisning og språk." ("Science Teaching and Language.") Universitetet i Oslo 1986.

Rioux, Jean-Pierre: *Erckmann et Chatrian. Ou le Trait d'Union.* Paris 1989.

Roeder, Peter Martin: *Zur Geschichte und Kritik des Lesebuchs der höheren Schule.* Weinheim/Bergstr. 1961.

Roksvold, Thore: "Holdninger i avisenes fotballreportasjer." ("Attitudes in Newspapers' Coverage of Football Matches.") Nordisk institutt. Universitetet i Oslo 1975.

Rolfsen, Nordahl: Verdenshistorien for de unge. *(World History for the Young.)* Oslo 1903.

Roll-Hansen, Nils: "'Naturhistorie for børn.' Introduksjon." ("'Natural History for Children.' An Introduction.") In: *Skolen 1988.* Oslo 1988.

Rosen, Harold: "The Language of Textbooks." In: Britton, James (ed.): *Talking and Writing.* London 1967.

Rosen, H., C. Rosen: *The Language of Primary School Children.* London 1972.

Rosenblatt, L.: *The Reader, the Text, the Poem.* Carbondale 1978.

Rothery, A., H. Shuard (eds.): *Children Reading Mathematics.* London 1984.

Rothery, Andrew: "Readability in Maths." In: Gillham, Bruce (ed.): *The Language of School Subjects.* London 1986.

Rönström, Thomas (ed.): Skolböcker 1–3. *(Schoolbooks 1–3.)* Ds 1988:22–24. Stockholm 1988.

Røsvik, Sindre: "I oppløpet for år 2000 – Status for innføring av datateknologi i skulen." ("Approaching Year 2000 - Status for the Introduction of Data Technology in Schools.") In: *Data i skolen* No. 1. Oslo 1990.

Sanderud, Roar: Fra P. A. Jensen til Nordahl Rolfsen. Et skolehistorisk bilde. *(From P. A. Jensen to Nordahl Rolfsen. A Portrait of Our School History.)* Oslo 1951.

Sanness, Anna Huse: "Grunnskolen: Fra planer til lærebøker." ("Primary Schools: From Curricula to Textbooks.") In: "Rapport fra NFF's seminar for lærebokforfattere på Leangkollen 1987." ("Report from NFF Conference at Leangkollen 1987.") Oslo 1987.

Sattler, Rolf-Joachim: *Europa. Geschichte und Aktualität des Begriffes.* Schriftenreihe des Internationalen Schulbuchinstituts. Band 16. Braunschweig 1971.

Schallenberger, Horst E.: *Untersuchungen zum Geschichtsbild der Wilhelminishcen Ära in der Weimarer Republik. Eine vergleichende Schulbuchanalyse deutscher Schulgeschichtsbücher aus der Zeit von 1888 bis 1933.* Ratingen 1964.

Schallenberger, Horst E. (ed.): *Das Schulbuch – Produkt und Faktor gesellschaftlicher Prozesse. Zur Sache Schulbuch.* Band 1. Kastellaun

1973.

Schillo, Michael Alloys: "Die Arbeit des Duisburger INSTITUTs FÜR SCHULBUCHFORSCHUNG e.V. an der Universität Duisburg 1977–1987." In: *IfS-Spectrum* No. 3–4 1987.

Schissler, Hanna: "Perceptions of the Other and the Discovery of the Self." In: Berghahn, Volker R., Hanna Schissler (eds.): *Perceptions of History*. Oxford/New York/Hamburg 1987.

School Textbooks in Japan. Japan Textbook Research Center. Tokyo 1991.

Schorling, Raleigh, J.B. Edmonson: "The Techniques of Textbook Authors." In: *The Thirtieth Yearbook of the NSSE. Part II*. Bloomington 1931.

Schramm, Wilbur: "The Publishing Process." In: Cronbach, Lee J. (ed.): *Text Materials in Modern Education*. Urbana 1955.

Schlesinger, I.M: *Sentence Structure and the Reading Process*. Haag 1968.

Schotte, Gustaf Victor: Lärobok i gamla tidens historia för allmänna läroverkens högre klasser. *(Textbook on Ancient History for Upper Secondary Schools.)* Stockholm 1877–1902.

Schubert, Ulrich: *Das Schulfach Heimatkunde im Spiegel von Lehrerhandbüchern der 20er Jahre*. Hildesheim 1987.

Schumacher, Gary M.: "A Reaction to 'Americans Develop Plans for Government'– 1." In: *Journal of Curriculum Studies* 17:3, 1985.

Schuyler, M.R.: "Readability Formula Program for Use on Microcomputers." In: *Journal of Reading* 25:6, 1982.

Schwier, H.-J.: "Methodische Überlegungen zur emotionalen Wirksamkeit von Lehrbuchabschnitten im Biologieunterricht." In: *Informationen zu Schulbuchfragen*. Heft 40, Halle-Köthen 1980.

Schüddekopf, Otto-Ernst: "Miller Elson, Ruth: 'Guardians of Tradition, American Schoolbooks of the Nineteenth Century'." In: *Internationales Jahrbuch für Geschichts- und Geographieunterricht*. Band X. Braunschweig 1965–66.

Schüddekopf, Otto-Ernst: "20 Jahre Schulbuchrevision in Westeuropa 1945–1965. Tatsachen und Probleme." In: *Schriftenreihe des Internationalen Schulbuchinstituts*. Band 12, Braunschweig 1966.

Schüddekopf, Otto-Ernst: "The Lesson Learned from History and History Textbook Revision." In: Schüddekopf, Otto-Ernst, Edouard Bruley, E.H. Dance, Haakon Vigander (eds.): *History Teaching and History Textbook Revision*. Strasbourg 1967.

Selander, Staffan: Textum Institutionis – den pedagogiska Väven. *(Textum Institutionis – The Educational Web.)* Lund and Stockholm 1984.

Selander, Staffan: Lärobokskunskap. *(Textbook Knowledge.)* Lund 1988.

Selander, Staffan: "Towards a Theory of Pedagogic Text Analysis." In:

Scandinavian Journal of Educational Research 34:2, 1990.

Selander, Staffan, Ewa Romare, Eva Trotzig, Annika Ullman: "Racism och främlingsfientlighet i svenska läroböcker?" ("Racism and Xenophobia in Swedish Textbooks?") In: *SPOV* No. 9, Härnösand 1990.

Selander, Staffan (ed.): Bilden av arbetsliv och näringsliv i skolans lærebøcker. (*The Image of Work, Trade and Industry in School Textbooks.*) Stockholm 1992.

Sewall, Gilbert T: "American History Textbooks. An Assessment of Quality. A Report Of The Educational Excellence Network." Columbia University, New York 1987.

Shaver, J.: "Reflective Thinking, Values of Social Studies Textbooks." In: *School Review* No. 73 1965.

Shaver, Davis, Helburn: "The Status of Social Studies Education: Impressions from Three NSF Studies." In: *Social Education*, Washington 1979.

Shayer, David: *The Teaching of English in Schools 1900–1970.* London 1972.

Shepardson, Daniel P., Edward L. Pizzini: "Questioning Levels of Junior High School Science Textbooks and Their Implications for Learning Textual Information." In : *Science Education* 75(6), 1991.

Shorish, Mobin M.: "Textbooks in Revolutionary Iran." In: Altbach, Philip G., Gail P. Kelly (eds.): *Textbooks in the Third World. Policy, Content and Context.* New York 1988.

Sigurgeirsson, Ingvar: "Inquiring into the Nature, Role, and Use of Curriculum Materials in Icelandic Schools." Reykjavik 1990.

Simensen, Aud Marit: Tekstforenkling. Et eksperiment. *(Simplification of Texts. An Experiment.)* Trondheim 1986.

Simonsen, Kathrine: Om lærebokvokabularet i den høyere skole. Hvordan elevene tilegner seg det. *(On the Vocabulary used in Textbooks in Upper Secondary School. How the Students Acquire It.)* Oslo 1947.

Sjøberg, Svein: Naturfag i søkelyset. *(Focus on Nature Studies.)* Oslo 1979.

Sjøberg, Svein: "Forfatterundersøkelse." ("Investigation of Authors' conditions.") NFF. Oslo 1987.

Skadberg, Kåre: "Lærebøkene – ein føresetnad for eit høgt utdanningsnivå." ("Textbooks – a Prerequisite for Educational Quality.") In: Mæhle, Leif, Einar Lundeby, Oddrun Grønvik (eds.): Fornying og tradisjon. *(Reform and Tradition.)* Norsk språkråd, Oslo 1987.

Skinningsrud, Tone, Magnus Haavelsrud: "Temaet likestilling mellom kjønnene i lærebøkene." ("The Topic of Equality of Status Between the

Sexes in the Textbooks.") In: Haavelsrud, Magnus (ed.): Indoktrinering eller politisering? *(Indoctrination or Politicization?)* Oslo 1979.

Skoog, G.: "Topic of Evolution in Secondary School Biology Textbooks: 1900–1977." In: *Science Education* No. 63 1984.

Skovgaard-Petersen, Vagn (ed.): Skolebøger i 200 år. *(Schoolbooks through 200 years.)* København 1970.

Slater, Frances (ed.): *People and Environments, Issues and Enquiries.* London 1986.

Sleeter, Christine E., Carl A. Grant: "Race, Class, Gender, and Disability in Current Textbooks." In: Apple, Michael W., Linda K. Christian-Smith (eds.): *The Politics of The Textbook.* London/New York 1991.

Sletvold, Sverre: Norske lesebøker 1777–1969. *(Norwegian Readers 1777–1969.)* Oslo 1971.

Smith, Dora V.: "Instruction in English." National Survey of Secondary Education Monograph No. 20. Washington DC 1933.

Smith, N.B.: "Patterns of Writing in Different Subject Areas." In: *Journal of Reading* 31:6, 1964.

Solheim, E.: "Kjønnsroller i liv og lærebøker." ("Sexual Stereotypes in Life and in Textbooks.") Universitetet i Oslo 1972.

Sosniak, Lauren A., Carole L. Perlman: "Secondary Education by the Book." In: *Journal of Curriculum Studies* 22:5, 1990.

Spalding, Willard B.: "The Selection and Distribution of Printed Materials." In: Cronbach, Lee J. (ed.): *Text Materials in Modern Education.* Urbana 1955.

Sperling, Walter: "Zur Darstellung der deutschen Kolonien im Erdkundeunterricht (1890–1914) mit besonderer Berücksichtigung der Lehrmittel." In: *Internationale Schulbuchforschung* No. 4, Braunschweig 1989.

SPOV. (Review on Pedagogic Text Research.) Ed.: Staffan Selander, Högskolan Sundsvall-Härnösand, Sweden. 1987-.

Spreng, Bernard: "La Problématique des Manuels Scolaires. Études sur les Manuels Scolaires." Institut Romand de Recherche et de Documentation Pédagogiques. Neuchâtel 1976.

Sprenger, Reinhard: "Das zweigeteilte Deutschlandbild – Deutschland im Geschichtsbuch der DDR." In: Sprenger, Reinhard (ed.): *Das Deutschlandbild in internationalen Geschichtsbüchern. Zur Sache Schulbuch.* Band 8. Kastellaun 1977.

Squire, James R.: "Textbooks to the Forefront." In: *Book Research Quarterly,* Summer 1985.

Squire, James R., Richard T. Morgan: "The Elementary and High School Textbook Market Today." In: Woodward, Arthur, David L. Elliott (eds.): NSSE Yearbook 1990: *Part I. Textbooks and Schooling in the United States.* Chicago 1990.

St. Lawrence, Francis: "Teaching Aids in Biology Texts." In: *Phi Delta Kappa* 33:5, 1952.

Starke, U.: "Zu Ergebnissen sprachstatistischer Untersuchungen von Lehrbuchtexten." In: *Beiträge zu Methoden der Schulbuch-forschung. Informationen zu Schulbuchfragen* No. 47 1983.

Starver, J., M. Bay: "Analysis of the Conceptual Structure and Reasoning Demand of Elementary Science Texts at the Primary (K-3) Level." In: *Journal of Research in Science Teaching* 24:6, 1989.

Stein, Gerd (ed.): *Schulbuchkritik als Schulkritik.* Saarbrücken 1976.

Stein, Gerd: *Schulbuchwissen, Politik und Pädagogik. Zur Sache Schulbuch.* Band 10. Kastellaun 1977.

Stein, Gerd (ed.): *Schulbuch-Schelte als Politikum und Herausforderung wissenschaftlicher Schulbucharbeit.* Stuttgart 1979.

Stene, Helga: "Portrayal of Women in School Textbooks. Historical Outline, Documents, and Publications. Norway 1956–1981." Paper. Conference held by the Ministry of Education. Oslo 1981.

Sticht, T.: "Understanding Readers and Their Use of Texts." In: Duffy, T. M., R. Waller (eds.): *Designing Usable Texts.* Orlando 1985.

Stodolsky, Susan S.: *The Subject Matters: Classroom Activity in Maths and Social Studies.* Chicago 1988.

Stodolsky, Susan S.: "Is Teaching Really by the Book?" In: *From Socrates to Software: The Teacher as Text and the Text as Teacher. Eightyninth Yearbook of the National Society for the Study of Education.* Chicago 1989.

Stortingsmelding No. 23 1982–83: See: Report to the Storting.

Stray, Chris: "Paradigms Lost: Towards a Historical Sociology of the Textbook." Paper. PEXU Conference, Härnösand 1991.

Struminger, Laura S.: *What Were Little Girls and Boys Made of? Primary Education in Rural France, 1830–1880.* New York 1983.

Strømnes, Å.L., N. Søvik (eds.): *Teachers' Thinking. Perspectives and Research.* Trondheim 1987.

Sudmann, Arnulf: "Kor mykje forstår borna av språket i lærebøkene?" ("How Much Do the Children Understand of the Textbook Language?") In: *Norsklæreren* No. 3 1978.

Sujew, Dmitri: *Das Schullehrbuch.* Berlin 1986.

Svingby, Gunilla: "Mål för lärarutbildning. Några principiella synpunkter." ("Goals for Teachers' Education. Some Principal Points of View.") DsU 1977:4, Stockholm 1977.

Svingby, Gunilla: "Läroplaner som styrmedel för svensk obligatorisk skola." ("Curricula as a Means of Controlling the Public Swedish School.") Göteborg Studies in Educational Sciences No. 26 1978.

Svingby, Gunilla: Sätt kunskapen i centrum! *(Focus on Knowledge!)* Stockholm 1985.

Svingby, Gunilla, Birget Lendahls, Dennis Ekbom: Omvärldskunskap. *(Knowing the World Around Us.)* Göteborgs universitet 1990.

Sødring-Jensen, Sven: Historieundervisningsteori. *(A Theory of History Teaching.)* København 1978.

Tarschys, Karin: Svenska språket och litteraturen. Studier över modersmålsundervisningen i högre skolor. *(Swedish Language and Literature. Studies on the Teaching of Swedish as a Mother Tongue in Upper Secondary Schools.)* Stockholm 1955.

Tartu Ülikooli Toimetised: *Problems of Textbook Effectivity. Papers on Education II.)* Acta et Commentationes Universitatis Tartuensis No. 926. Tartu 1991.

Tergan, S.-O.: *Textverständlichkeit und Lernerfolg in angeleiteten Selbststudium.* Weinheim und Basel 1983.

Thavenius, Jan (ed.): Litteraturvetenskap. *(Literary Science.)* Stockholm 1966.

The Norwegian Publishers Association: See Den norske Forleggerforening.

Thorson, Staffan: "Tendenser i efterkrigstidens läroböcker i svenska." ("Trends in Swedish Language and Literature Textbooks after WW 2.") In: Rönström, Thomas (ed.): Skolböcker 3. Den (o)möjliga läroboken. *(Schoolbooks 3. The (Im)Possible Textbook.)* Ds 1988:24. Stockholm 1988.

Tierney, Robert J.: "A Synthesis of Research on the Use of Instructional Text: Some Implications for the Educational Publishing Industry in Reading." In: Anderson, Richard C., Jean Osborn, Robert J. Tierney (eds.): *Learning to Read in American Schools: Basal Readers and Content Texts.* New York 1981. (NB: All quotations are from proof sheet.)

Tiller, Hanne, Andreas Lem Nordahl: "Metoder for fremtidens skolebokproduksjon." ("Methods for Producing Textbooks in the Future.") Norges Tekniske Høyskole. Trondheim 1988.

Tingsten, Herbert: Gud och fosterlandet. *(God and the Fatherland.)* Stockholm 1969.

Tischer, Heinz: *Geschichte des deutschen Volksschullesebuches. Von den Anfängen bis zur Mitte des neunzehnten Jahrhunderts.* Friedrich-Alexander-Universität. Erlangen-Nürnberg 1970.

Togeby, Lise: Den uopslidelige lærebog. En indholdsanalyse af folkeskolens samfundslærebøger. *(The Imperishable Textbook. A Content Analysis of Textbooks in the Social Sciences for Primary Schools.)* Aarhus 1978.

Tonjes, Marian J.: "Reading and Thinking Skills Required in the Subject Classroom." In: Gillham, Bruce (ed.): *The Language of School Subjects.* London 1986.

Toulmin, S., R. Rieke, A. Janik: *An Introduction to Reasoning.* New York 1979.

Tournier, Michèle, Michèle Navarro: *Les professeurs et le manuel scolaire.* Institut National de Recherche Pédagogiqe, Paris 1985.

Trecker, J.L.: "Women in U.S. History High School Textbooks." In: *Social Education* No. 35 1971.

Trott, Gerhard: "Anthologie-Rezeption in Zeitschriften des 19. Jahrhunderts." In: Bark, Joachim, Dietger Pforte (eds.): *Die deutschsprachige Anthologie 1–2.* Frankfurt am Main 1970.

Trotzig, Eva: "Den osynliga texten." ("The Invisible Writing.") In: SPOV 7, Härnösand 1989.

Tulley, M.A., R.Farr: "Textbook Adoption: Insight, Impact, and Potential." In: *Book Research Quarterly* 1:2, 1985.

Tulley, M.A., R. Farr: "The Purpose of State Level Textbook Adoption: what does the Legislation Reveal?" In: *Journal of Research and Development in Education* 18:2, 1985.

Tveterås, Harald L.: Et norsk kulturforlag gjennom hundre år. Aschehoug 1872–1972. *(A Norwegian Publishing House through One Hundred Years. Aschehoug 1872–1972.)* Oslo 1972.

Tveterås, Harald L.: I pakt med tiden. Cappelen gjennom 150 år. *(Keeping Abreast of the Times. Cappelen through 150 Years.)* Oslo 1979.

Tyson-Bernstein, Harriet: "The Academy's Contribution To the Impoverishment of America's Textbooks." In: *Phi Delta Kappan* 69:13, 1988.

Tyson-Bernstein, Harriet, Woodward, Arthur: "Why Students Aren't Learning Very Much from Textbooks." In: *Educational Leadership,* November 1989.

Ulvik, Synnøve: "Språkkløyvde lærebøker – bruk og konsekvensar." ("On and Consequences of Having Textbooks Written Partly in 'Bokmål' and Partly in 'Nynorsk'.") Statens bibliotek- og informasjons-høgskole. Oslo 1991.

Vail, Henry H.: *A History of the McGuffey Readers.* Cleveland 1911.

Verduin-Muller, Henriette S.: "The Textbook: A Knowledge Product."

Manuscript. Georg-Eckert-Institut, September 1990.

Vigander, Haakon: "Textbook Revision in the Nordic Countries." In: Schüddekopf, Otto Ernst, Edouard Bruley, E.H. Dance, Haakon Vigander: *History Teaching and History Textbook Revision*. Strasbourg 1967.

Vinje, Eiliv: "Utdanningsperspektiv på skriftkulturen." ("An Educational Survey of Written Culture.") Report. Nordisk institutt. Universitetet i Bergen 1990.

Vogt, Sidsel (ed.): Kjønnsroller i lærebøker. *(Sex Roles in Textbooks.)* Oslo 1984.

Von Laer, Hermann: "Das Thema 'Entwicklungsländer' im Geographie-Schulbuch." In: *Internationale Schulbuchforschung* No. 4, Braunschweig 1989.

Wain, Kenneth: "Different Perspectives on Evaluating Textbooks." Manuscript. Georg-Eckert-Institut, September 1990.

Walker, Kevin Richard: "SMILE Update". Paper. PEXU Conference, Härnösand 1991.

Weinbrenner, Peter: "Kathegorien und Methoden für die Analyse wirtschafts- und sozialwissenschaftlicher Lehr- und Lernmittel." In: *Internationale Schulbuchforschung* No. 3, Braunschweig 1986.

Weinbrenner, Peter: "Erziehungswissenschaft." In: Laubig, Manfred, Heidrun Peters, Peter Weinbrenner: "Methoden der Schulbuchanalyse." Universität Bielefeld 1986a.

Westbury, Ian: "School Textbooks. Research Report from The Curriculum Laboratory." No. 11, Urbana-Champaign 1982.

Westbury, Ian: "Textbooks, Textbook Publishers, and the Quality of Schooling." In: Woodward, Arthur, David L. Elliott (eds.): *NSSE Yearbook 1990: Part I. Textbooks and Schooling in the United States.* Chicago 1990.

Weymar, E.: *Das Selbstverständnis der Deutschen. Ein Bericht über den Geist des Geschichtsunterrichts der höheren Schulen im 19. Jahrhundert.* Stuttgart 1961.

Willinsky, John, Deanne Bogdan (eds.): *Embattled Books: The State of the Text.* Special Edition of JET – *The Journal of Educational Thought* – 24:3A, Calgary 1990.

Williamson, John H.: "Textbook Publishing: Facts and Myths." In: Cole, John Y., Thomas G. Sticht (eds.): *The Textbook in American Society.* Washington DC 1981.

Woodward, Arthur: "Taking Teaching out of Teaching and Reading out of Learning to Read: A Historical Study of Reading Teachers' Guides,

1920–1980." In: *Book Research Quarterly* No. 2 1986.

Woodward, Arthur: "On Teaching and Textbook Publishing: Political Issues Obscure Questions of Pedagogy." In: *Education Week* 6:17, 1987.

Woodward, Arthur, David L.Elliott, Kathleen Carter Nagel: *Textbooks in School and Society. An Annotated Bibliography and Guide to Research.* New York/London 1988.

Woodward, Arthur: "When a Picture Isn't Worth a Thousand Words: An Analysis of Illustrations and Content in Elementary School Science Textbooks." Paper. American Educational Research Association. SIG Group, San Francisco 1989.

Woodward, Arthur: "Selecting Elementary Social Studies Textbooks: An Analysis of Illustrations and Content in Elementary School Science Textbooks." Paper. American Educational Research Association. SIG Group, San Francisco 1990.

Woodward, Arthur, David L. Elliott: "Textbook Use and Teacher Professionalism." In: Woodward, Arthur, David L.Elliott (eds.): *NSSE Yearbook 1990: Part I. Textbooks and Schooling in the United States.* Chicago 1990.

Woodward, Arthur, David L. Elliott (eds.): *NSSE Yearbook 1990: Part I. Textbooks and Schooling in the United States.* Chicago 1990.

Woodward, Arthur: "Do Illustrations Serve an Instructional Purpose in US Textbooks?" To be printed in: Britton, Bruce, Arthur Woodward (eds.): *Learning from Textbooks.* Erlbaum Press 1993. (NB: Quotations are from manuscript 1991.)

Wright, Patricia: "Editing: Policies and Processes." In: Duffy, T.M., R. Waller (eds.): *Designing Usable Texts.* Orlando 1985.

Young, Jean M.: "Writing and Editing Textbooks." In: Woodward, Arthur, David L. Elliott (eds.): *NSSE Yearbook 1990: Part I. Textbooks and Schooling in the United States.* Chicago 1990.

Zahorik, John A.: "Stability and Flexibility in Teaching." In: *Teaching and Teacher Education* No. 6 1990.

Zahorik, John A.: "Teaching Style and Textbooks." In: *Teaching and Teacher Education* No. 7 1991.

Zückert, Ulrich: "The soft Revolution in the GDR and revolutionary Changes in History Teaching." Paper. Georg-Eckert-Institut, September 1990.

Oestreich, Klaus: "Deutsche Geschichte seit 1945 in Schulbüchern der beiden deutschen Staaten." Manuscript. Halle-Köthen 1990.

Åhlberg, Mauri: "Concept Mapping, Concept Matrices, and Argumentation Analysis as Tools of Textbook Analysis." Paper. Institut för Pedagogisk Textforskning. Härnösand 1990.

Åhlberg, Mauri: "Concept Mapping, Concept Matrices, Link Tables and Argumentation Analysis as Techniques for Educational Research on Textbooks and Educational Discourse and as Tools for Teachers and Pupils in their Everyday Work." In: Julkunen, Marja-Liisa, Staffan Selander, Mauri Åhlberg: "Research on School Texts." Research Reports of the Faculty of Education. University of Joensuu, No. 37 1991.

Aaneby, Sigrun: "Hvordan gjøre et godt lærebokvalg?" ("How Does One Make a Good Choice of Textbooks?") Manuscript. NFF (Norwegian Non-Fiction Writers' and Translators' Association) Conference, Oslo 1991.

Name Index

Bromsjö, Birger 163, 177, 179
Bruno, G. 33, 262, 364
Bulletin d'information sur les manuels scolaires 307, 321
Bünger, Friedrich 368
Byrne, M.A. 191

California Board of Education 152, 205
Cappelen 297–298
Carlson, Fredrik Ferdinand 241, 390
Carpenter, Charles 33, 366
Caspard, P. 59, 144
Chall, Jeanne S. 276
Chatrian, Alexandre 262–263
Charmasson, Thérèse 359
Chervel, André 51–52, 84, 203, 369–370
Chevalier, Jean-Claude 370
Choppin, Alain 58–60, 84, 150, 276, 296, 297, 299, 320, 358–359
Christiansen, Kurt Dahl 131
Christiansen, Torben Bergmann 384
Christian-Smith, Linda K. 284
Clark, Christopher M. 160
Cody, Caroline 293, 310
Coffey, W.L. 277
Cole, John Y. 97
Colloquium on Textbooks, Schools and Society 83
Comenius 13, 35
Cooper, B. 272–273
Cortázar, Julio 263–264
Coser, Lewis 271
Council of Europe 73, 86, 394
Crismore, Avon 153, 205–209, 215
Cronbach, Lee J. 78, 181, 245, 265, 315, 323, 327, 343–344

Dahl, Hans Fredrik 124
Dahlkvist, Ragnar 188–190
Dale, Johs. A. 217
Damerow, Peter 45, 289
Dance, E. H. 86, 133, 327
Danielson, Sylvia 193–194
Danielsson, Annica 39, 193–194
Darras, Francine 187

Subject Index